Hiking the
North Cascades

Hiking the North Cascades

Dr. Fred T. Darvill, Jr.

STACKPOLE
BOOKS

Published by
STACKPOLE BOOKS
5067 Ritter Road
Mechanicsburg, PA 17055
website: www.stackpolebooks.com

Printed in the United States

10 9 8 7 6 5 4 3 2 1

Maps and diagrams by Marjorie Domenowske
Cover design by Wendy Reynolds

IMPORTANT

The information regarding trail or campsite conditions, fees, and permits were accurate as of the publication of this book, but are subject to change due to any number of factors. Readers are responsible for consulting park information centers in preparation for any trip to the North Cascades.

Readers are also responsible for their own safety while in the backcountry. The author and publisher of this book take no responsibility for any adverse outcomes incurred by back country travelers using the information contained in *Hiking the North Cascades*.

Cataloging-in-Publication information

Darvill, Fred T., 1927–
      Hiking the North Cascades / Fred T. Darvill, Jr.—1st ed.
         p.   cm.
      Includes bibliographical references (p.) and index.
      ISBN 0-8117-2791-2
      1. Hiking—Cascade Range—Guidebooks. 2. Hiking—Washington (State)—Guidebooks. 3. Trails—Cascade Range—Guidebooks. 4. Trails—Washington (State)—Guidebooks. 5. Cascade Range—Guidebooks. 6. Washington (State) Guidebooks. I. Title.
GV199.42.C37D37   1998
917.97'504'43—dc21   98-13265
                                                                                                        CIP

This book is dedicated to those mountain lovers and conservationists whose dreams of preserving the splendor of the North Cascades and unceasing efforts toward that end resulted in the establishment of the North Cascades National Park; the Ross Lake, Lake Chelan, and Mount Baker National Recreation Areas; and the Glacier Peak, Pasayten, Alpine Lakes, Mount Baker, Henry Jackson, Lake Chelan–Sawtooth, Noisy Diobsud, and Boulder River Wilderness Areas. Generations to come will be grateful for their foresight, wisdom, involvement, and concern. Continued vigilance is necessary to protect these dedicated areas and to minimize environmentally unsound activities in the remaining splendid areas of the North Cascades still being administered by the Forest Service under the multiple-use concept.

This book is also dedicated to the many people, living and dead, who have walked the footpaths of the North Cascades with me over the past forty years. All are fondly remembered.

Lastly, I dedicate this book to my treasured wife, Ginny, who has been my trail companion for the past two decades.

Contents

Preface

I began my love affair with the North Cascades in 1957, when I spent the Labor Day holiday in the Mazama Park area and first visited the Park Butte Lookout. During those three days, I contracted a virulent case of "mountain fever," for which there is no known cure. The condition may be controlled, however, with frequent visits to the high country. In the course of treating my affliction, I began making observations and recording trail information for my own interest. Eleven years later, while in the White House witnessing the signing of the bill creating the North Cascades National Park complex, I decided to use the information I had gathered to produce a guide to the North Cascades. In late 1968, *A Pocket Guide to Selected Trails of the North Cascades National Park and Associated Recreational Complex* was published. As I continued to explore the area and accumulate additional information, further books on the Cascade Mountains followed: *A Pocket Guide to the North Cascades National Park* (1970), a two-volume guide to the park and associated areas (1972, revised 1975), *North Cascades Highway Guide* (1973 and 1986), *Stehekin, the Enchanted Valley* (1981 and 1996), and *Hiking the North Cascades* (1982).

This publication reflects forty years of personal experience in the North Cascades. Material from preceding publications—many now out of print—has been amplified based on additional personal experience plus, when appropriate, backup from experts in their fields (see the Acknowledgments).

As Lois Webster wrote about me in the Introduction to my first book on the Cascades in 1968, "He believes in the continuing need for protecting the North Cascades, and he would develop their recreational potential since he feels they are the most beautiful mountains in the world. He is pleased to be able to share his enjoyment of the high country with the readers of this booklet."

Acknowledgments

I am indebted to the following people and organizations that provided data, photographs, or expertise. Drafts of each section were reviewed by authorities in that field. Most of their suggestions were incorporated into the book, but I take full responsibility for the material that finally reached print.

ORGANIZATIONS
Whatcom Museum of History and Arts, Bellingham, WA
North Cascades National Park (NCNP)
Mount Baker–Snoqualmie National Forest
Wenatchee National Forest
Okanogan National Forest

INDIVIDUALS
History: Dr. A. D. Martinson, Pacific Lutheran University, Tacoma; Jim Harris, NCNP
Botany: Dr. Arthur Kruckeberg, University of Washington, Seattle
Geology: Dr. R. S. Babcock, Western Washington University, Bellingham; Cynthia Gardner and Larry Mastin, U.S. Geological Survey
Fire Lookouts: Ray Kresek, Spokane
Zoology: David Drummond, wildlife biologist, Nahkeeta Northwest
Entomology: Reed Glesne, NCNP
Ornithology: Bob Kuntz, NCNP; David Drummond, wildlife biologist, Nahkeeta Northwest
Archaeology: Bob Mierendorf, NCNP
Diagrams and Maps: Marjorie Domenowske, Seattle

Abbreviations

ALW	Alpine Lakes Wilderness
BRW	Boulder River Wilderness
CPP	Cathedral Provincial Park (British Columbia, Canada)
GPW	Glacier Peak Wilderness
HJW	Henry Jackson Wilderness
LCNRA	Lake Chelan National Recreational Area
LCSW	Lake Chelan–Sawtooth Wilderness
MBNRA	Mount Baker National Recreational Area
MBSNF	Mount Baker–Snoqualmie National Forest
MBW	Mount Baker Wilderness
MPP	Manning Provincial Park (British Columbia, Canada)
NCH	North Cascades Highway (State Route 20)
NCNP	North Cascades National Park (complex)
NDW	Noisy Diobsud Wilderness
NPS	National Park Service
ONF	Okanogan National Forest
PW	Pasayten Wilderness
RLNRA	Ross Lake National Recreational Area
SMW	Stephen Mather Wilderness (within the NCNP)
USFS	United States Forest Service
USGS	United States Geological Survey
VF	vertical feet
WNF	Wenatchee National Forest

"Sea of Peaks" effect. Only the airborne and the mountaineer are privileged to see the rocky "waves" of the North Cascades seemingly stretching to infinity.

PART I

About the North Cascade Mountains

General Information

Many people do not understand current terminology applied to federal lands dedicated in part or in full to recreational use. The following brief clarification may be of value.

National parks are spacious land and water areas of nationwide interest established as inviolable sanctuaries for the permanent preservation of scenery, wilderness, and wildlife in its natural condition. The unexcelled beauty and unique inspirational quality of the national parks distinguish them from all other areas. Park land is protected, through act of Congress, for human enjoyment, education, and inspiration for all time.

The National Park Service, a division of the Department of the Interior, was established in 1916 by Congress and directed to administer the national parks under the following directive: "To conserve the scenery and the natural and historic objects and the wildlife therein, and to provide for the enjoyment of same in such manner and by such means as to leave them unimpaired for the enjoyment of future generations."

National forests are federally owned forestlands administered by the U.S. Forest Service, a division of the Department of Agriculture. By law, all lands in the national forests are administered under the multiple-use policy. Theoretically, *multiple use* means the wise balancing of resource extraction (logging, mining, grazing), watershed protection, wildlife conservation, and recreation to produce the greatest good for the greatest number of people involved. (Unfortunately, at least in the past, conservationists have felt that commercial uses, particularly logging, have overshadowed important recreational uses.)

A *wilderness area,* generally under federal ownership, is a tract of land that is, by act of Congress, to be preserved in its wild state indefinitely. It is generally defined as an area essentially unchanged by human hands, although minor modifications of the environment (such as trails) are generally considered acceptable. Roads are prohibited, and all commercial development is banned, as is resource extraction such as logging. Unfortunately, mining claims established before 1984 may still be worked; new claims have been banned since 1984. Hunting, fishing, and all other recreational uses are allowed. Mechanized equipment may not be used in dedicated wilderness areas.

The *national recreation area* might best be described as a child produced by the union of a national park and a national forest; it has qualities of each. In general, resource extraction is prohibited, unless compatible with recreational use. Hunting is generally permitted. More intensive recreational development, even if it substantially alters the natural scenery, is also allowed. In short, these are playgrounds of national significance.

RULES AND REGULATIONS

With these definitions in mind, some of the rules relating to the various areas in the North Cascades will be more understandable. In the North Cascades National Park (NCNP), nothing is to be defaced or changed. Wildlife may not be disturbed; flowers may not be picked; specimens such as rocks may not be removed. In short, the area is to remain pristine and natural. It is a federal offense to deface or change the natural order of things within the park in any way. Mechanical equipment on trails is prohibited. Dogs and other pets are allowed only in areas that are accessible by road and on the Pacific Crest Trail (from near High Bridge to about 1½ miles from the North Cascades Highway) if they are leashed and continuously under control. Hunting is prohibited, but fishing is allowed. Buildings and other developments within the national park are kept to a minimum and are designed to harmonize with the environment.

Hunting is allowed elsewhere in the North Cascades, subject to the laws of the state of Washington. Certain animals, such as marmots and pikas, are protected throughout the year.

In the Lake Chelan and Ross Lake National Recreation Areas, dogs are allowed on the trails if they are leashed and under control at all times. In the Mount Baker National Recreation Area, dogs must be leashed or under voice control by their owners. In the Alpine Lakes Wilderness, dogs are not allowed in the Enchantment Permit Area or the upper Ingalls Creek drainage. Dogs must be leashed on almost all the trails off I-90 and Highway 2 west of Stevens Pass. Where leashes are not required, dogs must be under voice control at all times.

In the remainder of the areas covered in this book, dogs (and other pets) may accompany their owners subject only to the unwritten rules of outdoor courtesy. It is wise to keep dogs restrained if other animals are nearby. In addition, some people dislike dogs; pet owners should minimize the impact of their four-footed friends on canine-phobic hikers.

Within reasonable limits, specimen collecting is permitted outside of the national park, but it should be recalled that a picked wildflower does not reproduce and a removed rock will not be seen by subsequent visitors. One person's thoughtless act multiplied by the acts of many individuals can produce substantial destruction in areas of fragile beauty.

The national park complex currently requires permits for overnight camping anywhere within its jurisdiction. Permits are required for all entries into the Alpine Lakes Wilderness. Permits for day use only are available at the trailheads; permits for overnight use in certain locations must be obtained in advance, since quotas have been imposed to protect these areas from overuse. Additional areas will probably have quotas imposed as they become impacted by overuse in the future. Contact the ranger station with jurisdiction to ascertain present regulations before departing for the trailhead. At this time, permits are not required elsewhere in the national forests; however, a "Trail Park Pass" is now required to park at national forest trailheads.

The locations and phone numbers of all the land management agencies in the North Cascades (as of late 1996) are listed in the Resources section.

MAPS

A plethora of maps, both topographic and nontopographic, cover the North Cascades. The best overall map of the North Cascades National Park and Lake Chelan and Ross Lake National Recreation Areas is the 1:100,000 topographic map (metric) published by the U.S. Geological Survey (USGS), Branch of Distribution, Box 25286, Denver Federal Center, Denver, CO 80225. Standard topographic maps of the 7.5- and 15-minute series are also available; an index to the topographic maps of Washington and an order form can be obtained on request from the USGS. In addition, 1:100,000 maps of Robinson Mountain, Sauk River, Twisp, and Skykomish River and 1:250,000 scale maps of Concrete are available from the USGS.

Another excellent map of the North Cascades National Park complex is the topographic map available from Trails Illustrated, Box 3610, Evergreen, CO 80439; phone 800-962-1643.

Nontopographic maps are produced by each national forest. In addition, the Forest Service has produced topographic maps of the Glacier Peak Wilderness and the Pasayten Wilderness. The most recent maps have metric contour intervals and record trail distances in kilometers rather than miles. These maps are available at district ranger offices and national forest headquarters.

Topographic maps of the Canadian parks can be obtained from Map and Air Photo Sales, Ministry of Environment, Parliament Buildings, Victoria, BC, Canada V8V 1T7.

In addition, Green Trail Maps, PO Box 77734, Seattle, WA 98177, provides 15-minute-series topographic maps of the entire North Cascades, with all trails in the area marked in green. I prefer these maps to the USGS maps. To order, call 800-762-6277.

A topographic map is essential for any off-trail walking or climbing and is desirable for all visitors. The 7.5-minute maps give great detail but are relatively bulky, and often two or three maps are needed to cover one trail or one area. Maps covering larger areas offer less detail but are both less costly and more portable. Since maps are usually kept in outer pockets of packs, it is advisable to purchase a small plastic map container; soggy, wet maps are difficult to read and destruct easily.

Compass angle of declination in the North Cascades is 22 degrees east of true north.

The trails in this book are annotated to provide the name of the topographic sheets and the Green Trail maps that cover the trail area.

WEATHER

The North Cascades are the most elegant and splendid mountains on the face of the earth, when they can be seen. Mountain aficionados who are knowledgeable about the weather patterns here have stated, "If you can't see the mountains, it's raining; if you can see the mountains, photograph them immediately, since it's going to rain very soon." Or as one wet, bedraggled walker wrote on the register at a hut on New Zealand's Milford Track, "This is the only place in the world as wet as the North Cascades."

In an average year, the mountain range is reasonably visible one day out of six. In other words, about sixty days a year, the northwest Washington hills are relatively cloud free and glorious to behold.

Weather patterns are quite different east and west of the Cascade crest. Many days when storm clouds hug the peaks in the west, eastern weather is overcast but rain free. Occasionally there is a dramatic difference, with bright, warm sunshine in the east and a wall of wet rain clouds meeting travelers at the summits of the mountain passes. The difference in weather is due to the prevailing storm winds that sweep in from the southwest out of the great expanse of the Pacific Ocean. As the clouds are pushed upward over the peaks, they cool, releasing their moisture as rain in the summer and snow in the winter. Most of the moisture is lost before the crest is reached, less is available for the land beyond the crest.

Annual precipitation records are illuminating. Mount Baker receives an average annual snowfall of 516 inches and a yearly precipitation of about 110 inches; Diablo Dam, near the Cascade crest, receives about 72 inches of precipitation; Stehekin has an annual snowfall of 109 inches and annual precipitation of about 34 inches.

West-side weather in the lowlands consists of a six-month rainy season stretching from roughly November 1 to April 30; in the high country, this is the snow season. May and June are spring months; July and August summer; September and October fall.

West of the crest, the average high trail is 90 percent snow free in a normal year by July 15 and 100 percent snow free by September 1. Intermittent snow begins again about October 1. In an average year, snow closes the high country about November 1, although this can vary from October 15 to November 15. Snow can occur any day in the year above 5,000 feet. The best weather, year in and year out, is between July 15 and July 31. June is often wetter than May. Intermittent storms increase in frequency after Labor Day. The height of the alpine flower bloom is August 1, and the peak of the fall color is October 1. The hills are usually skiable by Thanksgiving; deep snow persists well into June.

Weather patterns in Stehekin are typical of the eastern foothills. Winter temperatures are generally cold, with the first snow usually falling about December 1 and melting off sometime in March. Spring comes relatively early; daytime temperatures are pleasant by late April or early May. Summer weather in Stehekin can be oppressively hot, with temperatures in the high 90s relatively common in late July and early August. September is perhaps the most delightful month; daytime temperatures are pleasant, and all trails are snow free. Autumn coloration adds zest to wilderness walking. People are less common on the trails and there is less competition for popular campsites after Labor Day. October is comfortable in the Stehekin valley but is cold at higher elevations.

The snow in the mountains east of the crest has generally melted enough for comfortable hiking by mid to late June. Afternoon thunderstorms are not uncommon in midsummer. Rain can occur at any time, particularly west of the crest, and storms may continue for several days, even in July and August.

Over the summits of Mount Baker and Glacier Peak, and less frequently over the summits of the high nonvolcanic peaks, a cloud cap may form. The presence of this persistent lenticular cloud, which is not blown away by the wind, is often an indication of deteriorating weather. The mechanism of the formation and maintenance of the cloud is interesting. As air is forced up and over the cold summit of the mountain by a prevailing wind, the air is cooled. The temperature change causes the water in the air to change from invisible vapor to visible cloud. When the air descends on the other side of the peak, warming occurs; the process is reversed, and the cloud disappears. Accordingly, a summit may be cloud-capped for several hours when there are few, if any, other clouds in the sky. The first indication of bad weather in the North Cascades is often the development of a wind out of the southwest. Since both wind and moisture in the air are necessary for cloud-cap formation, rain often follows within a few hours after the tops of the major peaks are obscured by these strange, stationary miasmas. When cloud-capped, the summits have an unusual scenic beauty. However, it is both unpleasant and dangerous to be in a cloud cap when climb-

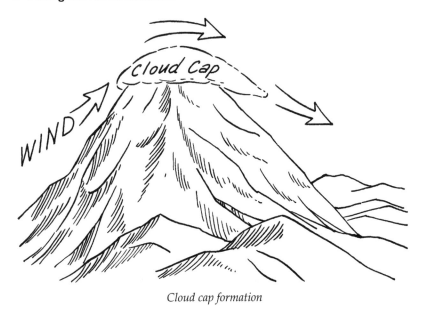

Cloud cap formation

ing a major peak, because wind velocity can be substantial, and the lack of visibility is hazardous.

CAMPING

There are many campgrounds in the North Cascades accessible by car. North Cascades National Park (NCNP) fee sites are located along the North Cascades Highway; they are operated on a first come, first served basis. Fee and free campgrounds, managed by the national forests, are located along most major roads. Advance reservations for some of the fee campgrounds in the three national forests may be made by phoning 800-280-2267 (USFS Reservation Center, PO Box 900, Cumberland, MD 21501-0900). USFS campgrounds also operate on a first come, first served basis. Desirable, and sometimes all, locations are often filled early in the day, particularly on summer weekends and the July 4 and Labor Day holidays.

All campsites for backpackers within the NCNP complex are designated. Strict rules govern camping (1 mile off trail) in other locations. In the Mount Baker National Recreation Area, all campsites are designated. Some locations in the Mount Baker National Forest (Chain Lakes, for example) are also designated, as are several locations in the Alpine Lakes Wilderness. The laissez-faire "camp wherever you like when you are ready" still applies within almost all the national forest land of the North Cascades. However, even there, no-trace camping is appropriate. Camp on mineral earth or sedge. Do not cut living trees or branches. Do not construct new campfire pits (if there is no pit, make no fire), and make no fires at all in the alpine meadows. Carry out everything that you take in.

Car camping information is given on the maps of the national forests. Information about campgrounds can also be obtained from the appropriate land management agency.

TRANSPORTATION AND ACCOMMODATIONS

There is no scheduled public transportation on Ross Lake. Arrangements can be made with the Ross Lake Resort (Rockport, WA 98283; 360-386-4437) for up-lake drop off and later down-lake pickup at a prearranged time. Canoes can be portaged from the highway or, more easily, taken between Diablo and Ross Lakes by boat and truck for a fee. All trailheads can be reached by land, except Little Beaver.

Boat transportation from Chelan to Stehekin is available daily in the summer, four times a week in the spring and fall, and three times a week in the winter. Contact the Lake Chelan Boat Co. (PO Box 186, Chelan, WA 98816; 509-682-2224) to obtain a schedule or other information. Charter air service is also available from Chelan; contact Chelan Airways (Chelan, WA 98816; 509-682-5555) for information and to make reservations. Flying time from Chelan to Stehekin is about 35 minutes.

Private boats can be launched on Lake Chelan at several sites. Canoe and small-boat users must use caution, because brisk winds often cause substantial waves, particularly in the afternoon.

For those preferring to enter the area on horseback, packers are available at Stehekin, Winthrop, and Merritt. The Forest Service will provide a listing of packers that serve the North Cascades and a list of resorts in the area.

The Pacific Crest Trail and all trails in the park and wilderness areas are closed to all vehicles. Trail machines are also officially prohibited on many of the other trails described herein. Rugged terrain throughout the entire range and mud west of the crest are natural limitations to their use, not to mention hikers' disapproval of their presence.

For accommodations at Stehekin, contact the North Cascades Stehekin Lodge (PO Box 457, Chelan, WA 98816; 509-682-4494) or the Stehekin Valley Ranch (PO Box 36, Stehekin, WA 98852; 509-682-2212). A 100-page guide to the Stehekin area is available locally or by mail (1819 Hickox Road, Mount Vernon, WA 98274) for $9.95 plus postage and handling.

HIKING

There are a number of day hikes that can be made in the North Cascades. Although there is little private land in the North Cascades, there are a few patented mining claims, plus the community at Stehekin. Roughly 600 acres in the Stehekin valley still remain in private hands; please respect the rights of private landowners in the Stehekin area.

Equipment

A small rucksack or day pack should be carried, containing a first-aid kit, a water bottle, food, insect repellent, and extra clothes. Temperatures can change dramatically in the high country within a few hours; you can start in a T-shirt in the heat and five hours later be in drenching rain, or even snow. It is important to be prepared for these sudden changes in temperature and precipitation.

Other useful items and emergency gear that should be in the pack of the mountain walker include a map and compass, waterproof matches and a fire starter, sunglasses, pocketknife, flashlight, and whistle.

Water is almost always available west of the crest, but the east side can be dry, particularly in the late summer and early fall. Carry water if in doubt, particularly if it is hot.

Overnight packers obviously need more extensive equipment. A light waterproof alpine tent is an essential in the North Cascades, in view of the unpredictable weather. Down sleeping bags are recommended but must be enclosed in a waterproof container to keep them dry. Fiberfill sleeping bags are heavier and not as warm as down but insulate better than down when wet. A waterproof pack cover that is durable and effective is also recommended. Fires are inappropriate or prohibited in many areas; a lightweight camp stove is an essential. Rain gear and extra clothing for warmth are also mandatory. Good boots, well broken in before arrival, are another important item. Trails on the east side are drier than on the west, but mud or snow can be encountered anyplace in the mountains. Nights are cool in the high country, even in midsummer. Remember that most trails start in valleys. Altitude is therefore gained when the pack is heaviest; a conditioning program prior to arrival is mandatory for comfortable exploration of the high country.

Stores providing camping, backpacking, and climbing equipment are located in Seattle, Everett, Mount Vernon, Bellingham, and Wenatchee.

Hypothermia

Hypothermia ("exposure" is a misnomer) has been appropriately termed the "killer of the unprepared." Loss of body heat can occur rapidly high in the North Cascades, even at temperatures well above freezing. Thin individuals are particularly susceptible to hypothermia; women lose heat more slowly than men.

The danger of hypothermia is greatest with a combination of physical exhaustion and wet clothing; failure to eat may be a contributory factor. This combination of circumstances should be avoided at all costs, since mental deterioration occurs when body temperature falls to about 89° F, leaving the individual unable to make rational decisions. Without help from companions, death can occur in a surprisingly short time.

To prevent hypothermia, obey the following instructions: (1) carry effective waterproof external garments and use them immediately if it starts raining; (2) be aware of the windchill factor (the greater the wind speed at a given temperature, the greater the loss of body heat); (3) bivouac before exhaustion occurs, and construct the most effective practical shelter; (4) carry extra food and eat frequently, particularly starches and sugars; (5) keep as warm as possible with a fire or by huddling together to conserve body heat; (6) wear appropriate clothing if adverse weather is probable (polypropylene, pile, and wool all retain heat well when wet); and (7) maintain fluid intake to prevent dehydration, drinking warm liquids if possible.

The initial symptoms of hypothermia are marked shivering, a fast pulse, rapid breathing, and paleness. As body temperature falls, the shivering stops, pulse and respiration slow, and the body begins to feel cold to the touch. Further body temperature drop is manifested by confusion and defective thinking. If heat loss continues, consciousness is lost; the heartbeat becomes irregular; and body functions progressively deteriorate. Death occurs when the core temperature falls to about 80° F.

The treatment of choice is to provide heat as rapidly as possible without burning the patient. Minor hypothermia responds to the replacement of wet clothing with dry, use of additional insulation, administration of warm fluids, and consumption of candy and sugar. More severe hypothermia requires the addition of heat from external sources. A simple method of providing warmth is to encase the patient in an insulated cocoon containing one or more non-hypothermic companions. Sleeping bags, tarps, clothes, or any other available material may be used to surround the bodies. (For additional information on this subject, see the Bibliography.)

Wild Animals

All overnight campers must protect food supplies from bears. Many of the campsites that have had bear problems in the past are equipped with bear cables or bars strung between trees or posts; some camps have stringers connecting the cable with the ground. Since stringers are supplied in only a few camps, all campers should carry about 40 feet of nylon cord. Before retiring for the night, all food supplies should be placed in the pack or other suitable container and strung over the bear cable. If there is no cable, hang the food on a tree limb at least 10 feet above the ground and 5 feet from the trunk of the tree

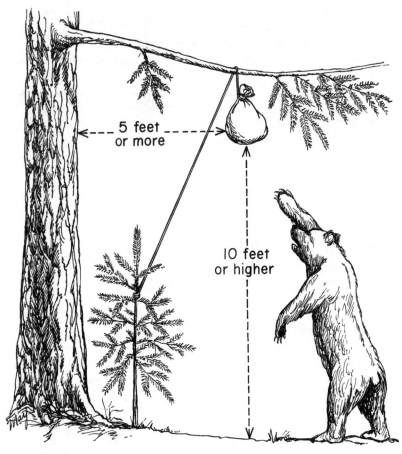

5 feet or more

10 feet or higher

Bear-proofing a campsite

(see diagram). Supplies left in camp during the day, if no one is present or if people are napping, should be protected in a similar manner. Here are some other suggestions for avoiding problems with bears: (1) never leave uneaten food in the camp area or, more importantly, in a tent; (2) place garbage in plastic to decrease odors, and be sure that the garbage is packed out of the camp area; and (3) do not feed any wild animals, particularly bears.

The black bear is far less dangerous than the grizzly; there are few, if any, grizzlies in the North Cascades. Although many campers have lost food to bears, injury from bear attacks in the Cascade Range has been negligible. However, it is always unwise to get between a mother bear and her cubs; the mother may attack if she feels that her cubs are threatened. (More information about bears is presented in the chapter on Animals.)

Rodents are present in many campsites. The bear-proofing method usually prevents rodent damage, as does storing food in metal or glass containers. Flocks of gray jays, Clark's nutcrackers, or ravens can also ravage a camper's food supply; in some areas, raccoons and skunks are a problem.

Remember that there are critters out there that would like to eat the food you have brought with you; good planning keeps your stomach full and their innards empty.

PHOTOGRAPHY

The North Cascades offer superb opportunities for quality mountain photography. However, camera enthusiasts in the North Cascades follow the rule that if you can see it, photograph it immediately, because you may not be able to see it later. Scenes with snow and ice in brilliant sunshine require ½ to 1½ f-stops downward compared with standard exposure (e.g., f/16 rather than f/11). Deep forest shots are difficult on sunny days, particularly with color film, in view of the marked lighting contrasts. In the woods, photography is best done on hazy or foggy days when the light is more uniform. Mountain photographs are much better when clouds are present than when the sky is a homogeneous blue. Unsettled weather often produces the best photographs, although the experience of surviving the inclement weather may not be as pleasant for the photographer as on a "bluebird" day. Wildflowers are best photographed against some sort of monochromatic background, such as a shaded area, rock, or log. Into-the-sun photographs can be effective in the mountains but require a much shorter exposure time and some good luck to avoid artifacts from the starburst effect of the sun.

Haze and clouds can sometimes produce unique photographic effects. A light meter is particularly useful at times of unusual lighting, such as sunrise, sunset, and various cloud conditions.

A wide-angle lens is occasionally helpful for recording broad panoramas. For example, the view of Mount Baker and the Black Buttes from the tarns a half mile east of the Park Butte lookout requires a wide-angle lens to photograph the mountain and its reflection in the water. Quality animal and bird photography generally requires a 135mm telephoto lens. This lens is probably the largest that can be used without a tripod, and most backpackers do not have the space for a tripod or the time to set one up when doing on-the-spot animal pictures. All other things being equal, the smaller the camera and lens, the less space they will occupy in the pack and the less weight to be carried on your back.

Climbing party on Mount Baker, 1908.

CLIMBING

Mountaineering opportunities abound throughout the North Cascade Range. Peaks of every degree of difficulty offer ongoing challenges to the mountaineer. An ardent climber could probably climb throughout a lifetime and not do all the routes on all mountains in the North Cascades. Some summits can be reached by simply a vigorous uphill walk; others involve great technical difficulty and require a high skill level. There are all gradations in between. Routes up a single peak vary from simple to very difficult. Those contemplating climbs should refer to a standard reference source in advance, such as the guides written by Fred Beckey (see the Bibliography).

Most climbs in the North Cascades involve an approach through a lowland valley, preferably by trail, less pleasantly by bushwhacking. There is generally a traverse across subalpine meadows. From the timberline, the ascent to near the summit generally involves crossing snow or glacier. Except for the volcanic snow cones, the final route to the summit usually involves a scramble, generally on rock. Most of the rock in the North Cascades is not solid; hand- and footholds must be tested in advance and retested to avoid serious falls.

The ice ax is an absolutely essential tool; the ability to do a self-arrest using the ax is mandatory. The ax has many other uses with which North Cascades climbers must be familiar. Crampons are necessary if any significant amount of ice must be traversed, and a quality climbing rope must be carried. Climbing parties should invariably "rope up" when crossing glaciers. The ice and rock of the arctic-alpine areas are hazardous to the inexperienced; those without climbing experience and proper equipment should restrict themselves to the trails.

Climbing parties should register at an appropriate Park or Forest Service office before climbing and sign out when they have descended.

Certain areas are restricted with regard to camping. Those planning climbs near these areas (Cascade Pass, for example) should discuss potential high camps with a ranger before departing from the Golden West Lodge in Stehekin or from Marblemount ranger station. High camps on ice, snow, and bare rock have no environmental impact and are allowed by the Park Service, even in areas otherwise closed to overnight camping.

Climbers should have experienced companions. Solitary climbing can be uniquely satisfying but is quite hazardous. Particularly in view of the unpredictable weather, a minimal climbing party should consist of three people, preferably four to six. All the climbers should have had the equivalent of a basic climbing course and, if crossing glaciers, should be experienced in crevasse rescue techniques.

Climbing courses, which include survival and wilderness travel training, are given in the Pacific Northwest by outdoor clubs and educational institutions annually, usually in the spring. Most classes are in the evening, with field trips on the weekends. Enrollment is strongly recommended for those interested in exploring the North Cascades.

The American Alpine Institute, Ltd. (1515 12th Street, Bellingham, WA 98225; 360-671-1505) offers both ice and rock climbing instruction and guided climbs in the North Cascades.

FISHING

Fishing is one of the pleasures of travel in the Pacific Northwest wilderness. Almost all the lakes and streams in the North Cascades contain trout.

Fishing at the head of Lake Chelan generally requires a boat, since the best lake fishing is at the mouth of the Stehekin River. However, it is possible to fish with some success from the docks around Stehekin or from places on the lakeshore where there is a fairly sharp dropoff into deep water.

Ross Lake trout fishing is legendary. Although it is not quite of the caliber that it was fifteen or twenty years ago, it can still be quite productive. The usual technique is to troll a series of spoons followed by a hook baited with worms or salmon eggs. Still fishing on Ross is not as effective. The best locations are at the mouths of the access streams. Boats can be rented from the Ross Lake Resort. Fishing in Diablo Lake is generally not as good as on Ross, but the lake is more accessible. Boats can be rented from the Diablo Lake Resort, or there is a launching area for private boats at the Colonial Creek Campground just off the North Cascades Highway at Thunder Arm. For stream fishing, worms, salmon eggs, and flies are commonly used lures. In the fall, the Stehekin River may yield large trout, often taken on mosquito flies. The thick brush that lines most rivers, particularly on the west side, is an impediment to fly-fishing. Hip boots or waders are suggested for avid fishermen.

Most of the high lakes have been stocked with trout. Two or three contain exotic species, such as the arctic grayling and the Sierra golden trout. Flies are generally the most effective lure, although bait is taken occasionally. Trout under 6 inches in length should be returned to the water with as little damage to their mouth parts as possible and with minimal exposure to air. A Washington fishing license is required; temporary licenses for nonresidents can be obtained at most sporting goods stores in good-sized towns; even small villages almost always have one location where licenses can be purchased.

Fishing gear for backpackers has become relatively miniaturized. A fly rod, reel, leaders, and flies fit into most backpacks without great difficulty. Supplementing a spartan backpacker's diet with fried trout is delightful.

As with fishing almost everywhere, the farther you get from a road, the more likely it is that quality fishing will be found.

Other fish in the rivers draining the western slopes of the North Cascades are the anadromous game fish, which include the steelhead and the various varieties of salmon (king, silver, humpback, chum, and sockeye). The steelhead is a seagoing rainbow trout that spends its infancy in the rivers and its maturity in Puget Sound or the Pacific Ocean. Both steelhead and salmon return to spawn in the small streams in which they were hatched. Unlike the salmon, which dies after spawning, the steelhead often survives and returns to the ocean. Apparently using subtle olfactory clues, these fish almost unerringly return to spawn in the small streams where they started their lives. A substantial fishery, both commercial and sport, exists for both types of fish. There has been much controversy over the past several years about what percentage of the catch should be reserved for the Indian tribes and what percentage may be taken by non-Indians. Pollution, overfishing, loss of spawning areas, and dams have reduced the fish runs to a fraction of their former magnitude. Nonetheless, the Skagit and its tributaries still contain substantial numbers of these fish. Dead salmon carcasses are a major food supply for the eagles that winter along the upper Skagit in considerable numbers.

HUNTING

Hunting is allowed everywhere in the North Cascades, except in North Cascades National Park. The most common animal hunted is the deer, but bears are also pursued. There are limited seasons on the mountain goat and cougar, and some hunters go after grouse. Certain animals such as the marmot and pika, and certain birds such as the eagle, are protected year-round.

In the early fall, there is a Cascades "high hunt" in certain areas of the mountains. During these times, hunters usually establish horse-packed base camps and use the pack animals to remove their kill. The regular deer season generally begins in mid-October and lasts through the first week of November.

Recreationists should use caution in all areas of the North Cascades, save in the National Park, during the fall hunting seasons. Stay on the trails if possible, and avoid bushwhacking through brushy areas. Wear high-visibility clothing, such as international orange, and make substantial noise (sing, whistle, carry a tinkling bell, or converse loudly with your trail partner).

A hunting license is required. Dates of the fall hunting seasons are set each year by the state of Washington; this information is available in almost all sporting goods stores.

WINTER SPORTS

Winter sports are also popular in the mountains of the Pacific Northwest. Downhill skiing areas are located at Heather Meadows (Mount Baker), Stevens Pass, Snoqualmie Pass, and Loup-Loup between Twisp and Okanogan. There are opportunities for cross-country (Nordic) skiing and snowshoe exploration away from the developed ski facilities. For the very experienced and well equipped, the summits still beckon, even in the dead of winter.

Only the main cross-mountain highways are plowed, limiting access to many backcountry areas between December and April. Snowmobiles can penetrate deeply into the wilderness, but most skiers and snowshoers find their noise profane and their tracks a technical problem. Conflicts between the machine users and the self-propelled exist both on the logging roads in winter and on the trails in summer.

Hypothermia and avalanches are substantial hazards to those who challenge the North Cascades in winter. The experienced can predict whether overall avalanche risk is minimal, moderate, or high, but no one can be sure of the safety of a route at any given moment. These snowy torrents can snap off 4-foot-diameter trees like matchsticks and deposit the debris 300 feet high on the other side of the valley; the speed of the snowslide can reach 200 miles per hour. A mere human has little chance of surviving if overwhelmed by megatons of rapidly moving snow.

The Methow valley is perhaps the best location for cross-country skiing in the North Cascades. Groomed trails are maintained by Sun Mountain Lodge near Winthrop. Elsewhere, the lack of level terrain and the frequent changes in snow quality as altitude is gained and lost make proper waxing of skis a greater problem than in most other areas. Many have turned to fish-scale touring skis as the best solution to North Cascades conditions.

Snowshoes should be fitted with special metal traction devices to improve performance on steep terrain.

Those interested in winter mountaineering and wilderness travel should consult the references listed in the Bibliography for additional information about routes, techniques, avalanche risks, and winter survival skills.

RIVER SPORTS

The North Cascades rivers offer a wide range of white-water experiences, including major rapids, breathtaking scenery, and riverside camping. There are two major points about these rivers deserving emphasis. First, all are fairly cold, even in late summer. As a result, hypothermia due to prolonged immersion in these rivers can be life threatening. Second, trees from the surrounding forest often fall into the rivers, and dangerous obstructions develop unpredictably. Tree limbs, submerged logs, and logjams increase the danger for boaters, even though the white water itself may be relatively mild. Consequently, the first time down a river for the season, extreme care should be taken, scouting ahead when necessary and obtaining advance information from other boaters.

There are runs other than those described here, but they have dangerous logjams or falls that must be portaged. All water classifications are American kayak I–VI scale.

The north fork of the Nooksack can be run from the Douglas Fir Campground down to Deming. The south fork can be floated from Doran to the confluence of the north and south forks.

The Stillaguamish is a good run for inflatables early in the spring; later in the year, low water makes it floatable only by kayaks.

The Skagit River system offers a wide range of boating experiences. The river below Marblemount is relatively rapid free and is at most Class II water. The woods and farmlands through which the river passes are attractive; in the background are the forested foothills of the North Cascades. Deer and other wildlife are often seen on the riverbanks, and eagles roost alongside the river in winter. Spawning salmon may be observed in tributaries in the fall. Fishermen may catch trout, steelhead, and salmon.

Above Marblemount, the Skagit is a little more challenging. The put-in is at Goodell Creek. There are several take-out points, located at Copper Creek, Bacon Creek, and Marblemount, allowing trips of 8, 10, and 14 miles, respectively. Most of the upper part of the river is large water with fairly obvious channels. The one major run of rapids, the famous S-turn, can be scouted from the road; usually Class III, this section of white water can reach Class IV at times. The majority of the trip, however, is Class II water, making the run the least demanding of the white-water transits in the area.

The Sauk River offers approximately 40 miles of river experience. Access points approximately every 10 miles make day trips convenient. Two- and three-day trips with overnight camps are also feasible. This river is only for the more experienced, in view of the logjams and Class IV to V rapids in places.

The lower 10 to 12 miles of the Suiattle can be run; rapids are considered Class II to III. From the river, there are excellent views of the nearby mountains, with scenic waterfalls descending from their flanks.

The Methow River drains the eastern portion of the North Cascades area and offers a striking contrast to the western rivers, because it flows through a desert environment. It can be run from Mazama down to its mouth at the Columbia River. Because there is a road close to the river most of the time, the boater does not get a feeling of traversing wilderness, but the roads and bridges allow for easy access to and from the river. Since precipitation on the east side of the crest is substantially less than on the west, by late summer and early fall, the water level is too low to make running feasible in most years.

ROAD ACCESS

Six west-side and four east-side roads provide access to the park and associated recreational areas, plus the two "water roads" of Lake Chelan and Ross Lake.

There is limited access to the area through Canada. Forking off from the Trans-Canada Highway a short distance west of Hope, a relatively primitive road reaches the north end of Ross Lake. Trails and fire roads from Canadian Provincial Highway 3 pass through Manning Provincial Park to reach the Cascade Crest and other trails. Cathedral Park is reached via the Ashnola Road, which branches off British Columbia Highway 3, 2 miles east of Keremeos.

Stevens Pass Highway (U.S. 2), open all year, provides access to the Pacific Crest Trail at the pass and to the Curry Gap section of the Crest Trail via Smith Brook Road just east of the summit. A number of other scenic trails are reached from the east section of U.S. 2 via State Highways 207 and 209. These latter roads depart from Cole's Corner and Leavenworth, respectively, to reach Lake Wenatchee and Trinity. The Stevens Pass Highway is moderately scenic. Tumwater Canyon on the east side is a pleasant drive, particularly in the fall, when the colors of the turning leaves make this section of the road impressive. There are extensive ski developments at the crest of the pass, heavily used in winter and unsightly in summer. There are no broad perspectives of the surrounding mountains without substantial walking.

U.S. 97 is the main eastern approach road. The eastern end of the Pasayten Wilderness is best reached via Tonasket and Loomis. State Routes 153 and 20 lead to Twisp and Winthrop, gateways to the Twisp and Chewuch valleys.

West of Winthrop is Mazama, gateway to both Harts Pass and the eastern portion of the North Cascades Highway.

Western road access, from the south northward, begins with the southern portion of the Mountain Loop Highway. The western terminus of this highway is at Granite Falls, where State 92 connects with State 9 and ultimately with Interstate 5. The pavement terminates at Barlow Pass about 30 miles east of Granite Falls. Good stream fishing is available at many areas along the highway on the south fork of the Stillaguamish River. The last few miles of the road offer spectacular mountain vistas. Monte Cristo is of interest to those concerned with North Cascades history. From Barlow Pass, the Mount Loop Highway continues northward through pleasant and occasionally impressive country. Side roads to the east allow one to reach trailheads on the Sauk and White Chuck Rivers. Each of these side roads is easily negotiable in a standard passenger car and offers a number of locations for car camping and fishing and, from time to time, spectacular vistas of the surrounding mountains. The Mountain Loop Highway terminates about a mile northeast of Darrington.

Darrington can be reached from Interstate 5, taking the Arlington exit and progressing eastward on State 530 approximately 30 miles. Fine fly-fishing can be had in the north fork of the Stillaguamish en route. From Darrington, it is possible to connect with the Mountain Loop Highway; there is also a good connecting road from Darrington to Rockport paralleling, in general, the Sauk River and offering opportunities for trout fishing in summer and steelhead fishing in winter. About midway between Darrington and Rockport, the access road up the Suiattle valley is intersected. A number of forest camps, good fishing, access to a number of trailheads, and some enjoyable scenery are available on the Suiattle Road.

The Mount Baker Highway (State 542) is a high-grade, all-weather, all-season road that terminates at Artist's Point. A Forest Service visitors' center is located near the road. Some of the most spectacular scenery in the North Cascades is available from this road without getting out of the car. Particularly striking are the splendid views across Picture Lake of Mount Shuksan, perhaps the most photogenic peak in North America. Also of interest en route are the Nooksack Falls, some very interesting basaltic lava formations with talus slopes beneath, and some fine views of Mount Baker. Tire chains are mandatory during the winter season on this road. It does, however, offer access to the high country, even when the snow is piled 25 feet deep at the Heather Meadows ski facility.

Probably the most spectacular access route to the park and associated recreational areas is the North Cascades Highway (State 20), completed in September 1972. This route leaves Interstate 5 at Burlington and progresses eastward through Sedro Woolley and Hamilton. Six miles east of Hamilton, and at Concrete, spur roads provide access to Baker Lake and to the scenic country on the south sides of Mounts Baker and Shuksan. There is a resort at Baker Lake. Fishing, hunting in season, forest camps, magnificent deep woods, and splendid mountain panoramas are available from the Baker Lake Road and its branches.

The North Cascades Highway continues northeastward through Rockport (where there is a connection with Darrington) to Marblemount. At this point, the Cascade Pass Mine to Market Road crosses the Skagit River and continues approximately 18 miles to the Cascade Pass trailhead. This road offers access to fishing areas along the Cascade River and passes a number of forest camps. Impressive scenery is visible from the road, providing an unusual opportunity to enjoy the mountains without leaving the car.

From Marblemount, State 20 continues northeastward through the Seattle City Light town of Newhalem. The Goddell Creek campground is located to the east of the road just before entering the City Light village. The Newhalem campground and the recently constructed visitors' center are accessed by a one-way bridge on the outskirts of the village. (Aggressive enforcement, particularly on weekends, of inappropriately low speed limits occurs in Newhalem and Concrete. Watch speed signs carefully and drive defensively in these areas.)

The road then enters the scenic Skagit River gorge, which it follows to near Diablo village, 1 mile off the main road. Employees of Seattle City Light, Seattle's electrical utility, live in Newhalem and Diablo. The utility built the three dams on the Skagit River. Note the major avalanche tracks that have necessitated road reconstruction. Near Diablo, the highway crosses Gorge Lake (the former Skagit River); another 1.3 miles farther, the turnoff to Diablo Dam is passed. The road then contours above Diablo Lake, passes Thunder Lake, and shortly thereafter crosses Thunder Arm, an extension of Diablo Lake. Fine camping is offered at this location in the Colonial Creek campground, staffed by the National Park Service.

About 5 miles beyond Thunder Arm, an impressive view northward over Ross Lake, with the Picket Range to the northwest and Jack Mountain to the northeast, merits a stop for photography and contemplation. The road continues eastward an additional 5 miles to the junction of Ruby Creek and Granite Creek and then climbs gradually an additional 13 miles up the Granite Creek valley. Fairly level Rainy Pass is reached, where there are several trailheads; from here, the road dips down slightly and then regains altitude to reach the Cascade crest at Washington Pass, immediately beneath the massive granite massif of Liberty Bell and its associated spires. A side road leads to a viewpoint and to an information booth. From the pass, the road switchbacks downward rapidly to reach Mazama and Winthrop.

In the Early Winters area, a Forest Service interpretive center is located about a mile west of Mazama.

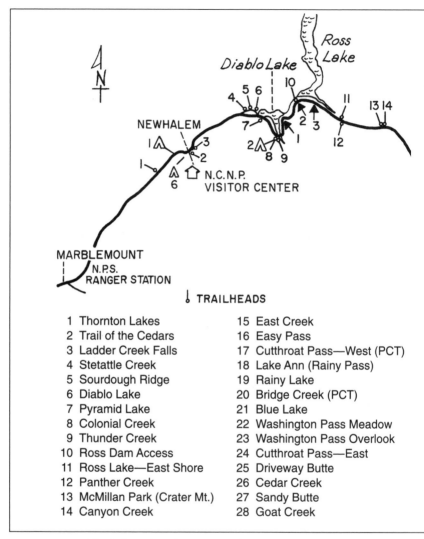

North Cascades Highway, Marblemount to Mazama

TRAILHEADS

1 Thornton Lakes
2 Trail of the Cedars
3 Ladder Creek Falls
4 Stetattle Creek
5 Sourdough Ridge
6 Diablo Lake
7 Pyramid Lake
8 Colonial Creek
9 Thunder Creek
10 Ross Dam Access
11 Ross Lake—East Shore
12 Panther Creek
13 McMillan Park (Crater Mt.)
14 Canyon Creek

15 East Creek
16 Easy Pass
17 Cutthroat Pass—West (PCT)
18 Lake Ann (Rainy Pass)
19 Rainy Lake
20 Bridge Creek (PCT)
21 Blue Lake
22 Washington Pass Meadow
23 Washington Pass Overlook
24 Cutthroat Pass—East
25 Driveway Butte
26 Cedar Creek
27 Sandy Butte
28 Goat Creek

The North Cascades Highway offers views as impressive as any in the United States from the road. The only comparable road in my experience is the one in Canada between Lake Louise and Jasper. Spectacular peaks, icy-blue glaciers, verdant forest, tumbling mountain streams, and the scent of Douglas fir make this a most scenic drive. This highway offers access to thirty fine trails, many of which are included in the trail guide section of this book. A detailed description of the highway, and of the thirty trails originating from it, is con-

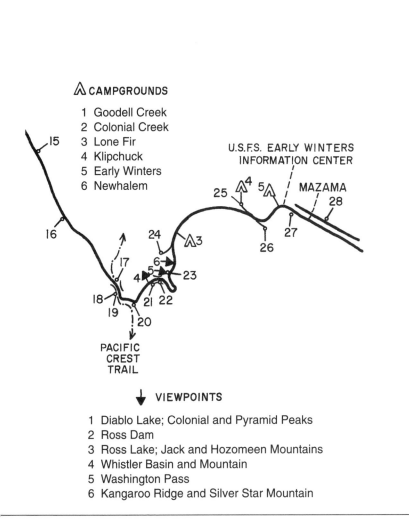

Ⓐ CAMPGROUNDS

1 Goodell Creek
2 Colonial Creek
3 Lone Fir
4 Klipchuck
5 Early Winters
6 Newhalem

U.S.F.S. EARLY WINTERS
INFORMATION CENTER

MAZAMA

PACIFIC
CREST
TRAIL

↓ VIEWPOINTS

1 Diablo Lake; Colonial and Pyramid Peaks
2 Ross Dam
3 Ross Lake; Jack and Hozomeen Mountains
4 Whistler Basin and Mountain
5 Washington Pass
6 Kangaroo Ridge and Silver Star Mountain

tained in the 62-page booklet *North Cascades Highway Guide* (2nd edition), published in 1986. Although a bit out of date, this publication is still the best guide to Highway 20 between Marblemount and Winthrop.

One road that certainly deserves mention and description is the 23-mile road beginning at Stehekin Landing and ending at Cottonwood Camp. This road has aptly been described as "beginning at the lakeshore and dead-ending at paradise." The road, paved for the first 4 miles, follows the lakeshore for a bit over a mile and then enters wooded country at the northwest end of the lake. At about 2 miles, the side roads to Silver Beach and the Stehekin River Resort fork off the main road to the left. The short spur road to Rainbow Falls forks to the right a little beyond the 3-mile mark, just past the historic one-room Stehekin school. Although supplanted by a newer school, the building and Rainbow Falls merit inspection. The 0.1 mile from the loop road head to the base of the falls can easily be hiked by anyone. Standing in the spray of the falls, particularly in the spring when the snowmelt is substantial, is an experience to be remembered. In May, blooming dogwood overhangs this trail. A little beyond the 4-mile mark, the road forks, with the left road leading to the Stehekin airport, Company Creek trailhead, and a number of residences on the southwest side of the river. The main road continues upriver at this point to reach the High Bridge Guard Station and shelter, the national park boundary, and multiple trailheads at a little past the 10-mile mark. From this point on, there are numerous established campsites along the road, some with shelters. Fishing is good in the Stehekin River from almost its source to the mouth in season (July through October). Beyond High Bridge, the quality of the road deteriorates. In addition to High Bridge, forest camps are located at Dolly Varden, Bridge Creek, Shady Creek, and Cottonwood Camp. The Bridge Creek, Park Creek, and Flat Creek trailheads are passed en route.

The Stehekin Road is currently served by a shuttle-bus system during the spring, summer, and early fall. Schedules change from year to year, so if you plan on using the system, particularly if hiking into the area, check with the Park Service to obtain the current schedule. Early in the season, the road may not be passable; making prior inquiry at a Park Service facility is highly advisable.

Magnificent mountain scenery, the clear and beautiful Stehekin River, the verdant forest, and the sense of isolation make driving the Stehekin Road a thrilling experience.

Floods intermittently damage the Stehekin Road. The greatest flood in history, in November 1995, caused major road damage between High Bridge and Cottonwood. Current plans are to repair the road to Flat Creek by mid–1998. Repair of the last 3 miles of road have been indefinitely deferred, pending natural changes in the Stehekin River watercourse.

The second edition of a 1996 guidebook to the Stehekin area is available locally or from the publisher (see the Bibliography).

Change is one of the laws of the universe. The human factor makes some errors in a book of this length almost inevitable. For both reasons, feedback from readers is welcome. If you find an inaccuracy meriting correction in future editions, please write to me care of the publisher. Carefully document the situation, using diagrams, photographs, or references.

The experience gained after forty years of involvement in conservation activities has convinced me that both eternal vigilance and self-sacrifice are the prices one must pay if wilderness and wild beauty are to be preserved indefinitely.

As sagely observed by a North Cascades aficionado, the current problems in several areas of the North Cascades (and in many other national parks and dedicated wilderness areas) are due to "too many people, and not enough mountains to go around." As the population increases, the adverse impact on all of the finite wild lands accentuates. Solutions to continued population growth merit the concern of everyone, particularly those people who value natural beauty and sojourns into pristine scenic backcountry.

All of us who love the mountains and the wild places of this earth must fight a never-ending battle to conserve and to protect. Serene, magnificent areas will not be left inviolate if corporate America can profit from their destruction. Since only disciplined political activity is effective in influencing the decisions of the land managers, it is imperative that those who love the wildlands continue to defend the values of beauty, wilderness, and solitude. A number of local and national conservation organizations are active in the cause of preservation of our national heritage; membership in one or more of them is therefore suggested (see the list in the Resources section). It is also suggested that you join an outdoor club if one exists in your area. Check with the Federation of Western Outdoor Clubs (c/o Northwest Conservation Representative, 1516 Melrose Avenue, Seattle, WA 98122) for information and for the address of the outdoor club nearest you.

Carbon dioxide accumulation likely will result in global warming in the next century, with major deleterious consequences. Ancient forests, both temperate and tropical, by taking up carbon dioxide from the atmosphere, are needed to mitigate the increase of this gas. The timber of the ancient forests of the North Cascades is subject to continual attempts by the logging industry to convert the trees to pulpwood and lumber. Since both lumber and old-growth forests are necessary to our welfare, environmentalists and the logging industry must seek compromises that minimize the cutting of ancient forests and rely instead on the reforestation of both public and private lands and state-of-the-art logging and milling techniques.

Having achieved the North Cascades National Park complex, the Mount Baker National Recreation Area, and the seven wilderness areas within the North Cascades, let us remember that eternal vigilance is required to preserve the remaining areas of beauty and wildness in the North Cascades and to safeguard all of Washington's magnificent wilderness for the benefit of posterity. These unsurpassed mountains must be kept pristine and wild indefinitely.

2

Archaeology

RESEARCH HISTORY

The first professional archaeological investigations in the North Cascades National Park (NCNP), beginning in the early 1970s, were surveys conducted to find and document archaeological sites. Few sites were found, as artifacts and other remains of the first people proved difficult to uncover in dense forests and rugged mountainous terrain. With little hard evidence to go by, it was generally thought that Native American people and their ancestors had made little if any use of the Cascades interior, except to pass between interior and coastal regions for purposes of trade. These views were held in spite of native elders' references to the use and knowledge of high-elevation resources.

Beginning in the early 1980s, the National Park Service (NPS) began to systematically gather field and archival data related to the earliest human uses of NPS lands in the Pacific Northwest. Beginning in 1984, annual archaeological projects have been conducted to inventory and assess the significance of prehistoric sites. This has resulted in the rapid accumulation of a large body of archaeological data. In 1984, only 17 archaeological sites had been inventoried within the NCNP; today there are 260 inventoried sites (237 prehistoric and 23 historic). Although ongoing, archaeological research and inventory at the NCNP are still in their infancy, and only about 5 percent of the 684,000 acres of the park complex has been surveyed to date. Although it will be a long time before the complete story of human use of the North Cascades can be told, the following sections describe what has been learned from recent archaeological studies in the most scenic and rugged of Washington's mountainous landscapes.

PREHISTORIC USE

The lands in today's park complex were occupied by human groups for at least the last 8,400 years, based on radiocarbon-dated archaeological sites. Distinctive styles of a few spear points suggest that humans may have used the North

Author's note: This section was prepared with the assistance of Robert R. Mierendorf, park archaeologist, North Cascades National Park, Marblemount, Washington.

Cascades for the last 10,000 years or so. It is probable that these people were the ancestors of today's Coast Salish and Interior Salish speaking peoples, particularly the various bands of the Upper Skagit, Sauk-Suiattle, Nooksack, Chilliwack, Nlakapamux (Lower Thompson), Chelan, Methow, Entiat, and Similkameen tribes.

Most of the archaeological sites in the NCNP consist of belowground remains of camps and resource use areas, where Indian people processed and cooked food, collected specific kinds of rocks and minerals for tools, hunted, fished, and collected plants. Some sites have aboveground remains and appear as rock shelters, rock art, bark-stripped trees, rock alignments and piles, and pits dug in the ground.

These sites are found throughout all environmental and elevational zones of the park complex, from the densely forested valley bottoms to above the timberline. Because some of the locations are so remote and adjacent to the steepest portions of the mountains, it is clear that prehistoric people were more than just traveling through; rather, they explored all portions of the mountains and used the locally available resources during their stay. Some parties traveled across the mountains for purposes of trade and social relationships, which lent great significance to the lowest passes, such as Cascade Pass; these provided the main travel routes across the range.

Although large and permanent villages have yet to be found in the park complex, remnants of these are likely to exist along the lower valleys of the largest rivers. Most of the camps that have been found represent short-term or seasonal occupation by relatively small groups of people. Some of these camps were occupied recurrently for thousands of years. The geographic distribution of camps within interior valleys shows a clear settlement pattern: not unexpectedly, camps are asymmetrically located in mountain valleys and tend to cluster in those parts of the valley offering maximal solar insulation and minimal exposure to avalanche slopes. This pattern is most clearly expressed in the Skagit River valley and Stehekin River–Lake Chelan valley.

NEW RESULTS FROM RECENT ARCHAEOLOGICAL SITES
The following data were derived from detailed study and analysis of about fifty archaeological sites within the park complex.

Radiocarbon Chronology
The chronology of prehistoric use of the park complex is based on a sample of fifty-two radiocarbon dates. The oldest site is a chert quarry in the Skagit River valley dated 8,400 years old (calibrated using dendrochronology); the youngest is a fishing encampment dated 170 years old. These radiocarbon dates are not uniformly spread across the last 8,400 years. Instead, they cluster into three

distinct time periods. The earliest period is 5,000 to 3,500 years ago, the next is 2,000 to 1,000 years ago, and the most recent is 600 to 200 years ago. The exact significance of these clusters is unknown. Generally, we can conclude that the park complex was used more or less continually over the last 8,400 or more years, but with three periods of more intensive activity.

Tephrochronology (Volcanic Ash Dating)

As in other geographic regions of the Pacific Northwest, native populations had to cope with the frequent eruption of Cascade volcanoes. Ash deposits from some of these eruptions are prominent within archaeological sites or the deposits below them. To date, four chemically distinct ash layers have been identified within the park complex. These include Mount St. Helens J (about 12,000 years old), Mount Mazama O (6,800 years old), Mount St. Helens Y (3,500 to 2,900 years old), and Mount St. Helens W (500 years old). Two additional ash layers have been found, but their source is unknown. Mount Baker or Glacier Peak, the two closest volcanoes to the park, may be the source for one or both of these layers. The effects of all these ashfalls on the lives of native populations are uncertain, but there is nothing in the archaeological evidence that indicates any effect at all.

Prehistoric Artifact Types

A wide array of tool types have been found in archaeological sites. Chipped stone tools include spear, dart, and arrow points; knives; scrapers; drills; gravers; microblades and microblade cores; and simple flake tools. Stylistically, these suggest that native groups in the North Cascades maintained direct or indirect relationships with groups widespread in the foothills and nonmountainous lands surrounding the northern Cascade range. Ground stone tools include adz blades; slate knives; soapstone pipe bowls, effigies, and decorative pieces; pestles and manos; and grinding tools and hammerstones. A few broken bone awl or harpoon tips were found at one site.

Other remains, called "features" by archaeologists, including living floors at camps, food-cooking pits and hearths, sweat lodges, salmon smoking and drying sites, vision quest locations, hunting blinds, and food storage locations. The oldest dated feature in the park complex is a subalpine campfire area that is 5,400 years old (calibrated using dendrochronology). Overall, the combined inventory of artifacts and features indicates extensive use of mountain landscapes for hunting, gathering, and fishing purposes, including the processing, cooking, and working of a wide variety of local resources.

With few exceptions, the artifact assemblages from throughout the park complex are dominated by utilitarian remains, the evidence of procuring, manufacturing, and processing the numerous locally derived resources pro-

vided by the mountain environment. Compared with artifacts from archaeological assemblages from nonmountainous environments, the evidence suggests that people in the North Cascades wasted little and tended to discard
tools only after they were worn out. These early people traveled light by
today's standards; nonetheless, they were able to move freely across all parts
of the mountain landscape.

Faunal and Floral Remains
Often in the excavation of archaeological sites, the remains of animals and
plants used by the inhabitants are found. Due to the moist, maritime climate,
which accelerates the decay process, and the acidic mountain soils, organic
remains are rarely preserved. To date, the best preservation environment, surprisingly, is in cooking hearths and other features where organic remains were
charred but not completely burned. Like charcoal, such charred remains are
chemically stable and can remain in the soil for thousands of years.

Animals, used for food and utilitarian purposes, have been recognized
from remains found in a few hearths. These include beavers, mountain goats,
elk, and deer. Other animal remains cannot be identified to the species level,
but numerous bones from birds, small mammals, and fish have been found.
One site that marks a fish smoking and drying location, dated 660 to 170 years
old, contains thousands of bones (spines, vertebrae, and teeth) of salmonids of
an as yet unidentified species.

Plant remains are preserved in sites as charred fragments or sometimes
complete specimens. At one site dated 475 years old, dozens of charred red
elderberry seeds were identified from a cooking hearth. Most of the charred
remains from archaeological features appear to be woody parts of trees and
shrubs used for fuel.

Shell remains are rarely found from park complex sites, the single exception being a complete *Dentalium* shell recovered from one site. *Dentalium* is a
seashell found in sand and mud habitats under 6 to 500 feet of water along the
Pacific coast. It was highly valued by native peoples and was used throughout
the Pacific Northwest as a form of currency.

Stone Procurement and Use
The North Cascades provided an incredible array of stone raw materials that
were used by native groups for tools and other utilitarian needs. These stone
materials include a variety of quartz called chert, slate, argillite, serpentine,
quartz crystal, soapstone, and obsidian.

In the northern portion of the North Cascades, numerous chert quarries
have been found, marking the places where chert fragments were hammered
from bedrock outcrops and glacial boulders. Artifacts made of this Hozomeen

chert have been found as far east as Lake Chelan and as far west as Puget Sound. In another part of the park complex, far removed from the chert quarries, were alpine and subalpine obsidian quarries. Although generally poor in quality, this distinctive material has been used for at least 5,300 years and is beginning to be found in archaeological sites far removed from its source.

Other varieties of high-quality obsidian have been found in archaeological sites in the park complex. Chemical analysis of these varieties indicates that they were derived from sources far to the south, in today's northern California and Oregon. It can now be said with certainty that native inhabitants of the North Cascades participated in a broad, intraregional trade network, through which they procured high-quality obsidian from such volcanic terrains as Newberry Crater, Glass Butte, and the Three Sisters, all located in central Oregon.

INTERPRETIVE EXHIBITS

A small display of prehistoric artifacts from the park complex is open to the public at the North Cascades Visitor Center, located a short distance south of Highway 20, just before Newhalem. The display shows original artifacts from eastern, western, and subalpine landscapes of the North Cascades, as part of a larger exhibit explaining the natural history of the park complex.

Presently, none of the archaeological sites in the park complex are open to public visitation. However, NCNP staff are presently planning for the exhibition of a small prehistoric rock shelter located not far from the visitor center. The project includes building a handicapped-accessible interpretive trail to a viewing deck that will overlook the rock-shelter floor. Interpretive panels will describe the significance of the rock shelter from archaeological and native perspectives. The shelter itself will be closed to the public to maintain the site and the surrounding forest in its natural condition. The trail and viewing deck will serve as the site of guided ranger programs about the first inhabitants of the North Cascades.

Native use of this shelter is radiocarbon-dated to 1,350 years ago, with occupation as recently as 250 years ago. This shelter was used to cook a variety of local food resources, and it may have served as a short-term camp for a small group of people. Most of the remains from the shelter are associated with hunting activities and include small stone arrow points and mountain goat bones. Other artifacts from the site indicate that most of the stone tools were manufactured somewhere else and brought to the site, where they were repaired and resharpened. Some of the animals brought to the site were butchered there, and the abundance of charcoal associated with small pit features indicates that food animals were cooked or smoked and were probably consumed at this location.

The completion date for this project is uncertain. Detailed project plans are currently under way, in consultation with the Skagit tribes. At this time, the NCNP is seeking funding support for development of the project. It is hoped that within the next few years, this interpretive facility will be open to the public.

SITE PROTECTION
The National Park Service and the North Cascades National Park are committed to protecting the archaeological resources under their jurisdiction. These resources are protected under the Archaeological Resources Protection Act of 1979 and its amendments and other federal regulations and guidelines. It is illegal to remove, destroy, disturb, or deface artifacts; to dig in archaeological sites; or to disturb or deface Indian burials or rock art. These activities result in the irretrievable loss of the nation's heritage. To ensure that this does not become a problem at North Cascades, the specific locations of archaeological sites are confidential.

FUTURE DIRECTIONS
Archaeological inventories and assessments of archaeological site significance in the NCNP are ongoing. If information gained in the next few decades is comparable to the accomplishments of the last two, much new knowledge about the past will be acquired. Increasingly, this information will be offered to the interested public through a variety of NPS interpretive programs and publications.

For more detailed information on some of the archaeological studies conducted in the NCNP, interested readers can visit the NCNP library, located at the park headquarters in Sedro Woolley.

History

3

Much of human history in the North Cascades, particularly during the early years of exploration, has been irretrievably lost. Accurate history depends on the preservation of records; unfortunately, much of the data of the early explorations were neither recorded nor preserved. The fragmentary records available to current historians have led competent observers to draw different conclusions. It is unlikely that these controversies about early North Cascades history will ever be firmly resolved.

First on the scene, of course, were the Indians. Early humans reached North America via the Siberia–Alaska land bridge. This route existed in the past when ocean levels were substantially lower than they are at present, presumably because considerably more water was locked in ice masses.

The coast Indians and the interior aborigines lived in substantially different environments and, as a result, evolved dissimilar lifestyles and customs. However, trails to facilitate trading between the two groups were developed over the centuries. Wild hemp, useful for making fishing nets, was exchanged for the Higua shell, which served as a medium of exchange for the inland Indians. Most historians concur that the most extensively used of the primitive transmountain routes was over the Cascade Pass, but Indian Pass, Snoqualmie Pass, and perhaps the route of the current North Cascades Highway were also traveled.

Stehekin is a corruption of an Indian word meaning "the way through." The word first appeared in George Gibbs's map in 1860 as S'cho-kehn; by 1866, the boundary survey map read Stcho-kin; by 1883, it had become Stehekin and has remained so since. Skilled professional investigation has discovered that the Skagit people extensively utilized the mountains even though little remains of Native American presence. Perhaps this should be considered to the credit of the first people here; they walked softly, lived within the carrying capacity of the land, and left few marks of their passage. Our culture has not done as well.

EARLY EXPLORATION

In 1790, while exploring Bellingham Bay, Spanish cartographer Lopez de Haro saw Mount Baker and named it Montana del Carmelo. Two years later, Captain George Vancouver, during his exploration of Puget Sound, renamed it after Third Lieutenant Joseph Baker, who first saw the mountain while on watch. The Indians knew the peak as Koma Kulshan. There is disagreement regarding the meaning of this. The generally accepted translations are "the great white watcher" or "the shining one"; however, Buchanan in 1913 wrote that "Kulshan is a Lummi word, indicating that the summit of the peak has been damaged or blown off in an explosion." If this translation is accepted, the mountain was probably named after the Indians witnessed a significant eruption of the peak. Each of the neighboring tribes also had its own name for this impressive ice-clad volcano, and these names translate into English as "white rock" or "white mountain."

Probably the first white man to traverse the North Cascades was Alexander Ross. Ross, a member of John J. Astor's Pacific Fur Company, arrived at Astoria in 1811 and was assigned to establish an interior fort for the organization. He founded Fort Okanogan (located where the Okanogan River joins the Columbia River) in September 1811 and was in charge of the fort for the next five years. In 1814, in the company of three Indian guides and companions, he set out to explore the region between the fort and Puget Sound and to determine "if that part of the country held out a good prospect for extending the trade."

On July 25, with a blanket, gun, compass, ammunition, and kettle, he set out to explore the unknown. Historians still conjecture as to his exact route, since his journal is less than clear. Probably he traveled up the Methow River by Indian trails, crossing into the Bridge Creek drainage via either Twisp or Copper Pass. Most historians presume that he descended Bridge Creek to its junction with the Stehekin, then turned west and crossed the Cascade crest on July 30, probably at Cascade Pass. It is also possible that he turned northward at Bridge Creek and followed the Rainy Pass route now traversed by the North Cascades Highway. In any event, on the west side of the crest, probably at the Mineral Park area near the Cascade River, he encountered difficulties. A guide became sick and was unable to proceed. Ross left the ill guide with a companion and pressed forward with the remaining Indian, who presumably knew the route to Puget Sound. On August 4, he reached a river junction, probably the junction of the Cascade and the Skagit, at the present site of Marblemount. The following day, a violent windstorm panicked his guide, and the Indian deserted during the night. Since there were no settlements to the west in 1814, and without the services of a guide, Ross reluctantly but wisely gave up and retraced his steps. He arrived back at Fort Okanogan one month after his departure. How far he progressed down the Skagit (or whatever river he may have been following) is unknown. Some historians believe that he may have gone as far as the present-day site of Sedro Woolley; others think otherwise. Regardless, it was a historic and memorable transit of the mountains and earned Ross a permanent niche in North Cascades history.

The army also had a part to play in the North Cascades. In 1853, territorial Governor Isaac Stevens directed young Captain George McClellan to undertake an exploration of the North Cascades to determine the feasibility of building a wagon road through the mountains. Apparently disliking this assignment, McClellan did not take advantage of the opportunity to investigate the Stehekin Valley and Cascade Pass, nor did he evaluate the Twisp Pass–Rainy Pass transmountain route. Based on what appears in retrospect to have been a suboptimal investigation, he reported that there was no satisfactory, economical route across the mountains. (Many historians believe that he was equally ineffectual as a Civil War general.)

In 1880, an army post was established at the site of the present town of Chelan. Colonel Merriam, in command, personally explored the area at the head of the lake and described the Indian pictographs across from the present Stehekin Landing. The army detachment was moved elsewhere within the year, so the colonel and his followers had no other role in North Cascades history.

Soldiers and prospectors arrived in the Stehekin valley at approximately the same time. In 1882, the U.S. Army expedition under the command of Lieutenant Henry Pierce left Fort Colville on August 1, 1882, and proceeded west, up the Methow to the Twisp River, then up to War Creek. He followed that valley to what is presently War Creek Pass and crossed the Juanita Lake meadow to a point where he could see the head of Lake Chelan, presumably at Purple Pass (or perhaps Boulder Butte).

He stated: "As I gazed westward from a height of 6,500 feet above the sea and 5,800 feet above the lake, a scene of remarkable grandeur was presented. To the south and west were the rugged peaks of the Cascade Mountains covered with everlasting snow. At our feet, reposed [Lake] Chelan in color like an artificial lake of thick plate glass, while the Stehekin River brought its clay-tinted waters with many a winding down the narrow canyon that opened to the North." After accomplishing the difficult descent to the lake, Pierce described the valley bottom as a "dense jungle of cottonwood, willows, firs, and underbrush with frequent lagoons covered by almost tropical growth of rush grass, ferns, and other marshy vegetation." Proceeding up the valley on a "most imperfect trail," Pierce noticed, as the party forded Bridge Creek, a crude bridge of drift logs, presumably used by Indians for crossing the creek.

Cascade Pass was crossed the morning of August 27. Quartz presumed to contain gold was found. (One of the upper tributaries of the Cascade River is called Soldier Boy Creek, and one of the mining claims in that area was named Soldier Boy.) The remainder of the trip down the Cascade River was uneventful. Near the mouth of the Cascade, an Indian summer lodge was found, and Indians were employed to take the party down the Skagit by canoe. By November 1, the patrol reached a logging camp near the present Sedro Woolley.

Pierce reported that a military road through that portion of the North Cascades was not necessary, since the mountain range itself was sufficient barrier to keep the interior and coastal Indians separated and prevent them from forming a successful alliance. Pierce's account and accompanying map gained public attention and publicized the area to the rest of the world.

The northern boundary of the North Cascades National Park coincides with the international boundary between the United States and Canada along the 49th parallel. In 1856, Congress authorized a boundary commission to survey the 49th parallel from the ocean to the Rocky Mountains. The British appointed a survey commission at the same time. The U.S. commissioner was Archibald Campbell; one of the topographers was Henry Custer. Custer became fascinated with the North Cascades and attempted to describe the magnificence of the mountains as he performed the more prosaic aspects of his assignment. The task was formidable. Even today, much of the boundary is difficult to reach. Chilliwack Lake was used as a base camp. Astronomical observations were used to determine the boundary line.

Custer first entered the area of today's park by traveling up the headwaters of Ensawkwatch Creek. He was among the first to describe the discomforts of breaking trail through a lowland Cascade valley. Custer climbed Middle Peak, elevation 7,464 feet, and made the following statement: "The view from here was fine and extensive to all directions of the compass. I leave it to a better pen to describe the sublimity of true mountain scenery in the Cascade Mountains. . . . It must be seen, it cannot be described. Nowhere do the mountain masses and peaks present such strange, fantastic, dauntless and startling outlines as here. Whoever wishes to see nature in all its primitive glory and grandeur, and its almost ferocious wildness, must go and visit these mountain regions." Custer also climbed one of the summits of Copper Mountain, traveled down the Little Chilliwack, climbed Easy Ridge, and crossed Whatcom Pass. He was impressed with the mighty Challenger Glacier, noting the "red snow" in that area. He also made the descent of Little Beaver Creek. At a later date, he ventured 20 miles down the Skagit River from the international boundary in an Indian canoe, reaching Ruby Creek. Custer intended to climb Hozameen Mountain as the climax of his explorations, but the smoke of an extensive forest fire precluded any view, and he abandoned the project.

Metal and cairn survey markers were placed by both the American and the British survey teams. In later years, surveyors made minor adjustments in the boundary. Eventually, a swath 20 feet wide (10 feet on either side of the line) was cut through the timber along the border. This denuded area still exists today. Metal pyramid markers, set in concrete, now mark each mile of the border; numbering begins in the west and progresses eastward. Both the monuments and the somewhat irrational cleared area are maintained by an international border commission.

Hikers can see monuments on both the Monument 78 and Monument 83 Trails, commencing in Manning Park (described later in this book). Other border markers can be seen on the Chilliwack River Trail (Monument 51). A short hike to the west across the river brings the hiker to Monument 50. Where the boundary crosses Ross Lake, Monument 72 stands at the eastern shore of the reservoir; Monument 71, to the west, can be reached by a brief walk.

MINING

The lure of gold next drew people to the North Cascades, as many came seeking mineral wealth. Fortunately (from the viewpoint of the recreationist), North Cascades mines produced little of value, although the dreams of elusive mineral riches have not totally died. The sale of claims probably produced more profit than the value of all the metal extracted to date from the mountains. However, for some years, mining was one of the most active industries in the North Cascades and resulted in a thorough exploration of the mountain wilderness and contributed to the settlement and development of the surrounding areas.

In the Skagit district, miners reached Ruby Creek in 1872. The creek was named for the garnet found in the riverbed. Six years later, Ruby Creek was the site of the first gold rush in the North Cascades when gold dust was found along Ruby and Canyon Creeks. By the spring of 1880, in spite of a 4-foot snowpack, 400 men were in the area. In 1891, gold was found on Slate Creek near Harts Pass. By 1894, the town of Barron on the west side of Harts Pass had a population of over 1,000. Shortly after 1900, Thunder Creek witnessed a great increase in activity. The Skagit Queen Mining Company erected a substantial camp along Skagit Queen Creek near the terminus of the Boston Glacier. A bunkhouse, mess hall, storehouse, powder house, barn, and electric generator were installed at the site. The logistics problems, although incredibly difficult, were solved by pack trains carrying equipment and food from Marblemount up Skagit and Thunder Creeks to the mine site (even today, it is a day and a half's walk one way to reach the mine area). Although this claim came under several ownerships, it was unprofitable for all.

In the early 1900s, a substantial mining community existed at Mineral Park. Almost all vestiges of this village had been reclaimed by the forest and the mountains by the mid-1960s.

Another active mining district was in the Twin Lakes area of Whatcom County. The current road to the lakes was constructed and is still maintained by miners. In 1980, in view of the increasing price of gold, some of the mines in this area were reexplored and reworked, to the detriment of the fragile and beautiful Twin Lakes–Winchester Peak area.

The substantial copper mining activity at Holden near Lake Chelan by the Howe Sound Mining company continued for many years. About twenty years ago, the ore played out, and the mining company withdrew from the area. Holden is now a Lutheran Church center that serves as a retreat and a place for ongoing theological activity. Accumulated tailings are still a major problem to the ecology of the Holden area and Railroad Creek.

Mining activity also brought the first permanent white settlers into the Stehekin Valley. Although a Mr. McKee may have prospected the area as early as 1875, brothers George and John Rouse made the first major ore discovery in 1886 on the edge of Doubtful Lake. Gold, silver, and lead were found. Multiple other claims were staked shortly thereafter, particularly in the Horseshoe Basin area. There also were claims on the North Fork of Bridge Creek.

Mining activity was substantial and vigorous in the 1890s, with many active claims at the head of the Stehekin Valley. To supply the mines, a road was constructed from the lakeshore and ultimately extended to Horseshoe Basin. The original road went up the hillside above the current site of High Bridge and can still be followed to this day. The road was actually passable by cars as late as 1948, when some of the mines in Horseshoe Basin, particularly the Black Warrior, were still being worked. (Erosion and overgrowth have closed the road between Cottonwood and Horseshoe Basin.) The ore never proved to be high grade. The difficulties of conveying the ore from mine to railroad, in conjunction with the short working season (considering the amount of snowfall at high elevations), made the mines economically unfeasible, and none are presently in operation.

There is still a substantial amount of abandoned mining equipment and debris in the Horseshoe Basin area, however. History buffs can imagine the courage and fortitude required to locate and work these "glory holes," particularly if one wintered over, as was done in 1909. A tunnel through the snow connected the sleeping cabin with the mine entrance. The Black Warrior mine is listed on the National Register of Historic Places.

The Rouses' mining camp stood approximately at the present site of the Basin Creek campground. Pieces of this structure and abandoned equipment can still be found in the area today.

At the junction of Bridge Creek and the Stehekin, a substantial community existed in 1892 to supply the mines; this community was still active in 1904. Presently, several cabins, the ruins of a sawmill, and the debris of several other structures can be found in and around the Bridge Creek area. Other camps and cabins were located up Bridge Creek and farther up the Stehekin. At one time, there were two cabins and a sawmill at Doubtful Lake. Most of these early structures have long since collapsed under the weight of the heavy winter snows.

The most classic mining story in the North Cascades began July 4, 1889, when Joseph L. Pearsall, while on a solitary prospecting trip, discovered the broad, glistening streak that was later to become the "1776 lode" on the side of the Wilmans Peak. He convinced himself that it was a large deposit of galena (lead sulfide), "as rich as Monte Cristo." The pass from which the deposit was first seen was later named Pearsall Pass.

After the ore was assayed and proved to have appreciable amounts of gold and silver, others became involved, including John Wilmans. Multiple claims were staked in both the Monte Cristo and the Goat Lake areas. Newspaper publicity about the area began in the spring of 1890, and by 1891, there were three small mining camps in the area and a post office. Road building commenced initially up the Sauk River and later through Barlow Pass. National mining interests ultimately became involved. Mining engineers evaluated the area in 1892, at the same time that actual construction began on the railway from Everett to Monte Cristo. The tracks reached Silverton in late June. The first engine of the Everett and Monte Cristo Railroad steamed into the mining camp August 25, 1893; the project cost $1.8 million. Four hours were required for the trip from Everett to the mines.

Meanwhile, the mining camp was developing rapidly, and by 1893, there were 1,000 people in the area. The first photographs were made in 1893, when the newly completed railroad allowed the cumbersome photography apparatus to reach the area. The construction of tramways to the mines also began in 1893 and was completed in 1894. The longest tramway was about 12,000 feet, running from the Comet Mine high on the side of Wilmans Peak to storage bins near the concentrator mill. At its maximal development between 1894 and 1897, there were four hotels, four restaurants, six saloons, two churches, a school, a hospital with one doctor, three barbershops, a drugstore, two butcher shops, a real estate office, a clothing store, one newspaper, and the usual mining camp brothels at Monte Cristo.

From the beginning, the economy was somewhat precarious. In 1893, a recession influenced financing. Floods in December 1896 damaged the railroad, but the coup de grâce was the flood of November 1897, which severely damaged trestles and tunnels and washed out much of the railroad. Rockefeller interests decided against further investment. The railroad was rebuilt in 1900, and the mines reopened, but the ore was still not rich enough. The population dwindled to 150 people by 1901. A landslide and tunnel cave-in in 1906, followed by a depression in 1907, caused Monte Cristo to be abandoned.

The railroad was revived in 1915, renamed the Hartford and Eastern Railroad, and served as an excursion access for the next fifteen years. The roadbed was again damaged in a severe flood in 1930, and in 1963 the railroad was totally dismantled. Most of the area has now returned to forest.

In summary, in the North Cascades, the story has always been the same. To be profitable, a mine must be near a railroad or waterway, and its ore must be high grade in order to pay the freight. With rare exceptions, North Cascades ore was not of high quality, nor was it easily accessible. The remote veins usually hugged the glaciers. The odds were too one-sided for even the hardiest turn-of-the-century prospectors.

As of 1997, 226 acres of private land remain within the NCNP and RLNRA. No mining or other activities incompatible with park policies are presently taking place at these inholdings. About 500 acres of private land remain in the Stehekin valley.

HOMESTEADING AND DEVELOPMENT

The topography of the North Cascades is such that the land offered little opportunity to homesteaders. The river valleys contained some arable areas suitable for farming, but land transportation, particularly on the west side of the mountains, was very limited. Waterways served as the initial transportation routes. Immense logjams existed on the Skagit River when the first settlers arrived in the Puget Sound area, and no upriver migration could occur until these impediments to boat traffic were removed from the river in the late 1870s.

With the influx of miners, the first real settlers came to sell goods to the prospectors, not to farm. A classic example is Mrs. Lucinda Davis, who initially was a storekeeper at Goodell's Landing and later moved farther upriver to Cedar Bar near the mouth of Stetattle Creek. The Davis family built cabins in the area, raised hay, and provided room and board for travelers brave enough to proceed up the Skagit on the Goat Trail. This trail began at Goodell's Landing and eventually terminated at the mines on Ruby or Thunder Creek. The Devil's Corner, a crude pathway bypassing an overhanging rock above the Skagit, was the most dangerous point on this primitive trail. Eventually, the original cabin was enlarged to a roadhouse containing eleven rooms. The land was later condemned by Seattle City Light to construct Diablo Dam. The area where the cabin stood is presently occupied by the village of Diablo.

Tommy Rowland also arrived on the upper Skagit in the 1880s, building a cabin and outbuildings at today's Roland Point (misspelled by the topographers), almost directly across Ross Lake from the mouth of Big Beaver Creek. Prospecting and growing hay and vegetables occupied most of his time. He also developed eccentric religious beliefs, eventually naming his homestead New Jerusalem and proclaiming himself the Prophet Elijah. His delusion is still documented on the topographic sheets, in the form of Mount Prophet. Eventually, he was committed to a mental hospital. The ruins of his cabin, barn, and root cellar can still be found near Roland Point.

Several other pioneers of the upper Skagit demand notice. One was Jack Durand, trapper, prospector, and miner, who worked Thunder Creek for many years during the summers. In 1893, he built the structure called Middle Cabin, a spot well known to the previous generation of hikers along Thunder Creek. This was used as a way station and hostel for miners, much as the Davis cabin functioned farther downriver. Neither the cabin nor a subsequent shelter still exists.

On the Cascade River near Cascade Pass, Gilbert Landre built a cabin in the early 1890s as a hostelry for other miners. Known then and now as Gilbert's Cabin, the ruins still stand.

John McMillan settled on remote Big Beaver Creek, where he made a living by packing supplies and trapping. He lived in his isolated valley until 1922. After his death, he was buried near his cabin. His grave marker, entangled by undergrowth, still stands. The Park Service no longer maintains the way trail to the site of his cabin, outbuildings, and grave.

There were also a mining development and eventually an inn at the junction of Ruby Creek and the Skagit River. The site is now under the waters of Ross Lake.

One of the most interesting and enigmatic North Cascades historical personages was "Mighty" Joe Morovits. His name, slightly misspelled, can be found on the topographic maps in the form of Morovitz Creek. This immensely powerful and stubborn man homesteaded in the Baker Lake area in October 1891. He lived alone in the area between Mount Baker and Mount Shuksan for twenty-seven years. He prospected the mountains, blazed trails into the area, made first ascents of many of the peaks, staked numerous claims, and kept looking for gold at the end of the Rainbow (Creek). It was common for him to pack 100 pounds on his back over the 32-mile trek between Birdsview on the Skagit River and his homestead. In addition, he is credited with moving a massive mortar weighing over a ton from Concrete to his Fourth of July Mine on Swift Creek. He accomplished this by winching it from tree to tree over his own crude trail; the task required two years.

In the early 1900s, Morovits started providing mountaineering guide service to the Seattle Mountaineers. His record of first ascents on Mount Baker is impressive: first ascent of the dangerous northeastern ice face in 1892; establishment of the Morovits route via the ridge between Park and Boulder Glaciers in 1984; first ascent of Sherman Peak, the southern secondary summit of Mount Baker, in 1907. He, along with the timber cruiser Vic Galbraith, established the first bathing place at Baker Hot Springs, 2½ miles from his ranch. A hole was dug and lined with logs as a crude bathtub, just long enough and deep enough for a good soak. Many have followed him into those warm waters. Unfortunately, the inundation of people, cultural conflicts, and alleged health hazards have caused the Forest Service to dismantle the bathing area at the hot springs. Such is the price of progress.

Joe disappeared from the mountains in 1918. His ultimate fate is unknown.

It is my understanding that he was the first white person in the splendid meadows immediately south of Mount Baker below the Park Butte Lookout. In recognition of his feats on Koma Kulshan, many of us have chosen to call these two areas the upper and lower Morovits Meadows.

An entire book has been written about the hydroelectric projects on the Skagit. Beginning in the early 1900s, there was a great deal of jockeying for hydroelectric dam sites on the Skagit River among individuals, corporations, and public utility districts. Eventually, Seattle City Light won out, and in 1918, work began on the river. First Gorge Dam, then Diablo Dam, then Ross Dam, and then a higher Gorge Dam were constructed. A dam on Thunder Creek remains a possibility for the future. Seattle City Light carefully cultivated favorable public opinion by conducting Skagit tours over many years. People were brought to Newhalem, originally on the railroad, and given combined land and water tours of the area, a practice that continues today, although access is by car rather than train.

Goodell's Landing is now occupied by the town of Newhalem and the Goodell Creek campground. The town of Diablo now occupies the location of the Davis Inn near the mouth of Stetattle Creek. A replica of the original Davis electrical powerhouse is still maintained by Seattle City Light. The Devil's Corner area can still be seen by parking near the road tunnel closest to Newhalem and looking downward from that point.

With the passage of the National Forest Act of 1906, further homestead claims were prohibited. Those already living on the land were forced to contest their right to remain. Ultimately, a fair number of people were forced from the land on which they had lived for years.

In 1891, the Forest Reserve Act became law. In 1897, President Grover Cleveland by proclamation established the Washington Forest Reserve, which included the present North Cascades. Administration of the reserve was initially the responsibility of the Department of the Interior. In 1905, the forest reserves were transferred to the Department of Agriculture and came under the direction of Chief Forester Gifford Pinchot. In 1908, the Wenatchee, Chelan, and Snoqualmie National Forests were carved out of a portion of the Washington Forest Reserve. In 1924, the balance of the reserve was renamed Mount Baker National Forest.

Meanwhile, on the east side of the mountains, the mining frontier in the hills beyond Stehekin created an immediate need for transportation facilities. This demand was met by the development of steamboat service on Lake Chelan and by the construction of roads within the Stehekin valley.

The first steamer on Lake Chelan was called the *Belle* and made its appearance on the lake in 1889. The *Stehekin*, the largest steamer on Lake Chelan at the time, at 100 feet long with a 16-foot beam, was commissioned in 1893 and

Lady of the Lake *(Chelan)* at the Stehekin Landing with McGregor Mountain in the background.

retired in 1904. In August 1900, the first *Lady of the Lake* was launched. This boat was 112 feet in length with a 16-foot beam. There has been an active *Lady of the Lake* on Lake Chelan since that date. The original boats were cordwood-burning steamboats; petroleum-powered engines did not appear until about 1914.

The *Speedway* was built on the lake and was functional when the Lake Chelan Boat Company was incorporated in 1929. The still-operational *Lady of the Lake* was built on the coast and served as a tour boat on Lake Roosevelt before being moved to Lake Chelan in 1945. The currently operating *Lady II* was built by the Lake Chelan Boat Company in the early 1970s and went into regular service in June 1976. It is licensed to carry 350 passengers.

Fuel, vehicles, building materials, and all goods either too large or too heavy to go on the regular passenger boat are transported on the freight barge, the *Allen Stone.* During the summer, the barge makes a regular weekly trip up the lake.

Overall, the steamboat era on Lake Chelan provided miners, homesteaders, and tourists with adequate service for many years, and it was one of the most colorful chapters in Stehekin's history.

In 1896, work began on the Cascade Wagon Road west of Cascade Pass and continued fitfully for many years. Although shown on some maps in the past, the road was never developed to the point where any vehicle could follow it to, much less over, the crest of the Cascades. Although a "mine to market" road was constructed in 1948 from east of Marblemount to within 2 miles west of the crest of Cascade Pass, no connection was ever built between this road and the Horseshoe Basin Road.

Excluding the crude and often steep access to the mines in the upper Stehekin valley, road building never went much beyond the 23 miles that exist today. Nevertheless, over half a century or so, several plans to link the valley with the outside were pursued with some seriousness. Even railroad interests considered building a railroad over Cascade Pass. The Stehekin Valley and the pass were surveyed in the course of evaluating routes for railroads, but eventually such plans were abandoned in favor of a route over Stevens Pass. The Cascade Pass route remains pristine today, insofar as automotive and railroad traffic is concerned.

The mineral discoveries in the late 1880s also attracted homesteaders in the lower Stehekin valley. Several of the first settlers were prospectors; others were engaged in supplying the men at the mines in the backcountry. Among the earliest settlers were miner J. W. Horton; hotelman George Hall; prospector Dan Devore; miner and homesteader Bill Buzzard; M. E. Field, hotel proprietor; F. F. Keller, prospector; and the W. F. Purple family (after whom Purple Point, Purple Creek, and Purple Pass were named), who arrived in the area in 1892.

Mr. Field first operated a small hotel, the Argonault, which was in operation in 1892. In 1900, Field began construction of a new hotel, which was opened in July and was known thereafter as the Hotel Field. This wilderness inn was later enlarged, and by 1910, it had developed into an elaborate three-story building whose fifty rooms could accommodate 100 guests. Indeed, it was one of the most well-known hotels in the Pacific Northwest. In those days, everyone who came up the lake had to stay overnight, since the boats were unable to make the round-trip in one day. Later, the building served as the focus of valley activities for almost two decades.

The hotel was demolished in 1927, shortly before the Chelam Dam raised the water in the lake to a sufficient height to flood the hotel site. The present Golden West Lodge, currently being used as an interpretive site by the Park Service, was partially built out of the material removed from the Field Hotel. The Golden West Lodge operated for forty-four years (1927–1971), the longest continuous operation in Stehekin's history.

In the early 1900s, another lodging place was started on the site of the present Stehekin. This inn, known as the Purple House (named after its owner), was less plush than the Field Hotel; both were in operation in 1910. In 1927, the small store and post office were also moved from the head of the lake to their present locations.

Curt Courtney operated lodging and restaurant facilities at Stehekin for a number of years before the transfer of land management responsibility from the Forest Service to the Park Service in 1968. Shortly thereafter, the buildings at Stehekin were acquired by the federal government, were renovated and remodeled, and are presently leased to concessioners to operate.

By 1892, there were enough children at Stehekin to justify the establishment of a school. A number of structures were used temporarily. The oldest known school building still standing is the Kronk Cabin (named after an early Chelan County commissioner), about 5 miles up the valley from the lake. In 1921, the citizens of the valley and the U.S. Forest Service reached an agreement to erect a permanent schoolhouse. The parents contributed their time and skill, and the current Stehekin School, originally one room built of logs, was established on Forest Service land near the spectacular Rainbow Falls. For a long time, it was the last one-room school still in use in Washington. The building still stands today, although it has been supplanted by a new and larger school nearby. The edifice is open for public inspection and contains memorabilia of interest to visitors.

Other historical buildings include the Buckner Cabin, originally constructed by William Buzzard in 1889. The Buckner Ranch can currently be toured with a Park Service guide.

Bill Buzzard and Henry Buckner were two of the many prospectors reaching the Stehekin valley in the late 1800s. The current Buckner Ranch was originally a homestead of 160 acres, first claimed by Bill Buzzard around 1900. Henry Buckner, after whom Buckner Peak was named, had a younger brother, William Van, who came to the valley and eventually bought the current Buckner Ranch from Bill Buzzard. Van's son, Harry, came to the ranch in 1911, at the age of sixteen, and never left the valley for any significant period thereafter except to serve in the army in World War I. His father turned the ranch over to Harry in 1918, and Harry Buckner was a Stehekin institution by the 1960s when I first reached the valley. At that time, he was continuing to operate his ranch, which obtained irrigation water from both Rainbow and Boulder Creeks. He also was the Stehekin postmaster until his death in the late 1970s.

Two buildings on the west side also merit mention. The road to Heather Meadows, east of Mount Baker and north of Mount Shuksan, was completed in the fall of 1926. The Mount Baker Lodge, constructed the following year, was an impressive edifice, comparable to the still existing Timberline Lodge near Mount Hood. A thirty-two-room annex was added in 1928. In August 1931, the main building burned to the ground, fortunately without loss of life. Thereafter, the annex, which survived the fire, and the Heather Inn, which included a fully equipped dining room, were used to house guests. The Heather Inn was eventually destroyed in the 1970s because it could not be adequately repaired. The annex remains today as housing for employees of the Mount

HISTORICAL PHOTO TAKEN BY J. JULEEN. USED WITH PERMISSION OF MT. BAKER-SNOQUALMIE NATIONAL FOREST

Big Four Inn and Mountain with ice caves at the base of the mountain. 1931.

Baker Recreation Company while the ski area is operating. The Heather Meadows area received national publicity in the winter of 1934 when *The Call of the Wild*, starring Clark Gable, was filmed at this location.

The ruins of the fireplace and crumbling sidewalks are all that remain of the historic Big Four Inn, which once stood at the trailhead of the Big Four Ice Caves trail. This land was homesteaded in 1897 by P. L. Prout. The land was later acquired by the Rucker brothers, who in 1920 began construction of a three-story, fifty-room hotel on the site. Water piped from Perry Creek ran a generator that produced electricity for the inn and cabins. Tennis courts, a nine-hole golf course, and a compound between the cabins and main hotel provided the amenities. There was a 1-mile boardwalk trail to the Big Four Ice Caves. A substantial swath was cut in the nearby wooded hillside for a winter sports area. The Forest Service was persuaded to construct trails up Perry Creek and Mount Dickerman to provide additional outdoor recreation opportunities. In 1924, the inn was visited by some 6,000 guests. It was an extensive and impressive operation, perhaps second only to the Field Hotel in Stehekin in size, architecture, and remoteness.

Extensive flood damage to the Everett and Monte Cristo Railroad in 1930 resulted in the permanent closure of both the railroad and the inn. The resort served as a rest and recreation center for the Coast Guard during World War II. The historic building was destroyed by fire in early September 1949. The site of the inn is now marked by a Forest Service sign.

FIRE LOOKOUTS

Forest fires have always been a part of North Cascades history. Henry Custer observed that the Indians sometimes set fires to clear underbrush from their trails and to improve hunting. Most fires in the old days were caused by lightning strikes during the summer thunderstorms. Human-caused fires, secondary to logging operations or from careless use of recreational fire, are now a substantial problem. The largest forest fire in recorded history in the North Cascades was the Big Beaver fire of 1926, which burned 40,000 acres, including the present east side of Ross Lake. Desolation Mountain was named because of the appearance of the area following this major conflagration.

Most of the trails in the North Cascades were not constructed for recreational use. Miners made the first footpaths. Later, the Forest Service constructed trails, primarily to facilitate fire control. These trails allowed more rapid access to roadless areas than was possible by cross-country bushwhacking, or they served as access routes to the fire lookouts.

The first fire lookout in Mount Baker National Forest was a tent station on Gold Hill across from Darrington, erected in 1915. It was abandoned after only one season, in favor of nearby Jumbo Mountain, elevation 5,880 feet, where a tent lookout was established on the summit in 1916. The Sourdough Mountain lookout was constructed by Glee Davis, using hand-split cedar, in 1917. It was a 12-by-12-foot structure with a 6-by-6-foot cupola on top. The Civilian Conservation Corps (CCC) replaced it with the current standard 14-by-14-foot lookout in 1933. Active construction of lookouts continued through the 1930s; forty-three lookout stations were built in Mount Baker National Forest during that time. Most were constructed in the early 1930s, including Crater, Desolation, Park Butte, and Hidden Lake.

Before the construction of telephone lines, army heliographs were used to send messages. This device consisted of a mirror and shutter mounted on a tripod. By reflecting sunlight, Morse code messages could be sent as a series of flashes to a distant observer. Communication was then by telephone for a number of years, but annual maintenance problems with the telephone lines were formidable. Currently, the lookouts use two-way radios for communication.

Before the logging roads pushed closer to the summits, some of the lookout houses were in remote locations, requiring two vigorous days of hiking to reach them. The personnel manning the lookout stations were generally unusual people, self-sufficient and able to tolerate prolonged solitude. Occasionally, married couples both worked and lived in the structures; in 1937, a couple spent their honeymoon in the Three Fingers lookout station. Loneliness was combated to some degree by the evening "lookouts' hour"; during that hour, unless the fire hazard was extreme, the lookouts could indulge in personal radio communication with one another. At the center of each structure was a range finder, an instrument for precisely locating fires. When not fire watching, the lookouts fetched water, maintained the lookout structures, did trail work, read, and cursed the insects.

As aircraft became more reliable and safer to operate, aerial fire patrol flights were thought to be cheaper and more efficient. Gradually, the lookouts were phased out, and many of the buildings were burned. Many currently existing pathways to high points originally were constructed to build and supply the fire lookout system.

Fire lookouts still staffed on a regular basis during the summer include Copper, Sourdough, Desolation, Goat, Granite Mountain, Lookout Mountain (Twisp), Sugarloaf, Alpine, and First Butte. Lookout houses in reasonably good condition that are manned intermittently, usually at times of great fire danger, remain at Green Mountain, Monument 83, North 20 Mile, Leacher, Thorp Mountain, Lookout Mountain (Cascade River), Slate Peak, Miners Ridge, Tyee, and Steliko. Lookouts currently maintained by volunteer groups include Park Butte, Hidden Lake, Winchester, Three Fingers, Pilchuck, Evergreen, Heybrook, and Red Top. Green Mountain repairs are planned for 1998.

Outdoor organizations or groups of individuals have "adopted" some of the lookout shelters and maintain them for the use of their members and for public use. The Everett Mountaineers maintain the lookouts on Pilchuck and Three Fingers. The Skagit Alpine Club of Mount Vernon leases and maintains the lookout at Park Butte. A group known as the Friends of the Lois Webster Memorial Shelter, also headquartered at Mount Vernon, maintains the Hidden Lake lookout.

The history of the lookout on McGregor Mountain is rather typical of all the lookouts. McGregor was first used as a lookout site in 1918 or 1919. The lookout person lived in a small tent camp at the foot of the summit rock, where the Park Service campsite is presently located. A 1,100-foot tramway was constructed in the early summer of 1923 to move materials from the horse camp to the summit; the lookout house was built later that summer. It was a 12-by-12-foot framed cupola cabin located on the summit. The tramway was not too practical, as each year it had to be repaired and restrung, due to damage from the ice and snow of winter. It was eventually abandoned, and material from the horse camp was backpacked to the lookout.

Early communication was by heliograph from the lookout to the Stehekin Ranger Station. Eventually, a telephone line that ran from Stehekin to High Bridge was extended to the lookout. This line was still in use when the station was abandoned in the late 1940s, although two-way radio use had been instituted at about that time.

Thirty to forty gallons of kerosene were used each season for cooking, heating, and melting snow and ice from the Sandalee Glacier on the northeast side of the peak; snow and ice were the only readily available water source.

During lightning storms, the person in the lookout sat on a stool that had glass insulators on all four legs. All lookouts had lightning rods and conducting wires to ground electricity, since mountain peaks are high-risk places for lightning strikes. At night during electrical storms, the metal on the station would sometimes glow with an eerie light, due to the buildup of static electricity. A humming sound, likened to the buzzing of a bee, often accompanied the Saint Elmo's fire.

During World War II, the lookouts, including McGregor, also served as aircraft identification stations. McGregor was manned by two persons during the war, each standing twelve-hour shifts to monitor the skies for enemy planes.

The McGregor lookout was destroyed and burned in 1953. Visitors to the area can find rusting metal, fused glass, and a square platform at the summit; there are sharp drop-offs in all directions. The location has to be one of the most incredibly beautiful and dreadfully lonely places in the world.

Fortunately, the remaining lookouts are beginning to be regarded by the public, and by the land management agencies, as historic structures. Many are now over half a century old. It is hoped that further senseless destruction of these buildings will cease; the cabins have a function both for historical interpretation and as shelters in inclement weather. Many are now listed on the National Register of Historic Places.

LAND USE

In the beginning, western Washington had only three colors: the blue of the sea, the green of the forest, and the white of the ice- and snow-capped peaks. Loggers have changed that. From 1860 until about 1883, loggers started harvesting the timber at the seashore and worked inland. They were able to select timber at will during those years. After 1883, most of the land had been claimed, and loggers had to either own the land or pay private or governmental third parties for the privilege of cutting the timber. By 1888, there were sixteen logging camps employing 400 men and producing 800 million board feet of timber a year operating along the Skagit alone. Gradually, the seemingly inexhaustible stands of old-growth timber were harvested. The supply had seemed so plentiful that reforestation was not even considered for many decades. Ultimately, little timber was left in private hands, and what remained was under the jurisdiction of major corporations. Loggers more and more looked toward the timber on the federally owned lands within the national forest. Clear-cuts appeared at a rapid rate and in locations that led to major conflicts with other users of Forest Service land. Loggers and timber companies have provided the major opposition to the establishment of parks and wilderness areas in the North Cascades. The conflict between the users and the conservers continues today and will no doubt last as long as trees grow on the slopes of the mountains.

Sheep and cattle grazing once played a small but important role in portions of the North Cascades and is still allowed in the Okanogan National Forest and in the Pasayten Wilderness Area, in spite of the adverse effects on the delicate ecosystems of the higher elevations.

MOUNT BAKER MARATHONS

Established in 1910, the Mount Baker Club of Bellingham was organized for the purpose of attracting the nation's attention to the incomparable snow peak in the city's backyard and to secure inclusion of the mountain and the surrounding area within the national park system. To publicize Mount Baker and the North Cascades, the club sponsored the most unusual sporting event ever staged in the Pacific Northwest: the three Mount Baker marathons in 1911, 1912, and 1913, in which hearty buckoes from the logging camps raced from Bellingham to the 10,778-foot summit and back to Bellingham. The unusual nature of these races attracted international attention. European press service reports crossed a continent and an ocean to flash news of the sporting event taking place on a mountain that few in the United States—much less readers in Europe—had ever heard of before.

The publicity generated by the marathons led to the filing of national park legislation in Congress. However, the attention of Congress and the nation was distracted by the advent of World War I, and the proposals were shelved until slightly over half a century later. Nonetheless, the marathons accomplished one of the goals envisioned by the Mount Baker Club, that of "opening up this wonderland with road and trail to the northernmost fire peak of the Cascade Mountains, 30.3 crowflight miles from Bellingham."

The starting point for the marathons was the Chamber of Commerce building in downtown Bellingham. Runners could choose one of two routes. The first was through the village of Deming, an approach to the mountain from the west over a 16-mile-long trail; the other route via Glacier was more rugged but 4 miles shorter. Both trails met at the "saddle," a low point between the Black Buttes to the west and the main peak to the east. Those going to Glacier rode a special logging train provided by the Bellingham Bay and British Columbia Railroad. Those taking the Deming route rode hopped-up cars over winding wagon roads up the Middle Fork of the Nooksack River to the road end at Heisler's ranch house. The first person to return to Glacier preempted the train for a wild dash back to Bellingham. Those on the Deming route left cars and drivers waiting for them at Heisler's barn. Only those who have climbed Mount Baker or a similar peak can comprehend how arduous a task it is to run up an icy, steep, cold, dormant volcano.

Luck played a part in the outcome. In 1911, Harvey Haggard, the first one back to Glacier, reached the train exhausted; by all rights he should have won, but the engine derailed after colliding with a bull. Indomitable Haggard pressed on, first on foot, then by horseback, wagon, and car. His time was still fast enough to finish second to Joe Galbraith, an Acme logger, whose time via the Deming route was an astonishing 12 hours and 28 minutes.

The 1911 race was so successful that plans were immediately made for a repeat the following year. Prize monies were substantially increased, with the winner to receive $500 rather than the $100 in gold awarded the first year; awards decreased to $75 for fourth place, and the leader on the trail not used by the winner would receive a prize of $200. To entertain the throngs that came to see the race and to finance the extravaganza, the town contracted for a carnival and circus to be in the vicinity simultaneously. Judges climbed the mountain beforehand and set up a tent on the summit to certify that each contestant reached the top of the mountain. The increased prize money drew more interest, and this time, the runners practiced on the various trails. Shortcuts, concealed from the other contestants, were constructed. On the glaciers, prerace examination determined the shortest, easiest routes to the summit and the best locations for jumping crevasses when descending. The substantial prize money also attracted a Finnish professional marathon racer and mountain climber name Paul Westerlund.

It should be noted that the glaciers on the mountain extended downward approximately a mile farther in 1912 than they do today. Data from historical sources indicate that the routes across the ice were far less crevassed and, therefore, less hazardous than they are presently; this is logical, since there should be fewer crevasse problems if the ice is thicker and deeper. Since the contestants could glissade (slide) down the ice to a lower elevation with reasonable safety, the downward descent was substantially more rapid than it would be under current conditions. This factor accounted for the phenomenal round-trip times established. Nonetheless, it was fortunate that none of the runners died by plunging into a hidden crevasse on the peak, a fate that has befallen a number of unroped climbers since the marathons were discontinued.

Dreadful weather, not uncommon in the North Cascades, forced a postponement of the 1912 race. When the race finally began, the knowledgeable local racers allowed Westerlund to break trail through fresh snow all the way to the summit and passed him on the descent. The race was won by Harvey Haggard of Maple Falls, who set an incredible time of 9 hours and 48 minutes from Bellingham to mountaintop and back to Bellingham.

The publicity of the Mount Baker marathons had spread to all parts of the country and focused attention on Bellingham. The town boosters were enthusiastic, and the local hiking club was pleased because the Forest Service had agreed to improve the mountain trails. Everyone decided that the marathon should be an annual affair, with each year bigger and better than the one before. The 1913 marathon was the most heavily promoted of all. This one was to be run entirely in daylight hours; previous races had started in the evening to allow racers to cross the hazardous parts of the mountain in the early morning when the ice was most solid and the risk of avalanche the least. To avoid charges that the Deming trail handicapped the racers, it was ruled that the racers had to go up one trail and down the other. The Finnish professional returned, an English professional entered, and other outsiders also became contestants.

On the day of the race, the weather was dreadful. It was snowing heavily at the saddle. The judges gave conflicting advice to the contestants because of the bad weather. Some were told that they only needed to reach the saddle and return; others were advised that the race still included reaching the peak. Both trails were quagmires of mud. The mountain was dangerous and almost impassable. There was a strong wind, and visibility was often less than 10 feet. One of the contestants fell into a crevasse but was found and extricated before he became significantly hypothermic. Not surprisingly, racers who went only as far as the saddle arrived back in Bellingham first and were declared the prize winners. Later, those who had gone all the way to the summit returned and protested that they had completed the race as planned and should be considered the winners. Eventually, famed Finnish marathoner Paul Westerlund, first up and over the saddle and back in 9 hours and 48 minutes, and John K. Magnusson, a timber cruiser, first to the snow-swirling summit and back in 11 hours and 51 minutes, were declared co-winners. All ended on a happy note, with no one killed on the mountain or in the automobiles and trains.

There was never a fourth Mount Baker marathon. The mountain race came to an end not for lack of eager contestants, but because of cries of "barbarism" and "human horse races" thundered from the pulpit and repeated in newspaper editorials. The death of the president of a British Columbia mountain club in 1913 due to a fall into a Mount Baker crevasse may have been a contributing factor. It appears that the Mount Baker marathon committee, shaken by the bad weather of 1913, harassed by adverse publicity, and concerned because of the death, decided not to press its luck too far.

I have climbed Mount Baker twice and found the recorded times unbelievable. Even considering the special transportation arrangements and the different condition of the glaciers, it is improbable that anyone today could achieve the same results in similar times. Perhaps that is fortunate, for the racers took great risks by traveling unroped, and sooner or later, had the race continued, someone would have been killed.

TRAILBLAZING AND MOUNTAIN CLIMBING

The first trail built in the Mount Baker region by the Forest Service was the Swift Creek Trail in 1904. The Mazama–Wells Creek Trail was built in 1906 to allow access for the Mazama (a mountaineering group) outing that year. In 1909, the Forest Service collaborated with the Bellingham Chamber of Commerce and the citizens of the town of Deming to construct an 11-mile trail along the Middle Fork of the Nooksack to reach the Mazama Park area on the south slopes of Mount Baker. The following year, this trail was extended by the Forest Service over Baker Pass and down Sulfur Creek 10 miles to connect with the Bear Creek Wagon Road from Concrete.

The first recorded penetration of the North Cascades solely for the purpose of climbing a mountain occurred in 1866, when Coleman, Brown, and Darwin attempted to reach the peak of Mount Baker via the Skagit River. After bypassing the famous logjam about 6 miles up the Skagit River, they had to abandon the climb at the mouth of the Baker River, where a tribe of Indians refused to let the three men pass.

A month later, Coleman tried again with companions Bennett and Tennant, this time following the Nooksack River. Coleman and Bennett reached the saddle but, after two attempts, were unable to surmount the wall of ice immediately beneath the summit plateau. An unpleasant overnight bivouac was spent in the saddle between the two attempts.

The first successful ascent occurred in August 1868, when Coleman again returned, with companions Stratton, Tennant, and Ogilvey. Coleman was living in Victoria at the time and traveled by Indian canoe to Bellingham Bay. He followed the path of the Nooksack River to its middle fork, portaging areas of logjams. Ascending the middle fork as far as possible by canoe, his party then proceeded farther upstream by land. They ascended the ridge at the head of Wallace/Thunder Creek, gaining some 3,000 vertical feet, to the subalpine meadow areas west of the Black Buttes, which they named Lincoln and Colfax

Peaks. The party feasted on marmots that evening. After roping up, the party progressed to the saddle between the main peak and the Black Buttes. The ascent from the saddle to the summit was accomplished in two hours on August 17, 1868, and the summit was named Grant Peak after General Ulysses Grant. The south subsidiary summit was also ascended and named after General William Sherman.*

Some of the party inspected the crater, which appeared to be ice and snow free at that time, suggesting that the level of volcanic activity was substantially greater in the mid-1800s than presently. The men returned to their meadow base camp at eleven o'clock at night, after some difficulty in retracing their ascent route in the feeble twilight.

Coleman was the first person to use an ice ax in the Northwest. He also used spiked "creepers," a forerunner of modern-day crampons. Coleman used colored glasses, and others in the party blackened their faces around their eyes to prevent or reduce snow blindness.

The Mazamas (Spanish for "mountain goats"), still an active mountaineering group, were organized in the Mount Hood and Portland area of Oregon in 1894. Five years later, a group of forty club members arrived at Stehekin by boat and proceeded up the valley. Hiking up through Horseshoe Basin, the enthusiastic climbers scaled a peak that they named Sahale, an Indian term for "celestial." The mountain still bears that name.

Later, the same organization constructed a cabin in Mazama Park, immediately beneath the south slopes of Mount Baker. Mazama members named a substantial portion of the places surrounding Mount Baker as they explored, often using the Mazama cabin as base camp.

As detailed earlier in this book, it is undisputed that Joe Morovits climbed Mount Baker many times and by many routes. Whether he made the first ascent of Mount Shuksan in 1897 is highly controversial, and it is improbable that this issue will ever be resolved. Harvey Manning writes that Morovits's claim is "generally accepted"; Fred Beckey believes strongly to the contrary. No one denies that two Mazamas, Price and Curtis, climbed Mount Shuksan in 1906; they reported no human traces on the summit at the time of their climb and presumed that theirs was the first ascent of the peak. Other first ascents in the North Cascades are as follows:

Glacier Peak: 1898 by T. G. Gerdine and four others (USGS)
Boston: 1938 by Cox, Bressler, Clough, and Meyers
Twin Sisters: 1891 by Hegg, Harris, and Edson

---

*It appears clear that the four explorers did not ascend what is currently known as Sherman Peak, a point of 10,150 feet on the south rim of the active crater. The name changes of the two high points of the peak are attributed to errors of later cartographers.

Goode: 1936 by Bauer, Dickert, Hossack, MacGowan, and Halwax
Liberty Bell: 1946 by Beckey, Welsh, and O'Neil
Mount Challenger: 1936 by Dickert, Hossack, and MacGowan
Bonanza: 1937 by Leuthold, Ijames, and James
Sloan: 1921 by Bedal and Skaar

Any discussion of the history of climbing in the North Cascades must devote some space to Fred Beckey, without doubt the most persistent and aggressive aficionado of the sport in the history of the range. Author of all the authoritative climbing guides to the area and a legend in his time, Beckey has climbed hundreds of North Cascade peaks. Many of the routes have been first ascents. This colorful and unusual man has evoked mixed reactions throughout his mountaineering career. No one denies, however, his contributions to the accumulation of climbing wisdom and the documentation of historical data about the North Cascades cordillera.

FOREST SERVICE MANAGEMENT
The federal lands in the North Cascades originally became part of the public domain in 1846, when the United States established title to the Oregon Territory. The Washington Forest Reserve was created in 1897. After numerous boundary and name changes, the Washington Forest Reserve in the North Cascades eventually became the Mount Baker–Snoqualmie, Wenatchee, and Okanogan National Forests. In 1926, 75,000 acres around Mount Baker were designated as a recreation area, although other uses were permitted to continue. In 1931, a 234,000-acre area around Glacier Peak was established as the Glacier Peak–Cascade Recreation Unit. In 1935, areas north and east of Mount Baker were established as the North Cascade Primitive Area. In the early 1960s, the Glacier Peak Wilderness Area was established, and special management was accorded to the Cascade Pass–Ruby Creek area by direction of the secretary of agriculture. The Multiple Use–Sustained Yield Act of 1960 specifically provided that outdoor recreation be among the purposes for which the national forest lands should be administered and singled out wilderness areas as being consistent with such purposes.

Between 1950 and 1963, 332,000 acres of national forest timberland in the north and central Cascades were logged under Forest Service management.

A number of the early rangers in the North Cascades will long be remembered. These included Tommy Thompson, who served on the Skagit between 1907 and 1943, and C. C. McGuire, who was in the area between 1908 and 1918 and again from 1925 to 1939. McGuire later wrote his memoirs of his early days on the western slope of the mountains, thus preserving history that would otherwise have been lost.

The single most important historical figure in the Pasayten area was topographer Lage Wernstedt, who, during 1925 and 1926, single-handedly mapped almost all of the present Winthrop Ranger District. During the course of his work, Wernstedt took over a thousand photographs. Many are still on file at the Winthrop Ranger Station, and some are part of the Northwest Collection maintained at the University of Washington library. In addition, combining work with pleasure, he made the first ascents of over a hundred peaks. Wernstedt named many of the topographic features of the northeast Cascades. For a time, some historians thought that the Picket Range was named after General George Pickett of Civil War fame, who lived in Bellingham for a time. However, that opinion has generally been discarded. H. M. Majors, in his book *Exploring Washington* (1975), states that the Picket Range was named by Wernstedt because "its serrated peaks resembled a picket fence." All agree that the area has an appropriate title.

The first ranger stations in Mount Baker National Forest included Bacon Creek, Babcock Creek, Reflector Bar, Ruby Creek, and the boundary station near the mouth of Little Beaver Creek. The McMillan and Rowland homesteads were also used as ranger stations. The Backus station was built in Marblemount in 1909. There was a CCC camp at Bacon Creek in 1933.

Early-day forest rangers were not pampered with large budgets. They were jacks-of-all-trades who could build cabins, run a pack string, fight forest fires, and devise ingenious means of killing mice.

As forestry became a subject taught in colleges, rangers gradually began to be professionally trained in silviculture. Living in the local areas, they were attuned to the needs of the loggers and were trained to cut trees. However, for several decades, they had no formal training in recreational management. From 1920 to 1960, it was uncommon for rangers to care enough about the land to be concerned with the recreational aspects of managing the forest. Fortunately, colleges and universities are now teaching recreational management as well as commercial use of the forests.

In the early 1970s, the Mount Baker and Snoqualmie Forests were merged, presumably in the interest of economy. Forest headquarters was transferred from Bellingham to Seattle at that time.

CREATION OF THE NATIONAL PARK

The grand argument to create a national park within the "wilderness alps" of the North Cascades, pronounced by a federal study team "the most breathtakingly beautiful and spectacular mountain scenery in the 48 contiguous states," lasted for sixty-two years. A national park was first proposed by the Mazamas, Portland's famed mountaineering club, while camped at Galena Chain Lake near Mount Baker in the summer of 1906, a full decade before the National

Park Service was established. Four years later, the Mount Baker Club of Bellingham was organized for the purpose of securing the peak's inclusion on national park rolls. Bills introduced in Congress, assisted by the publicity of the Mount Baker marathons, seemed headed for passage. Then World War I came, and the proposed national park in the North Cascades was forgotten.

The dreamers would not give up. Other efforts to acquaint the nation with the incomparable Northwest mountain wilderness were made, and by 1937, an investigating committee of the Department of the Interior reported that "the area is unquestionably of national park caliber, is more valuable used as such than for any other use now ascertainable, and should receive park status. . . . It will outrank in its scenic, recreational, and wildlife values any existing national park and any other possibility for such a park within the United States." Still the legislation was passed over, perhaps because another great war preempted the concern of Congress.

Many northwesterners feel a deep personal involvement with the Cascade Mountains, born of wet boots squishing in soggy forest duff, of lenticular cloud caps streaming from icy summit domes, of the solipsistic experience of warming oneself over the first tiny rockbound campfire ever lighted in a hidden hanging valley, of acceptance into a magical plant and animal ecology. Cascade mountaineers know that dawn in a high Cascades pass is as dreamlike as waking up on a Nepalese col, face-to-face with the great peaks of the Himalayas. People have spent lifetimes exploring the Cascades, worlds within worlds; yet there are still meadows that have never known a bootprint or a backpacker's high mountain tent, lonely vantage points from which to grasp the powerful statement of the mountains. Such people do not give up easily.

The final effort to establish a national park, which culminated in success, began in about 1956 with the organization of the North Cascades Conservation Council. This group spearheaded the twelve years of continuous effort required to create the North Cascades National Park and its associated recreational areas; assisting organizations included the Sierra Club, the Seattle Mountaineers, and the Federation of Western Outdoor Clubs and its affiliated organizations in the state of Washington. Washington Congressman Thomas Pelly filed the initial bill for the creation of the park in Congress. After years of further effort, a joint study team sponsored by the Departments of Agriculture and the Interior evaluated the area and held public hearings. The five-person study team produced a substantial book containing its findings and recommendations; the *North Cascades Study Report* still makes interesting reading today. The Senate Interior Committee held hearings when the bills to create the park and recreational areas were filed in the Senate by Washington Senator Henry Jackson and in the House by Washington Congressman Lloyd Meeds. The final bill as adopted was a compromise between the conflicting interests of those desirous of preserving the area for its recreational and aesthetic values and those concerned with extracting resources, particularly timber, from the area. As a result of this compromise, although many superior areas now have legal protection, a number of equally fine locations are without any protection whatsoever. Perhaps someday some knowledgeable author will describe in detail the complex political maneuvering that took place between 1956 and 1968, culminating in the North Cascades National Park bill signed by President Lyndon Johnson on October 2, 1968. Suffice it to say that the creation of a national park requires a great deal of work and effort by many dedicated, highly motivated individuals. Among those making outstanding contributions to the establishment of the North Cascades National Park were Patrick Goldsworthy, Phillip Zaleskey, Polly Dyer, Grant McConnell, William Halliday, Mike McCloskey, Brock Evans, David Brower, Harvey Manning, and Charles Hessey. Martin Litton, Brock Evans, Pat Goldsworthy, and I were privileged to watch President Johnson sign the North Cascades National Park bill in the White House. Space prohibits listing the scores of other people who made substantial contributions to the establishment of the North Cascades National Park complex.

CHANGE AND PROGRESS

The park and associated recreational areas have now been in existence for thirty years. The Park Service has had time to write its own historical saga in the North Cascades. Projects initially planned that have been abandoned include the road from the North Cascades Highway to the shore of Ross Lake, an aerial tramway from the North Cascades Highway to the top of Ruby Mountain, "high camps" in the recreational areas, and a ferry on Ross Lake. Changes instituted by the Park Service include the closure of the alpine passes (Cascade, Park Creek, Easy, and Whatcom) to camping and an effort to reestablish the alpine flora of these areas (see the chapter on Plants). Trails have been reopened (Desolation Lookout, Goode Ridge, and McGregor Mountain). Over half of the private land in Stehekin has been acquired by the Park Service.

Sadly, there has been little if any progress by Chelan County in establishing zoning regulations for the Stehekin Valley that would prohibit inappropriate development in that special place. Park Service enforcement of the "compatibility standards" has been suboptimal in my opinion.

A visitors' center near the Newhalem Creek campground is now operational. Accessed over a one-way bridge from the Seattle City Light village of Newhalem, it offers displays, programs, information, and sales of books, postcards, and so forth. Hours fluctuate with the seasons (daily in the summer; weekends in the winter). A permanent park complex headquarters is located at State Route 20 about ¼ mile west of the town of Sedro Woolley.

The concept of designated campsites has been introduced, as well as the camping permit system requiring preregistration for overnight visits within the park and recreational areas. A Park Service office has been established at Chelan, and a visitor center has been opened at Stehekin.

A shuttle-bus system to transport visitors and residents between Stehekin Landing and Cottonwood Camp has been instituted. Rangers patrol the backcountry trails on a regular schedule to assist visitors and to enforce Park Service regulations. Park rangers patrol both Lake Chelan and Ross Lake by boat. Campgrounds have been established or expanded at Goodell Creek, Newhalem Creek, and Colonial Creek along the North Cascades Highway. One of the two roads initially leading into the North Cascades National Park has been closed and converted into a trail. The only road presently entering the park from the west is the road to Cascade Pass. The dead-end Stehekin Road enters the park from the east. Fires have been prohibited at many high camps within the park complex.

In 1932, Californian C. C. Clarke proposed a trail along the summit divide between the Canadian and Mexican borders through the states of Washington, Oregon, and California. The idea caught fire, and five years later, the CCC had done sufficient work so that the 2,156-mile trail could be traveled, though with difficulty. The northern portion of the trail was called the Cascade Crest Trail. In 1968, this trail was established as a national scenic trail and is now called the Pacific Crest Trail. Although almost completed in Oregon and near completion in Washington, substantial sections in California still await permanent trail status. In the North Cascades, the trail is presently complete between Snoqualmie Pass and British Columbia Highway 3. A number of changes in the trail have taken place since 1982, and further revisions are probable in the future. Reroutes generally move the tread from the lowlands to the higher, more scenic locations.

The North Cascades Highway began as part of the construction involved in building Ross and Diablo Dams. Initially, access to the upper Skagit area was by railroad only. After the dams were completed, the railroad was dismantled, and a highway was constructed. In many places, the highway followed the railroad grade and used several of the one-lane train bridges. The old railroad bridges at Bacon and Goodell Creeks have been replaced by two-lane modern highway bridges, but the old railroad bridge is still used in crossing Stetattle Creek to reach the community of Diablo.

The road dead-ended at Diablo for many years. After World War II, interest in a route through the North Cascades wilderness was again generated by businesspeople in the Twisp-Winthrop area and in the Skagit Valley. An organization called the North Cross State Highway Association vigorously applied political pressure. Ultimately, funds were appropriated, and the North Cascades area was resurveyed. The Cascade Pass route was abandoned, and it was decided that the Granite Creek–Harts Pass route was not feasible because of the substantially higher elevation at Harts Pass. Ultimately, the current route via Rainy and Washington Passes was established, since it was thought to be the easiest to construct and maintain. Construction began in 1960 and terminated with the opening of the road for limited use in September 1972 and for full use in 1973.

Highway construction posed formidable problems because of the difficult terrain and the high annual snowpack. Winter avalanches are a particular hazard; there are over sixty major avalanche paths along the highway route. Heavy snows and avalanches normally force closure of the road between mid-November and mid-April. One winter, light snowpacks allowed the highway to remain open almost all year.

The highway was called the North Cross State Highway during its construction phase but was renamed the North Cascades Highway when the Ross Lake National Recreation Area and the North Cascades National Park were created by an act of Congress in 1968.

Many people think that the highway passes through the North Cascades National Park; that is incorrect. The highway passes through the Mount Baker–Snoqualmie National Forest, the Ross Lake National Recreation Area, a small portion of the Wenatchee National Forest, and the Okanogan National Forest. The park itself is both to the north and to the south of the highway.

The highway has caused a major change in the Winthrop and Twisp areas. The former quiet country towns are now inundated by visitors, particularly on summer weekends. Winthrop has responded by "westernizing" its business district, and without question, the town has reaped a bonanza from the tourist trade. However, many who initially favored the highway have had second thoughts.

The Thunder Creek Dam will significantly and adversely affect the area if it is constructed. Certainly history would be changed if one of the volcanoes entered a major eruptive phase. Most of the changes associated with the establishment of the park have come to pass. Major changes have been occurring with frequency in the forty years that I have been familiar with the North Cascades. Perhaps now that most of the major environmental battles are being fought in other locations, relative stability will come to these mountains. Land management decisions, however, continue. It is important that people who love these mountains keep the National Park and Forest Service decision makers apprised of their continuing concern. Detrimental management proposals must be fiercely opposed.

Geology

North Cascades geology is complex. Several years of study are necessary to begin to understand the descriptions in the professional literature with regard to the origins of the North Cascades.

In the material that follows, definitions are provided that may be helpful to readers without a geological background. Following that, the two volcanoes in the area are discussed. The effects of North Cascades glaciation are reviewed, especially the actions of the ice sheets on the Methow and Stehekin Valleys. The origin of the rocks and mountains of the North Cascades is then discussed, with particular reference to the geology visible from the North Cascades Highway.

DEFINITIONS

Certain terms must be understood before the reader can begin to understand North Cascades geology, or geology anywhere.

Igneous rock: rock formed from the solidification of magma

Magma: molten rock

Metamorphic rock: rock that has been transformed in the solid state by the application of pressure and heat without undergoing disintegration or melting (like bread converting to toast)

Sedimentary rock: rock formed by deposits of particles, such as fragments of other rock; precipitation from solution; or the remains of plants and animals

Fault: a break in the crust of the earth along which substantial movement has occurred

Schist: a metamorphic rock in which the minerals are stacked up parallel to one another like sheets of paper

Gneiss: a metamorphic rock that consists of alternating layers of dark and light minerals

Diorite: an igneous rock consisting of almost equal amounts of dark and light minerals with grains large enough to be seen without magnification

Batholith: a large body of igneous rock formed deep in the earth's crust under pressure, which later becomes exposed due to erosion removing the surrounding less resistant rock

Dike: a sheet of igneous rock that has been injected while molten into a fissure

Graben: a depressed segment of the earth's crust bounded on at least two sides by faults

Glacier: a slowly flowing mass of ice formed by countless years of accumulation of winter snows in greater amounts than are lost by summer melting

Moraine: rock debris accumulated along the lateral margins or advancing front of a glacier, which has been scoured from areas higher on the mountain where the glacier originated

Cirque: a deep, steep-walled basin on a mountain shaped like half a bowl, which has been carved by glacial action

Crevasse: a crack or fissure in a glacier formed where it flows over an irregular area of the underlying rock

VOLCANOES

Both Mount Baker (Indian name Koma Kulshan) and Glacier Peak are volcanoes. The current theory of volcanic formation is that a large plate of rock from the Pacific Ocean seafloor is continuously being forced beneath the continental crust. Complex physical and chemical reactions occurring at the area where the two plates converge (the subduction zone) cause the already hot rocks in this area to liquefy. This molten rock, or magma, moves upward toward the surface, accompanied by associated volatile gases.

Eventually, subsurface rocks are displaced or assimilated to form an underground reservoir called a magma chamber. In the magma chamber, heavier crystals settle downward, and lighter components, including volatile gases and steam, rise. When a major weakness in the rock above is encountered, or when the volatile pressures exceed the gravitational and cohesive forces of the overlying rock, an opening is blasted to the surface, and an eruption occurs.

Explosive eruptions produce clouds of gas, volcanic ash, and fragmental material. Relatively quiet eruptions produce lava flows. There are four common types of lava: basalt, andesite, dacite, and rhyolite. Each has a different chemical composition and a different viscosity. For example, basalt is highly fluid and may flow rapidly over great distances. Dacite is pasty and viscous when molten and tends to form bulbous, steep-sided domes. One form of rhyolite is obsidian (volcanic glass).

Both Mount Baker and Glacier Peak are composite, or strato, volcanoes. In other words, they are composed of lava flows, fragmental material, and ash, reflecting alternating explosive and quiet eruptions.

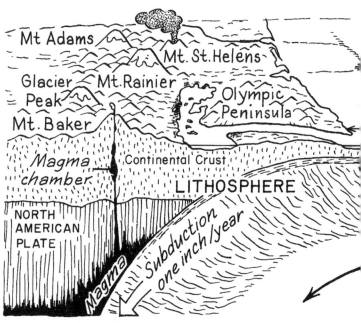

North Cascades volcano mechanism

The ash distribution from eruptions (as exemplified by the ashfall from Mount St. Helens in 1980) has been used to date geological events over wide areas, since bits of carbonized wood found with the ash can be analyzed for age using the carbon 14 dating method. By using these techniques, eruptions from Mount St. Helens 175 years ago, from Mount Mazama (forming Crater Lake) 6,600 years ago, and from Glacier Peak 12,000 years ago have been reliably documented. The latter eruption, or perhaps nine eruptions closely spaced in time, laid down a layer of dacite pumice up to 12 feet thick as far as 12 miles downwind from the crater and deposited lesser amounts of dust and ash over thousands of square miles of what is presently Washington, Oregon, Idaho, Montana, and Alberta. After the major pumice eruption, a glowing avalanche devastated the Whitechuck Valley.

Glacier Peak produced several smaller eruptions between 5,000 and 6,000 years ago. There is evidence of small tephra (ash) eruptions 200 to 300 years ago. The volcano otherwise appears to have been inactive. There are no fumaroles or evidence of the escape of heated gases at the summit. However, there are three hot springs on the flanks of the peak (Gamma, Kennedy, and Sulfur), presumably heated by underlying magma. Glacier Peak is not considered dormant by the U.S. Geological Survey (USGS) in view of an eruptive history

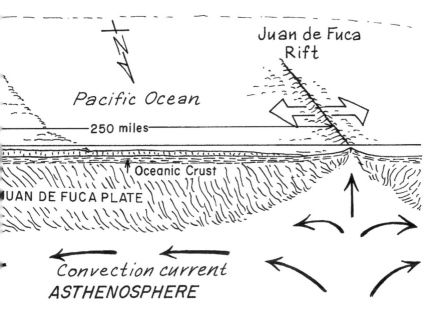

similar to that of Mount Mazama, the Oregon peak that blew its top away, forming Crater Lake in the process. During its many years of quiescence, Glacier Peak has been lowered and extensively modified by erosional processes, particularly glaciation.

The earliest eruptions in the vicinity of Mount Baker about one million years ago culminated in the formation of a caldera comparable to Crater Lake. Mount Baker's later eruptive centers are now occupied by the Black Buttes. These subsidiary peaks to the current snow cone are the basalt and andesite core remnants of the primal Koma Kulshan volcano; when the fires below moved eastward, erosion and intense glaciation carved them to their present shapes.

There are several locations around Mount Baker where lava flows (which originally flowed down stream valleys) can be found capping high ridges. In one location, the flow is 800 feet above the stream level, suggesting that erosion has removed the intervening material since the flow occurred. Dating by radioactive methods indicates an age of 400,000 plus or minus 100,000 years for this flow, which probably issued from the Black Butte area. Overall, lava flows from Mount Baker substantially exceeded ash production.

There is geological evidence of persistent eruptive activity of Mount Baker over the past several thousand years. At least one flow of hot gas and fragmental material extended down the Baker River Valley almost to the Lake Tyee junction (junction of Burpee Hill and Baker Lake Roads). The youngest lava flow from Mount Baker issued from the cinder cone located in the Sulfur Creek valley. The remnants of the cone can be seen today half a mile from the end of the Schrieber's Meadow Road; for well over a half mile, the road is cut through red cinders deposited downwind from the eruption. The lava flow poured down the original Sulfur Creek valley, splitting the stream into the currently existing Sulfur and Rocky Creeks. This eruption took place between 6,600 and 10,350 years ago, as determined by ash measurements. Logic suggests that the event occurred after the last major advance of the Easton Glacier.

Mount Baker has sported steam plumes since it was first seen by white explorers. Data suggest that up to six eruptions occurred between 1843 and 1884.

In 1975, fumarolic activity within the summit crater increased nearly a hundredfold, and the mountain was subjected to rather intense scrutiny and investigation for several years. However, since no major eruptions occurred, scientists and the public became more accustomed to the increased summit activity, and less attention was paid to the mountain, particularly after Mount St. Helens became active in the spring of 1980. A 160-by-230-foot shallow acidic lake formed in the summit crater, and there was substantial melting of the crater ice pack. When most active, the summit steam vents spewed clouds over 2,000 feet above the crater rim. The amount of sulfur-containing gas released by the volcano increased greatly.

It is probable that significant eruptions of Mount Baker will occur in the future. It is improbable that such an eruption will occur in a given visit or a given year or, for that matter, in a given decade or perhaps a lifetime. It should be remembered, however, that Mount St. Helens was considered inactive for 137 years—four generations, as humans reckon time, but a mere instant in the history of the earth.

Interestingly, the greatest danger from these volcanoes, should they awaken, is not from lava but from floods and mudflows (lahars). These mixtures of hot rock, debris, and water from melted snow and ice can travel up to 50 miles an hour, destroying everything in their path. Equally dangerous to those close to the mountain are vulcanian eruptions, such as the explosive initial blast on Mount St. Helens, and glowing eruptions, immense burning clouds that totally consume whatever they encounter. This type of eruption is more typical of Glacier Peak than of Mount Baker.

It is impossible to accurately predict which of Washington's five volcanoes will erupt next. If probability is based on known eruptive activity for the past 10,000 years and on the assumption that those with the most activity in the past will exhibit the most activity in the future, there is a consensus that Mount St. Helens is most likely and Mount Adams least likely to erupt. Where

PHOTO BY THE SKAGIT VALLEY HERALD, MT. VERNON, WA

Two-thousand-foot-high steam emission from the Mount Baker crater, 1977.

to rank the other three is questionable. For example, Mount Baker has never shown the same explosive history as Glacier Peak, but has exhibited more activity in recent times. What appears to be a certainty is that one or more will erupt again sometime in the future.

Future eruptions of magma from Mount Baker are likely to be preceded by changes that can be detected by modern volcano monitoring techniques. The USGS continuously receives data from a network of earthquake monitoring devices on and around Mount Baker. If movement of magma was suspected, additional seismic, deformation, and gas monitoring studies would be carried out. Full-scale monitoring and hazard communication during the volcanic episode would continue until further eruptive activity was unlikely.

GLACIERS

Having dealt with fire, let us now consider ice. The North Cascades glaciers today, extensive as they are, are only tiny remnants of the alpine ice that once covered a much greater area and extended to much lower elevations. The evidence on which this statement is based is substantial and includes the characteristic U-shaped cross-profile of the North Cascades valleys; the semicircular basins (cirques) with nearly vertical headwalls at the upper ends of the valleys from which the glaciers originated; the grooves or striations of exposed bedrock surfaces produced by abrasion from stones transported in the bottom layer of the moving ice; the erratics, rocks deposited on the valley floor that clearly originated many miles up the valley; occasional locations of glacial polish; and the embankments of glacial material (moraines) along the sides and floors of the valleys. The terminal moraine (the deposit farthest down the valley) marks the maximal extent of the former glacier. These embankments consist of till, a mixture of pebbles, sand, silt, clay, and sometimes larger rocks deposited directly by the glacier and not rearranged by running water. The most recent period of maximal glaciation was about 14,800 years ago. The ice sheet, a mile deep in the Bellingham area, extended a bit to the south of Olympia. Stream flow from the mountains was blocked by the ice, causing extensive lake formation. (This was a continental ice sheet originating in Canada rather than alpine glaciers from the Cascades.)

Exact details of the glacial events of the North Cascades as a range are not known. The glacial sequence has been worked out fairly reliably in a few valleys. Knowledge is greater about the most recent glaciation than about previous ones, primarily because each glaciation destroys much of the evidence of the preceding ice accumulation. Correlating one valley sequence with another is much more of a problem, since the glaciers in an area do not wax and wane in unison. For example, at the present time, some North Cascades glaciers are advancing and others are receding.

Two fairly clear examples of prior North Cascades glaciation are described here. The first is the Methow Valley, through which runs the North Cascades Highway, Washington State Route 20. This valley has steep walls and a broad, flat floor, giving it a Yosemite-like quality. The Methow Glacier was derived in part from ice that flowed south from British Columbia and rather incredibly surmounted 7,000-foot-high Harts Pass, and in part from alpine glaciers that formed in the surrounding mountains. The Methow Glacier extended all the way to the Columbia Plateau at Brewster and Pateros. Impressive terraces (called kames) deposited between the stagnating glacier and the valley wall can be seen today lining the sides of the lower Methow Valley. The current valley floor is filled with glacial debris.

Beginning about one million years ago, alpine glaciers periodically grew and descended the Stehekin valley; at its longest, this glacier reached from Cascade Pass to the Columbia River. Lake Chelan lies in a classic example of the U-shaped glacial trough; stream-carved valleys, in contrast, are classically V-shaped. The glacial ice scoured and scooped deeply along much of the lake, in places gouging 583 feet below sea level. The ice was approximately a mile deep at the time of its maximal advance. There is evidence that in places the depth of glacial excavation exceeded 2,000 feet; in other words, the preexisting valleys were cut down and deepened substantially by the ice. Geologists are still unsure how many times the alpine glaciers descended the valley; based on data obtained about ice advances elsewhere, it is thought that there were several advances, probably four.

The Chelan or Alpine Glacier had receded well up the lake to approximately 25 Mile Creek by the time of the farthest advance of lowland ice across the Columbia Plateau (the Continental Glacier). This glacier invaded the lower end of the already excavated valley and blocked the exit of water. The lake level was raised hundreds of feet as a result. Eventually, water spilled out of the lake into the Columbia River via the Knapp and Navarre Coulees.

In its early, more vigorous existence, the Continental Glacier added a final dimension to the shaping of the lower Chelan valley. Later, as the climate warmed, the ice lost its power to erode the land. Present today in the lower valley is an extensive series of terraces, formed during a late static phase of ice wastage as the glacier receded. Further evidence of the presence of the inland ice mass is the basalt (lava) erratics, known locally as haystack rocks, which are scattered over the lower valley; no such rock exists between Cascade Pass and the lower valley, so the rock had to be brought in from central Washington rather than down the Stehekin valley.

While traveling on Lake Chelan, one cannot fail to be impressed with the power of the almost 1-mile-thick ice sheet that created the trough. When coming up the lake, notice 4,000-foot Domke Mountain on the west near Lucerne and 4,397-foot Round Mountain on the east. Both of these hills were smoothed and rounded by the ice of the Lake Chelan, Railroad Creek, and Fish Creek Glaciers as they joined together in this area.

In an effort to understand the complex forces that caused the ice sheets to wax and wane, current investigators are studying North Cascades glaciers. For example, the South Cascade Glacier, one of the largest ice accumulations in the range, has been under intensive study for some years. USGS scientists, operating out of a snug helicopter-supplied outpost adjacent to the ice mass, measure the rate of ice flow, chart precipitation, gather core samples for study, and perform other experiments that will serve to clarify the young science of glaciology.

Perhaps a bit less scientific, but in progress since the early twentieth century, has been a study of the Easton Glacier* on the south side of Mount Baker. The 1907 Mount Baker quadrangle map places the terminus of the Easton Glacier at an elevation of about 4,100 feet, roughly 1 mile northwest of Schrieber's Meadows. Photographs taken at the time are confirmatory. By 1917, the glacier

---

*The Easton Glacier was named by the Mazama Mountaineering Club at its 1909 outing after Charles F. Easton, the historian of the Mount Baker Club in Bellingham.

PHOTO BY AUSTIN POST—U.S.G.S.

South Cascade Glacier, one of the largest glaciers in the North Cascades, 1960.

had receded an estimated 500 feet. Photographs taken in 1925 show a terminus elevation of about 4,800 feet. Recessional measurements conducted by the mountaineers between 1934 and 1941 show recessions between 116 and 429 feet per year, averaging 161 feet during this seven-year interval. By 1952, the terminus elevation was at 5,500 feet. Measurements at that time showed a recession since 1934 of 2,210 feet; for an eighteen-year period ending in 1952, the glacier had melted back at an average rate of 123 feet per year.

I have been observing this glacier since 1957 and have been measuring it annually since 1970. From 1970 until 1984, the glacier advanced substantially. The terminus was stable for the next five to six years. Over the past six to seven years, the ice has retreated about 150 feet. In spite of this withdrawal in 1996, ice 400 to 500 feet wide and perhaps 200 feet deep filled the area that marked the snout of the glacier in 1970.

ROCKS AND MOUNTAINS

Volcanism and glaciation, as has been demonstrated, have contributed to the topography of the North Cascades. To understand the underlying core of the range, consideration must extend much farther backward into the immensities of geological time.

In the past, extensive volcanic flows covered central Washington to great depths. Lava covered the areas now occupied by the Cascade Range. Over the past five to six million years, the range has risen more than 10,000 feet in elevation; the extent of the elevation was greater in the northern part of the cordillera and reached its maximal height in the region of the current U.S.–Canadian border. Because of its greater elevation, the northern part of the range was more aggressively eroded by both ice and water than the southern portion. As a result, most of the volcanic material has been removed from the North Cascades, exposing the underlying complex rocks. To the south, however, these older igneous and metamorphic formations are still beneath the lava cover. In the substantially uplifted and highly eroded northern end of the North Cascades, the exposed rocks that were formed well below the surface of the earth are of two varieties: recrystallized or metamorphic rocks (schists and gneisses) modified by high temperature and pressure, and associated igneous intrusions (granites) that cooled slowly under pressure and are therefore coarsely crystalline. Both of these rock groups are relatively resistant to erosion and therefore persist as the steepest and tallest peaks of the range. Examples include many alpine summits between Snoqualmie and Stevens Pass, eroded from the Snoqualmie batholith; Sloan, Del Campo, and Gothic Peaks of the Monte Cristo group etched in granodiorite; Snow King and Mount Buckindy, sculptured in granite; Dome Peak, also formed of intrusive granite; and the orange granitic peaks in the Liberty Bell–Early Winter Spire area, sculptured from the Golden Horn batholith.

Resistant metamorphic rocks include the gneisses of the Cascade Pass area (Sahale, Forbidden, Boston, Buckner, and Goode Mountains) and the Picket range in the north section of North Cascades National Park. The Pickets are carved in general from strongly metamorphosed Skagit gneiss. The highest of all the nonvolcanic summits in the North Cascades, Bonanza Peak, is composed of granitic gneiss.

The dominant bedrock at the upper end of Lake Chelan is called Skagit gneiss. It is a classic example of the type of "mixed" igneous and metamorphic rock known as a migmatite. The various components of this coarse-grained, banded rock appear to be of substantially different ages and to have developed asynchronously and by different mechanisms. The cliffs around Stehekin were probably originally sediments and lava flows, which have been slowly changed by powerful earth forces (metamorphosed) and then intruded by granite dikes.

The oldest rock in the North Cascades is the Yellow Aster Complex, a bit over one billion years old. This material was moved up along faults from very deep in the earth and eventually exposed by the erosional process. The formation can be seen today as patches on Winchester Mountain, rock blocks in the Yellow Aster Meadows, and at the Park Butte lookout area.

El Dorado Peak is composed of a gneiss that is 90 million years old. The Skagit Metamorphic Suite, 60 to 90 million years old, can be seen in Ripsaw Ridge and in Snowfield Peak. Mount Triumph lies near the contact between the Skagit Suite and the Chilliwack Batholith.

It is mind-boggling to realize that Mount Shuksan was moved at least 15 miles upward and westward in an incredible geological convulsion called the Shuksan thrust; the entire mountain rests on a totally different kind of underlying rock called the Chilliwack formation. Perhaps even more difficult to believe is a current theory that the Chilliwack, a sedimentary rock containing fossils similar to those in ancient Asian seas, was transported to its present location over the past 200 to 300 million years by "drifting" across the Pacific Ocean. Another thrust of similar magnitude moved Jack Mountain 6 miles, where it too presently sits on a different type of base rock.

Another interesting area of the Cascade range is the Twin Sisters area between Mount Baker and Puget Sound. Composed primarily of a homogeneous igneous mineral commonly known as olivine (scientifically termed peridotite), it is the largest single exposed mass of this material in the world. Newly exposed olivine is a light green color; weather rock is orange, accounting for the rusty color of the peaks. This formation does not support as much vegetation as surrounding slopes. Many geologists believe that this rock is an exposed sample of the mantle (the part of the earth that underlies the crust), moved to its present position by the Shuksan thrust fault.

The geology of the North Cascades Highway, otherwise known as State Route 20, is both interesting and complex. Between Marblemount and Newhalem, Marblemount meta-quartz diorite, mica and talc schist of the Cascade River Schist Formation, various quartz diorites of the Chilliwack Batholith, and Skagit Gneiss in the Newhalem area are exposed.

The road between Newhalem and Ross Dam lies entirely within the Skagit Gneiss. Dikes and faults are numerous. Pink garnets are found in outcrops in the gneiss, especially in the area immediately southwest of Diablo Dam. In the Rainy Pass area, the older (about 88 million years) Black Peak Batholith is transected by the highway. These coarse-grained, intrusive rocks, principally granodiorite and quartz diorite (granitelike rocks differing mainly in their potassium feldspar content), make up the ridge above Blue Lake as well as Black Peak. Just south of the Early Winter Spires is the contact zone between the Black Peak and Golden Horn Batholiths. The latter is a true granitic inclusion dating to the Early Tertiary period (about 50 million years ago). Spectacular Liberty Bell, the Early Winter Spires, and Silver Star are composed of reddish granite and are part of the Golden Horn Batholith. For several miles east and west of Washington Pass, the road is carved out of this material. Sedimentary rocks of the Cretaceous era lie against the east side of the Golden Horn Batholith within the Methow valley, which is a graben.

The effects of glaciation, as seen from the highway, are obvious; witness the U-shaped valleys through which the road passes. The high alpine lakes, of which Lake Ann and Rainy Lake are good examples, are gouged from the headwalls of the surrounding mountains by glacial action (cirques). When the glaciers melted, the small, lovely, jewel-like lakes were left nestled high among the peaks.

A number of the numerous active glaciers still present in the North Cascades can be seen from Route 20. Ice is visible on the Picket Range to the west and on Jack Mountain to the northeast, as seen from the Ross Lake viewpoints. There is also an active crevassed glacier on Colonial Peak, best seen from the Diablo Lake overlook.

LIFE ZONES

The original concept of life zones reflected the relative latitude of a given area. The names identified these equator-to-pole locations (Lower and Upper Sonoran, Canadian, Hudsonian, Arctic). Later it was realized that life zones change in a similar way with increasing elevation. In the North Cascades, the amount of precipitation also exerts a significant effect. The types of trees and plants and, to a lesser extent, animal species in a given location vary according to life zone.

Because precipitation is less east of the Cascade crest, life zone boundaries on the east side of the range are more sharply demarcated than on the wetter west side.

On the east side, five life zones are encountered between desert and mountaintop:

The steppe zone, below 1,000 feet elevation, is treeless, with bunchgrass and sagebrush predominant.

The yellow pine forest zone occupies the foothills between 1,000 and 3,000 feet. This zone is distinguished by its dominant tree, the ponderosa pine.

The grand and Douglas-fir (Canadian) zone extends from about 3,000 to 4,500 feet; western larch and lodgepole pine are the other two common trees in this life zone.

The subalpine fir (Hudsonian) zone ranges from 4,500 to 6,500 feet. Common trees are the mountain hemlock, white bark pine, Engelmann spruce, Alaska cedar, and Lyall's larch. In this zone are the splendid alpine meadows. At the upper limits of this zone, the trees become brushy shrubs (krummholz)

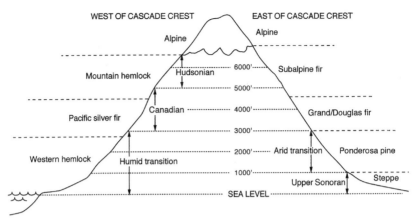

Life zones of the North Cascades

as a result of the struggle to survive the extremes of temperature and the violent winds common at these elevations.

The alpine zone includes all the terrain above timberline, at about 6,500 feet. Specialized flowers—moss campion, Lyall lupine, and the golden fleabane—survive and reproduce above the tree line, as do shrubs such as dwarf willows and common juniper.

On the west side, there are only four life zones. The western hemlock, or humid transition, zone extends from sea level to about 2,800 feet. Other trees found here include the Douglas-fir, western red cedar, and alder. The Pacific silver fir (Canadian) zone extends from about 2,900 to 4,400 feet. Alaska yellow cedar, western white pine, and Douglas-fir are also found here. The mountain hemlock (Hudsonian) zone is from roughly 4,500 to 6,100 feet; subalpine fir and white bark pine are other common trees. The alpine (Arctic) zone extends from timberline (about 6,200 feet) upward to the perpetual snow and ice.

5

Plants

Hikers or climbers who are so intent on reaching their destinations in the mountains that they pay little or no attention to the plethora of plants and trees along the way are missing some of the greatest pleasures of the North Cascades. Wilderness plants or blooms should not be picked. Flowers can be taken home in memory or on film. Slow-growing subalpine trees are fragile and must not be cut for firewood.

WILDFLOWERS

Three plants that often form the ground cover in forested areas are trillium; bunchberry, or ground dogwood; and queen's cup, or bead lily. Trillium is a conspicuous and well-known plant. The stem is about a foot high and supports three parallel-veined, prominent green leaves that form a base for the single large, white, three-petaled flower. The flower has a pleasant fragrance. As it ages, the flower becomes progressively colored, ultimately reaching purple before it withers. The process of blooming and withering lasts approximately a month. This flower is highly adaptable, being found from sea level to almost 5,000 feet. The trillium can tolerate deep shade in the lowland forests and seems equally adaptable to sunlight, since it grows well at the junction of the Pacific silver fir and mountain hemlock zones. It blooms in April in the lowland forests, but bloom is deferred in the high areas until the snow has melted and late spring warmth has reached the high country. For example, the first few hundred yards of the Sauk Mountain Trail is surrounded by impressive numbers of blooming trillium in mid to late June.

The bunchberry is also aptly named the ground dogwood. The blooms are small miniatures of the bracts of the flowering Pacific dogwood. Frequently found in conjunction with fallen timber and decaying wood, this plant is very attractive with its dark green foliage and showy white blooms, which often cover extensive areas of the forest floor. The semiwoody stems creep along the ground, rooting at the nodes and producing upright branches. Flowers are produced in the late spring; by midsummer, attractive and edible, though not particularly tasty, red berries mature where the bracts were two to three months earlier.

The queen's cup, or bead lily, is often found in the same locations as the bunchberry. It is a distinctive and beautiful mountain flower with three large, green leaves forming a base for a six-petaled white flower that usually blooms in July. As the flower matures, it is replaced by a blue berry about 1 centimeter in diameter, which is probably not edible. This plant, like the bunchberry, is a middle-elevation plant generally seen between 2,000 and 4,000 feet.

The deep forest is the habitat of some curious plants that are devoid of chlorophyll. Since they do not require light for survival, they can live in deep shade, where there is insufficient light to support plants dependent on photosynthesis. Fungi probably act as intermediaries in relaying nutritional materials from decaying vegetation to these plants.

A number of species of these unusual plants can be found on the forest floors of the North Cascades. Three species of coral root, all members of the orchid family, flower in late spring. Pinesap and Indian pipe have a similar appearance; they are yellow-white in color, with heads suggesting the bowl of a pipe. Indian pipe is found only in low-level, dense forests. Another plant of this group is the red and white barber pole, sometimes called a candy stick. The tallest group member, pine drops, is a white or pink plant with urn-shaped flowers.

The pinkish red, chest-high flowers of fireweed are ubiquitous in open areas in the North Cascades, particularly those of recent origin. The plant is commonly found in areas of blowdowns, clear-cutting, and man-made or natural fire burns. Its name comes from its ability to be the pioneer plant in an area following a forest fire. Fireweed is able to do this for two reasons: it can start from root stalks sufficiently deep beneath the ground to survive the fire; and the seeds are small and light, with a tuft of long whitish hair, enabling them to move long distances when picked up by the strong fall winds. Since fireweed is not fussy about soil or moisture, it grows almost anywhere and can even be found in the subalpine meadows. Fireweed begins flowering at the base of the stalk, and the blooms gradually progress to the top of the stalk by late summer. Flowers are located above the narrow green leaves. Since pioneer plants require light and heat, other plants maturing in the area often shade them out as the years pass.

Perhaps the most beautiful flower in the North Cascades is the calypso orchid, otherwise known as lady's slipper or fairy slipper. These small flowers, perhaps 4 inches high, are elegant both in their lavender coloration and in their structure. There are several spurs superiorly and an open saclike lower petal with white, yellowish, or darker reddish spots. Each plant has a broad, parallel-veined leaf and a single, fragile stem topped by its splendid flower. The capsule of this plant produces thousands of minute seeds that lack stored food. The germination of the seeds and subsequent establishment of the seedlings is dependent on fungi, which provide a source of nutrition. Therefore, despite its prolific seed production, the calypso orchid reproduces inefficiently. Excessive flower picking has led to its virtual elimination from many areas where it was previously common. It now occurs sporadically from the lowlands to perhaps 2,500 feet in elevation and grows in moist humus on the floor of rich coniferous forests, where it is often hidden by underbrush. The plant flowers in mid-spring. These blooms must not be picked under any circumstances. The best place to see this plant in the North Cascades is along the first several miles of the Thunder Creek Trail in the month of May. In this location, the plant is sufficiently common so that several may be present within the same square foot of ground.

Mountain heathers are usually about 9 inches high, with broad green leaves and cheery red or white flowers. White and red heather, although both members of the heath family, are not members of the same genus. Both are found in the high subalpine meadows, generally on granitic soils that do not support much in the way of other wildflowers. White heather produces small nodding bells growing singly on little stalks. The leaves are small and closely compressed around the branches. Red heather also has small leaves and bell-shaped pink flowers. Both heathers tend to grow up and over large rocks to better reach the sunlight. Both red and white heathers tend to be found in the same areas and are often intermixed. A far scarcer yellow heather has similar leaves and a few greenish yellow closed bell flowers. This plant occurs at higher altitudes than the red and white varieties. Heathers are rather fragile plants and should not be walked or encamped on.

Several kinds of Indian paintbrush are found in the North Cascades. Flower color varies from a pale pink to a deep scarlet; less colorful blooms are ivory or yellow-white. Exact identification of the various species requires inspection by an expert botanist. Species of this plant grow from seashore to timberline. They are relatively easy to distinguish from other kinds of flowers by their hairy leaves and clumped blossoms at the top of the plant. Leaves are narrow and pointed at the tips. Although vigorous in the wild, this plant does not transplant well or thrive in city gardens, since it is a partial parasite.

The mountain daisy grows in a number of western states and is common in the high Cascade meadows. The plant, about a foot high, usually has only one flower head that is yellow in the center with a number of surrounding violet petals. This plant is a member of the composite, or sunflower, family, so named because there are two kinds of flowers—disk flowers centrally, and ray flowers radiating out from the central disk.

Yellow-flowered glacier lilies are wide ranging in the Pacific Northwest. Most commonly found in the mountain meadows, the glacier lily blooms immediately after the snow melts, or it sometimes sprouts and blooms right through the last 1 or 2 inches of melting snow. These plants are capable of growing at low temperatures, heated by their own metabolism. On the east side of the Cascades, the plants bloom at lower elevations earlier in the spring. If you see glacier lilies in bloom, you can be sure that snow has left the area very recently. The plant blooms and withers early, and by midsummer, there is little evidence of its presence. Nonetheless, as the first high-meadow wild-flower to bloom, it has a special place in the hearts of Northwest backpackers and climbers. The saying "Any day on which you see a glacier lily cannot be a bad day" says much about the flower and the Northwestern high country devotee. The glacier lily is far more common in the North Cascades than its close relative, the white-blossomed avalanche lily.

The Columbia tiger lily is one of the most beautiful and easily observed wildflowers of the North Cascades. It is a tall, impressive plant; its height allows it to stand above associated vegetation, so it has less competition and is more easily seen by hikers. The leaves are fairly large and attractive, with one or more whorls. Flowers are multiple, usually six to eight on a stalk, and the showy orange petals that bear conspicuous red to purple spots are bent backward and upward. This plant has an unusual elevational range, since it is found from sea level to about 5,000 feet. It is common in the moist, lush, sub-alpine meadows, where it generally flowers about August 1.

The columbine is another relatively tall flower, usually 2 to 3 feet high. Leaves are compound, in multiples of three-lobed leaflets. The brightly colored flowers with red spurs and yellow blades are impressive. Stamens are numerous. This flower is very attractive to both hummingbirds and bumblebees, both of which seek nectar from a small gland at the base of the spur. The bumblebee chews through the spur and laps up the nectar; the hummingbird is able to hover near the flower and extract the nectar by extending its pointed beak into the opening of the spur. Like the Columbia tiger lily, this plant often towers above the rest of the meadow flora and is easily visible to passersby.

There are two varieties of monkeyflower, or mimulus, in the North Cascades. Both are found only in moist or wet areas. Look for them around small streams and in seepage areas of the mountain meadows. The red variety is the larger of the two, generally between 12 and 18 inches high. The flowers are bright red, with the petals fused into a tube with five lobes projected outward—two upward and three downward. The inside of the tube is marked by two linear yellow hairy ridges; the contrasting colors make the flower very attractive. Yellow monkeyflower is a smaller plant with densely matted succulent stems and large impressive flowers. Again, there are two upper and three lower petal lobes projecting from a tubular base. The lower lobes are usually splotched with red, contrasting sharply with the otherwise bright yellow color and providing an attractive landing area for the nectar-seeking, pollinating mountain bumblebee. Both varieties flower in midsummer.

The many kinds of lupine can be found in practically every habitat and climate in North America. These hardy flowers bloom from the southern tip of Baja California to as far north as the timberline in the Arctic. Members of the pea family, they produce individual flowers and distinctive seedpods. The leaves have a starlike design, with each of the many leaflets radiating from a central point. Most produce blue flowers, but yellow or white flowers are seen on occasion.

Two species of lupine commonly occur in the mountains of the Pacific Northwest, and both flower during early summer. The first and more common is the broad-leafed or subalpine lupine. A rather tall plant, usually over a foot high, it is found throughout the lush meadows of the subalpine zone. Less commonly seen, since it generally occurs above the timberline, is the considerably smaller alpine lupine. This plant can thrive in the sandy or gravelly soils of the Arctic-alpine zone. Blue blossoms are borne on the ends of the spreading branches of this ground-hugging wildflower.

The broad-leafed lupine is probably the most common flower in the high meadows of the North Cascades. At prime blooming time, acres of blue ripple in the summer winds. Occasionally, when the air is still, a subtle fragrance suggestive of sweet peas is noticeable. The lupine dies back to the ground in the fall but springs up again after the snow melts. Depending on location and altitude, blooming time may be from mid-July until mid-September but on average occurs about August 1.

Other fairly common shade-tolerant plants found in lower-elevation forests are the aster, arrowleaf balsamroot, bear grass, wild bleeding heart, wild currant, false lily of the valley, pipsissewa, white rhododendron, Oregon grape, salal, skunk cabbage, and pioneer and evergreen violets. Nonnative plants are the foxglove and the oxeye daisy.

Alpine wildflower species include the orange agoseris, western anemone, broad-leafed arnica, bellflower, bistort, cinquefoil, cow parsnip, elephant head, false hellebore, golden fleabane, Lyall's goldenweed, moss campion, Jacob's ladder, lousewort, marsh marigold, penstemon, various saxifrages, stonecrop, spring beauty (also found in the lower woods), edible thistle, Sitka valerian, dwarf fireweed or red willow herb, Jeffrey shooting star, spreading phlox, and luetkea (partridge-foot or Alaska spirea).

TREES

The common lower-elevation trees of the western North Cascades are the Douglas-fir, western hemlock, western red cedar, alder, and vine maple; eastern trees are the ponderosa (yellow) pine and the dogwood. At middle elevations, on the west are the mountain hemlock and Alaska cedar; on the east is the aspen. Western subalpine meadow trees, each with a definite preferred niche, are the subalpine fir and the white bark pine; on the east, the Engelmann spruce and the subalpine larch are also present. There is overlap between zones. Other trees that may be seen occasionally include the big-leaf maple; birch; black cottonwood; willow; Pacific yew; noble, grand, and Pacific silver firs; western larch; and lodgepole and western white pine. Near the upper range of timberline, trees become dwarfed and stunted and assume atypical bushy forms; this phenomenon is called krummholz (from the German meaning "crooked wood").

The most familiar and common tree in the North Cascades is the Douglas-fir. This tree grows elsewhere in the western United States but reaches great size only west of the Cascade crest in Oregon and Washington. Only the giant sequoias of California are larger.

The Douglas-fir has confused botanists since its discovery by Menzies in 1791 and its rediscovery three decades later by Douglas. It has features of firs, spruces, and yews; its name is a misnomer, since it is not a true fir.

In the North Cascades, the tree occurs between sea level and 5,000 feet in elevation. In favorable sites, it attains heights of over 200 feet and diameters up to 8 feet. The trees have unmistakable cones with three-pronged bracts. Other identifying characteristics are the corky-textured bark, the elongated growth buds, and the distinctive aromatic fragrance of fresh-cut foliage. The largest Douglas-fir discovered to date was over 13 feet thick and slightly over 302 feet tall.

The thick bark and the long, clear trunk of adult trees provide considerable protection against fire; paradoxically, forest fires and massive blowdowns help perpetuate stands of Douglas-fir. Since these trees are less tolerant of shade than the western hemlock and western red cedar, the Douglas-fir is not the climax tree in the forest, unless there is some form of disturbance every several hundred years. Douglas-fir germinates rapidly in devastated areas and outstrips its competitors to gain dominance in the area. It is relatively resistant to drought, long-lived, tough, durable, and more shade tolerant than Ponderosa pine, western larch, and lodgepole pine. It is the tree most valued by western timbermen and makes good firewood.

Squirrels, chipmunks, mice, and shrews eat the seeds, as do birds such as crossbills, winter wrens, and song sparrows. Deer may eat the new shoots, and black bears may strip the bark of vigorous young trees to eat the sap layer. The tree is preyed upon by various insects, including the western budworm, tussock moth, and Douglas-fir beetle. Other parasites include dwarf mistletoe and several root- and stem-rotting fungi. In spite of these handicaps, the Douglas-fir does splendidly in this area.

The western red cedar, a commercially valuable tree, grows between sea level and 3,500 feet elevation in the North Cascades. It is characteristically a tree of moist habitats, growing best in cool, cloudy summers and wet, mild winters in the Pacific Northwest. It was by far the most valuable tree to the coast Indians, who used cedar wood for shelters, clothing, and dugout canoes. It is still highly valued commercially as a source of shingles, shakes, and boards for exterior siding.

The trees have conical trunks: gray, stringy, fibrous bark; and shallow but widespread root systems. It is not uncommon for old-growth trees to be 10 feet in diameter and grow to a height of 200 feet. Two trees over 20 feet in diameter are known, and one tree 19 feet thick and 178 feet tall still grows on the Olympic Peninsula.

The foliage is distinctive, with tiny, flat, scalelike leaves about ⅛ inch long. Broken boughs have an aromatic, sweet odor. Small, brown, oval cones produce very small seeds (400,000 per pound); the tree produces a prodigious number of seeds each year, but only a few seedlings survive.

This tree is more tolerant of shade than any of its principal associates, except for western hemlock. Because of its large size and longevity, it remains a member of undisturbed stands indefinitely, even when competing with the western hemlock. Cedars seldom dominate forest sites, other than in very wet places, where hemlock does poorly.

Cedar wood has a straight grain, allowing it to be split easily into shakes, fence posts, and kindling. The wood is also decay resistant, due to the presence of a natural fungicide. Since the wood is easy to carve and work, it was used exclusively by Northwest Indian artisans for totem poles. Cedar burls are used to make attractive furniture.

The tree is durable: insects generally do not attack it, snow inflicts little damage on its resilient boughs, and it is relatively resistant to wind throw, despite its shallow roots. Because of its thin bark and low branches, it is easily damaged or killed by fire, but major conflagrations seldom sweep through the wet sites where it grows most abundantly.

A closely related tree, the Alaska cedar, is usually found between 2,500 and 6,500 feet in elevation in the North Cascades. It does best in areas of high rainfall, extensive winter snowfall, and relatively mild winters. Since it is slow growing and relatively shade intolerant, it is most common on poor, rocky soils, where its competitors do not grow well. Krummholz forms of this tree are often seen at timberline. Although easily damaged by fire, major fires do not occur where this tree grows. Since it also is resistant to fungi and insects, it may be the longest-lived tree in the North Cascades, with older trees possibly reaching a life span of 2,000 years or more. Because of its inaccessible location, slow growth, and relatively small size, it is less important as a source of timber than the western red cedar.

The ponderosa pine, named by David Douglas because of its great size, averages 3 feet in diameter and 120 feet in height in old-growth forest. The largest recorded specimen is nearly 9 feet in diameter and over 161 feet tall. Although there are scattered trees west of the Cascade crest, east of the crest at lower elevations it forms a vast forest, covering the foothills of the Cascades. The tree is very drought resistant, having made a number of adaptations, including an immense root system, to gather water.

Once the vulnerable sapling has grown sufficiently large to develop thick, attractive, dark red bark, the tree becomes highly resistant to fire. Wounds caused by brush fires are usually sealed with pitch, which prevents damaging insects and decay organisms from gaining entry. Frequent minor natural fires consume duff on a regular basis, thus preventing fuel buildup to dangerously high levels that might cause a holocaust that would kill and consume mature trees. Minor ground fires, therefore, are ultimately beneficial to the mainte- nance of healthy stands of ponderosa pine.

Ponderosa pine is intolerant to shade and generally requires a lot of grow- ing space; stands of the trees are typically open. Large old-growth pines are valued by timbermen, since the wood is of good quality. Younger trees are knotty and of substantially less value. The wood rots fairly rapidly when in direct contact with the ground. Needles are 5 to 8 inches long in bundles of three. Cones are distinctively egg shaped, 3 to 5 inches long.

Cold and frost seem to be the limiting factors above 4,000 feet, as is lack of water in the steppe deserts of central Washington. (Ponderosas are often seen growing close to small streams in otherwise treeless sagebrush country.)

Hikers in the upper valleys in the fall will be impressed by the brilliant color of the vine maple and Douglas maple. Vine maple has seven to nine sharp-pointed lobes on leaves that are 3 to 4 inches across. The leaves may begin to turn red or yellow as early as midsummer. They produce an unforget- table display of color in October. When it grows in clearings or in avalanche chutes, vine maple can form a bushy, multistemmed tree that is 20 to 30 feet tall. The vine maple is tolerant of shade and grows as forest undercover, whereas the Douglas maple needs open sunlight. The Douglas maple leaf is a bit smaller, with only three to five main points. Both maples are a favorite food of deer.

The leaves of the quaking aspen, bright green above and silvery beneath, tremble and whisper when stirred by the slightest breeze. Small groves of aspen are found tucked away in the high valleys of the North Cascades. Their leaves turn yellow, golden, and occasionally even reddish in the fall, making the mountain landscape more splendid. Aspen can be identified by the pres- ence of leaf motion with even minimal winds; the tree makes a gentle rustling noise when its leaves are trembling. The bark is smooth and cream-colored.

A common and spectacular tree in the lower valleys is the Pacific dogwood. There are a large number of these trees in the Stehekin area; one scenic specimen can be found at the base of Rainbow Falls. There is also a large grove of trees at the Rainbow Creek Bridge 2 miles from the valley floor. This is the most beautiful flowering tree in these mountains, although its true "flowers" are small, greenish, and inconspicuous. These plain flowers, however, are set in a cluster of creamy white floral leaves, creating the effect of a cream-colored blossom 4 to 6 inches across. By fall, the inconspicuous true flowers have ripened into a cluster of bright red fruits about 1 inch across, nestled among leaves that have turned red and purple. Occasionally, a dogwood even flowers again during an extended Indian summer.

This tree is unusual because it is able to survive and bloom in the forest understory. It is very shade tolerant and needs little sunlight. The tree is a hardwood, and apparently the wood was considered especially suited for skewers or "dags"; in time, dagwood became dogwood. In most areas, the trees bloom maximally about Memorial Day.

There are four alders in the North Cascades: red alder is the largest and most plentiful; the Sitka, or "slide," alder is found in avalanche paths; white alder occurs almost exclusively east of the Cascades; and thin-leaf alder grows along watercourses east of the Cascades. These members of the birch family form a distinctive group of trees. Alders have nodular growths on their roots that are able to convert atmospheric nitrogen into soil nitrogen. Much of this "fixed" nitrogen is made available to the forest soil through decomposition of alder leaves each fall. Alders are therefore important to the health of the forest because of their unique ability to enhance soil fertility.

The red alder is also a pioneer tree. It seeds readily on logged and devastated areas and outgrows even the Douglas-fir for the first twenty-five years after germination. Seeds are extremely light, produced in profusion, and showered over practically the entire west-side landscape by the southwest storm winds. The tree grows rapidly and can reach 15 feet in five years, 35 feet in ten years, and 75 to 80 feet in twenty-five years. A maximal height of 100 to 110 feet is obtained at about sixty years of age. Alders are very intolerant of shade and seldom live over a hundred years. In short, this pioneer tree primes the forest floor. As the alders die out, shade-tolerant conifers, taking advantage of the enriched soil, supplant them. Alders grow from sea level to about 3,000 feet in elevation. Large trees have smooth, gray bark. The leaves have rounded teeth and short hairs on their undersides and are approximately 5 inches long. The fairly hard wood is useful for furniture making and is also valuable for firewood.

Sooner or later, cross-country hikers in the North Cascades will tangle with the "slide alder," with its intertwined, slanted, tough, springy trunks that generally incline downhill in the direction of winter avalanches. Because of their elasticity and direction of growth, these trees can survive snow avalanches that would uproot most other trees. This 10- to 15-foot-high shrubby tree characteristically pioneers fresh gravelly sites at the foot of retreating glaciers. Sitka, or "slide," alders form almost impenetrable clumps at midelevation on the steeper slopes of the range.

The western hemlock is the climax tree of the west-side forest. It is not as dramatic a tree as the Douglas-fir or western red cedar and grows more slowly. However, because of its prolific seed crops and remarkable shade tolerance, it will ultimately dominate, assuming that no disaster such as fire, blowdown, or logging occurs. After perhaps a thousand years, the forest, if undisturbed, will be primarily pure western hemlock, with perhaps an occasional red cedar.

The tree grows from 3,500 feet in elevation down to sea level. In dense climax forests, the canopy is so thick that minimal light penetrates, which makes the forest undergrowth very sparse.

The needles are small, of unequal length, flat, and short. The cones are also small and delicate. Smaller trees can easily be recognized because the growing tips droop downward like an inverted J. Seeds possess a membranous wing, which allows them to travel substantial distances on only light winds. Moisture is essential for the growth of this tree. Old-growth trees can be 3 to 4 feet thick and up to 200 feet tall and can reach an age of about 500 years. Hemlocks are susceptible to fungi, mistletoe, insects, fire, and windthrow. The wood is moderately useful as lumber and is excellent for producing pulpwood and eventually paper products.

Clearly, the most unusual tree in the North Cascades is the alpine or Lyall's larch, commonly known as a tamarack. This member of the pine family grows in small, open stands and is rarely found below a mile in elevation. The needles are a soft, pale, luxuriant green in the summer. This tree is one of the very few deciduous conifers (cone-bearing trees that lose their needles in the winter). The other two such trees native to North America are the western larch and the bald cypress. One of the magnificent sights in the North Cascades occurs in the last week of September and the first week of October (in an average year), when the larch turns a golden yellow before it drops its needles. When backlit by the sun, the trees glow. Anyone who has walked in a golden larch forest in the fall will never forget the experience.

Larch is found only in a north-south distance of 120 miles in the Cascades—roughly from Wenatchee on the south into Manning and Cathedral Parks on the north. The tree is never found below 5,000 feet and cannot be grown in cultivation in lowland areas, presumably because it is intolerant of heat. It is of interest that of the world's ten larch species, nine grow at timberline either in the high mountains or in the arctic tundra; the exception is the western larch.

Since alpine larch grows only at higher elevations, it is seldom seen from the car. A few trees can be seen underneath Liberty Bell and the Early Winters Spires from the Washington Pass overlook. The Harts Pass Road leads into stands of this tree, as does the road in Manning Park that goes to the north side of Blackwall Peak; however, to really appreciate this splendid tree, one must walk the high country east of the Cascade crest.

This tree is able to eke out an existence on sites that are too cold, too rocky, too boggy, or too snow covered for other trees; however, it is shade intolerant and cannot compete with evergreen conifers on more favorable sites. Like the alder, alpine larch is a pioneer species, meaning that it can colonize sites such as moraines at the foot of active glaciers, where no other tree can gain a foothold.

Larch trees may reach 3 feet in diameter and 70 to 80 feet in height, with an age of 500 to 700 years. The largest known alpine larch is in a steep rocky basin at 6,200 feet elevation above Lake Chelan; it is 6 feet 3 inches in diameter and 94 feet tall. As with other subalpine trees, growth rates are slow because of harsh conditions. A ten-year-old alpine larch may be only 2 inches high.

The larch has thin bark and is rather easily killed by fire; however, fire is not a great risk to the tree because of the sparse fuel and short burning season where it grows. Purplish new cones emerge with the first foliage about June 1, but most are destroyed by adverse weather. Successful cone crops are rather exceptional, but in spite of that, the tree successfully regenerates once in a great while when seed crops and survival conditions are ideal. Lyall's larch is the favorite tree of many mountaineers and backpackers, including me.

Mountain hemlock grows almost exclusively in the uppermost zone of the forest, from about 3,500 to 6,000 feet. It is a tree that survives best in mountains with heavy snowfall. Rather surprisingly, it does not have a compact, narrow crown but is still able to tolerate the huge quantities of snow that collect on its branches in the winter. The needles are plump and spread out in clusters. Cones are about 2 inches long. Bark is thick and furrowed. It is relatively shade tolerant, allowing growth to heights of 150 feet below elevations of 4,000 feet. In the meadows, the tree is smaller and stouter, with wind-battered upper branches and thick, gnarled trunks. At the tree line, krummholz forms resemble huge, sprawling shrubs. The mountain hemlock can grow in the rockiest of soils, as long as moisture is adequate. The species reproduces both by seeds and through branches that reach the ground, take root, and then grow erect to become independent mature trees (layering).

The subalpine fir joins the alpine larch as the other majestic and distinctive high-country tree. These trees grow in clusters, shaped like splendid gothic cathedral spires, at hundreds of locations across the subalpine meadows of the North Cascades. It is the most widespread true fir in North America. It is found between 4,000 and 7,000 feet in the North Cascades. It is also known as alpine fir—a misnomer, since no trees occur in the true alpine areas above timberline. Although it is shade tolerant, it is unable to compete with the dense, taller trees of the lower forest zone. Its shape is well suited for survival in areas of heavy snowfall. The branches are stiff but exceedingly tough, short, and densely packed together; the crown resembles an A-frame snow roof. Unlike most other trees in this area, it is limbed all the way to the ground and can reproduce by layering. This is one of the reasons that this tree often grows in clusters at timberline. Sizable seed crops are produced, but germination and survival of new trees are precarious propositions. Growth rates in the high country are very slow in view of the brief summers and the prolonged winters, during which small trees are snow covered.

The bark is smooth. In late summer, cylindrical blue-gray cones project upright on short, rigid boughs. The needles are about an inch long and deep green in color, with fine white bands on all sides.

Trees 5 to 6 inches thick are often 100 years old or more. The tree is relatively short-lived, seldom surviving more than 250 years. Its thin bark and combustible lower limbs almost assure destruction in even a low-intensity forest fire; fortunately, it does not grow in areas where fire is common. The trunk is brittle and rot susceptible, and the tree is often extensively damaged by the spruce, or western, budworm. It is also parasitized by snow molds that give limbs emerging from the snowpack a matted, blackish, diseased appearance. Winds and major temperature variations can damage trees significantly. Krummholz forms seldom grow higher than the usual depth of the winter snowpack. Shoots that grow above this protective blanket are pruned by the winter ice blast. Because of lack of access, small size, and frequent knots, the tree has little commercial value.

The Engelmann spruce is one of the high-country trees east of the Cascade crest. It is usually found in moist locations between 3,000 and 7,000 feet. Old-growth trees can be 3 feet thick and up to 140 feet tall. The tree grows slowly but steadily. It has a tall, narrow crown; thin bark with loose scales; and, like all North American spruces, prickly needles.

It produces purple half-inch-long pollen cones. Seed cones are about 2 inches long. The tree is vulnerable to windthrow, since it lacks deep or extensive roots. The wood is of moderate commercial value, for both lumber and wood pulp.

White bark pine is another common tree of the high country, more common on the east side of the Cascade crest than the west. It has a number of varied growth forms. At low altitude, it can be slender and straight. At higher elevations, it develops a short, stout trunk and a large, spreading crown. The average tree is smaller and shorter as altitude is gained. Near timberline, the white bark pine may assume a massive, sprawling krummholz form. At the very highest elevations, the tree may be a small, wind-pruned shrub perhaps only a foot high; these stunted varieties may be found as high as 8,000 feet. The bark of young trees has a whitish color, presumably accounting for the common name. The color does not persist as the tree ages. White barks grow slowly but may reach trunk diameters of 3 to 4 feet by the time they are 600 years of age. Needles are stout, stiff, and yellow-green and come in bundles of five. Cones are small and disintegrate on maturity. Pine nuts are an important food source for squirrels and the Clark's nutcracker.

East of the Cascades, many large white bark pines have been killed by mountain pine beetle infestation. Their skeletons form picturesque gray-white snags along many lofty ridges.

FUNGI AND ALGAE

Fungi are common at lower elevations in the North Cascades. A variety of mushrooms grow in the valleys and foothills, particularly on the west side. Detailed descriptions of most varieties are beyond the scope of this book (see the Bibliography). Chanterelles have a uniform egg-yolk yellow color and are found in late summer to late fall beneath the conifers of old- or second-growth forest.

In August and September, chicken-of-the-woods may be observed growing from rotting logs and stumps. Their brilliant sulfur yellow appearance is an unexpected sight in the forest understory, particularly on a gray day.

Also visually impressive and common in the area is the fly amanita, with its brilliant red-orange cap speckled with creamy white warty particles. They are found most commonly in the fall on the forest floor beneath the conifers. These fungi are enjoyable to look at, a pleasure to photograph, but gastronomically disastrous. When eaten, they produce nausea, diarrhea, an intoxicated madness, and in severe cases, convulsions and coma. Fortunately, the taste is repugnant, so it is seldom ingested.

Another form of fungus commonly seen in the North Cascades is the bracket fungus. These woody or leathery relatives of the mushroom have no stalk. The cap is attached by one side to the wood on which it feeds. There are several genera and many species of bracket fungi; precise identification is difficult, even for experts. In the Cascade Range, most of these unusual organisms can be found clinging to dead timber and are most commonly seen on snags alongside the trail. Smaller species commonly grow on downed timber. Watch for them on the cut ends of the wind-thrown deadwood sawed out of the footpath by trail crews. Only rarely do bracket fungi grow on living trees.

Although the bracket fungi have an obvious family resemblance, the various species vary tremendously in size, color, and appearance. When young, they are frequently soft and pliable, but as they age, they become more tough and leathery, and many of them end up being as hard as the wood on which they grow; the upper surface may have the consistency of hardened leather or resin. Their mechanism of attacking the wood on which they grow varies, but the ultimate effect is the same—a general softening and crumbling of the timber.

Mountain climbers and, to a lesser extent, high-country hikers who cross snowfields may be startled now and then to note the presence of red snow beneath their feet. The coloration is due to high concentrations, or "blooms," of microscopic algae plants. Investigators have identified more than 100 species of snow algae, many of which have a worldwide distribution. Probably the most common and widely distributed species is *Chlamydomonas nivalis*; great numbers of these organisms produce the watermelon color commonly observed on alpine snowfields not only in the North Cascades but also elsewhere in the world.

As in most plants, the cells contain chlorophyll and use solar energy for photosynthesis. Pigments other than chlorophyll are responsible for the appearance of colored snow. The organism is extremely hardy and resistant to cold and may survive frozen in ice for long periods. These organisms obtain nitrates, phosphates, and other chemicals essential for plant growth from the snow itself. Liquid water is essential for plant growth, which explains why the organism does not flourish during the winter. Because the dark red pigments of the algae absorb solar energy, the cells melt their way into the snow, deepening "sun cups" and increasing the melting rate of snowfields.

How the algae are "reseeded" on the surface after each winter's snow accumulation is unclear. Possibilities include transportation of spores by wind from adjacent snow-free land areas, transportation by birds either in their intestinal tracts or on feet and feathers, or the production of motile cells by resting spores in the deeper layers of the snowpack that migrate to the surface and grow. The last is the most probable explanation. Surprisingly, other organisms are found in association with snow algae communities. These include snow and ice worms belonging to the genus *Mesenchytraeus*. These worms feed on the snow algae. Various species of protozoans, rotifers, nematodes, spiders, and springtails are other members of the snow community. Birds form the final link in the food chain by feeding on the snow worms and springtails.

REESTABLISHING NATIVE FLORA

When the North Cascades National Park was established by act of Congress in October 1968, the new park administration inherited from the U.S. Forest Service some problems of severe overuse. The backpacking boom of the late 1950s and 1960s had brought ever-increasing numbers of hikers and climbers into the high country of the North Cascades. There were no Forest Service restrictions on campsites, fires, or party size, and the fragile subalpine vegetation of the scenic passes rapidly began to show signs of wear. Cascade Pass, in particular, was a sad example of the inability of subalpine vegetation to withstand the impact of concentrated use. Always a popular destination because of its superlative surrounding peaks and glaciers, the pass was subjected to greatly increased visitation when the Forest Service extended the Cascade River Road and constructed a new high-standard trail in the late 1960s. Sunny summer weekends found as many as fifty parties camping in the vicinity of the pass, digging out the heather to level their tent sites and hacking at the ancient mountain hemlocks and subalpine firs for their campfires.

In 1969, the park's first summer, the NCNP administration contracted with forest ecologist Dale Thornburgh to survey the impact at Cascade Pass and make management recommendations for its rehabilitation. Based on his suggestions, the pass was closed to camping and fires at the start of the 1970 season. Later that summer, the superintendent persuaded two volunteer research biologists, Margaret and Joseph Miller, to undertake a long-range program of revegetating the worn-out campsites and myriad trails of Cascade Pass.

Over the next ten years, the Millers experimented with a number of horticultural techniques designed to restore native plants to the area. They finally concluded that, because of the scarcity of meadow vegetation suitable for transplanting, Cascade Pass could best be revegetated by propagating plant material at a lower elevation from cuttings and divisions collected from the pass area. The National Park Service constructed a large greenhouse at the Skagit District Ranger Station in Marblemount in which native plants are grown and later carried—usually in backpacks, but occasionally by helicopter—for replanting at Cascade Pass. Eventually, the Park Service plans to use its Marblemount greenhouse to grow plants to place in other damaged areas within the park complex. Plants will be segregated by areas of origin to avoid the mixing of gene pools.

Although Cascade Pass is the park's "showcase" of successful subalpine revegetation, many other areas have received less intensive rehabilitation efforts. All the popular subalpine passes were closed to fires and camping in the early 1970s, but more than the cessation of recreational impact was needed to restore these damaged areas. Jute netting was flown by helicopter or carried on pack frames to several locations and laid on worn-down campsites to retard erosion and discourage illegal camping. Revegetation through transplanting has been carried out at Park Creek Pass, Lake Juanita, Copper and Egg Lakes on Copper Ridge, and Boundary Camp below Hannegan Pass.

In addition to work in the subalpine areas, many of the old closed camp-grounds in the lowland valleys have been successfully replanted with young trees and shrubs from adjoining damaged areas. In these lower elevations with longer growing seasons, revegetation proceeds much more rapidly than in the harsh subalpine climate.

The success of the revegetation program of the North Cascades National Park, both in the subalpine zone and in the lower closed-canopy forest, depends ultimately on the cooperation of visitors. Several years of work by seasonal backcountry rangers and volunteers can be wiped out by one thoughtless camper who erects a tent or builds an illegal fire in a revegetation plot. All visitors to the North Cascades should understand the significance of the presence of jute netting and cooperate with the efforts to restore the backcountry to its pristine state.

Animals

6

As described in the section on botany, North Cascades vegetation zones are sharply demarcated on the east side of the Cascade Crest, whereas boundaries are less distinct on the west.

Each vegetation (life) zone in the North Cascades also tends to have a distinctive animal population, subject to seasonal variations. As snow melts in the spring, many mammals migrate upward into the high country, where they spend the summer and early fall. These animals return to the valley floors when early winter storms begin to fill the high meadows with the usual 15 to 25 feet of snow that accumulates in the high country by late spring.

The animals most likely to be seen by hikers or cross-country travelers include deer, black bears, golden-mantled ground squirrels, raccoons, chipmunks, pikas, marmots, and porcupines. Animals of significance in the North Cascades, but less likely to be seen, include the cougar, mountain goat, and coyote. Rattlesnakes are not uncommon at lower elevations on the east side of the range.

DEER

The animal of substantial size most likely to be seen by hikers in the North Cascades is the deer. Black-tailed deer are more common on the west side of the crest; mule deer predominate on the east side of the range. Black-tailed deer have Y-branched antlers and an all-black-on-top tail. Typical mule deer have a dark horseshoe patch on the forehead, larger and wider-spreading antlers than the black-tailed deer, and a tail that is mostly white with a black tip. All deer have plumed tails that they use as signaling devices. While running, the tail of the black-tailed deer is held straight out, whereas the tail of the mule deer is held down. Although the mule deer was named for its large, mulelike ears, there is little difference in the ear structure of the black-tailed, white-tailed, and mule deer. Crossbred animals, found particularly on the west side of the range, have features of both species.

Deer are found in season from sea level to timberline. They migrate upward to the lush high meadows in the summer, returning to the lowland valleys in the winter. Male deer have horns, more precisely called antlers. A buck grows his first set when he is a yearling. These antlers are without branches, hence the term "spike buck." Antlers start their growth in the late winter or early spring. By fall, they attain full growth, lose their blood supply, and harden. After the fall rutting season, the antlers drop off. Each succeeding year, the antlers become larger and heavier and add additional tines until the male deer reaches his prime.

Deer are browsers (herbivores) and feed on available vegetation. Baby deer, called fawns, are born in the spring, usually singly but occasionally as twins. Fawns are almost odorless and are dappled in coloration during the first few months of life; when threatened, they lie motionless. These adaptations grant some degree of protection from their natural enemies, the cougar and bobcat. Small fawns, when temporarily separated from their mothers, make a bleating noise until mother and progeny are reunited. Deer tend to sleep during the day; therefore, these animals are most easily seen at dawn and at dusk.

During the fall rut, bucks literally "lock horns." The stronger animal acquires a harem of does; the weaker male returns to a solitary existence. Fierce as these mating battles are, it is rare for either animal to be killed, although occasionally their horns lock together, dooming the combatants to a slow death together.

BEARS

The American black bear is a relatively common animal in the North Cascades. This animal is seldom seen in the winter, since bears sleep most of the time from December until March; available data suggest that they do not truly hibernate. In spite of its name, the black bear can have cinnamon or dark brown fur, as well as black. The black bear stands 2 to 3½ feet high at the shoulders and weighs between 200 and 500 pounds. It has short, curved, non-retractable claws, enabling it to climb trees. It can be distinguished from the grizzly bear by the shape of the head seen in profile; the upper line of the muzzle arches slightly upward in the black bear and downward in the grizzly bear. Grizzly bears have long, curved claws.

Half-pound black bear cubs, usually twins, are born in midwinter of alternate years in the den or other protected location where the mother is overwintering. Between birth and spring, the mother bear nurses them to viable size. When spring arrives, she introduces the young bears to the outside world. She teaches them survival skills, including climbing, and cuffs them if they disobey. Cubs rapidly learn to climb trees if the mother signals the presence of danger. Cubs remain with their mother for about the first year and a half of their lives.

Bears tend to be more active at night, but in undisturbed wilderness, they also range widely by day. The bear is omnivorous, eating everything it can find, including berries, roots, grasses, insects, rodents, honey, yellow jacket nests, skunk cabbage, huckleberries, blueberries, dead animals, fawns, salmon, and if given the opportunity, garbage and campers' food supplies. Although black bears normally withdraw when they become aware of people nearby, sows with cubs and problem bears that are habituated to camper food can be dangerous. Never come between a mother bear and her cubs; to do so is to invite an attack. Backpackers should protect their food supplies from this opportunistic and potentially aggressive animal (see the General Information chapter on how to bearproof a camp).

The more aggressive grizzly bear existed in limited numbers in the North Cascades early in the twentieth century. A five-year study was recently conducted by a wildlife biologist to determine whether grizzly bears still inhabit the North Cascades. A definite conclusion could not be drawn, since the researcher never saw or photographed the great bear; however, based on less tangible evidence, grizzlies were thought to be present in small numbers from time to time. Indigenous grizzlies are appropriately protected by law from harm wherever they are found, since they are considered endangered in the lower forty-eight states. Measures to reestablish the grizzly in the North Cascades are being considered, but transferring the great bear from other areas to these mountains is controversial; a final decision has not been made as of this writing.

SQUIRRELS

The Cascade golden-mantled ground squirrel, roughly 10 inches long, resembles a large chipmunk. Its behavior is quite chipmunkish and it shares a habitat with the yellow pine chipmunk. However, this squirrel is less dependent on seeds and nuts for sustenance, subsisting on other foods such as mushrooms, roots, flowers, and berries. The ground squirrel is less arboreal than the chipmunk and is a true hibernator, spending long winters underground with all bodily functions reduced to a minimum. Breeding occurs shortly after reawakening; one litter is produced in the spring of the year. Its habitat is usually the subalpine zone.

This animal lives in an underground burrow with protected access areas. It is found in both pine forest and mountain forest clearings. These squirrels frequently visit campsites and picnic areas, happily accepting handouts during lunch or disposing of food scraps afterward.

Other animals of similar appearance and habits commonly found in the same or lower areas include the Douglas squirrel, or chickaree, and the north flying squirrel; the latter is rarely seen, since it is nocturnal.

Chipmunks, the smallest of the Pacific Northwest squirrels, are charming, active, and frequently seen in the North Cascades. Their size is about halfway between that of a mouse and a rat. Although there are other species of chipmunks in the Pacific Northwest, only two are commonly seen in the North Cascades. The larger, darker-colored, and less active Townsend's chipmunk prefers the dense Douglas fir and hemlock forests of the west-side lowlands and the higher hemlock forests of the Cascade mountains. The lighter-colored, smaller yellow pine chipmunk is a denizen of the ponderosa pine zone of the more arid east-side mountains and foothills, although this animal can also be found in mountain meadow areas near timberline. Both species are diurnal.

The Townsend's chipmunk, an agile climber, subsists on a varied diet of seeds, bulbs, roots, berries, nuts, flowers, and fungi. It buries food stores in caches, which it uses periodically during the winter, when the animal remains underground beneath the snow cover.

Yellow pine chipmunks are curious, vociferous animals, not averse to stealing food from campsites. The agile little animals are fine tree climbers. Nests are usually placed at the end of a short burrow or in a small cave. Mating occurs in April, and young are born thirty to forty days later in May or June. This chipmunk feeds on insects and any available plant food during the spring; seeds, particularly from conifers, are standard food items later in the year.

When startled, these animals make shrill, high-pitched cries, often accentuating their verbalizations with vigorous twitches of their tails. Chipmunks are characteristically observed scampering up trees as hikers approach; normally, they spend much of their time on the ground or in the low bushes foraging. These small mammals often fall prey to various predators, including coyotes, foxes, bobcats, rattlesnakes, and less commonly, bears and cougars.

These vigorous little animals are the most commonly seen mammals in the North Cascades. They can be identified easily by their coat of sharply contrasting black and white stripes set against a brown or gray background.

RACCOONS

The common North American raccoon is a remarkable form of wildlife that has adjusted to the impact of civilization. The animal can be found in the heart of the North Cascades wilderness and is apparently equally comfortable in the Seattle metropolitan area. Raccoons are usually 30 to 36 inches long, weigh 10 to 30 pounds, and are clearly identified by their black masks and bushy, ringed tails. Raccoons subsist on almost any type of food. They defend themselves well from most predators, fighting ferociously when cornered. When clearly outclassed, they escape enemies by climbing trees. Also predaceous themselves, these animals are tough and aggressive. They tend to be nocturnal but are sometimes seen in the early evening or early morning hours.

The talented hands of the raccoon rival the skilled manipulative abilities of primates. These animals can sit on a creek bank and deftly sort crayfish and snails from stones. Dabbling is a fixed motor pattern of raccoons when searching for food in the wild. This habit was misinterpreted, leading to the false idea that coons washed their food before consuming it.

Mating occurs in midwinter; about nine weeks later, three to six kits are born. Raccoons do not hibernate but typically experience a variable period of winter dormancy.

PIKAS AND MARMOTS

The two characteristic mammals of the high country are the pika, affectionately known as the coney, and the marmot. Pikas are fluffy, little, egg-shaped animals with small, rounded ears. They live in communities beneath the loose rocks of talus slopes. Individual coneys can often be located amid the boulders by zeroing in on the high-pitched cheeping sounds that these animals make with frequency. Pikas collect masses of grass and other vegetable matter, making hay racks outside their holes in the rocks where they dwell. This is their food, and they spend much of their lives caring for it—carrying it below if rains are threatening, and bringing it out to dry again when the bad weather passes. They feed on this food in the winter, when they live in their rocky homes buried under 20 to 30 feet of snow but are active nonetheless. They bear four or five young at a time.

The hoary marmot, or whistler, also inhabits talus slopes in the Hudsonian and Arctic-alpine zones. Weighing about 10 pounds and a bit over 2 feet long, it has thick grayish fur, a compact body, short legs, small ears, and a moderate-sized, fairly bushy tail. Hoary marmots hibernate during the winter, awakening in late spring. They are vegetarians, feeding on the grasses and flowers of the high alpine meadows. They live in holes excavated under rocks and in talus slopes. Marmots often sit on rocks or outcroppings near their holes or dens and survey their domain; when disturbed, they emit a shrill whistle that rises in pitch as whatever is disturbing them comes closer. When danger threatens, they rapidly disappear underground, only to reappear shortly thereafter, as these animals are very curious.

A typical marmot colony consists of a dominant breeding male, three to five adult females, and up to twenty young. The male is territorial and defends the females from marauding males. Young marmots are born in early July. Because the summer season is short, they do not grow very much the first year; full growth is reached in the middle of their second summer. At this time, males are driven away by their fathers. Some females stay; others depart.

Marmots and pikas are sometimes shot by trigger-happy hunters. Both are protected animals, even outside of the park boundary, and a substantial fine can be levied on anyone who kills them.

PORCUPINES

The porcupine is often seen on trails and roads within the forested area of the North Cascades. Although slow moving and defenseless against an armed human, they have been provided by nature with a formidable means of warding off attack by carnivorous predators. An unwary aggressor receives a paw or face full of spines that pierce the skin as they pull out of the porcupine. Although these spines are never "shot," once they are firmly implanted, they are difficult to remove (as many dog owners know). In the wild, animals so unwise as to attack a porcupine may develop serious or lethal infections around the implanted quills; death may also occur if a migrating spine penetrates a vital organ.

Porcupines are rodents with tremendous jaw power. They crave salt, such as that from human sweat, and at night, they may chew on unprotected boots, pack straps, handholds on staffs, and so forth. They have a quill-less underbelly, an Achilles heel for an attacking cougar or fisher.

Porcupines are considered pests by foresters, because they kill trees by gnawing through the bark and superficial wood layers circumferentially. This "ringing" is done to obtain the sap for nourishment, but it is destructive to the forest. Porcupines usually bear one young in the spring. These animals may be seen all year, since they do not hibernate.

COUGARS

The cougar, also known as the puma or mountain lion, is the most widespread terrestrial mammal except for humans. The cougar ranges from southeastern Alaska to Patagonia. Still unprotected in some states, and still a bounty animal in Texas, the cougar is now partially protected in the Pacific Northwest, where it is considered a game animal, with season and kill limits. The mountain lion is secretive and elusive. Many persons who have spent years in the wilderness (including me) have never seen one. The cougar population of Washington State is presently estimated at 1,500 animals (admittedly, there is no way to accurately determine mountain lion populations).

Cougars lead solitary lives. Adults of both sexes live alone and fend for themselves, except when the female is in heat. The female raises a litter of two to three kittens for about two years with no assistance from other adults. The kittens are able to kill small prey, such as rabbits, when only a few weeks old. Usually, only one or two kittens per litter survive to adulthood, at which time they may have trouble locating suitable territory. Both sexes are territorial; females defend their 5 to 15 square miles against other females. Males wander over and protect larger areas, often overlapping the territories of two or three females. A displaced or young male searching for his own territory may have to fight for living space.

The scream of a cougar, likened to a woman's scream, generally indicates that a female is in heat. After mating, the pair remains together for about a week and then separates. The litter is born about three months later, usually in the late spring or early summer.

Cougars kill an average of one deer every seven to ten days. They also kill smaller, more abundant prey, such as rabbits and porcupines, more frequently. The killed animal is often cached, and the cougar returns and feeds later. One of the advantages of cougar predation is that the lion tends to select the easiest prey—the infirm and diseased—thus maintaining a healthier population of prey animals. One of nature's ongoing systems of checks and balances occurs among cougars and deer populations. If deer herds increase, the number of cougars increases; more cougars kill more deer, and the deer herds decrease to within the limitations of the available forage; the cougars then also decrease. This feedback cycle prevents deer herds from becoming so numerous that they starve and keeps the herds healthy by culling the diseased, injured, and aged animals.

Cougars rarely attack people. Campers in the North Cascades are more likely to be struck by lightning than to be assaulted by a mountain lion. If confronted by a cougar, however, it is best to advance slowly toward the animal making lots of noise and waving arms, staff, or ice ax; *do not turn and run.* Barking loudly like a dog may also back off a mountain lion. At close quarters, fight back. Strike the beast with fists, knife, staff, club, rock, or ice ax. Children are at the greatest risk of attack by the big cat and should be closely supervised at all times when in lion country.

MOUNTAIN GOATS

Mountain goats are the true monarchs of the mountains. These splendid animals are found only in northwestern North America. They are lone American representatives of a resilient tribe of Old World antelopes; their closest relative is the chamois found in the Eurasian mountains.

The North Cascades goat is a stocky, bearded animal. The average weight of the female is 120 to 150 pounds; large males may reach 300 pounds. The goat has a pronounced shoulder hump; a long, narrow head; and permanent horns that extend backward and upward and are about 1 foot in length. Its body is well protected from the harsh winds and cold by a long, yellow-white outer coat of guard hair that overlies a dense wool undercoating. Both coats are shed in the spring. Males shed in late May to early June; lactating females do not shed until late July. Both coats are regained in full by early fall. The hooves are adapted to rock climbing in precarious places. The sole of each toe is concave, perhaps creating a suction-cup effect; bulbous heel pads provide added traction. This animal tends to be found on or near massive rock outcrops where escape routes are available. In these locations, it grazes on a variety of grasses and herbs not available to other competitive but less adept climbers, such as deer and elk. However, the best grazing is in the alpine meadows. Goats can be found in these lush grasslands in the summer if they feel safe from predators. The cellulose in their forage is converted into amino acids and eventually into protein by microorganisms in the rumen (stomach).

These animals spend most of their lives in the high country. They are able to make their way with safety over rock faces and cliffs that would tax the ability of the most skillful human mountaineer. During the summer, they rarely descend lower than the alpine grasslands, staying up in the barest and bleakest mountaintops and cliff sides in all weather. However, during the winter, when the snow is deep, they may descend to areas that are protected by a coniferous canopy. Here they feed on lichens, mosses, evergreen branches, and whatever other stunted vegetation is available. In addition, they use their strong legs to break through deep or crusted snow to obtain dried herbs and grasses. In the North Cascades, occasionally a goat herd is seen in the lowland country in the winter or early spring, particularly near the shores of Lake Chelan.

The animals generally graze in the morning and in the evening, with a rest period following each feeding, during which they bed down and chew their cud. Dusting areas are a prominent part of the mountain goat's habitat. Dusting appears to help the molting process and to rid the body of ticks and other insect pests.

In the November rutting season, dominant males acquire a harem of females, primarily with bluff and threat behavior. There is rarely physical contact between males contesting for dominance; however, occasionally males inflict damage with their horns. Eventually the dominant billy mates with a number of nanny goats. When not contesting for supremacy, males rub their horns against shrubs and rocks. Large glands at the base of each horn release an oily secretion believed to be an attractant to females. One or two young are born between mid-May and mid-June; kids are able to stand on spindly legs minutes after birth.

Coyotes, cougars, bobcats, and eagles have been reported to attack mountain goats. Actual predation of healthy adults is probably uncommon; kids are more vulnerable. Injuries associated with accidental falls from the rocks are not infrequent. Snow and rock avalanches may cause injury or death. Wounds inflicted by other goats do occur but are not common. Heavy worm infestations and malnutrition may also weaken the animals to such a degree that they cannot survive the winter. Outside of protected areas such as national parks, limited hunting is allowed.

COYOTES

Although coyotes are common in the North Cascades, they are infrequently seen, thanks to the inbred wariness that enables them to survive human attempts to eradicate their species. Nevertheless, their howls, generally at night, document their presence in the area. The animal is about 32 inches long, muzzle to rump, with a tail of about 14 inches. The usual height at the shoulder is 25 inches, and the weight varies considerably between 20 and 50 pounds. Clearly canine in appearance, this gray member of the dog family prefers to eat rodents and birds but is omnivorous during hard times and is able to subsist on grasshoppers, fruit, carrion, or fawns. To catch rabbits, coyotes employ the fastest running speed of any American predator. They occasionally kill livestock, leading ranchers to shoot them on sight. They hunt alone or pair up cleverly with their mates; one partner decoys or flushes prey to where the other lurks. An average litter produces seven pups, so coyotes are able to reproduce rapidly whenever their population has been depleted by governmental predator-control personnel. The secrets of their survival in many dissimilar environments include intelligence, prolific reproduction, and the ability to survive on a wide variety of foods.

WOLVES

Wolves have recently reinhabited the North Cascades. Adults with pups were first seen in 1990 in the Hozameen area; since then, biologists have seen three separate groups of adult gray wolves with pups. Gray wolf is a misnomer; the usual color is light tan mixed with brown, gray, and white. Wolves are carnivores (meat eaters); in these mountains, they eat deer, beavers, marmots, and smaller mammals. They generally attack prey with handicaps, which are easier to kill. Wolves live in packs, and the adult animals have a defined social status within the pack. The pack hunts together, thus increasing the likelihood of bringing down the hunted animal. Wolves avoid contact with humans. There are no documented instances of wolves attacking humans in North America (except for one assault by a rabid animal). Hikers and campers need not fear the wolf in the North Cascades. Further data on wolves are contained in the booklet *Wolves in the North Cascades*, available from the North Cascades National Park.

SASQUATCH

Far more unseeable than grizzly bears, wolves, or cougars is the Sasquatch, or Bigfoot, the phantom of the Pacific Northwest forests. Whether this creature is a figment of the imagination or a giant bipedal ape skilled at avoiding contact with humans is an unsettled mystery. A number of large, presumed footprints have been found by various backcountry users. Sightings have been reported by others at various locations. I have seen in the distance a large, dark body that did not appear to be a bear moving across a snowfield at dusk. Thirteen depressions in another snowfield, believed to be large tracks, but too far apart to be made by a human, were also observed but not explained. Do we live in a land still wild enough to conceal giant apelike creatures? A Bigfoot research project hopes to clarify this enigma. Should you have an observation to contribute, phone 800-BIGFOOT.

OTHER MAMMALS
Other relatively common mammals found in the North Cascades are the beaver, weasel, rat, mouse, mole, and shrew. An occasional moose, wolverine, lynx, marten, or fisher may also be encountered. There is a substantial elk herd in the Twin Sisters–Dock Butte area.

All animals within the national park are protected. Injuring or killing any animal within the park boundaries is a federal offense, punishable by fine or imprisonment. Hunting is allowed in season for game animals in the remainder of the North Cascades, subject to the laws of the state of Washington.

RATTLESNAKES
Rattlesnakes are often found at lower elevations in the eastern foothills of the North Cascades; they rarely venture above the upper boundaries of the yellow pine zone (3,000 feet). Although there are approximately thirty-two species of rattlesnakes throughout the world, the Pacific Northwest rattlesnake, a subspecies of the western rattler, is the only pit viper inhabiting the area covered by this book. Although they can swim without difficulty and occasionally climb trees, the western rattlesnake is most commonly encountered on the ground.

The rattle serves to frighten or warn larger creatures that might harm the snake. The sound is produced by vibrations of the tail, the speed of which varies with the ambient temperature. The rattles are composed of horny material similar to that of fingernails; a new segment is produced with each skin shedding, not annually, as was once believed. The approximate rate of rattle accumulation is three to four times a year in young snakes and twice a year in adults. The rattles are subject to loss by wear and tear, so very long strings are rare even in older snakes. Although most snakes rattle before striking, this is not always the case.

Rattlesnakes have a moderately keen sense of vision, particularly for moving objects. They also have an acute sense of smell and are sensitive to ground tremors, although they lack a sense of hearing. The rattlesnake is a pit viper; the facial pits are organs of acute sensitivity to minor differences in temperature.

This is a valuable asset to the snake for preying on small warm-blooded mammals, particularly at night.

The body temperature of the rattlesnake is dependent on air and ground temperatures. The rattlesnake seeks refuge when its body temperature is below 55° F (13° C) or above 100° F (38° C). Rattlesnakes are most active with a temperature range between 75 and 80° F and tend to be nocturnal when ambient temperatures at night are in this range.

Snakes mate in the spring; the young are born in the fall. There are usually between three and twelve young. The newborn rattler is encased in a membrane that it slits with a special tooth. The mother abandons her young within a few hours, leaving the small rattlers to fend for themselves.

The average rattlesnake lives ten to twelve years. Natural enemies include coyotes, foxes, bobcats, hawks, and king snakes. Deer and goats sometimes kill rattlers by deliberately stamping on them with their hooves; however, by far the greatest killers of rattlesnakes are the guns, clubs, and motor vehicles of humans.

All rattlesnakes are venomous and therefore dangerous; however, almost all snakes will go out of their way to avoid a human if given an opportunity to do so. Use caution in snake country, particularly at night. Wear high boots and long pants. The treatment for a bite with evidence of poisoning consists of the immediate use of the Sawyer extractor, a suction device that can remove venom from the wounds made by the fangs. Incision and suction to remove venom are no longer thought to be of value. Thereafter, treatment consists of rest and reassurance, immobilization of the bitten extremity, elective use of a constricting band (not a tourniquet) applied between the wound and the body, and most importantly, immediate evacuation to the nearest hospital for antivenin treatment.

Birds

Bird lovers will find traveling in the North Cascades a rewarding experience. Birds are found in all life zones—from lowland valleys to alpine peaks. Because of altitude and climate, the crest of the Cascades forms a geographic barrier. Many birds on the eastern slopes belong to the Rocky Mountain races; those on the west belong to the Pacific Coast races. Many birds wander after the breeding season, migrating both vertically and laterally.

A number of birds of interest in the North Cascades are discussed at some length here, either because they are commonly seen or because they are unusually interesting. These include the grouse, ptarmigan, Rosy Finch, Canada Goose, Rufous Hummingbird, Water Ouzel (dipper), eagle, Harlequin Duck, Clark's Nutcracker, Gray Jay, Spotted Owl, Marbled Murrelet, Pileated Woodpecker, Steller's Jay, Varied Thrush, and Common Raven. An up-to-date bird checklist can be purchased at NCNP headquarters in Sedro Woolley. Dedicated bird-watchers will have substantial opportunities to add to their life lists while visiting the North Cascades.

HARLEQUIN DUCK
If you are fortunate, you may observe a Harlequin Duck bobbing on the rapids of a mountain stream. This uncommon and shy duck spends the summer on swift western rivers. The two most likely locations to spot this aquatic bird are on Thunder Creek and on the Stehekin River. The duck winters in the heavy surf along rocky ocean coasts and around Puget Sound shorelines. This swimming bird is distinctively marked with a combination of red, blue, white, and black plumage. The female is smaller than the male. Nests are composed of feathers, dried leaves, moss, and lichens. The bird, when inland, feeds chiefly on aquatic insects. Along the coast, it eats crustaceans, mussels, and other marine animals.

RUFOUS HUMMINGBIRD
The male Rufous Hummingbird has a brilliant, fiery red and orange throat. These birds migrate fantastic distances, appearing in the foothills in the spring, summering in the meadows, and departing in the fall for Mexico and Central America. They are found from sea level to the highest peaks in the

range. They are attracted by red colors and may closely approach a person wearing red apparel. They are marvelous fliers, being able to hover in one place like a helicopter or to dart here and there with miraculous speed and coordination. Nesting occurs from early May to early July. A second brood may be raised later in the summer. Nests are covered with fresh green moss. Courting hummingbirds may fight fierce and angry battles, and may even attack other, larger birds. Hummingbird feeders, containing sugar, are frequently used by the birds, particularly early in the spring, before much vegetation is in flower. Their standard diet, however, is nectar obtained from various flowering plants.

WATER OUZEL (DIPPER)
Perhaps the most unusual bird in the North Cascade mountains is the Water Ouzel, or dipper, a bird slightly smaller than a robin. The dipper is classically seen on an exposed rock in the middle of a turbulent stream; every few moments it dips or curtsies, a movement characteristic and unmistakable. It is seldom seen far from water. Occasionally the gray-blue bird disappears into the rushing water of the rapids; it can move effectively underwater. Insects that live on the stream bottom are its source of nourishment. The nest of the ouzel is usually located under a waterfall or in a rock crevice alongside the home stream. The dipper is undaunted by cold water and may be seen in mountain streams in midwinter. It is a rewarding experience to sit beside a cascading torrent and watch a dipper negotiate the turbulent water in search of food. Often the bird's lilting song is audible over the sound of the rapids.

CANADA GOOSE
In the spring and early summer, there are usually Canada Geese nesting at the upper end of Lake Chelan; goslings can almost always be seen from May through July. Food for the Canada Goose consists primarily of vegetable matter. Grain from stubble fields and grass with the roots are the staples of their diet. In the summer, they may eat small animals found in their favorite marshes, such as snails, tadpoles, and minnows. One of the thrilling sights and sounds of fall is to see a long, V-shaped line of migrating geese and to hear the repeated honking noises they make while flying. Adults are roughly 40 inches long. The head, neck, rump, tail, and quills are black; the body is deep gray and the ventral region is white.

GOLDEN AND BALD EAGLES
The Golden Eagle is sometimes seen in the timberline regions of the Cascades wherever there is suitable habitat. An expanse of open country with an abundance of prey and a rocky ledge, cliff, or large tree on which to nest are necessary. Eggs are laid in the spring; incubation takes about six weeks. Eagles are

large birds, about 30 to 35 inches long, with a wingspread of 6 to 8 feet. In spite of their size, eagles may be harassed by smaller, quicker birds, such as crows. Eagles have extraordinarily sharp vision. They are able to see prey from substantial distances. Watch an eagle soaring on high when it is hunting. It is impressive to see it suddenly plunge with wings partly folded, shooting earthward after its victim. Quarry includes rabbits, pikas, marmots, chipmunks, squirrels, mountain beavers, and other rodents.

The Golden Eagle's close relative, the Bald Eagle, is primarily a fish eater, although it does eat carrion and sometimes catches crippled waterfowl. In the winter, Bald Eagles congregate near the Skagit and other rivers flowing westward from the North Cascades. Salmon die after they spawn, and Bald Eagles feed on the carcasses (as do crows, seagulls, and ravens).

GROUSE

Three species of grouse inhabit the North Cascades: ruffed, blue, and spruce. The Ruffed Grouse is chicken sized and inhabits deciduous woodlands and bordering coniferous forests. The male's spring display consists of drumming, a series of hollow, low-pitched noises made with wing strokes. The female raises the chicks alone. Berries and fruits are summer fare; in winter, buds, catkins, and twigs are consumed.

The Blue Grouse inhabits subalpine forest clearings. In the spring, the resonant sound of the displaying male Blue Grouse is often heard by hikers. With good fortune, the territorial male may be seen making his courtship display by alternate inflation and deflation of the sound-magnifying pouches on each side of his neck. His neck area distends as the air sacs inflate and collapses as air escapes. The female cares for the chicks. In summer, insects, seeds, and berries are eaten; in winter, pine needles are consumed.

The Spruce Grouse inhabits coniferous woodlands. The male displays by fanning his beautiful semicircular tail feathers. Its numbers are dwindling due to loss of habitat and because its tameness makes it an easy target for hunters.

Females tending grouse chicks are occasionally seen in the late spring. The mother grouse is fearless in protecting her brood. On two separate occasions, I have been struck in the chest by a defending female. The mother grouse may also feign injury in an effort to lead a person or an animal away from the chicks; I have witnessed this behavior several times. A disturbed grouse sometimes bursts upward with a loud whirring noise, startling an oncoming hiker.

WHITE-TAILED PTARMIGAN

The White-tailed Ptarmigan is one of the most handsome and most approachable avian species in the Cascade Mountains. In the summer, it is a mottled brown color; in the winter, it is pure white. This alpine grouse remains in the high country all year and does not descend in the winter, except in the face of overwhelming storms. The birds are very tame; many times I have walked within 2 to 6 feet of ptarmigan without spooking them.

The ptarmigan is a classic example of protective coloration, since its plumage harmonizes with the background in both summer and winter. The birds often react to danger by becoming motionless until the danger passes. This reliance on camouflage presumably accounts for their apparent tameness. Nests are usually located at elevations between 5,000 and 8,000 feet and are ordinarily found in the open, surrounded by heather or other alpine plants. Eggs are laid late in the spring, and with luck, an observer can encounter two to ten chicks in the high country during the summer. By the middle of September, the chicks are almost full grown. As with the blue grouse, the mother ptarmigan may attack humans if she believes that the chicks are in danger.

This alpine bird subsists on insects and plant products, including the leaves and flowers of the tiny alpine buckwheat, leaves of Lyall's lupine, huckleberries, and leaves and flowers of white and red heather. Ptarmigan are scarce and should never be harmed. One of the real thrills of the alpine meadow is to encounter one of these "mountain grouse."

ROSY FINCH

The rocky, windswept, and often snow-covered Arctic-alpine zone is a harsh place to live, but another bird has adapted to the rigors of existence in this area. The gray-crowned Rosy Finch lives in the high country much of the year, descending to lower elevations in midwinter. This bird feeds mainly on minute alpine plant seeds and insects borne by the wind from lower elevations and plucked directly off the snowfields. It is about 6 inches long with a black forehead, gray crown, and pink shoulders and rump. It nests in cavities in high cliffs above 7,000 feet.

VARIED THRUSH

The Varied Thrush, commonly known as the Snow or Mountain Robin, is a permanent resident throughout the dense forests of western Washington; in summer, it can be found from forested lowlands to timberline. In appearance and size, the male is much like a robin, except that the underparts are a rusty brown rather than a bright red. The adult female is similar in appearance, but with a duller color. This bird is comfortable with shade and moisture. Its food and nest requirements, habits, and colorations are all adapted to existence in the subdued light of the moist temperate forest. During the nesting season, the Varied Thrush sings vigorously much of the day. Its song is remarkable, best described as a trill that possesses a mysterious and faraway quality, making it unique. The sound has been described as a prolonged note of a few seconds' duration in a minor key, repeated at short intervals. Spring forest walks in the western North Cascades are almost invariably accompanied by the song of the Varied Thrush. The birds feed on the larvae and insect life living on the forest floor. Thrushes migrate vertically, descending in the fall and ascending to the upper levels of the forest in the spring.

CLARK'S NUTCRACKER AND GRAY JAY

Since they are approximately the same size and have similar coloration and habits, it is fairly easy to confuse the Clark's Nutcracker with the Gray Jay. Both are members of the crow family and are roughly 1 foot in length. Both species are found near camps and picnic areas, where they beg and steal food scraps. Of aid in telling the birds apart is the long, pointed bill of the Clark's Nutcracker and the uniform gray color of the head; in contrast, the Gray Jay has a substantially shorter bill and contrasting black and white head markings as an adult.

The Clark's Nutcracker has a guttural cry that sounds like a drawn-out or grating "kr-a-a-a-a." The bird nests very early in the year, depositing two to six green-spotted eggs in a stick nest located in a coniferous tree. The nutcracker has a special relationship with the white bark pine tree. It subsists mainly on white bark pine seeds, some of which it eats immediately, and some of which are buried for retrieval in the winter. It can hold a number of pine seeds in a special pouch under the tongue, in addition to those it carries in its beak. In poor pine seed crop years, nutcrackers irrupt in great numbers into the lowlands in search of substitute food.

The Gray Jay also nests early, producing three to five eggs in a bowl of twigs lined with feathers or other soft material. Its call produces a variety of notes. Formerly called the Canada Jay, and popularly called the Camp Robber in the United States and the Whiskey Jack in Canada, it can be a feathered pest in campsites. When not dining on pilfered food, it subsists on conifer seeds, berries, and insects. Some Gray Jays are sufficiently tame to take offered food morsels from an outstretched hand. But note that feeding wild birds and animals human food may be hazardous to their health.

COMMON RAVEN

A raucous, croaking "kraack," the call of the Common Raven, is often heard by hikers in the North Cascades. A backpacker, looking upward to identify the sound, will see one or more large black birds. The harsh croak of the raven is unique and, once heard, clearly identifies the bird thereafter. Ravens are often present in the subalpine and timberline meadowlands. About 21 inches long, with a wingspread of 48 inches, the raven is a masterful aerialist. It is also an intelligent bird, which accounts for its success as a skilled camp robber. Ravens are omnivores, eating seeds, rodents, nestlings, eggs, carrion, and trail food left accessible by hikers and backpackers. Ravens nest on the sides of cliffs or in large trees. They may forage up to 15 miles away on a daily basis. Watching playful ravens rolling and soaring through the sky can make the viewer wish for the ability to fly. Northwest Indians considered the raven to be a trickster. In many creation myths, the raven is a powerful supernatural being. Also, these birds were revered and feared as spiritual beings who were believed to be harbingers of doom.

SPOTTED OWL

The Spotted Owl is about 18 inches long. It is dark brown with white spots above, and brown with spots below; it has no ear tufts and has fluffy plumage. The most common call is two to three short hoots, followed by a more prolonged and louder sound suggestive of a dog barking. Nesting takes place in tree cavities or in nests abandoned by other birds. Rodents are its usual diet. The Spotted Owl lives only in contiguous stands of ancient forest (old growth), and except for unusual circumstances, nowhere else. This owl is presently considered an endangered subspecies in the Pacific Northwest and therefore merits special protection of its habitat. Put another way, the Spotted Owl is an indicator species of the adequacy and health of the ancient forest and its wildlife communities. Clear-cuts of old growth, with the associated logging roads, have been linked to the disappearance of these birds in and around the areas of habitat disturbance. Environmentalists concerned about the further destruction of old growth have successfully used the declining status of the Spotted Owl to limit further logging of the ancient forest. Lawsuits brought under the endangered species laws have contended that ecosystem and sustainable forestry management practices are needed to perpetuate the owl and other species dependent on ancient forest. Substantial controversy has been associated with this litigation. Additional information about the Spotted Owl follows, reprinted with the permission of Daniel Mathews from his book *Cascade–Olympic Natural History*.

The spotted owl, though never commonly seen anywhere, is currently a media star and a pawn in political chess, because it needs extensive old-growth forest for habitat. (This is doubtless true of many species, but best-proven of this one.) The species will almost certainly die out if all old-growth forests outside of present parks and Wilderness Areas are cut before others mature to replace them. The Endangered Species Act enables environmentalists to use the spotted owl as a legal tool to protect old-growth. Much data suggests that the acreage of old-growth needed for the species survival is equal to or even greater than what now exists. High government officials have replied that, at $300,000 a year per bird in lumber value foregone, the Forest Service cannot afford spotted owls. A wide range of estimates are quoted by partisans of one side or the other as to how many spotted owls survive today, how many are needed for the species to survive, how many hundreds of acres each pair requires, how much use they can make of second-growth as part of their habitat, how widely separated their parcels of old-growth can be, and so on. Further research should provide better data on these issues and, most important, better establish that it's not just spotted owls, but a whole, almost inconceivably intricate ecosystem, and the productivity of the lumber and fishery industries themselves, that are endangered by disregard for the value of extensive old-growth.

Larger owls are involved in the threat to the spotted owl. Its range in the Northwest is being invaded by its close cousin, the barred owl, which is more aggressive, bears larger broods, and seems to require less territory. Barred owls were virtually unknown in our range until the 1980s, but are spreading with astonishing speed. One hypothesis is that the replacement of old-growth with clearings and second-growth enlarges the range of great horned owls, which prey upon spotted owls, while barred owls are able to occupy nearly the same niche as spotted owls, and are just large enough to stand their ground against great horned owls.

MARBLED MURRELET

The Marbled Murrelet is a pigeon-sized seabird, brown above and gray-marbled light brown below in the summer; in the winter, it is white below and black above. The northwest population of this bird is classified as threatened by both the U.S. Fish and Wildlife Service and the state of Washington.

The murrelet is an interesting summer inhabitant of old-growth forest because of its nesting habits. The female prefers to lay her single egg on a moss-covered limb of an ancient forest tree. Two nests were recently found on western hemlocks in an old-growth stand in the Mount Baker–Snoqualmie National Forest 26 miles from Puget Sound. The farthest inland nest detected was 45 miles from the nearest salt water. One nest was identified in the vicinity of the Verlot Public Service Center, located below Mount Pilchuck. Stands in the North Cascades frequently used by nesting murrelets are old-growth coniferous forest less than 3,000 feet in elevation and located less than 40 minutes from salt water. These stands are also prime candidates for clear-cut logging. Therefore, as with the Spotted Owl, there is a conflict between the needs of this threatened bird and the logging industry. I consider the ancient forest ecosystem to be a dwindling resource meriting indefinite protection.

WOODPECKERS

A number of woodpeckers are present in the North Cascades, including the Northern Flicker, Lewis' Woodpecker, Hairy Woodpecker, Downy Woodpecker, Three-toed Woodpecker, and Red-breasted Sapsucker. The most dramatic bird in this family, and indeed the largest woodpecker in the United States, is the 17-inch-long, red-crested Pileated Woodpecker. The neck and face are white; the rest of the body is black. Males have a red mustache, which females lack. The call is a loud "kak-kak-kak-kak." The bird gives the appearance of power, whether in flight or active on the trunk of a dead tree. This splendid woodpecker makes a loud noise in the course of acquiring food from insect-infested tree trunks. The blows of its bill produce a sound so loud that it has frequently been mistaken for the noise made by a hammer or ax in the hands of a vigorous logger. It excavates substantial cavities in its search for carpenter ants, termites, and other wood-boring insects. It obtains its food mostly from dead rather than living trees. Since it is not common in the North Cascades, it is a fortunate hiker who observes this impressive bird at work on a tree trunk.

STELLER'S JAY

The Steller's Jay, sometimes known as the Mountain Jay, is a common permanent resident in the forests of western Washington, usually found in the western hemlock or humid transition zone. It is conspicuously crested, with the crest and upper body a blackish gray and the tail and lower body a purplish blue. The bird is about 11 inches long. Calls are low-pitched, raucous, and varied. Nests are built of twigs 8 to 25 feet above the ground, usually on a side branch of a small Douglas-fir. These birds can be scavengers and also may destroy the eggs and young of smaller birds. Jays can imitate the cries of various hawks; presumably, this skill has some survival value.

BIRD-WATCHING SAMPLER

Bird-watchers traversing in the North Cascades from west to east, via the Skagit and Stehekin drainages, might make the following observations of other avian species during their trip. Entering via the lush riparian Skagit Valley, you will notice that bird life in these areas is rich and varied as you traverse this leafy woodland. Band-tailed Pigeons feed on red elderberries. Common Mergansers nest along the rivers in spring and summer. Willow, Pacific-slope, and Hammond's Flycatchers swoop out from perches. Various warblers glean the treetops; Brown Creepers, the tree trunks; Black-capped and Chestnut-backed Chickadees and Golden-crowned Kinglets, the branches. American Robins, Swainson's Thrushes, Song Sparrows, and Red-eyed Vireos vie in song. Warbling Vireos and Yellow, Black-throated, Gray, and Wilson's Warblers nest within this area. Barred Owls inhabit the alder and big-leaf maple groves along the Skagit River from Hamilton to Thunder Creek.

As you ascend the thickly timbered western slopes, you may see Pine Siskins and Cedar Waxwings. The tiny Winter Wren gives forth a bubbling song from the forest floor. The Belted Kingfisher and Spotted Sandpiper share the stream. A small lake may harbor coots, Tree Swallows, Vaux's Swifts, Common Loons, and Barrow's Goldeneye ducks. Solitary Vireos and Yellow-rumped and Townsend's Warblers are summer residents in this region, as are Evening Grosbeaks. At the upper limits of forest, the Red Crossbill, a bird specialized for feeding on pine cone seeds, may be seen occasionally.

In the open meadows amid the alpine fir copses, the Townsend's Solitaire and the Hermit Thrush sing from the treetops. Townsend's Warblers, Dark-eyed Juncos, and Lincoln and Fox Sparrows flit through the thickets, and Olive-sided Flycatchers call their "quick, three beers" from dead treetops. Gray-hooded MacGillivray's Warblers slink through the dwarf willows and alders in gullies. Horned Larks feed on the grassy ridges and fly high with tinkling notes of song. In the lower tarn-dotted basins, American Pipits walk and bob from boulders. During fall migration times, raptors and passerines may be seen passing over mountain ridges. Abroad at night are Common Nighthawks, Great Horned Owls, Northern Pygmy Owls, Spotted Owls, and Western Screech Owls. Cooper's Hawks are common accipiters of the coniferous forest. Sharp-shinned Hawks, American Kestrels, and Black Swifts scan the land from above, seeking prey.

As you descend into the drier life zones on the eastern slopes, new birds may be encountered. In the semiarid yellow pine forest are the Ruby-crowned Kinglet, Mountain Bluebird, Cassin's Finch, Red Crossbill, Pine Grosbeak, Red-naped Sapsucker, Dusky Flycatcher, Williamson's Sapsucker, Evening Grosbeak, Warbling Vireo, North Goshawk, Mountain Chickadee, and House Wren. Calliope Hummingbirds may also be seen.

On Lake Chelan are found the Mallard, Great Blue Heron, Western Grebe, Common Goldeneye, Western Bluebird, Brown-headed Cowbird, American Goldfinch, House Finch, and Western Tanager.

8   Insects

After God created the North Cascades, He saw that they were perfect.
Since perfection by divine decree cannot be allowed in this world,
it was necessary then to create the mosquito,
the horsefly, and the yellow jacket.

Insects are one of the major drawbacks of the North Cascades. With the exception of the yellow jacket, the universal rule in these mountains is that if an insect lands on you, slap it immediately. Yellow jackets, unfortunately, may sting even though killed; the best technique for dealing with these aggressive insects is to take a deep breath and blow them off. Avoid leaving food attractive to yellow jackets near areas of human activity. Other common annoying insects are the no-see-ums, or biting gnats, horseflies, deerflies, blackflies, and the ubiquitous mosquitoes.

YELLOW JACKETS

Yellow jackets, hornets, and paper wasps are known for their potent sting and for their production of paper nests. The group is known as the social vespids. Nests are constructed underground, where there is insulation from cold, or on branches, on tree limbs, or under the eaves of houses. The yellow jacket queen hibernates during the winter in a sheltered spot. In the spring, she slowly comes to life, crawls forth into the sunshine, and flies away, seeking a suitable place for a home. After drinking deeply, she begins construction of a small nest with a few cells. When the cells are finished, eggs are laid in each, and when the eggs hatch, she hunts insects or other sources of food to feed the developing workers. Nectar, fruit juice, or other foods are all acceptable to the omnivorous yellow jacket.

Once the first generation of workers emerges, they take over all the work and the queen becomes simply an egg layer. If the nest is underground, more earth is removed, and the cavity is enlarged. Regardless of the nest location, more wood and fiber are collected, and more tiers of brood cells are added. Paper walls always enclose and protect the entire structure. By autumn, the nest may be as large as a pumpkin and contains 2,000 or 3,000 short-tempered inhabitants. There is no defense for the unfortunate person who blunders into a yellow jacket nest; the all-important response under those circumstances is immediate, rapid flight from the area.

Nests are practically impregnable during daylight hours but can be dealt with in almost total safety by approaching after dark, when all the inhabitants are inside and inactive. There is usually only one queen, although occasionally there is competition between queens for a nest; this contest ends in the death of one queen. In the fall, new queens and drones are produced and fly away and mate. The drones die, and the queens seek places to hibernate. The parent colony gradually becomes less and less active, as the cold penetrates the earth and food is no longer available. Eventually, all the workers in the colony die, thus ending another annual chapter in the life cycle of the yellow jacket.

There is no good remedy for the yellow jacket sting, which feels like the penetration of a red-hot needle. Discomfort lasts from twelve hours to several days. Serious allergic reactions to stings may occur in susceptible individuals and can be life threatening. Multiple stings can produce severe illness requiring hospitalization. Removal of the stinger (if visible), cold applications, and over-the-counter pain medicine (such as aspirin) are the treatments of choice. Antihistamines may help somewhat.

MOSQUITOES

There are no malaria-carrying mosquitoes in the North Cascades. Contracting a serious disease from the bite of this insect is improbable here, although mosquito-borne viral infections of the brain affected over 2,000 people in the United States in 1975.

The common *Culex* mosquito lays its eggs in floating rafts anywhere there is stagnant water. Sites can include holes in trees, minor depressions in the forest floor, and rain barrels; boggy and swampy areas remaining after the high spring runoff are common breeding areas.

The larvae, or wrigglers, are aquatic; they feed on algae and microscopic bits of organic debris. They project a respiratory tube through the water surface film to get air. The pupae, the next stage of development, also come to the surface for air. Both larvae and pupae are important food sources for fish and aquatic insects. The adult mosquito emerges from the pupa. Adults mate soon after emergence, after which the males die. Only the females suck blood; both sexes feed on plant juices.

The high-mountain snow mosquitoes of the western United States are Ice Age left-behinds. These mosquitoes lay their eggs once a year in pools formed from melting snow. Originally adapted to the harsh, cold climate of the Arctic, these insects were pushed south by advancing glaciers; they were forced to move up into the mountains following the postglacial warming trend. At this time, isolated at high elevations, they are the principal mosquito species of the coniferous forests of western North America. Deet-containing insect repellents are effective for mosquitoes.

MIDGES AND FLIES

Biting midges are small to minute mosquitolike insects that breed in aquatic and semiaquatic environments. The no-see-ums, sand fleas, and gnats are included in this group. Since they are small, the adult insects are not easily seen and may be able to penetrate screens that are effective barriers for mosquitoes and larger biting insects. A blood meal is required for egg production; both males and females also obtain nectar from flowers. Most species lay their eggs in a gelatinous mass in or near the water; the larvae develop in these damp places, feeding on decaying organic matter, dead insects, or the newly hatched larvae of other insects.

Blackflies also attack humans. Immature stages are aquatic. Deerflies and horseflies are large, stout-bodied, powerful insects most commonly found around lakes, bogs, streams, and ponds. The eggs of most species are laid in masses on vegetation over or near the water. The larvae mature in damp or wet soil; in general, the larvae are also predaceous and cannibalistic. The adult females obtain nourishment from both blood meals and plant nectar, since sugar is necessary for their metabolism.

Commonly used insect repellents are ineffectual against the biting flies. Fortunately for campers, the flies are active during daylight only; in general, the hotter the weather, the more prevalent the flies.

BUMBLEBEES

Bumblebees are common in the North Cascades but are not aggressive; therefore, bumblebee stings are rare. The bumblebee is easily identified by its large size and yellow and black (or sometimes partly red) coat of long hair. Unlike most bees, bumblebees favor cold climates and therefore range northward far beyond the Arctic Circle in Canada, Alaska, and Siberia, in addition to being common in the high mountain areas of the western United States. Their large size and ample insulation ensure that they can remain warm enough to fly at unusually low environmental temperatures. Some alpine plants, such as the louseworts, are pollinated only by bumblebees.

The bumblebee life cycle starts in the spring when the queen emerges from the burrow in the ground where she spent the winter hibernating. The emergence usually coincides with the bloom of the first flowering plants. After sucking nectar, the queen hunts for clumps of dry grass, old bird nests, or ground excavations of mice or other rodents. A honey pot is made, and eggs are laid. The eggs hatch in three to four weeks. The first workers are very small because of underfeeding. As the workers take over their tasks of gathering nectar and pollen, enlarging the nest, and caring for the brood, the queen can devote more of her time and energy to egg laying, although she still makes occasional trips to visit flowers. The colony grows, and toward the end of the season, the production of males and young queens begins. As the cold of autumn comes to the high country, the colony disintegrates. The males, the old queen, and the workers die; the young queens scatter and seek places underground in which to hibernate. The cycle repeats itself annually.

Perhaps the bumblebees are nonaggressive because they do not compete directly with other bees or with humans for food supply. They do, however, have the capacity to sting, as do other bees, and some caution is appropriate.

BUDWORMS AND MOTHS

The western spruce budworm is the most destructive forest defoliator in western North America. In the North Cascades, this insect attacks principally Douglas firs and the true firs. Some outbreaks flare up and subside naturally within a few years; others persist as long as twenty years. In these mountains, the insect is presently active in the Bridge Creek area and accounts for the substantial defoliation noted along that segment of the Pacific Crest Trail.

The budworm larvae feed principally on the buds and foliage of the current year. Sustained heavy attack causes nearly complete loss of needles in four to five years. Epidemics can cause the death of trees in extensive areas. Adult insects are generally a mottled orange-brown, with a wingspread of roughly 25 millimeters. Eggs are light green and are laid in shinglelike masses on the undersides of the needles. Eggs are laid in July and August and hatch in about ten days. The larvae spin silken shelters after hatching and hibernate throughout the winter. The next spring, they bore into the buds and feed on the expanding needles. Parasites, predators, adverse weather, and starvation tend to hold the budworm in check and to control outbreaks naturally. About forty species of insect predators feed on the budworm; about ten exert significant control.

When major outbreaks develop despite these natural checks and balances, measures to control infestation may be attempted in national and commercial forests. (Within national parks, insect activity is considered a natural event; only under unusual circumstances would intervention by park personnel be appropriate.) Even under the best of circumstances, control of this pest is exceedingly difficult. Insecticides applied from the ground are relatively ineffectual; access to involved areas is almost always limited. Spraying or dusting from airplanes has been effective, but this is costly and not entirely satisfactory. Concentrations of the spray sufficient to be lethal to the budworm also destroy much of the other animal life in the forest. Calculated introduction of predators, such as parasitic wasps and flies, may offer hope of more effective control of major outbreaks without substantial environmental side effects. Another destructive defoliator is the tussock moth. Five species parasitize western forests. The Douglas-fir tussock moth attacks Douglas-fir, grand fir, and subalpine fir. Outbreaks develop explosively and usually subside abruptly after about three years.

TICKS

Ticks exist in the lower portions of the North Cascade Range, on both sides of the crest. Worldwide, there are several species that transmit diseases to humans and other animals. The Rocky Mountain wood tick, common throughout western North America, transmits Rocky Mountain spotted fever, Colorado tick fever, and other illnesses to humans. This tick normally requires one or two years to complete its life cycle. Adults feed mostly on large animals such as horses, cattle, sheep, deer, bears, and coyotes. Nymphs and larvae feed on small mammals, such as rabbits, squirrels, woodchucks, and chipmunks. All three stages may feed on intermediate-sized animals such as jackrabbits and porcupines. Fertilization occurs on the host; later, the greatly distended, fully fed female drops to the ground, where she lays a large mass of 6,000 to 7,000 eggs. Eggs hatch after about five weeks; the larvae emerge, find suitable hosts, and feed for a few days. Then they drop off and molt, emerging as nymphs one to three weeks later. Nymphs that find a host will feed, molt, and winter over as adults. If they do not feed, the nymphs hibernate and then seek hosts the following spring. All ticks are markedly resistant to starvation and can live for months without food.

Humans are usually bitten only by adult ticks. The creatures are small prior to feeding; the blood-engorged tick is beanlike in form and may reach up to 2 centimeters in length, perhaps three to four times its size before eating.

Ticks position themselves on brush adjacent to, or hanging over, trails. When an inadvertent host passes by, they transfer from the brush to the body of the host. There is a time lag between the transfer and the tick's attachment to the skin. If possible, ticks should be found and removed prior to attachment. Surprisingly, the attachment process is frequently painless. If a tick embeds itself in the skin, it should be removed as soon as possible. However, removal is not simple, and most common folklore remedies with regard to tick removal are ineffectual. The body of the tick should not be crushed during removal. The best method of removal is for a professional to surgically remove the head of the tick, using local anesthesia to control pain. Researchers in 1963 found that 0.6 percent pyrethrins in methyl benzoate and camphorated phenol greatly reduced the force required to detach embedded ticks; application for at least twenty minutes before detachment and the use of a slow and steadily increasing pulling force were recommended.

Tick paralysis is also transmitted by the Rocky Mountain wood tick. On a weight basis, humans appear to be more sensitive to tick paralysis than any other mammal. Some animals—moose, bighorn sheep, mountain goats, and bears—seem totally resistant to this condition. Susceptible animals include cattle, horses, sheep, dogs, and marmots. In humans, tick paralysis is characterized by a flaccid ascending weakness that can cause death by respiratory failure. The disease is caused by a toxin produced during feeding by some female ticks. It takes five to nine days after attachment for this material to be produced in sufficient quantities to cause paralysis. Removal of the tick before the paralysis has proceeded too far leads to rapid and complete recovery. Any unexpected weakness during or following hikes should lead to a search for a feeding tick.

Fortunately, deer ticks, which transmit Lyme disease, are not common in the North Cascades. Nonetheless, occasional cases of this illness have occurred in the state of Washington. Since ticks rarely transmit any illness for twenty-four to forty-eight hours after attachment, prompt discovery and timely removal of ticks are important for everyone who enters these mountains.

INSECT STUDY

Since 1994, NCNP personnel have been developing methods for monitoring lakes and streams within the park in a unique way. The status of aquatic and terrestrial arthropods (insects and spiders) is a major component of this program. Arthropods are important components of biological diversity and are integral to the maintenance of ecosystem processes. Insects and spiders are ideal study organisms because of their short generation times, rapid population growth, and unique adaptations. These qualities make them ideal as early-warning indicators of environmental change and for assessing the recovery of disturbed sites. The goal is to find a more accurate method of evaluating overall biological integrity. Do not be surprised if you see a uniformed ranger, nose to the ground, doing important environmental research.

PART II

Trails

General Trail Information

Of the approximately 400 trails in the North Cascades, I have selected about 100, based on my forty years of experience in the area, that I believe reflect the experiential essence of hiking in the area. To some extent, I was arbitrary and capriciou, in selecting my favorite trails. My preference for high trails with vistas over lengthy deep-woods walks is reflected in the trail selection. Other considerations included selecting representative trails in the subsections of the North Cascades, so that at least four or five trails are described for each area. I also made an effort to describe trails that range from easy to strenuous. Several trails are described primarily because they can be explored in the early spring or late fall. The likelihood of obtaining solitude and a wilderness experience was also considered in the trail selection process.

Trails requiring substantial uphill hiking with little scenery during the elevation-gaining process have generally been omitted. Walking four hours up, spending half an hour in a beautiful location, and walking three hours down is not the most splendid form of hiking; however, many of the North Cascades footpaths require this type of commitment if done as a day hike.

I have walked all the trails described in this book. In the course of preparing for this publication, I reinvestigated a number of trails in 1996 and 1997. I was surprised to discover the extent of the changes that had occurred in the past five to fifteen years. Some changes were due to acts of God, such as floods, avalanches, and forest fires. More commonly, changes were caused by actions of the administrators of the land. Since these types of changes will continue, the date when the trail was last walked is included at the end of each trail description. The longer the time from that date to the present, the more important it is to check with the land management agency involved to determine if there have been changes in that trail. Every effort has been made to ensure accuracy as of 1997. However, astute readers will inevitably find some errors. Feedback via the publisher would be appreciated so that corrections can be included in future editions.

TRAIL DATA
Either in the text or in the tabular summary, an effort has been made to provide the following information: length of trail; altitude gain, which includes

ups and downs from the trailhead to the destination; high point; and walking time to the destination and walking time back, which are rarely equal in the North Cascades, since there is almost always more altitude gain in than out. The USGS topographic sheets that show the trail are also listed, as are the relevant Green Trail maps.

The difficulty of a given trail is, at best, an educated estimate. A steep, long trail may be considered moderate if you have a light day pack and do not hurry. Conversely, even a moderate footpath can be difficult if you are carrying an 80-pound pack and hurrying to locate a campsite before dark. If you know the distance involved and the altitude to be gained, and then factor in your age and physical condition, you can make a reasonable assessment of a trail's difficulty. Almost always, hiking times are my actual clocked times. (However, my current times are slower than those of ten to twenty years ago; this should be considered in computing estimated time.) After hiking one or two trails, you can compare your time to the hiking time given and establish a ratio, which should be applicable to all other trails in this book. For example, if you take three hours to walk what I walked in two hours going up, you can probably assume that you will take six hours to walk what I walked in four hours, and so forth. This is more true for up-times than it is for down-times, since most people can maintain a speed close to 3 miles an hour when hiking on level ground or going down.

Mileages are determined by my estimates of distance, based on timing by watch, personal experience with my hiking speed, plus the use of land management agency values, when available. All mileages given thus are approximate but can be considered reliable within a 5 to 10 percent margin of error.

All trail distances are given in miles. The following conversion table may be helpful to those who use the metric system:

> 328 feet = 100 meters
> 0.1 mile = 528 feet = 161 meters
> 0.62 miles = 3,281 feet = 1,000 meters, or 1 kilometer
> 1 mile = 5,280 feet = 1.61 kilometers

Forest Service road numbers are organized in a "trunk-branch-twig-leaf" manner. For example:

Arterial road	6100000
Collector road	6110000
Local road	6110110

The full seven digits are seldom posted on the ground. In the example above,

6100000 would be posted as 61
6110000 would be posted as 6110
6110110 would be posted as 110

Accessibility estimates are based on an average year. Usually, the mountains open about July 1 east of the Cascade Crest and about July 15 west of the crest. Snow accumulation during the winter varies from year to year. Access can be two to three weeks early or two to three weeks late in any given year. Snow remains longer on north-facing slopes than on hillsides with a southern exposure. Local microclimates also influence snowpack. Snow closes the hills on average about November 1. October is a snow and thaw month; a foot of snow may fall, only to melt in one to three days. If a trail is usually snow free earlier or later than average, that information is noted in the footpath description.

Certain trails in the North Cascades are crowded almost all the time. Some are so rarely used that solitude can almost be guaranteed.

High-use trails include the following:
Cascade Pass
Heather Meadows (all trails except for Panorama Dome)
Thunder Creek (near the Colonial Campground)
The Enchantments
Kennedy Hot Springs
Chain Lakes Loop and Table Mountain
Lake Ann (near both Mount Shuksan and Rainy Pass)
Rainy Lake
Heliotrope Ridge
Pilchuck Mountain
Big Four Ice Caves
Blue Lake (between Rainy and Washington Passes)
Melakwa Lake
Snow Lake
Pacific Crest Trail (north from Snoqualmie Pass)

Low-use trails include the following:
Sourdough Lookout
Buck Creek Pass
Cady Point
All trails in the Pasayten, except the Pacific Crest Trail and
    Horseshoe Basin
Desolation Lookout
Windy Peak
Copper Glance

Pyramid Mountain
Emerald Park
Goat Peak
The Pacific Crest Trail and all trails in the national park and the wilderness areas are closed to trail machines. Vehicles, and in some cases horses, are banned from other trails; this information is usually included with the individual trail descriptions.

Following is a list of lowland trails in the North Cascades that are not described in this book but are usually accessible in the late fall and mid to late spring, and occasionally in winter. Almost all involve deep-woods walking with little in the way of views. They offer options when the high country is snowbound. To assist in locating them, the Green Trails map showing their location is listed in parentheses after the name of the footpath.

Boulder River (Oso and Granite Falls)
Pyramid Lake (Diablo Dam)
Ross Dam Trail (Diablo Dam)
Diablo Lake Trail (Diablo Dam)
Happy Creek (Diablo Dam)
Newhalem Creek (Diablo Dam) (may not be maintained by the NCNP; check at the visitors' center in Newhalem)
Stetattle Creek (Diablo Dam)
Domke Lake (Lucerne)
Stehekin trails:
Rainbow Falls (Stehekin)
Buckner Homestead (Stehekin)
Imus Creek (Stehekin)
McKeller Cabin (Stehekin)
Bullion Loop (Stehekin)

A "scrabble trail" is a nonconstructed and nonmaintained footpath whose tread was produced by the repetitive passage of a walker's feet over a period of time. In other words, like Topsy, it just growed. Abandoned trails were initially constructed by the land management agency but are no longer maintained. Damaged tread is not repaired, and trees fallen over the trail are not removed by the trail crews. These trails are no longer shown on current maps but are often depicted on out-of-date maps. They are often passable for a substantial time after maintenance has been discontinued.

SAFETY

Please don't die in these mountains! Every year some people do, usually because of carelessness or ignorance. A minor danger is the presence of rattlesnakes up to

Self-arrest with an ice ax

perhaps 3,000 feet in elevation on the east side of the range. A major danger is hypothermia. It can snow any day of the year above 5,000 feet in the North Cascades. Weather changes can be abrupt, unpredictable, and extreme. Overnight hikers should be prepared to cope with rain, snow, or wind. A combination of exhaustion and wet clothing, perhaps complicated by lack of food intake, can cause body temperature to drop rapidly. Brain function deteriorates when body temperature falls to about 89° F. Shock due to injury accelerates heat loss. Death can occur rapidly if body temperature falls further. Always carry extra food, extra clothes, matches, fire-starting material, and a good-quality waterproof tent or, less desirably, a tarp; your life may depend on it.

Glaciers are also hazardous. An unroped fall into a crevasse is usually lethal. Beware when traveling on glacial ice.

Until mid-July on the east side and late August on the west side of the Cascade crest, portions of almost all the high trails are obliterated by snow. Early-season hikers should carry an ice ax routinely and should know how to kick steps into fairly deep snow slopes and how to do a self-arrest if a step pulls out. This is particularly important if there is no "runout" below the trail—if there are rocks at the bottom or a cliff you'll go over if you don't stop. Every year, many people are injured as a result of uncontrolled slides down steep snow slopes; deaths are not rare. Be cautious.

FEES AND REGULATIONS

As of June 1, 1997, Trail Park passes are required to park at almost all the trailheads of the Mount Baker–Snoqualmie, Okanogan, and Wenatchee National Forests. The passes will cost $3 per day or $25 per year; 50 percent discounts apply for Golden Age and Golden Access Passport holders. Most of the money from this program will be used to improve trails and trailheads. National Forest trail volunteers may receive a gratis annual pass. The passes will be sold at National Forest offices and other locations in nearby communities.

In 1997, the MBSNF will charge to enter the Heather Meadows Recreational Complex. A three-day parking permit will cost $5; an annual permit for unlimited access, $15. Individuals with Trail Park passes will be required to pay the entry fees. Fees collected at Heather Meadows will be used for a variety of needs at the Meadows, including trail maintenance, providing drinking water, staffing the visitors' center, and providing interpretive programs.

A permit will be required to enter the Alpine Lakes Wilderness from May 15 to October 31. Day-use visitors may obtain free self-issued permits at the trailheads or at a ranger station. Overnight backpackers to all the ALW except the Enchantments can also obtain permits at the trailhead. (Snoqualmie Pass overnighters can anticipate that advance reservations will be required in the future; contact the North Bend Ranger Station at 425-888-1421 for current regulations.)

Overnighters in the Enchantments (which includes Snow, Nada, and Colchuck Lakes) must obtain limited-use permits for entry from June 15 to October 15; Reservation procedures follow: In early February, call 509-548-6977 or write the Leavenworth Ranger Station for a wilderness permit application form. On or after February 21, not before, submit the application with a check for $3.00 per person per night. Applications received in February will be processed randomly beginning March 1. When all have been processed, the next set of reservation requests will be addressed. This procedure will continue until no reservations are available for June 15 to October 15. Twenty-five percent of available permits will be dispensed by lottery each day between June 15 and October 15 at 7:45 A.M. at the Leavenworth Ranger Station.

It is likely that this routine for 1998 will be followed in 1999 and thereafter, however, in view of this significant change between 1997 and 1998 permit application procedures, it would be wise to contact the ranger station early to confirm what requirements must be met before your visit.

An eight-page newspaper called the *Alpine Lakes Trip Planner* may be obtained from the MBSNF or the WNF. This contains considerable additional information about the ALW.

Predictably, further regulations will be instituted in the future. Consult the appropriate ranger station well in advance to ascertain the restrictions in force for the year you plan to visit the ALW.

RESPECT FOR THE LAND
Wilderness areas, like people, suffer if they are loved by too many.
Wild places are increasingly scarce. It is essential that everyone entering the North Cascades leave them unspoiled for future generations. What was standard practice in the past is no longer acceptable, since the subalpine meadows are too fragile to tolerate intensive use, particularly by the inconsiderate and destructive. Therefore, walk softly in the wilderness. Stay on the trail at all times; do not shortcut switchbacks, because doing so creates substantial erosion problems. If you brought it in, carry it out, unless you can burn it. Camp in designated campsites or in places previously used for camping. Use fire pits already in existence; do not build new ones. Use only dead wood. Carry a chemical or gasoline stove for cooking. If there are no obvious campsites, camp on sedge grass rather than on heather, wildflowers, or other fragile flora. Do not cut tree limbs, pick wildflowers, or otherwise change the natural scene. Disturb the natural world as little as possible. Develop a deep awareness of the permanent impact of your presence on any alpine environment and act accordingly, recognizing that simply by being there, you are causing some changes to occur.

The dictum of ten years ago, "Take only photos; leave only tracks," is now "Take only photos; leave nothing." May the peace and tranquility of these most beautiful of all mountains be yours.

As Mark Twain said, "There is no opiate like alpine pedestrianism."

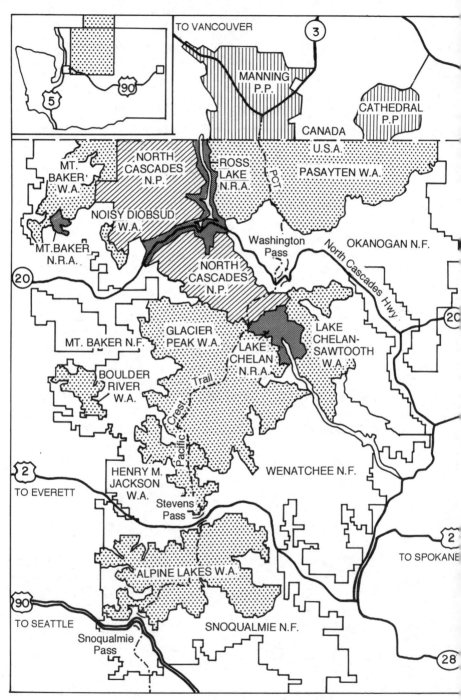

The North Cascade Mountains

Maps and Trail Descriptions

The first map in this book is the overall map of the North Cascades, which also depicts the route of the Pacific Crest Trail (PCT). The areas covered are divided into twenty-four sections for cartographic convenience; there is a map for each section. Each map title includes the name of the primary land management agency; sometimes a secondary agency is listed. Occasionally, maps include more than two administrative areas; these minor inclusions are not listed.

Many North Cascades trails cross land management boundaries; under these circumstances, the footpath is described in the section that is most representative of the particular route. Some footpaths are shown on more than one map; if so, the trail is described in the more appropriate section.

Some trails shown on the maps are not described herein. Data about these footpaths may be obtained from other guidebooks listed in the Bibliography or from the land management agencies listed in the Resources section.

All trails described are listed in the Index. Some trails have two or three names or significant locations. Secondary names are listed in parentheses in the heading and are also listed in the Index.

The *Washington Back Country Almanac,* updated and published annually by the Seattle Mountaineers, contains current information about the North Cascades, including present regulations and permit requirements. To order, call 800-553-4453 or write to The Mountaineers Books, 1101 SW Klickitat Way, Suite 201, Seattle, WA 98134.

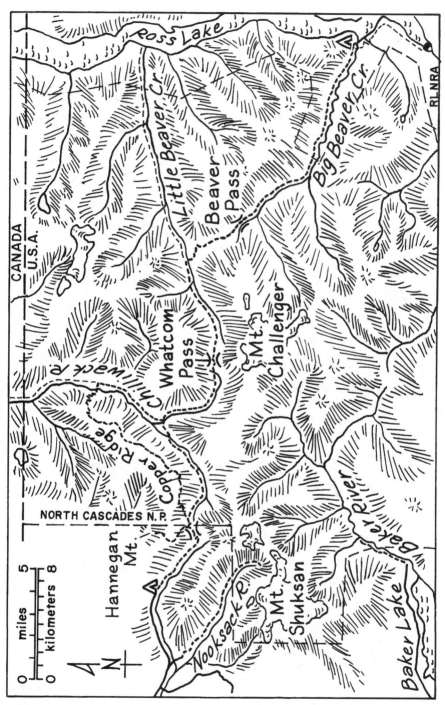

North Cascades National Park–North

North Cascades National Park–North

BAKER RIVER
Elevations
    Trailheads: 780 feet
    Destination: 900 feet (Sulphide Camp)
Altitude Gain   350 feet (including ups and downs)
Walking Time   In: 1 hour   Out: 55 minutes
Trail Length   2.4 miles one-way
Accessibility   Mid-March to early December
Difficulty   Moderate
Pack   Light
Topographic Sheets   USGS: Mount Shuksan
        Green Trails: Mount Shuksan

From State Route 20, drive up the Baker Lake Road to the bridge at Sulfur Creek just inside the Mount Baker–Snoqualmie National Forest boundary. Follow the main paved road to the right after crossing the bridge; a mile farther, continue past the Koma Kulshan Ranger Station on the left fork of the road (do not go right to Baker Dam). Continue on this paved and then graveled road, crossing the Boulder Creek Bridge and then passing the access road to the Baker Lake Resort. Note the odometer at the Swift Creek Bridge 0.2 mile past the resort. From the bridge, it is 5.3 miles to the signed turnoff to the left (east); road quality deteriorates after the turnoff. Follow the road 0.4 mile to a large, graveled, open area, which accommodates about forty cars. The trailhead is at the northeast end of the parking area.

Baker River is adjacent to the parking lot. For orientation before starting the walk, step over to the riverside. The surrounding peaks and ridges can be better appreciated from the riverbank than from the forested trailhead. Hagan Mountain is the peak to the southeast.

Also adjacent to the parking area are several level places to camp or park an RV. Two square, graveled tent sites are located 0.1 mile from the trailhead 50 feet to the right (south) of the footpath.

Deep and splendid ancient forest is a feature of this trail. Huge, impressive western red cedar trees abound. Moss is everywhere (on the rocks, beside the footpath, on the forest floor, and hanging from the trees). Ferns grow from the trees in this rain forest.

The first 0.25 mile of this walk is on a wide, graveled path. Thereafter, the tread close to the riverbank was washed away in places by the November 1995 flood. By May 31, 1998, an additional 0.3 mile of the footpath will be widened and made wheelchair accessible.

At 0.45 mile, a short way trail descends to the beach adjacent to the river. There are views here and logs to sit on while eating lunch.

The new bridge over the Baker River, which accesses the East Bank–Baker Lake Trail, is reached at about 0.6 mile from the trailhead.

At 0.7 mile, a washout has made it necessary to bypass a large boulder. A temporary reroute has been created. Construction of an easier way around was planned for 1997; until this is in place, use caution here.

At about 1 mile, the path turns to the north and gains about 100 feet above the river; for 0.3 mile, the tread is slick in places.

After descending, you must cross two creeks. A footlog, slick when wet, bridges the second creek. Another washout in this vicinity may require rock hopping or, in higher water, a ford.

A swamp is adjacent to the footpath on the right at 1.6 miles. Peaks to the east can be seen over the wetland.

At 1.7 miles, you enter the NCNP. Boundary markers, usually present here, were not seen in late June 1996. (Pets cannot legally proceed farther.)

At 1.9 miles, the tread is only a foot or so about the marsh. There are views here, and rocks on which to sit; it is another preferred lunch stop.

Soon after this point, the path enters deep woods and remains in the forest until Sulphide Creek is reached at 2.4 miles. From the riverbank, there are views to the north of the southeastern slopes of Mount Shuksan.

A campground is present near the creek in the dank forest. There are three tent sites, one by the river upstream and two in the woods 150 feet from where the access trail ends at the riverbank. A privy is accessed from the main trail 20 feet past a deteriorating signpost.

From Sulphide Camp, it is possible, with some difficulty, to follow the creek bed, hike through the forest, or do some combination of both and reach the junction of the creek and Baker River. A gravel bar here can be sunny in season. A deep, long run of the river here will tempt fishermen.

This path is intermittently snow free throughout mild winters. Indeed, it is a more enjoyable walk in late fall, winter, and early spring, since views of the surrounding peaks and ridges are more easily seen when the leaves of the deciduous trees have fallen. The footpath is brushy in places; be prepared to cope with wet undergrowth and to avoid stinging nettles. Many muddy areas of the tread merit appropriate footgear.

Overnight stays at Sulphide Camp require a permit issued by the NCNP. (June 1996)

COPPER RIDGE
Elevations
Trailhead: 4,424 feet (NCNP boundary)
Destination: 6,260 feet (Copper Ridge lookout)
Other Significant Locations: Silesia Camp, 5,690 feet
Altitude Gain   2,750 feet (including ups and downs)
Walking Time   In: 3 hours   Out: 2 hours
Trail Length   5.2 miles one-way
Accessibility   Late July to October
Difficulty   Moderately strenuous (Hannegan trailhead to lookout)
Pack   Full
Topographic Sheets   USGS: Mounts Shuksan and Challenger
   Green Trails: Mounts Shuksan and Challenger

See Hannegan Pass–Whatcom Pass on page 132 for access information to the national park boundary 5 miles from the Hannegan trailhead. From the junction, the trail again turns upward and reenters timber. After a number of switchbacks, the trail breaks out of the timber briefly under a large rock at about 7.6 miles, where there are views of Icy, Ruth, and Shuksan Mountains. Two-tenths of a mile farther is a false top-out; 0.1 mile beyond that is a somewhat technical rock and snow crossing over a slide area (the head of Hells Gorge). A tenth of a mile farther, the ridge top is reached. Walking time from the junction with a full pack to the ridge top is almost an hour and a half. The trail then goes up and over a knob; until August, it is possible to cut steps in the snow to the left or north and thus save some elevation gain, but there is some exposure and an ice ax is required. The trail then drops down and goes up and around a second knob immediately thereafter. Near the east side of the second knob, there is a trail pole indicating Silesia Camp to the right. There are two sites there, with space for three tents. All are excellent places to spend the night. Water can be obtained from melting snow close to the trail post, 50 yards below and northwest of the camp.

Two-tenths of a mile farther along the trail, after dropping downward, the post indicating Egg Lake Camp is intersected. The lake is 0.4 mile and about 300 vertical feet below this post. There are several designated campsites at the lake. (July 19, 1980, these tent sites were snow free, although Egg Lake was still approximately 90 percent snow and ice covered.)

The main trail goes up slightly, then drops down several hundred vertical feet, then climbs roughly a thousand feet in altitude over the last linear mile to the lookout. From the lookout, there are unexcelled views in all directions, including Mount Redoubt, Red Face Mountain, a portion of Mount Challenger,

Whatcom Peak, Mineral Mountain, Mount Blum, Icy Peak, Ruth Mountain, Mount Shuksan, Mount Baker, Hannegan Peak, and Copper Mountain.

Beyond the lookout, if you are interested in climbing Copper Mountain, drop down to a saddle to the left. The ridge to the first summit (6,855 feet) looks fairly easy; there is further altitude gain, and the ridge looks more technical between the first summit and the second true summit (7,142 feet), but it is not a difficult climb.

The Copper Ridge footpath drops down through meadow and snow patches, losing about 400 vertical feet over the next 0.6 mile. There is a stopping point here where hikers can look down an additional 600 vertical feet to Copper Lake nestled below in its granite amphitheater. The trail switchbacks down steeply to the lake in late summer (probably 0.6 mile more). However, as of July 19, 1980, the trail could be found only approximately 10 percent of the time, and the descent to the lake required glissading or plunge-stepping down fairly steep snow with occasional heather transits (the process had to be reversed on the return, mostly by kicking steps up steep snow slopes).

There is a trail post east of the lake, saying that the camp is to the left, or west. There are myriad trails in this area, certainly justifying the revegetation and rehabilitation project being attempted by the Park Service. Several designated tent sites are present. The main trail turns right at the trail post. There is no visible tread for about 100 feet. Look for a large boulder with a cairn on top, and expect the trail to disappear between several dead, silver trees on the left of the trail and a live tree on the right. The footpath, where the tread is more apparent, drops down another 100 feet, crosses the outlet creek from Copper Lake, gains a few feet, and then contours across a partially timbered area. About 0.5 mile past the lake, there is a mildly difficult stream ford; look up to see a nice waterfall 75 feet above.

Nine-tenths of a mile past the lake, the trail goes through an area of granite talus, through which runs a small creek. Follow cairns if you cannot find the tread. Immediately beyond this area, switchbacks go up to the ridge top. Tread quality declines after passing Copper Lake. A half mile farther, having gained a bit over 3,000 vertical feet in altitude, the footpath tops out on the ridge crest. Turn left or west at this point and follow the trail upward another 100 vertical feet. From here, the trail again turns northward and isocontours through snow and talus for half a mile, then proceeds levelly across a green meadow several hundred feet below a two-knobbed ridge.

The walking time, light packed, from Silesia Camp to the ridge top is 2 hours and 20 minutes; the return time is a bit greater, primarily due to the altitude gain coming up out of Copper Lake.

To make the descent to Copper Lake, an ice ax is mandatory until late

August, and the skills to plunge-step, glissade, and kick steps in the snow are necessary to make the descent and ascent safely in this area.

The down-time to Egg Lake from the main trail is 10 minutes; the up-time is 20 minutes. There are a fair number of mosquitoes and no-see-ums, but deerflies are not a major problem.

On the return trip, a loop option for experienced cross-country hikers presents itself. To reach Hannegan Mountain cross-country, cut upward off the trail 0.1 mile west of the second large rock above the trail, roughly 0.4 mile after beginning the descent from Copper Ridge. If done in the right place, a scrabble trail will be intersected 50 feet upward; this can be identified by cut log ends. Follow this trail progressively upward to the ridge crest. The tread is faint to nonexistent in places. Once on the ridge crest, simply follow the crest over minor ups and downs on snow and heather. The route is fairly level for roughly half a mile and then progressively steepens. The last 100 yards upward is steep, traversing snow and heather; use caution crossing a roughly 30-foot patch of scree and loose rock, which is a bit treacherous. As soon as possible, cut left out of this area to heather and more solid earth and continue westward on much less steep and more solid ground to the Hannegan Mountain trail immediately to the south of the summit. From here, it is but a few feet to the top, where the hiker is treated to one of the splendid views in the North Cascades. Baker, Shuksan, Ruth, Icy, Sefrit, Granite, Blum, Mineral, Whatcom Peak, Challenger, Whatcom Pass, Red Face Mountain, Mount Fury, and the remainder of the Picket Range surround the viewer. The Copper Mountain lookout can be seen in the distance, and beyond it is Mount Redoubt.

There are two campsites on top in the krummholz trees on the very summit. There is meltwater from snow patches 50 and 300 feet to the northwest of the summit. Watch for mountain goats between Copper Ridge, Hannegan Peak, and Granite Mountain.

It takes 1 hour to walk from Copper Ridge trail to the summit of Hannegan Peak. See Hannegan Pass for further data about the descent to the pass. Halfway down, there is one good campsite with water available from a small tarn fed by a snow patch nearby. The down-time from Hannegan Peak to the pass is 30 minutes.

No pack animals or fires are allowed on Copper Ridge. NCNP innovative compost toilets are located at Silesia Camp, Egg Lake, Copper Lookout, and Copper Lake.

The low point on the Chilliwack trail just before starting up to the north end of Copper Ridge is roughly 2,200 feet; the trail tops out at roughly 5,200 feet, so there is a 3,000-foot altitude gain in that segment of trail. Currently, this segment of the trail is not being maintained.

Trail mileages from the Hannegan trailhead are as follows: Hannegan Pass, 4; NCNP boundary, 5; Hannegan Peak, 5; crest of Copper Ridge, 7; Silesia Camp, 8; Egg Lake, 8.4; Copper Ridge lookout, 10.2; Copper Lake, 11.4; top of the Chilliwack trail, 14.5; Chilliwack trail junction, 18.4.

The scenery between the Copper Ridge lookout and Hannegan Peak is superb. The surrounding alpine grandeur rivals that available anywhere in the world.

(July 1980)

HANNEGAN PASS–WHATCOM PASS
Elevations
    Trailhead: 3,100 feet (Hannegan)
    Destination: 5,206 feet (Whatcom Pass)
    Other Significant Locations: NPS boundary, 4,424 feet; Chilliwack Ford (low point), 2,468 feet; Hannegan Pass, 5,100 feet.
Altitude Gain   4,800 feet in; 2,600 feet out (including ups and downs)
Walking Time   In: 8–10 hours (2 days)   Out: 7–9 hours
Trail Length   17.6 miles one-way
Accessibility   August 1 to October 1
Difficulty   Strenuous (Whatcom Pass)
Pack   Full
Topographic Sheets   USGS: Mounts Shuksan and Challenger
    Green Trails: Mounts Shuksan and Challenger

Take State Highway 542 eastward from Bellingham to Glacier. Drive 13.1 miles from Glacier to the highway maintenance shops on the left (north) side of the road. Continue 0.3 mile farther, and 100 feet or so before the bridge crossing the Nooksack River, turn left off the pavement onto an unsigned gravel side road. Three-tenths of a mile after the turnoff, look southward for a superlative view of Mount Shuksan framed over the Nooksack River. The road forks at 1.4 miles; take the left fork (the right fork goes to the Nooksack Cirque trailhead). The Goat Mountain trailhead, elevation 2,500 feet, is passed at 2.5 miles.

The potholed, one-way road ends at 5.4 miles; drive this road carefully. There is parking for twenty-five to thirty cars at the trailhead. There are also a campground, a dilapidated shelter, a privy, and picnic tables near the trailhead. Other campsites are available at pullouts beside the access road. This trail is for hikers, horses, and llamas and is closed to all machines.

The Mount Baker Wilderness is entered at 0.4 mile. There is thick brush overhanging the trail for the first 1.5 miles. During or following a rain or heavy dew, contact with the brush wets clothing up to chest high. Stinging nettles must be carefully avoided by hikers wearing shorts. At present Forest Service funding levels, it is unlikely that the trail will be brushed in the future. As compensation, many varieties of wildflowers bloom adjacent to the footpath.

For the first 0.5 mile, the trail follows the course of an abandoned wagon road; the path then narrows and proceeds gradually upward on the north side of the scenic Ruth Creek valley. Several creeks must be rock-hopped. There are intermittent views of Ruth Mountain, improving as altitude is gained. Several washouts of the footpath must be cautiously bypassed. At 3.4 miles, new tread has replaced the old pathway. At 3.6 miles, a side trail to the right leads to the Hannegan campsite, accessed by a boardwalk and a creek-hop. There are eight tent sites scattered over the first 0.2 mile; several of the lower sites are soggy. There is one privy, and a cooking area at the seventh and eighth tent sites.

Back on the main pathway, tread switchbacks up a lovely meadow with fine views of Ruth Mountain at 3.9 miles. Hannegan Pass, elevation 5,100 feet, is reached at 4.1 miles, after a walk of 2 hours and 20 minutes. There is a privy 75 feet east of the pass to the left. Three trails depart from Hannegan Pass: (1) the trail to the NCNP, Copper Ridge, and Whatcom Pass contours to the northeast and enters the forest shortly; (2) a footpath to the right accesses the base of Ruth Mountain; and (3) pathway to the left ascends Hannegan Mountain. This recently constructed tread switchbacks up through meadows with a plethora of blooming avalanche lilies. Tread has slipped in two areas, one of which is slick when wet. It takes slightly less than an hour to walk the 1.2 miles to the rounded summit, where there are two wind-sheltered tent sites among the low trees. Pack water up if you plan to camp here after the snow has melted. Views from the 6,186-foot peak are glorious in all directions; it is certainly a suitable location for a vision quest. Visible mountains include Ruth, Shuksan, Granite, Goat, Copper, Indian, Easy, and Mineral.

Leaving Hannegan Pass going eastward, the trail has been rerouted into the forest to the north; the prior trail that descended directly into the Chilliwack River valley has been closed. The trail loses 700 vertical feet in altitude over the next mile. Five miles from the trailhead, the national park boundary is reached, and simultaneously, the trail forks. The left fork leads to Copper Ridge, Copper Mountain lookout, and Copper Lake. A sharp right turn leads to Boundary Camp, 50 feet below and 100 feet away from the trail, located immediately above the headwaters of the Chilliwack River.

The trail to Whatcom Pass goes less sharply to the right at the park boundary junction. At 5.4 miles, deep forest is entered. At 6.2 miles, the lower portion of Hells Gorge is crossed. Hells Gorge is a large rock-slide area, starting almost at the Copper Ridge crest and extending downward to the Chilliwack River. At 7.5 miles, the trail crosses Copper Creek; notice the waterfalls to the left of the trail. Both are reliable sources of water. To the right, a substantial waterfall tumbles down the Chilliwack River. A designated camp is located in this area. The junction with the Easy Ridge trail is 9.3 miles, and the U.S. Cabin designated campsite is 10.1 miles. In the early 1970s, there was a substantial trail shelter at this site, accounting for the name of the camp. The cabin has been demolished by the Park Service. Water is available to the south of the camp. Both bears and rodents are problems at this campsite, and all food must be protected. This camp is located in deep woods, with little or no view.

It is 10.9 miles to the Chilliwack River crossing. The NPS has constructed a cable car at this location to eliminate the dangerous ford here. At 11.8 miles, Brush Creek is reached; 0.1 mile farther is the junction with the Chilliwack trail extending northward into Canada. At 14.1 miles, the designated Graybeal campsite (elevation 3,600 feet) is reached. Unfortunately, this location has problems. The area is not scenic. Brush Creek frequently changes its course, inundating tent sites. The NCNP plans to relocate this camp as soon as possible. From here, the trail climbs more steeply to Whatcom Pass, elevation 5,206 feet. Trail reconstruction west of the pass added about 0.5 mile to the length of the footpath, so Whatcom Pass is now about 17.6 miles from the Hannegan trailhead. A new campsite was built in the west basin 0.25 mile from Whatcom Pass in 1988; the camp has two tent sites with water nearby. It is reported to be an elegant place to overnight.

If proceeding northward on the Chilliwack trail, it is 3.5 miles to the junction with the north portion of the Copper Ridge trail, 5.3 miles to the Bear Creek campsite, 7.7 miles to the Little Chilliwack campsite, 8.7 miles to the Canadian border, and about 10.5 miles to the trailhead at Chilliwack Lake.

Walking times are as follows: trailhead to Hannegan Pass, 2 hours; pass to park boundary, 25 minutes; park boundary to U.S. Cabin campsite, 2 hours (losing approximately 2,500 vertical feet from Hannegan Pass to U.S. Cabin). From U.S. Cabin to Graybeal is about 2 hours, and from Graybeal to Whatcom Pass is an additional 2 hours and 15 minutes. From the pass, the trail drops down several hundred feet in meadow and then loses altitude very dramatically via switchbacks as it descends 2,000 vertical feet into the Little Beaver valley below.

From Whatcom Pass, there is a scrabble trail going to the north, allowing access to the Tapto Lakes for fishermen and to Red Face Mountain for climbers. To the south, a walk of 0.2 mile and a gain of several hundred vertical feet brings one to a small pond with a magnificent view of Mount Challenger to the southeast and Whatcom Peak directly to the south. Two faint trails lead off from this point. One stays fairly level and leads to the access route to Mount Challenger and Perfect Pass; the other goes upward fairly steeply onto the arm north of Whatcom Peak. Vistas progressively improve as altitude is gained. Camping at other than the designated campsite is not allowed in the Whatcom Pass area.

Both Hannegan and Whatcom Passes are quite splendid. The route between them is mostly deep-forest hiking and is not too scenic. Preferred campsites are at Hannegan Pass, Boundary Camp, U.S. Cabin, and the west basin of Whatcom Pass.

(Hannegan Pass to Whatcom Pass, September 1972; trailhead to Hannegan Mountain, July 1996)

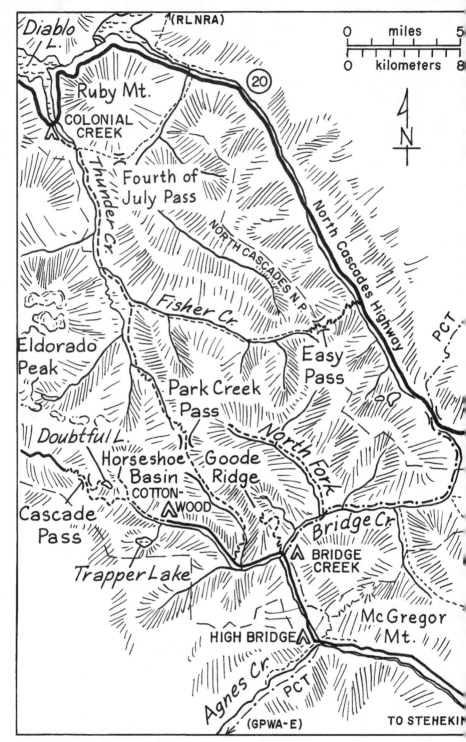

North Cascades National Park–South

North Cascades National Park–South

BRIDGE CREEK (PACIFIC CREST TRAIL)
Elevations
Trailhead: 2,200 feet (Stehekin Road)
Destination: 4,400 feet (North Cascades Highway)
Altitude Gain   2,400 feet (including ups and downs)
Walking Time 6 hours valley to highway   5 hours highway to valley
Trail Length   12.2 miles one-way
Accessibility   Mid-June to mid-October
Difficulty   Moderately strenuous
Pack   Light
Topographic Sheets   USGS: McGregor Mountain, McAlester Mountain, Washington Pass
    Green Trails: McGregor Mountain, Stehekin, Washington Pass

At the present time, this 12.2-mile trail is a section of the Pacific Crest Trail. From the valley, the trailhead is 0.2 mile before the Bridge Creek bridge. The trail ascends through deep forest, gains a moderate amount of altitude, and then drops to a well-constructed bridge over Bridge Creek. From here it switchbacks up, gaining 400 feet to reach the junction with the North Fork trail at 3 miles. The North Fork Camp is at the junction of Bridge Creek and the North Fork; there are good campsites here for fifteen people beside the rushing water.

At 4 miles cross, Maple Creek on a bridge 50 feet above the site of the old ford. The access trails to the bridge on either side may not be apparent; however, the bridge can easily be seen from either direction as one approaches the creek. Sixmile Camp is indeed at 6 miles. The trail to this camp goes down to the river, where there are a number of campsites beneath the trees. Mud is a problem here in wet weather.

For better campsites, continue 0.8 mile to South Fork Camp. There are several nice campsites by Bridge Creek. A footlog permits access to Rainbow Lake 6 miles away. (See Rainbow Lake trail for description.) At 8.5 miles, Hideaway Camp (on Bridge Creek) is recommended as a bivouac site only. A bridge crossing 0.5 mile farther allows access to Fireweed Camp on the other side of Bridge Creek. Here is the junction to the trails to Twisp Pass, McAlester Pass, Stiletto Meadows and Peak, and Copper Pass.

At 10.8 miles is the north border of the North Cascades National Park. From this point it is 1.4 miles to the North Cascades Highway and 2.4 miles to Rainy Pass.

The old trail that passed the old mine site at Crocker Cabin and the spur trail to Copper Pass and the Stiletto Meadows trail have been bypassed. Bridge Creek is now crossed on a sturdy bridge, eliminating the footlog/ford required on the old trail.

A substantial portion of the Bridge Creek trail is in deep forest, particularly at each end of the trail. In between, it passes through a number of avalanche slopes and open areas where views are possible. In season, there are flowers (particularly lupine and Indian paintbrush) along the route. The trail is muddy in places but well maintained throughout. Wood supplies are adequate at all campsites. Water is not a problem. Birdsong speeds your way along the trail. There are often many butterflies in the area.

If walking in from the North Cascades Highway, park your car at the lowest portion of the highway between Rainy and Washington Passes; this will save 1 mile of deep-woods walking by taking the 100-foot way trail from the road to reach the Pacific Crest Trail at this point.

Of the two access routes to the valley from the west, the Cascade Pass route is preferable to Bridge Creek, since it is more scenic, and shorter, assuming that the Stehekin Road is passable to Cottonwood. However, Bridge Creek is snow free several weeks earlier than the Cascade Pass route.

(June 1990)

CASCADE PASS: WEST APPROACH

Elevations

Trailhead:	3,700 feet	
Destination:	5,400 feet (Cascade Pass)	

Altitude Gain   1,750 feet (including ups and downs)

Walking Time   In: 1 hour 45 minutes   Out: 1 hour 15 minutes

Trail Length   3.7 miles

Accessibility   July 15 to October 15

Difficulty   Moderate

Pack   Light

Topographic Sheets   USGS: Good Mountain, Cascade Pass

Green Trails: McGregor Mountain, Cascade Pass

To reach the west trailhead, leave Interstate 5 at Burlington and drive State Highway 20 to Marblemount. Cross the Skagit River and follow the road to its end; the last 2 miles are rough, steep, and inadvisable for trailers. The trail begins on the north side of the parking lot at the end of the road. This trail, constructed in 1967, switchbacks gradually but seemingly endlessly upward, culminating in half a mile of almost level traverse, followed by a 0.2-mile uphill segment that reaches Cascade Pass. Sections of the trail are almost invariably

PHOTO BY MIKE BARNHART

View of Pelton Basin from Cascade Pass

muddy. Thick forest cover obscures views, with only occasional glimpses of the surrounding peaks until meadow is reached at about 3.2 miles. Water is available along the entire route. Watch for pikas and marmots in the talus and meadow areas along the last mile of the trail.

Views from the pass are extraordinary. Below to the east is Pelton Basin and the beginning of the Stehekin Valley. Below to the west is the valley of the North Fork of the Cascade River. Beginning in the west, the 360-degree circle of peaks includes Hidden Lake, Eldorado, Forbidden, Sahale, Buckner Mountain, Booker, McGregor, Glory Mountain, Trapper Mountain, Magic Mountain, Mix-up Peak, the Triplets, and Johannesburg Mountain.

Camping is allowed at both trailheads, Basin Creek, and Pelton Basin. Climbers can make special arrangements for high camps on snow when they obtain their backcountry permits. This day-use-only policy is necessary to preserve this fragile area, which was being "loved to death" before these protective measures were taken. Wilderness rangers regularly patrol the pass and surrounding areas.

A variety of other options confront the hiker, wilderness traveler, and mountaineer after reaching Cascade Pass. Data about these alternatives follow.

Cache Col. It is possible to follow a mountaineers' trail beginning at the pass and traversing upward to the southeast across steep snow and talus slopes to a promontory 0.5 mile above the pass. This is a dangerous trail and should be attempted only by those experienced in climbing techniques. From this promontory, descend about 100 feet; after reaching the snow or ice, begin the 0.9-mile ascent on the glacier to reach Cache Col to the southeast. Just above this col, there is a spectacular but exposed campsite from which to watch the mere mortals below. There is also camping 1 mile farther at Kool-Aid Lake, 1,000 feet lower. Basic snow and ice climbing skills are required to reach the col safely.

Trapper Lake. To reach Trapper Lake from the pass, descend on the footpath to Stehekin 0.5 mile. Take the lower (right) fork of the trail and descend into Pelton Basin, crossing to the south side of the creek. Ascend a moderately apparent scrabble path at the southeast side of Pelton Basin, gaining about 500 vertical feet to a nice camping area overlying the Stehekin Valley. From here, two traverses over scrabble trails lead to the ridge overlooking Trapper Lake after an additional walk of 1 mile. A steep descent of 0.2 mile (easy early in the season when snow is present, but a difficult bushwhack late in the season) brings one to the west end of Trapper Lake. Fishing and campsites are available at both ends of the lake. (The east end of the lake is best reached via a strenuous cross-country trek beginning at Cottonwood Camp.)

Doubtful Lake. One hundred yards east of the crest of Cascade Pass, the footpath to Sahale Arm and Doubtful Lake leaves the main trail; turn northward. This steeper secondary footpath then switchbacks up Sahale Arm, gaining 1,000 feet in 0.7 mile. At the top of the arm, descend the steep north side of the arm and lose about 1,000 feet to reach Doubtful Lake. Note the evidence of the mining activity that took place here in the late 1800s. Fishing is generally good, although the lake is rather heavily fished in the summer. The scenery features magnificent views of Sahale to the north and McGregor to the east. Total distance from the pass is 1.5 miles.

Sahale Arm. Instead of descending to Doubtful Lake, it is possible to continue higher on Sahale Arm by following the mountaineers' scrabble trail to an elevation of 8,000 feet. At this point, it is necessary to traverse a glacier, and those without experience in climbing should turn back. Sahale Arm features spectacular views of the surrounding "sea of peaks."

(1988)

CASCADE PASS: EAST APPROACH
Elevation
  Trailhead: 2,750 feet
  Destination: 5,400 feet (Cascade Pass)
Altitude Gain   2,900 feet (Cascade Pass)
Walking Time   In: 3 hours   Out: 2 hours
Trail Length   5.4 miles
Accessibility   July 15 to October 15
Difficulty   Moderately strenuous
Pack   Light
Topographic Sheets   USGS: Goode Mountain, Cascade Pass
                         Green Trails: McGregor Mountain, Cascade Pass

The east trailhead begins at Cottonwood Camp at the end of the Stehekin Road. The trail initially ascends gradually along the Stehekin River, detouring upward briefly to avoid the avalanche debris from the cliffs to the south, which dammed the Stekehin River and obliterated the old trail in the 1970s. It is 1 mile to Basin Creek Camp, where there are five or six established, scattered campsites. A bear cable has been placed in this area to help campers preserve food supplies from marauding bruins.

Cross Basin Creek on a cable suspension bridge (one person at a time). The footpath climbs more steeply from this point, switchbacking upward on the deteriorating Mine to Market Road toward Horseshoe Basin (see that description). The Cascade Pass trail forks left after several switchbacks and then goes gradually upward to reach and cross the Doubtful Creek waterfall 1 mile beyond the junction. Above this point, there are thirteen switchbacks, ending in the woods above Pelton Basin. The trail then goes through timber for 0.4 mile. After breaking out in meadow, it ascends across a talus slope and then zigzags upward through meadow to reach Cascade Pass a bit over 5 miles from Cottonwood Camp.

Moderately strong hikers can arrive on the first shuttle bus from Stehekin, reach Cascade Pass from the east in time for lunch, and return to catch the late afternoon bus back to the village. For a more leisurely exploration of this area, those coming from the east should plan to spend the night at Basin Creek or, more desirably, at the designated campsite for hikers in the forest above Pelton Basin 1 mile east of the pass.

The November 1995 flood washed out the road between Flat Creek and Cottonwood Camp. As of June 1997, the park superintendent decided to temporarily close this section of the Stehekin Valley Road. If and when the channels of the Stehekin River move away from the roadbed, the road will be rebuilt. This decision will be made annually hereafter. In the meantime, access from Flat Creek to Cottonwood is by trail only.

Until the road is rebuilt, trail distances to Cascade Pass, Horseshoe Basin, and Trapper Lake are 3 miles longer and 500 vertical feet higher; walking time in would be 1 hour and 15 minutes longer, and out time would increase by 1 hour. This would make a round-trip in one day (via shuttle bus to and from the road end at Flat Creek) to the three above locations possible only for the very fit.

Hikers planning trips to these areas should check the current status of the road at the Golden West Visitor Center beforehand.

Active and aggressive attempts to replant damaged areas at Cascade Pass continue. A greenhouse for growing high alpine plants has been constructed at the Marblemount Ranger Station. Green netting has been placed in many areas of the pass in an effort to retain seeds and support plant growth; it is important not to walk on any areas where netting is visible. Everyone visiting the area should remain on the designated trails.

(July 1995)

EASY PASS

Elevations

Trailhead:	3,700 feet
Destination:	6,500 feet (Easy Pass)
Other Significant Locations:	Fisher Camp, 5,200 feet

Altitude Gain   2,800 feet (including ups and downs)

Walking Time   In: 2 hours   Out: 1 hour 20 minutes

Trail Length   3.7 miles one-way

Accessibility   Late July to early October

Difficulty   Moderately strenuous

Pack   Light

Topographic Sheets   USGS: Mount Arriva 7.5'
                          Green Trails: Mount Logan

The trailhead is 46 miles east of Marblemount. A paved road extends 0.1 mile to the west of the North Cascades Highway, where it dead-ends; the Easy Pass trailhead is at the end of this road. There is parking for eight to ten cars near the road end and parallel parking along the spur road for perhaps twenty more. The footpath goes westward, dropping a few feet initially and then proceeding on the level for approximately 0.15 mile to Granite Creek. The creek must be forded (uncomfortable at any time, but dangerous in spring high water); footlogs upstream and downstream are present intermittently. After crossing the stream, the trail proceeds upward on a moderate grade through deep forest with no views until about 1.5 miles from the trailhead, where it suddenly breaks into an avalanche meadow. From here on, there are views all the way to Easy Pass. The trail crosses this meadow, meeting Easy Pass Creek—which can be forded or rock-hopped—in mid-meadow. The trail then turns to the southeast, again gaining altitude. Shortly thereafter, it passes through avalanche debris and then contours upward beneath an unnamed peak to the south. From about 2 to 2.4 miles, the trail crosses beneath a headwall to the west and then starts switchbacking up this headwall. The next 0.6 mile is in switchbacks up the headwall, eventually topping out by a small creek in a relatively level area, where there are possible campsites. The trail proceeds upward through meadow, eventually switchbacks under the rock face north of the trail, and then contours to the west over talus and scree slopes to reach Easy Pass. From the pass, it is 22 miles to Diablo Lake via the Fisher and Thunder Creek trails.

There are few good campsites along the Forest Service portion of the trail. Easy Pass itself is closed to overnight camping. Since the trail contours under a north slope and is shaded by a steep rock ridge, it is a late-opening and early-closing trail due to snow. An ice ax is essential in most years until about Labor Day.

The views from the pass are elegant, particularly the last weekend in September and the first weekend in October, when the larches are golden yellow. Ragged Ridge to the northwest, Mount Logan to the west, Mount Hardy to the east, and Mount Arriva, Fisher Peak, and Black Peak to the south are most impressive. There is room to ramble on progressively higher ridges toward the southeast. A trailless walk to the north, gaining about 800 vertical feet in altitude, brings you to a splendid viewpoint on the east end of Ragged Ridge.

Those desiring to overnight can proceed onward and downward a short 2 miles from the pass to the designated Fisher campsite located in the deep timber in the valley below; some 1,300 feet of altitude is lost in the process. Fisher Camp itself is not located in a scenic area. It is possible to cross-country to the southeast into the Fisher Creek basin. Any campsite more than a mile from the trail in the basin is acceptable to the Park Service. At either location, overnight camping permits are required. Campfires are prohibited at Fisher Camp and within the Fisher Creek basin; backpackers' stoves should be carried. The walking time down is 45 minutes; up-time is 1 hour and 15 minutes. The alpine flowers in the area are most enjoyable. There is open subalpine meadow for about a mile west of the campsite.

(Fisher Camp, August 1976; Easy Pass, September 1994)

HORSESHOE BASIN (STEHEKIN)

Elevations

Trailheads:	2,800 feet (Cottonwood); 3,600 feet (junction with Cascades Pass trail)
Destination:	4,800 feet (Horseshoe Basin)
High Point:	4,800 feet
Altitude Gain	1,200 feet (including ups and downs)
Walking Time	1 hour 30 minutes from the junction with Cascades Pass trail
	4 hours from Cottonwood Camp
Trail Length	3 miles round-trip
Accessibility	Late June to early October
Difficulty	Moderate
Pack	Light
Topographic Sheets	USGS: Cascade Pass
	Green Trails: Cascade Pass

The November 1995 flood washed out the road between Flat Creek and Cottonwood Camp. As of June 1997, the park superintendent decided to temporarily close this section of the Stehekin Valley Road. If and when the channels of the Stehekin River move away from the roadbed, the road will be rebuilt. This decision will be made annually hereafter. In the meantime, access from Flat Creek to Cottonwood is by trail only.

Until the road is rebuilt, trail distances to Cascade Pass, Horseshoe Basin, and Trapper Lake are 3 miles longer and 500 vertical feet higher; walking time in would be 1 hour and 15 minutes longer, and out time would increase by 1 hour. This would make a round-trip in one day (via shuttle bus to and from the road end at Flat Creek) to the three above locations possible only for the very fit.

Hikers planning trips to these areas should check the current status of the road at the Golden West Visitor Center beforehand.

Horseshoe Basin can be reached by continuing on the abandoned Mine to Market Road (now a trail) 2 miles west of Cottonwood Camp or 3 miles east of Cascade Pass. (This is a less rigorous one-day trip from the Cottonwood trailhead than the trip to Cascade Pass; although not as scenic, it is an enjoyable alternative for hikers physically unable to make the trip to the pass between the first and last shuttle buses of the day.)

There is a gain of 1,200 vertical feet in 1.5 miles to the large cirque between Sahale, Boston, Ripsaw Ridge, and Buckner Mountains. Note the many active waterfalls cascading down from the snow and ice fields above. The trail now ends at the Black Warrior Mine, easily located by the extensive tailings below the mine shaft entrance.

During most of the summer, there is a snowfield just below the mine, which may present problems to the inexperienced; use considerable caution in this area. If in doubt, go down about two switchbacks, cross the snowfield at that point, and work your way back up the talus slope, staying to the right of the creek and to the left of the mine trailings.

This mine is now listed on the National Register of Historic Places. The Park Service has done restoration work on the mine shafts; nonetheless, there are hazards both outside (snow crossings, rockfall) and inside. Carry at least two flashlights. Watch both your head and your feet. The shaft in places is only 5 feet high, and there are pipes and rough areas over which you can easily trip. At the mine entrance, notice the stove, hot water tank, and room just inside the mine shaft, which presumably served as a warming and cooking area. Allow your eyes to adjust to the darkness. The shaft penetrates the mountain perhaps 150 feet, and then the main shaft turns left an additional 75 feet; further penetration is thought to be unsafe by the Park Service, and there is a screen preventing more exploration at this point.

All artifacts are protected within the national park. You should not collect, mark, or disturb the materials left from the human activities of years ago.

Although there is lumber and other debris outside the mine, there are no standing cabins, since winter avalanches have decimated the area with regularity. Wildflowers are profuse, particularly mimulus, along the trail. The jagged "sawteeth" of Ripsaw Ridge above are also impressive. The area is designated for day use only; the nearest camp is at Basin Creek, 2.3 miles away. The trail has been brushed and is in good condition, although parts are muddy and follow a streambed. There is no problem obtaining water in the basin.

Near the junction with the Cascade Pass trail, there is a splendid proliferation of succulent yellow blooming rock plants (sedum, or stonecrop) along the trail in late July.

Before leaving this area, let your imagination go back to the winter of 1909, when miners wintered over here, going between cabin and mine shaft through tunnels dug underneath the 30-foot snowpack.

(July 1980)

PARK CREEK PASS

Elevations

Trailhead:	2,340 feet (Park Creek Camp)
Destination:	6,140 feet (Park Creek Pass)
High Point:	6,140 feet
Altitude Gain	4,000 feet (including ups and downs)
Walking Time	8 hours
Trail Length	16 miles
Accessibility	July 15 to early October
Difficulty	Moderately strenuous
Pack	Heavy or light
Topographic Sheets	USGS: Goode Mountain
	Green Trails: McGregor Mountain

Take the shuttle bus (or walk) 18 miles up the road from Stehekin, or 4.5 miles down the road from Cottonwood Camp, to the trailhead. An unobtrusive sign is located where the trail takes off north of the road; there is an unimproved camping area near the creek to the right of the start of the trail.

After 100 yards, the trail goes moderately steeply upward. At 1 mile, there is a viewpoint and a small spring from which water can be obtained. One-tenth of a mile beyond, a 50-foot walk to the right to a rocky knob permits splendid views up the Flat Creek valley. One hundred yards or so beyond this viewpoint, the trail tops out, and there are again views over the Stehekin valley from a rock a few feet to the right of the trail.

From this point, the trail drops gently downward to reach Twomile Camp. Hiking time to the camp, full packed, is 1 hour from the trailhead. There is a toilet on the hillside above the camp, and there is space adjacent to Park Creek for about three tents crowded rather closely together.

The trail forks at this point, with the horse trail going left. The hiker trail crosses a sturdy bridge to the north side of Park Creek. The trail then goes sharply up for several hundred yards and gradually upward thereafter. Fully packed, it takes an additional 1.5 hours to reach Fivemile Camp. There are good views in the open areas, and water is available at the 4-mile mark.

Most of the Fivemile Camp is in timber without views, but campsite #4, 50 yards beyond, is splendidly located in open meadow with a spectacular view of the great cirque beneath Booker and Buckner Mountains. Wood is scarce. Water is available from a small creek. Bear cable is available, but without stringers.

The hike from Fivemile Camp to Park Creek Pass takes about 1.5 hours, lightly packed. The trail first goes through the brushy valley floor for 0.5 mile, then goes up the hillside, crosses a stream, and at 7 miles, breaks out into meadow. After it leaves the valley floor, it goes steeply upward. It is a long 8 miles to the 0.2-mile-long pass, which is snow-filled at the bottom. The trail contours above and on the northeast side of the pass. Views down Thunder Creek from the place where the snow abruptly terminates on the north side of the pass are quite spectacular. Grouse, marmots, and pikas inhabit the area. The down-time from the pass to Fivemile Camp is slightly more than an hour, and from Fivemile Camp to Stehekin Road is about 2 hours. There is adequate water between Fivemile Camp and the pass.

Park Creek Pass is closed to camping. In fact, legal camping must be 1 mile off the trail for 3 miles on either side of the pass. However, campsites are available cross-country both south of the pass and to the west on the high ridge leading to Mount Buckner.

The trailhead is at 2,340 feet. There is a 1,000-foot gain in the first 1.5 miles. Twomile Camp is at 3,500 feet, Fivemile Camp is at 4,100 feet, Park Creek Pass is at 6,140 feet, and Buckner Mountain is at 9,112 feet. Storm King Mountain can be seen from the trail 4 miles from the Stehekin Road. Beyond the pass, the trail follows Thunder Creek north 20 miles to the North Cascades Highway and Colonial Creek Campground.

The pass area is splendid and relatively isolated and uncrowded. It is possible to travel cross-country into the cirque beneath Buckner Mountain or to go higher on the mountain for ever-improving views.

(August 1987)

THUNDER CREEK
Elevations

Trailhead:	1,220 feet
Destination:	6,040 feet (Park Creek Pass)
Altitude Gain	6,300 feet (including ups and downs)
Walking Time	In: 9–12 hours (allow 2 days)
	Out: 6–8 hours (allow 1 full day)
Trail Length	19.1 miles one-way
Accessibility	June to October (first 6.5 miles); July 15 to October 1 (entire trail)
Difficulty	Moderate (first 6.5 miles); strenuous (entire trail)
Pack	Light (first 6.5 miles); full (entire trail)
Topographic Sheets	USGS: Ross Dam, Forbidden Peak, Mount Logan 7.5′ Green Trails: Diablo Dam, Mount Logan

The trail begins about 0.1 mile south of the North Cascades Highway via the paved Colonial Creek Campground Road. There are parking places for approximately thirty-five cars in the large parking area northeast of the trailhead. At 0.1 mile is the start of the nature trail. The trail runs on the level along the west shore of the Thunder Arm section of Diablo Lake to the lake end at about 0.7 mile. At about 0.6 mile, notice a number of beautifully burnished silver cedar trees that have died due to flooding from the lake but are still standing; their color and texture against the mountains in the background are notable. At 0.9 mile, a large metal bridge crosses Thunder Creek. Watch for Harlequin Ducks here in the late spring. From the bridge, the trail proceeds upward on the east side of Thunder Creek, gaining altitude gradually. The trail forks at a signed junction at about 1.3 miles. The right fork goes an additional 0.1 mile to a hiker camp (Thunder), consisting of three sites with fire grates. This section of the river offers good fishing (using waders or hip boots) late in the year after the spring runoff. The left fork at 1.3 miles is the main trail. One and a half miles from the trailhead, the Fourth of July Pass (Panther Creek, Ruby Mountain) footpath departs eastward and upward.

From about 1.5 miles, the trail remains high on the east canyon wall until the 4.3-mile mark; access to the river is very difficult over this 2.5 miles. Between 3.9 and 4.4 miles, the trail passes through a burn area, offering views of the river below and Colonial and Tricouni Peaks above. From 4.3 miles on, the river can be reached with relative ease or, at worst, with moderate difficulty. The trail crosses a number of small creeks, but these can usually be jumped or rock-hopped, even at high water. At about 5.3 miles, there is easy access over a pleasant grassy knoll to the river; note the maidenhair fern on the riverbank in this area.

Other campsites on the Thunder trail include Neve Camp at 2.1 miles (three sites), McAllister Camp at 6.5 miles on the right side of the river (five sites), Tricouni Camp at 7.6 miles (three sites), Skagit Queen Camp at 13.6 miles (four sites), and Thunder Basin Hiker Camp at 17.5 miles (two sites); no campfires are allowed in Thunder Basin. The horse camp at Thunder Basin is about half a mile closer to the trailhead than the hiker camp.

The Middle Cabin shelter was formerly located 5.5 miles from the trailhead, very close to the river in a pleasant wooded area. Originally built in 1893 by Jack Durand as a way station for early miners, it was dismantled by the Park Service in the early 1970s. This location is now called Miner's Rest Stop and is closed to camping. A horse camp is located 0.2 mile past the rest stop.

The way trail to McAllister Creek leaves to the right at about the 6-mile mark. It is necessary to cross the river and go downstream perhaps half a mile to reach the McAllister campsite. The trail ascending McAllister Creek is difficult to locate and no longer maintained.

The altitude gain to McAllister Creek is about 700 vertical feet in total; many ups and downs make the actual altitude gain easily 1,000 feet. Walking time to McAllister Creek is about 2 hours and 45 minutes in and about 2 hours and 30 minutes out. This is an enjoyable walk, mostly through deep forest and lush undergrowth. There are occasional views of the surrounding peaks through clearings in the forest. Bunchberry, trillium, calypso orchids, and large cedar and Douglas fir trees are found in the area. Wood and water are plentiful.

Seattle City Light still has a license to build a dam at about the 5.3-mile mark. Construction of this dam would markedly change the Thunder Creek area. The utility has given no notification to the NCNP that it intends to actually construct this hydroelectric project. Environmentalists strongly oppose the dam in view of the adverse consequences construction and flooding the reservoir would cause upstream from the site.

From McAllister Creek, the trail runs approximately 2 miles almost level, then switchbacks up steeply for the next 2 miles to reach Junction Camp, 9.5 miles from the trailhead. One-tenth of a mile from the camp is the junction with the Fisher Creek trail (from this junction, via the Fisher Creek trail, it is 9.1 miles to Fisher Basin, 10.5 miles to Easy Pass, and an additional 3.7 miles to descend from the pass to the North Cascades Highway). There are views near the campsite of waterfalls dropping from Tricouni Peak. Boston Glacier is also visible.

Continuing up the Thunder trail, the next 0.7 mile is fairly level. After about 0.3 mile, a 1-mile way trail descends steeply to Historic Meadow cabin. The Thunder footpath contours downward, losing about 800 vertical feet, and then gradually regains the elevation by the time the Skagit Queen campsite is reached. Tent sites are to the right or west of the trail. There is a way trail to water 0.1 mile east of the trail. This campsite is in deep, dank woods. Two-tenths of a mile past the campsite, the ruins of a building, machinery, and a deteriorated metal flume are passed. This was the generator for the Skagit Queen Mine located 1.5 miles to the south many years ago. The trail to the mine can be followed with difficulty for about 1 mile and is then lost in brush.

From here, gentle switchbacks gain altitude for the next mile, and views become progressively better. Two miles of fairly easy walking bring the hiker to the first view of Park Creek Pass from the Thunder Basin Meadow. Substantial reconstruction work has been done on the tread both in the Skagit Queen area and for 3 miles in the Thunder Basin area, which has substantially improved the squishy tread in the wetlands of the basin. A last hump upward for about 0.8 mile brings the hiker to the top of Park Creek Pass.

Views are limited until the Fisher Creek junction. Tricouni, Primus, and Klawatti Mountains and the Klawatti Glacier can be seen across the Thunder Creek valley. Farther to the south, Forbidden and Boston Peaks and their glaciers come into view as the hiker goes higher. On the left in the upper valley,

Mount Logan towers above, with the Fremont Glacier clinging to its steep flanks. Directly to the south, the Thunder Glacier seems to almost overhang the trail. Be sure to look back just before you enter the slot of Park Creek Pass; the view down the Thunder Creek valley is most impressive.

The entire Thunder trail lies within the Ross Lake National Recreation Area or within the NCNP; the boundary between the two is at about 6.8 miles. Park rules apply beyond this point. Permits are required for overnight camping in both areas, and camping is restricted to designated campsites. Camping is not permitted within 1 mile of the trail in the Park Creek Pass alpine area.

See Park Creek Pass for a description of the footpath between Park Creek Pass and Stehekin Road.

(August 1987)

North Cascades National Park–North and South

HIDDEN LAKE

Elevations

Trailhead: 3,560 feet

Destination: 6,890 feet (Lookout Shelter)

Other Significant Locations: Hidden Lake Peak, 7,000 feet; Hidden Lake, 5,733 feet

Altitude Gain   3,400 feet (including ups and downs)

Walking Time   In: 3 hours   Out: 1 hour 45 minutes

Trail Length   3.9 miles one-way

Accessibility   August and September

Difficulty   Moderately strenuous

Pack   Full

Topographic Sheets   USGS: Eldorado Peak, Sonny Boy Lakes 7.5

Green Trails: Diablo Dam, Cascade Pass

Take State Route 20 to Marblemount, cross the Skagit River, and drive about 2 miles past the Marble Creek bridge. Turn left here; the junction is presently signed. Drive 5.2 miles on the one-way rough road to the road end. The parking area accommodates about twenty cars; on weekends, turnaround space may be limited. Note data on the trailhead bulletin board. Follow the abandoned logging road to timber at the end of the clear-cut. Two creeks must be crossed; during unusually high water, a ford may be required. In the forest, the trail ascends moderately steeply for about 1 mile and then breaks out into the Sibley Creek meadow. For the next mile, the footpath is often difficult to find through the meadow due to lush overgrowth. If wearing shorts, watch for stinging nettles in this segment of the footpath. Forest Service trail crews brush back the meadow fairly regularly, but this work is often done late in the summer season.

Switchback up an additional 1.2 miles to the head of Sibley Creek, and then cross the creek and traverse gradually upward for approximately 0.5 mile through delightful meadowland. (At the head of Sibley Creek, there is an interesting juncture of granite with sedimentary rock and an equally abrupt botanical shift from verdant thick meadow to alpine heather.) From here, an additional 0.9 mile of fairly steep ascent brings you to a notch between Hidden Lake Peak and the unnamed spire on which the Hidden Lake Lookout sits.

The boundary between the national forest and national park is located at this point. From this notch, there are impressive views of Hidden Lake below and of the Cascade Pass area to the east. From this point, the hiker can drop

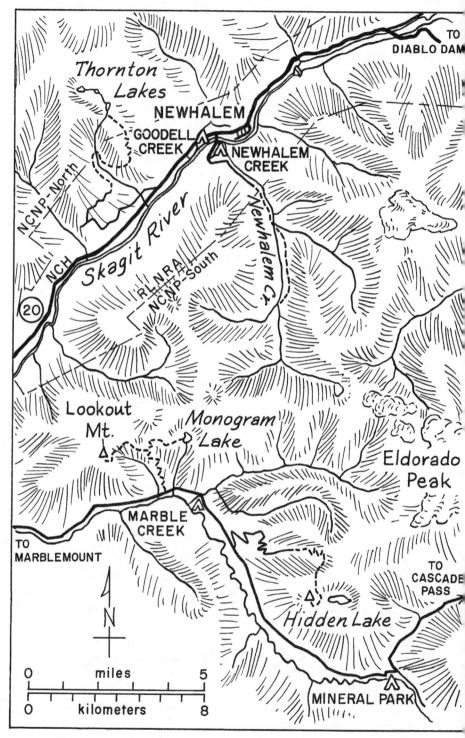

North Cascades National Park–North and South

down over the trailless, fairly steep talus slopes to several good campsites on a bench midway between the notch and Hidden Lake. The altitude loss to the bench is about 400 feet and to the lake itself is an additional 400 feet. The safest access route to the lake bears to the far left (north) on the descent and is not the route directly below and east of the camping areas. There are no campsites near the lakeshore at the west end of the lake. Water is no problem at the designated Hidden Lake campsite, since there is a permanent creek nearby. Campfires are prohibited.

Ptarmigan are often seen in and around the notch, campsite areas, and ridge crest. They are generally quite tame, and it is often possible to approach within a few feet for observation and photographs.

From the notch, the trail goes upward an additional 0.3 mile to the Lois Webster Memorial Shelter (formerly the Hidden Lake Lookout). The structure is no longer a fire observation station; when not being used by work parties, it is available for occupancy by the general public as a shelter. The building is maintained by a group of individuals who respect the structure both for its historic value and as a place for protection from inclement weather. Assistance in maintaining the structure is welcomed; volunteers should contact the Friends of the Lois Webster Memorial Shelter, 1819 Hickox Road, Mount Vernon, WA 98274. If you use the old lookout building, please show good outdoor manners and leave the building and contents in better condition than you found them. A register is located inside the shelter for those who wish to document their presence or to make comments or observations. The lookout is listed on the National Register of Historic Places.

There is no easily obtained water on the lookout spire. Snow, 200 feet or so from the shelter, can be used as a water source well into August. After the snow melts, the closest water is the tarn 0.2 mile west of the notch and about 200 feet south of the trail; a small way trail leads to the tarn. There is also a good campsite at this location.

It is difficult to reach the east end of Hidden Lake from the west end. To reach the east end, where there are splendid campsites near the lake, go one notch to the south after reaching the top of the Sibley Creek col. From there, go southeast cross-country; gain a bit of altitude and pass above a small, unnamed lake. Turn south and proceed several hundred yards; two obvious routes to the southeast bring you to the south end of the lake, where there is an outlet stream, two good campsites with fire pits, and absolutely gorgeous views in every direction. This route to the lake is as easy as the route described earlier and offers the best fishing, since the lakeshore is not steep on the east end, as it is on the west. The altitude gain to the lake via this route is roughly 2,500 feet in and 1,000 feet out. From the notch to the east end of the lake, it takes about 45 minutes down and 1 hour and 15 minutes out. The route is easy early in the season, when snow is present. It probably offers no difficulties after the snow is melted, but it has not been personally inspected in the snow-free state.

This trail opens later than most, and the seasons for use are from approximately August 1 to September 30. Substantial snow is not uncommon in October.

On the Forest Service side of the crest, there is a campsite in the forest about 0.8 mile from the trailhead. Once the headwaters of Sibley Creek are crossed, multiple campsites are available between Sibley Creek and the tarn 0.2 mile west of the saddle. Permits are required for overnight camping around Hidden Lake; no permit is required for camping in the national forest.

From the lookout, on a clear day, you can see forever. Glacier Peak and, indeed, Mount Rainier are visible to the south, as is Snow King Mountain in the nearer foreground. Sauk, Bald, Lookout Mountain, T-Bone Ridge, Mount Shuksan, Eldorado, Mount Baker, Hidden Lake Peak, and the Cascade Crest surround the mountaintop. The panorama of Boston, Sahale, Johannesberg, Spider, and Formidable Mountains is most impressive. Cascade Pass itself cannot be seen from the lookout, but it can be seen from the top of Hidden Lake Peak or from the crest of the Sibley Creek col.

An optional descent route is to climb Hidden Lake Peak and then follow the ridge crest downward to the Sibley col, descending from the col to the trail at that point. This is more easily done early in the season, when snow is present, than later in the year, when the steep meadow makes descent technically more difficult.

(July 1997)

LOOKOUT MOUNTAIN AND MONOGRAM LAKE

Lookout Mountain
Elevations
Trailhead:	1,200 feet
Destination:	5,719 feet (lookout building)
Altitude Gain	4,600 feet (including ups and downs)
Walking Time	In: 3 hours (light pack); 3 hours 30 minutes (full pack)
	Out: 1 hour 40 minutes (light pack); 2 hours (full pack)
Trail Length	4.7 miles
Accessibility	July 15 to October 15
Difficulty	Strenuous
Topographic Sheets	USGS: Marblemount
	Green Trails: Marblemount

Monogram Lake
Elevations
    Trailhead: 1,200 feet
    Destination: 4,900 feet (Monogram Lake)
    Other Significant Locations: Junction with Lookout Mountain trail, 4,300
               feet; ridge crest above and west of lake, 5,400 feet
Altitude Gain   4,400 feet in, 500 feet out
Walking Time   In: 3 hours 15 minutes (light pack); 4 hours (full pack)
                 Out: 2 hours 20 minutes (light pack); 2 hours 45 minutes (full
                 pack)
Trail Length   5 miles
Accessibility   July 15 to October 15
Difficulty   Strenuous
Topographic Sheets USGS: Marblemount
                   Green Trails: Marblemount

Follow the road as for Cascade Pass; drive about 7 miles east of Marblemount and roughly 0.5 mile past the entrance to the Mount Baker–Snoqualmie National Forest. The unobtrusive but signed trailhead is located on the north side of the road, 0.1 mile past a bridge. There is parking for four or five cars across the road from the trailhead. The first 2 miles of trail switchbacks up steeply and remorselessly through deep forest. At about 1 mile, several large, mossy rocks are passed; at times, there is an impressive growth of maidenhair fern on these boulders. At 1.5 miles, water is available via a 50-foot scrabble trail to the west. At 1.8 miles, an avalanche track is quite apparent to the west of the trail. At 1.9 miles, there are two campsites; water is available 25 feet to the east of the lower site. The elevation gained in the first 2 miles is about 2,500 feet. The trail then goes 0.3 mile through a small clearing, which is often overgrown in the summer before the trail is brushed. If wearing shorts, watch for stinging nettles in this segment of the footpath. Back in forest, the trail to the lookout continues northward and then westward. The tread breaks out into an open alpine area at about 3.7 miles, switchbacks across and up the meadow, crosses a saddle, and then switchbacks up the steep ridge to the lookout building itself. The tread in the meadow is not well maintained. A flat area just below the lookout offers several good tent sites. Water is available from a spring 0.3 mile below the summit.

    The no-longer-manned fire lookout, elevated on pilings about 30 feet above the mountaintop, is in fair condition. The roof was repaired in 1996; more work is needed to upgrade the structure. The view from the catwalk of the structure is impressive. The valleys of the Skagit and Cascade Rivers lie below. The jagged summits of the Picket Range are seen to the north. T-bone Ridge, Little and Big Devil Peaks, Eldorado, and Hidden Lake Peaks lie to the east; Sauk and Bald Mountains are to the west; and to the south loom the peaks of Snow King and Mount Chaval. Unfortunately, clear-cutting on the surrounding mountains has been extensive; the gaps in the forest cover detract from what would otherwise be a splendid 360-degree view.

The junction with the Monogram Lake trail is reached 2.9 miles from the trailhead; the intersection is marked with a trail post. Turning eastward, the Monogram Lake footpath scrambles up through forested hillside for approximately 1 mile, entering North Cascades National Park 0.2 mile from the junction. After about 1 mile, the trail breaks out into a lovely high meadow, crosses a branch of Lookout Creek, and angles south and up across a prominent ridge. From the ridge crest, there is an impressive view down into the Monogram Lake basin below and to the east. From the meadow to the ridge is about 0.4 mile, and from the ridge to the lake an additional 0.7 mile. There is about a 400-foot ascent from meadow to ridge and a 500-foot descent from ridge to lake.

There are three NPS designated campsites at Monogram Lake. Just before reaching the lake, the trail forks. The right fork leads to campsite #1 right beside the lake. The left fork leads to campsite #2, 0.1 mile north of campsite #1. From site #2, follow the scrabble trail 0.15 mile farther around the bluff and then up a knoll to reach isolated campsite #3 above the lake, where water can be obtained from a small stream 35 feet to the north. Fires are prohibited at Monogram Lake; stoves must be carried.

The lake outlet can easily be crossed on downed timber. A scrabble trail follows the lakeshore southeastward, passing a rock that juts into the lake (a good fishing site) and two prepark campsites that are currently being revegetated. The trail then turns upward and gains 100 feet in altitude to reach a bench above the lake, where there are several shallow tarns. The tread deteriorates progressively after the footpath leaves the lake. Eastward from the first bench, there is another flat area 100 feet higher, where there are more tarns. Intermittent faint tread continues eastward. Cross-country travel beyond this point brings the hiker to a saddle east of the lake, from which an unnamed ridge to the south can easily be climbed. For the more vigorous, it is possible to proceed northward on a moderately steep meadow to reach a knob at 6,844 feet near the summit of Little Devil Peak, located a bit farther north. Fishing in the lake is generally good, and the water is sufficiently warm to permit swimming on hot days.

Strong hikers can make the round-trip to lake or lookout in one day; only the very fit can do both in the same day. Most visitors prefer to overnight at one of the campsites mentioned. National park restrictions apply at Monogram Lake but are not applicable to the main trail or to Lookout Mountain. The lower portions of the trail are best avoided if the weather is hot; carry water, since there is none available for the first 1.5 miles of the trail. Bugs are often annoying, particularly in hot weather; carry repellent. The lookout, if unlocked, offers a refuge in inclement weather (check lock status at the Sedro Woolley Ranger Station before ascending). If you use the building, leave it in better condition than you found it.

Ptarmigan are common in the lookout area. Coyotes are sometimes seen near Monogram Lake.

Once you reach alpine meadow on either trail, the scenery rapidly improves. The high-country portions of both trails (beyond 3.8 miles for Lookout Mountain and 4 miles for Monogram Lake) are most enjoyable.

(August 1981)

THORNTON LAKES
Elevations
Trailhead:	2,700 feet
Destination:	4,500 feet (Thornton Lake)
High Point:	4,900 feet

Other Significant Locations: Unnamed peak above lakes, 6,234 feet

Altitude Gain	2,300 feet (including ups and downs)
Walking Time	In: 3 hours Out: 2 hours 30 minutes
Trail Length	5.2 miles
Accessibility	July 15 to October 15
Difficulty	Moderately strenuous
Pack	Light
Topographic Sheets	USGS: Marblemount
	Green Trails: Marblemount

The side road leading from the North Cascades Highway (NCH) to the trailhead is currently signed. Turn west near milepost 117, 3.6 miles from the main intersection in Newhalem, or 11.2 miles from Marblemount. In July 1981, it was a fair backcountry road and was passable without difficulty in a standard car. At 3.8 miles after the turnoff, take the right fork. After about 4 miles, there are impressive views to the east from the road. The road ends abruptly 5.3 miles from the NCH, where large boulders have fallen into the road; there is a bulletin board at this location. At 5.2 miles, there is a parking area for approximately twelve cars. Turnaround space, previously limited, has been improved. A vault toilet is located at the trailhead.

The trail begins at the road end and follows a rapidly deteriorating logging road. There is sufficient brush for the trail to be uncomfortable when the vegetation is wet. Water erosion has been substantial, and in places, the outer edge of the road has fallen or is in the process of falling away into the valley below. The footpath goes up at a moderate grade for roughly 1 mile, crosses Thornton Creek, and goes up more steeply for an additional mile. At this point, there is a promontory; good views from here may be obscured by brush growth. Follow the roadbed past this point about 200 feet. There is a trail post where the footpath leaves the abandoned road and rather unobtrusively enters the forest. There are views of the impressive peaks to the east (T-bone Ridge) from this section of the trail. It is 2.1 miles from the trailhead to where the footpath leaves the old road.

The initial trail to the lakes was probably created by fishermen. The portion of the trail within the recreational area remains a scrabble trail; the tread is slick and muddy and interlaced with multiple tree roots. This portion of the trail is in deep timber, without views. The North Cascades National Park is entered 3.4 miles from the trailhead.

Three-tenths of a mile farther, a bridge crosses a small stream. There is a dependable water supply at this point. Beyond this point, the tread substantially improves. The trail bypasses a bog and then switchbacks upward. After an additional half mile, there is a trail post; go right. One-tenth of a mile farther, note that the rehabilitation efforts made by the NCNP fifteen to twenty years ago to revegetate the steep scrabble trail to the lakes have been quite successful. Two-tenths of a mile farther, there is a trail post; go left. One-tenth of a mile farther, there is another trail post; again go left. One-tenth of a mile farther, the trail tops out on the ridge above lower Thornton Lake. (The old 50-degree gully scramble upward has been bypassed by the new switchbacks.) There is a splendid view of the lake below and the mountains in the distance from this point. Trappers Peak, 5,964 feet, is to the right of the lake. Mount Triumph, a 7,270-foot peak in the Picket Range, looms beyond the lake to the northwest.

A steep, muddy, slippery descent, occasionally over steps blasted out of the granite, brings one to the outlet creek of lower Thornton Lake. A mildly difficult descent on granite boulders brings the hiker to creekside, where the stream is easily crossed on either boulders or downed timber. Just past the crossing is the designated campsite, where there is space for a maximum of five alpine tents; an additional tent site is available 100 yards above on flat granite for tents that do not require stakes. Campfires are prohibited at this location, and camping is not allowed anywhere else from trailhead to snow on the ridges above the lakes.

The formal trail ends at the lakeshore campsite. From here, it is possible to scramble up and down for several hundred yards to another gulch; an indistinct way trail can be used if located. This trail contours around the lake, giving access to various fishing areas. There are two higher lakes, and those who wish to explore or fish them or to climb to the peaks beyond should contour upward to the left from this last gulch, gaining about 1,000 feet in altitude. It is possible to drop down to any of the lakes in the valley below or to continue to an unnamed peak, elevation 6,234 feet, to the west of the lower lake. This is also the route to the southeast ridge of Mount Triumph. It is possible to drop down from the unnamed peak and "ridge-run" a high heather and meadow crest for half a mile or so to the south.

Views from the high point are impressive. Thornton Lakes lie below. Mount Triumph is to the north. Blum, Hagan, and Damnation Peaks can be seen to the west. To the south and east are T-bone Ridge and Lookout Mountain; to the east, Pyramid and Colonial Peaks.

Allow two hours light-packed from the lower lake to the summit of the unnamed peak. The altitude gain is roughly 1,700 feet.

Early in the year, if snow is present, a more direct route would be to go up via the Thornton Creek valley, from the point where the abandoned road crosses the creek, directly to the lower lake; however, without snow, this is a formidable bushwhack through slide alder and vine maple and is not recommended.

(July 1981)

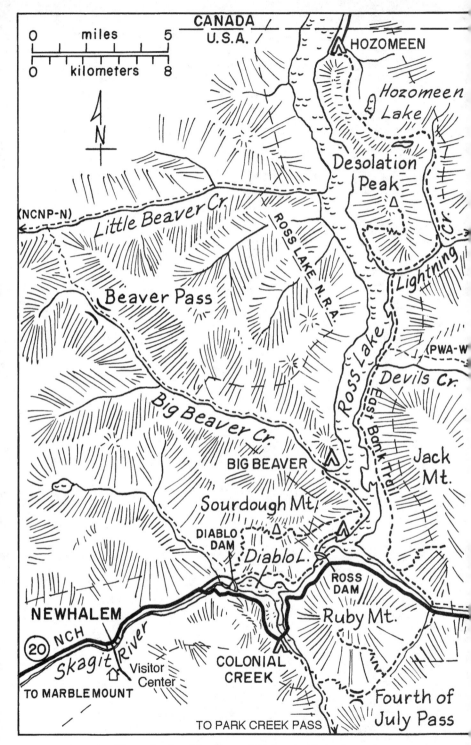

Ross Lake National Recreation Area

Ross Lake National Recreation Area

ROSS LAKE—EAST (EAST BANK, LIGHTNING, WILLOW LAKE)

Elevations

Trailhead: 1,800 feet (NCH) ; 1,650 feet (Hozomeen)

Destination: 2,900 feet

High Point: 2,900 feet (Willow Lake)

Other Significant Locations: Hidden Hand Pass, 2,500 feet; Nightmare Camp, 2,150 feet

Altitude Gain   2,800 feet (including ups and downs)

Walking Time   In: 2–3 days   Out: 2–3 days

Trail Length   30 miles

Accessibility   Mid-April to mid-November

Difficulty   Moderate throughout, but long

Pack   Full

Topographic Sheets USGS: Hozomeen, Skagit Peak, Pumpkin Mountain, Ross Dam, Crater Mountain

Green Trails: Ross Lake, Jack Mountain, Diablo Dam, Mount Logan

The south trailhead is located along the North Cascades Highway (NCH) 8.2 miles east of the Thunder Arm Bridge and 33 miles east of Marblemount. There is parking for fifty or sixty cars on the north side of the highway.

From this point, it is 30.1 miles to the trailhead at Hozomeen. Since most hikers start at one trailhead or the other rather than making the entire trip, the south portion of the trail is described to Lightning Creek. The north portion of the trail from Hozomeen to Lightning Creek is then discussed.

From State Route 20, the trail drops down to the Ruby Creek bridge 0.2 mile away. Turn left at this point and follow the trail along the north side of Ruby Creek. After about 0.1 mile, the trail forks; the upper, broader trail is the correct one. A 2.6-mile walk, taking about 50 minutes, brings you to the junction with both the East Bank and the Little Jack Mountain trailheads; from here, the East Bank trail goes north (left), and Little Jack goes east (hard right). There are minimal views and little change in altitude along the Ruby Creek trail segment. The Hidden Hand campsite is located 0.5 mile past the junction toward Ross Lake.

From the junction, the East Bank trail goes upward into a saddle (Hidden Hand Pass) at about 1 mile, gaining about 800 feet in altitude in the process. It then gradually loses altitude until it reaches the Roland Creek campsite 3.7 miles from the junction. Only an occasional glimpse of the surrounding vistas can be seen throughout this segment of the trail. Beyond Roland Creek, the trail remains near the lakeshore, and scenic vistas continue until Lightning Creek is reached. From Roland Creek, it is 1.3 miles to the May Creek campsite; from May Creek, it is 0.9 mile to the Rainbow Point campsite. From Rainbow Point, it is 2.3 miles to Devils Creek.

From 1 mile south to 0.5 mile north of Devils Creek are the best views along the trail. From Devils Creek, it is 1.4 miles to the junction with the Devils Dome trail and the way footpath to reach the Devils Junction Camp about 0.2 mile to the west. From the junction to Lightning Creek is 3.5 miles. From the Lightning Creek bridge, it is 0.1 mile to the Lightning Creek trail junction and an additional 0.1 mile to the Lightning Creek Camp. From the trailhead to the Lightning Creek trail junction is 16 miles.

Since this is a lowland trail, it is generally snowfree from April to November. In light snow years, it may even be accessible periodically during the winter. It therefore offers a conditioning trail for spring and fall use when the high country is closed. There are fine views of Jack Mountain, Hozomeen Peak, the Pickets, and, of course, Ross Lake from the trail. Unfortunately, in the spring, the substantial drawdown of the Ross Lake reservoir creates an aesthetic eyesore.

A few yards past the junction with the Lightning Creek trail is the junction with the Desolation Peak trail. It is 2.1 miles up this trail to Jack Point. See Desolation Peak for information beyond the Jack Point lakeshore.

Hiking time is six to seven hours from the trailhead to the Lightning Creek Camp, with an additional hour to reach the Desolation trailhead.

There are two precautions with regard to this area. First, ticks are prevalent in the area; hikers should inspect one another frequently and remove any ticks before they embed themselves. Second, *Giardia,* a protozoan parasite that causes diarrhea and other symptoms, is prevalent in the area around Ross Lake. All water should be boiled or treated appropriately with iodine before drinking. Water access is not a problem.

Campfires are allowed at all designated campsites. Since firewood gathering has an adverse impact on all campsites, considerate campers will keep fires small or omit them altogether. Bears are fairly common, particularly at the Lightning Creek Camp. Be sure to bear-proof food supplies.

The north trailhead at Hozomeen is reached by driving the Trans-Canada Highway east from Vancouver; shortly before reaching the town of Hope, turn right (or south) on the Silver-Skagit Road immediately before a highway bridge; when visited in 1975, the road was signed Ross Lake. The road runs 39 miles from this turnoff to the trailhead. Immediately after passing the old City Light bunkhouse, follow the side road that goes upward, turns back to the north, and passes through a substantial part of the Hozomeen Campground; the trail begins immediately east of a cabin at the road end loop, about 0.2 mile on the side road from the main road. The driving time for the 39 miles is about 1 hour. Twenty-six miles from the Trans-Canada Highway is the Silver Tip Campground. From the trailhead, it is 3 miles to the Hozomeen Lake trail junction, 5 miles to Willow Lake, and 7.7 miles to Nightmare Camp. The walking time to the Hozomeen Lake trail junction is about 1 hour and 15 minutes; the side trail to the lake is 0.6 mile in length, takes about 15 minutes to walk, and terminates in a campground on a promontory out into the lake, where there are spaces for about ten campsites. From this promontory, there is an impressive view of the lake and the two peaks of Hozomeen Mountain looming up in the background to the northeast. Fishing is good in the lake; fly-fishermen will want to bring some sort of portable raft, since the forest comes right down to the lakeshore.

Two miles (45 minutes walking time) away from the junction is the Willow Lake Camp, altitude 2,900 feet; this is the highest point of this trail. At either end of Willow Lake, there are good views of the peaks to the east and west.

East of Willow Lake, the snow tends to stay late in the spring; look for yellow metal blazes on the trees for help finding the route. One hour farther away, and 2.7 miles distant, is Nightmare Camp. East of Willow Lake, the trail drops fairly sharply, goes about 0.2 mile through a beautiful little canyon paralleling a mossy stream, and then suddenly breaks out high above a hanging valley. Near this point, if you move off the trail 20 to 30 feet under a grassy knoll, there is an excellent view of Mount Hozomeen to the northwest. Indeed, the only good views of Hozomeen are at Hozomeen Lake and at this point. Nightmare Camp is set in a grove of huge cedars close by Lightning Creek trail. Skagit Peak to the east can be seen from this area.

The trail crosses Lightning Creek on a well-constructed bridge east of Nightmare Camp and proceeds southward along the east side of the river in deep forest. From the bridge, it is about 2.5 miles to Deerlick Camp. For those interested in fishing, the river can be reached without major difficulty along most of the route. The path is mainly in the deep forest; views of the surrounding peaks are difficult to obtain. Walking time is approximately 1 hour; altitude loss is a bit over 200 feet.

A trail post marks the way trail to the west to Deerlick Camp; a 0.1-mile side trail leads to the river. There are two campsites by the creek, dank even in good weather conditions; two additional campsites lie on a bench above the creek; and a backcountry toilet is near the upper camp areas. There is also a cabin here, often used by NCNP trail crews. This is a pleasant sylvan campsite; two huge cedar trees tower above the cabin and bridge.

Two-tenths of a mile farther, the trail post marking the junction with the Boundary (Three Fools) trail is encountered. From this point, it is 0.8 mile to the Pasayten Wilderness boundary and 3 miles to the Little Fish shelter to the east, and 4 miles to Ross Lake to the west.

Going westward from the bridge and cabin, the trail goes upward for roughly 0.9 mile, gaining about 350 vertical feet. Near the cabin, the trail is in dank, deep forest. Shortly thereafter, it is in dense, young forest; the homogeneous growth at this point is probably due to uniform regrowth following a burn. A bit farther on, a number of extensively branched lichens (Old Man's Beard) can be seen hanging from most of the tree limbs in the area.

The trail levels off about 500 feet above Lightning Creek and continues westward for a bit over 2 miles without gaining or losing much altitude. About 1 mile away, and approximately 900 vertical feet above the Lightning Creek Campground, it begins a switchbacking descent to the lake. At the high point, there are good views of the lake to the west and south, of the Eastbank Trail bridge directly below, and of Mount Prophet to the west. The junction with the Desolation Peak trail is 0.15 mile from the campground, and marked by a trail post. A few yards on, also marked with a trail post, is the junction with the Eastbank Trail, running to the south and across a sturdy suspension bridge over the mouth of Lightning Creek. A short trail 0.1 mile long leads from this junction to the Lightning Creek Campground, where there are tables, rest rooms, and campsites for five or six parties.

Walking time from the Deer Lick Cabin to the campground is 1 hour and 30 minutes. From the campground, the NCH can be reached via the East Bank trail (described elsewhere). Alternatively, arrangements can be made in advance for a boat pickup to return the hiking party to the Ross Lake Resort, located about 1.5 miles from the NCH.

The nicest campsite without question is at Hozomeen Lake. There is about a 1,200-foot altitude gain from the trailhead to Willow Lake. The walking time is about 3 hours to Nightmare Camp from the trailhead. Wood is scarce at the Hozomeen site but adequate at the other campsites. Campfires are allowed at all campgrounds.

An early-spring low-water alternative for experienced hikers is to walk the lakeshore about 9 miles on beaches, ledges, and occasionally class 2 rock between Hozomeen and Lightning Creek. This route is impossible when the lake is full.

Birds are frequent alongside the trail; birdsong echoes through the trees as the hiker passes. Grouse, deer, and occasionally bears are seen along this trail and at the Lightning Creek Camp. Wildflowers, particularly Indian paintbrush, are often seen in late spring.

(South trail, spring 1971; north trail, June 1975)

DESOLATION LOOKOUT

Elevations

Trailhead:	1,600 feet
Destination:	6,100 feet (Desolation Lookout)
Altitude Gain	4,500 feet (including ups and downs)
Walking Time	In: 4 hours 15 minutes Out: 2 hours
Trail Length	4.7 miles one-way
Accessibility	July 15 to early October
Difficulty	Strenuous
Pack	Full
Topographic Sheets	USGS: Hozomeen Mountain 7.5'
	Green Trails: Ross Lake

The trailhead is on the east side of Ross Lake, 2.1 miles from the junction with the Lightning Creek trail; the lakeshore trailhead is about 0.3 mile south of Jack Point and 1.25 miles north of Cat Island. Four switchbacks up from the lakeshore, the way trail intersects with the trail from Lightning Creek. The Desolation Lookout trail then switchbacks up moderately steeply through dry, fairly open country for about 1 mile, offering good views up and down Ross Lake intermittently. The trail then enters brush and small trees; there are minimal views until you break out in the meadows between 2.5 and 3 miles. The only water is at one small spring at about 2.5 miles. The fourth mile is in meadow, switchbacking up fairly steeply until the ridge crest is reached. From there, the trail swings north through gorgeously blooming wildflowers to the false summit of Desolation Peak, dips down slightly into a saddle, and then ascends several hundred feet to the true summit where the lookout is situated. Grouse and hummingbirds are commonly seen along the trail. The pleasant noise made by crickets is also heard by the wayfarer.

In a normal snow year, all snow has melted from the summit ridge by August 1, and obtaining water thereafter is a substantial problem. For this reason, June and July are the best months to visit this area. The Park Service has established a designated campsite on the summit ridge 1 mile south of the fire lookout. The camp meets "bear standards," having separate sleeping and cooking areas. There are three tent sites. If snow is not available, water must be carried up from a spring about 2 miles below. Fires are prohibited.

From the summit, there are magnificent views down into the Ross Lake basin and into the Little Beaver valley to the west. Ruby, Colonial, and Pyramid Peak are easily seen to the south. To the north are the black fangs of Hozomeen Mountain. To the east and south in the Pasayten Wilderness are Castle Peak, Skagit Peak, Spratt Mountain, Devils Dome, and Jack Mountain. Mount Baker and Mount Shuksan are also visible beyond the Pickets to the west. Surprisingly, hikers can hear the water plunging into Ross Lake from waterfalls on the far side of the lake, at least 3 miles away. Tame deer are common in the lookout area. Unfortunately, deerflies are a substantial problem in midsummer.

The best means of access is to arrange in advance at the Ross Lake Resort for lake transportation to and from the trailhead. It is a two-day, one-way walk to reach the area from either Hozomeen or the North Cascades Highway.

Warnings: Ticks are common in the lower part of the trail, and *Giardia* is prevalent in water in the area. Boil water or treat it with iodine.

It is possible to cross-country down the north slope of Desolation and climb two other somewhat lower peaks to the north.

The lookout is manned in the summer. With the exception of the fire watcher, people are uncommon in the area, in view of the access difficulties. There is accordingly a sense of remoteness and isolation, offering the opportunity to get away from people and the problems of civilization. However, NCNP staff advise that this walk is increasingly used as a day hike by organized groups on leisurely East Bank hikes or on Ross Lake canoe trips. A permit is required for overnight camping.

(July 1967)

FOURTH OF JULY PASS–RUBY MOUNTAIN
Elevations
Trailhead: 1,300 feet
Destination: 3,700 feet (Fourth of July Pass)
Other Significant Locations: Ruby Mountain, 7,408 feet
Altitude Gain   2,500 feet (including ups and downs)
Walking Time   In: 2 hours 30 minutes   Out: 1 hour 45 minutes
Trail Length   3 miles one-way
Accessibility   Mid-May to early November
Difficulty   Moderately strenuous
Pack   Light
Topographic Sheets   USGS: Ross Dam, Crater Mountain
                            Green Trails: Diablo Dam, Mount Logan

The trailhead is 1.5 miles from the Colonial Creek Campground on the Thunder Creek trail; see Thunder Creek for more information on access to the trailhead.

This trail gives access to Fourth of July Pass, Ruby Mountain, and the Panther Creek trail, which descends to the North Cascades Highway. The trail leaves to the left, or east, ascending moderately steeply via switchbacks on fair-quality tread for about 0.7 mile. After crossing a creek, the trail traverses to the southeast for about 0.4 mile and then again switchbacks up moderately steeply, topping out about 2.9 miles from the trail junction. A large rock immediately to the left of the top-out point is an excellent place to stop for a breather or for lunch and offers excellent views of both Colonial Peak and Snowfield Peak to the west. A short walk 0.1 mile farther up the trail and then 100 feet south to a knoll offers striking views of the Eldorado massif to the southwest; Colonial and Snowfield Peaks can also be seen at this point. The designated Fourth of July Pass campsite is located approximately 100 yards to the north from the top-out point, roughly 3 miles from the junction. The first tent site is roomy and level and has a fire pit, but trees limit views. The second site, 0.1 mile north, is smaller and slopes, but it has a view. Water is available 0.1 mile north of the second site; follow a faint trail to a stream.

Several creeks are crossed en route, so access to water is no problem, at least in the spring. This is when calypso orchids bloom in profusion along the trail. Trillium, Oregon grape, and yellow wood violets also bloom along this trail in May.

Through breaks in the forest cover, Diablo Lake can be glimpsed occasionally. Heat can be a problem for those ascending the trail if the weather is warm.

Although the average hiker and camper stops at Fourth of July Pass, there are other options. Hikers can proceed eastward; initially, the trail loses altitude gradually. About 1 mile beyond the top-out point, there is a poorly signed junction. The trail to the right continues down Panther Creek to the North Cascades Highway about 5 miles away. The less apparent trail to the left leads to the summit of Ruby Mountain.

Those having two cars could make the loop down Panther Creek or, alternatively, take their chances hitchhiking back to the trailhead at the Colonial Creek Campground from the Panther Creek trailhead; the road distance between the two trailheads is 8.5 miles. The Panther Creek trail is not described in this book but is reported in the *North Cascades Highway Guide* (see the Bibliography).

Only the experienced wilderness traveler in good physical condition should attempt the ascent of Ruby Mountain. The trail is not maintained, and the tread is quite difficult to locate in places. Route finding is a constant problem, and the inexperienced can easily become lost.

Fourth of July Pass (June 1996)
Ruby Mountain (August 1972)

SOURDOUGH MOUNTAIN

Elevations

Trailhead: 900 feet; via Pierce Mountain Way, 2,100 feet
Destination: 5,997 feet (lookout)
Other Significant Locations: Sourdough campsite, 5,000 feet; Pierce Camp,
                    5,100 feet

Altitude Gain   5,250 feet; via Pierce Mountain Way, 4,100 feet (including
                    ups and downs)

Walking Time   In: 3–4 hours (to campsite)   Out: 2 hours (from campsite)

Trail Length   5.2 miles; to campsite, 3.8 miles; via Pierce Mountain Way,
                    5.1 miles to lookout; 4.4 miles to Pierce Camp (one-way)

Accessibility   July 15 to October 15

Difficulty   Strenuous

Pack   Full to campsite; light from campsite to lookout

Topographic Sheets   USGS: Diablo Dam, Ross Dam 7.5'
                    Green Trails: Diablo Dam, Ross Lake

Take the North Cascades Highway from Marblemount to Diablo; take
the left fork before the highway crosses Gorge Lake and continue into Diablo
proper. The trail begins immediately behind the plastic-covered swimming
pool in Diablo. Monotonously steep switchbacks make the first 2 miles unpleasant, particularly if the day is hot. At about 0.5 mile, the trail breaks out over a
rocky bluff, giving a nice view of the town of Diablo and Gorge Lake. At about
0.9 mile, there is scrabble access to water from a small creek to the west. About
1.5 miles, there is a small stream in the middle of the trail. At about 2.2 miles,
a 100-yard side trip brings you to a rocky bluff overlooking Diablo Lake; there
is a good view from this point. This is an excellent stopping point for lunch or
for those who do not wish to continue further; a way trail marked by blazes and
a cairn indicate where to leave the main trail. The national park is entered
at 2.5 miles. There is water at 2.6 miles. At about 2.7 miles, the trail breaks
into meadow and becomes less steep, although the tread quality deteriorates
thereafter.

The trail then goes almost directly northward, reaching the cleft between
the access ridge and Sourdough Mountain at about 3.8 miles. The Sourdough
campsite is located here at about 5,000 feet elevation. Water is available from
Sourdough Creek, which is crossed without difficulty. In the fall, this is the last
available water. Earlier in the season, water can generally be obtained from
snowfields along the summit ridge and small creeks en route upward.

From this point, the footpath to the lookout ascends via switchbacks up
the meadow, goes moderately upward and eastward until about 0.25 mile west

of the lookout, and then again switchbacks up through the meadow to the top of the ridge; for the last quarter mile, the trail traverses the ridge crest. The view from the lookout is spectacular. Five great valleys radiate out from the lookout like the spokes of a wheel (upper and lower Skagit, Ruby, Thunder, and Big Beaver). Diablo Lake immediately below sparkles in the afternoon sun. Ross Lake is an azure ribbon cleaving the mountains to the north. Sourdough Lake is visible to the northwest. Grouse, eagles, bears, marmots, pikas, ptarmigan, and hawks frequent the area. Deer are common and may be pests in the camp areas. The fall colors on the ridge blaze red and yellow when backlit by the sun. Meadow flowers are superb in season.

Cross-country travel from the Sourdough campsite up the Sourdough Creek col brings you without great difficulty to the ridge crest, where there is a fine view of the Picket Range to the northwest. From here, it would probably be possible to reach Sourdough Lake by dropping down about 1,000 feet and traversing cross-country to the northeast; the lake is not accessible from the lookout area itself.

One of the lookouts prior to 1965 had left the following quotation within the building: "Under the shadow of the pine and plum tree sleeps Unkuku, the Holy Mountain Man, on a high rock; He counts not the years, for there are no calendars in the mountains."

There are few more miserable trails in the North Cascades than the first 2 miles of this route. The hike should be attempted only by those in excellent physical condition, preferably on a cool day. In midsummer, in addition to heat, the deerflies are quite unpleasant. The best times to explore this area are in late September and early October when it is cooler, there are fewer bugs, and the fall color is at its most splendid.

An alternative but longer route to the lookout, which I have walked only from the lookout to the Pierce campsite, involves dropping down from Highway 20, crossing Ross Dam, and proceeding along the Big Beaver trail to the Pierce Mountain Way trailhead, roughly 3.8 miles from the highway. From there, it is 4.4 miles to Pierce Camp, altitude approximately 5,100 feet, and an additional 0.7 mile to the lookout. The altitude gain is roughly 600 vertical feet less, but the distance is about 3.7 miles greater. With the use of two cars, or by hitchhiking along the North Cascades Highway, it is possible to make a loop trip, ascending by one trail and descending by the other. Between the campsite and the lookout, the Pierce Mountain Way trail is difficult to locate; follow cairns or simply climb rock, heather, and snow to the top. If starting at the top, head for the flat tarn area below and to the northeast. A forest fire several years ago ravaged a portion of the lower trail area; you should inquire at the Marblemount Ranger Station about the condition of the Pierce Mountain access route, since it is a secondary trail and maintenance may vary from year to year. Estimated hiking times from the highway to the lookout via Pierce Mountain Way are 6 to 7 hours in and 4 to 5 hours out.

Campfires are not allowed at either of the campsites in the area; accordingly, a small stove must be backpacked if hot food is to be prepared.

When inspected in July 1981, the two tent spaces at both designated campsites were substandard. The walk between the two camps, however, is glorious. Experienced backcountry travelers can also follow the Sourdough Ridge westward, connecting cross-country with the Sourdough campsite.

The original lookout house was built in 1917 and rebuilt in the mid-1930s. The structure, presently in excellent condition, is manned only at times of high fire danger. If a fire watcher is on duty, you will usually be welcomed inside for a cool or hot drink, an inspection of the equipment, and an explanation of the lookout's duties.

(July 1981)

Lake Chelan National Recreation Area

AGNES CREEK (PACIFIC CREST TRAIL)

Elevations

Trailhead:	1,700 feet
Destination:	5,843 feet (Suiattle Pass)
High Point:	5,843 feet

Altitude Gain   4,400 feet (including ups and downs)

Walking Time   In: 10 hours 30 minutes   Out: 8 hours
(allow at least 3 days)

Trail Length   19.8 miles

Accessibility   July 15 to early October

Difficulty   Moderately strenuous

Pack   Full

Topographic Sheets   USGS: McGregor Mountain, Mount Lyall, Agnes Mountain, Holden
Green Trails: McGregor Mountain, Holden

A tenth of a mile beyond High Bridge (10.5 miles from Stehekin Landing) is the Pacific Crest Trail (PCT)–Agnes Creek trailhead, well signed and easily reached from the bus stop at the High Bridge guard station.

The trail descends 0.1 mile to cross Agnes Creek on a sturdy bridge and then switchbacks upward for an additional mile, gaining altitude but minimal westward distance. At 1.5 miles, it passes through a grove of large cedar trees. At 2.5 miles, the footpath leaves Lake Chelan National Recreation Area and enters the Glacier Peak Wilderness. There is a campsite on the right at 3 miles and a scrabble route to the south side of Agnes Gorge. At 5 miles, Pass Creek is crossed on a bridge; there are two good and three fair but buggy campsites immediately past the bridge. A tenth of a mile past the bridge is the junction with the trail accessing the west fork of Agnes Creek. Fivemile Camp is located here on a fairly flat, grassy bluff with scattered small scrub pine trees and a fair view; there are many places to pitch a tent here. Walking time from the trailhead is 2 hours.

At 6 miles, the trail crosses a high, rocky bluff and turns southward. From the bluff, there is a good view of the Agnes River canyon below and of Agnes Mountain above. At 6.5 miles, there is a campsite on the right. Swamp Creek is crossed on a bridge at 8.6 miles; there are a number of campsites here in the deep woods adjacent to the creek. Just past the bridge is the junction with the primitive Swamp Creek trail. Walking time from Fivemile Camp to here is 1.5 hours.

At 9.5 miles, there is a campsite on the left with a fire pit and enough

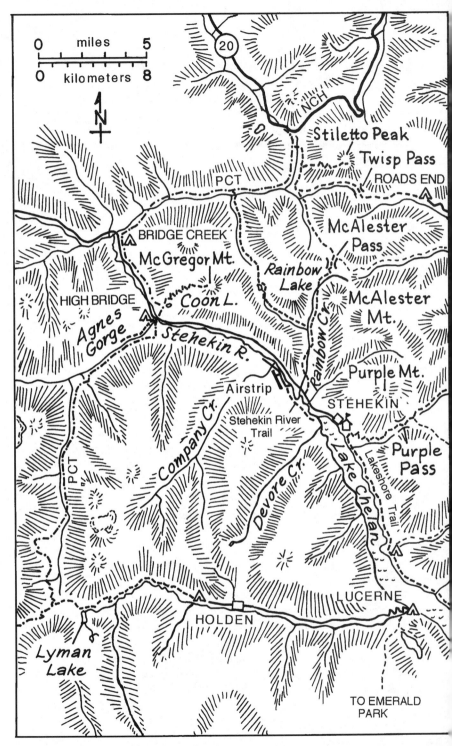

Lake Chelan National Recreation Area

space for two tents (probably Cedar Camp). This pleasant place is adjacent to the south fork of Agnes Creek.

Hemlock Camp (HC) (13.1 miles, 3,600 feet) is located alongside the creek in deep, pleasant woods. Amenities are four to five tent sites, two fire pits, and a wilderness privy. Unfortunately, flies and yellow jackets infest the area. Glimpses of Needle and Dark Peaks to the east can be had through the trees. The sun sets early beneath the high rock cliff at the base of Bannock Mountain, shading the camp. Deer wander through the camp intermittently. Walking time from Swamp Creek to here is 1 hour and 45 minutes.

A few feet south of HC is the junction of the PCT and the south fork of the Agnes trail leading to Cloudy Pass. The older route up the creek is shorter but less scenic. The PCT crosses Agnes Creek on a footlog 0.1 mile from the junction. When wet, consider a ford rather than walking the log. A few feet after the crossing, there is an overhanging granite boulder suitable for a rain shelter. Fifteen minutes from HC, the PCT breaks out into the first of a series of treeless areas, allowing the hiker to obtain the first unimpeded view of the surrounding countryside (campers at HC could come here to watch the last rays of the sun illuminate the spires of Dark and Needle Peaks). The footpath gains altitude steadily after the creek crossing. At 14 miles, the tread passes underneath a high granite wall to the west. There is water at about 14.5 miles, and 0.1 mile past the water, there is a signed way trail to a campsite below the trail on the left. (All tent sites between HC and Suiattle Pass are located off the trail. Tent symbols on posts mark the way to the camping areas, which cannot be seen from the PCT.) The next camping area is 0.2 mile farther. At 15.1 miles, cross a creek on a bridge in an unnamed basin; look for tasty blueberries on either side of the stream. The tread goes upward for the next mile. About 2 hours out of HC, note the view down the Agnes valley. About 4 miles out of HC, there are several campsites both above and below the footpath as the trail contours around the northeast flank of Sitting Bull Mountain; this is the high point of the trail at about 17.1 miles. After 0.2 mile in trees, cross a flowered talus slope. At 18 miles, the tread drops about 300 feet on switchbacks and then crosses an impressive talus bowl. Look upward to the west and observe the scar from which avalanched this immense amount of rock. There is a campsite below the trail on the south side of the valley. Three hours and 45 minutes out of HC (19.3 miles), the junction with the tread descending to the Agnes basin is intersected. At 4 hours, there is a campsite off the trail to the right. Ten minutes farther, Suiattle Pass is reached, approximately 19.8 miles from the trailhead. The distance from HC to Suiattle Pass is about 6.7 miles; walking time is a bit over 4 hours. From the pass, a short scramble up to the northeast leads to a viewpoint overlooking the upper Agnes valley. Visible peaks include Plummer, Sitting Bull, Cloudy, North Star, Dark, Needle, and Goode in the distance.

There is no water at the pass, but water can be obtained a short distance to the west or acquired on the ascent after passing the talus bowl.

From Suiattle Pass, trails lead to Holden, Miners Ridge, and Image Lake, and south via the Pacific Crest Trail.

(August 1985)

AGNES GORGE

Elevations

Trailhead:	1,700 feet
Destination:	2,000 feet
High Point:	2,000 feet
Altitude Gain	300 feet
Walking Time	2 hours
Trail Length	5 miles
Accessibility	May to October
Difficulty	Moderately easy
Pack	Light
Topographic Sheets	USGS: McGregor Mountain, Mount Lyall, Agnes Mountain
	Green Trails: McGregor Mountain

The trailhead is 0.2 mile above High Bridge and 0.1 mile beyond the Pacific Crest trailhead. The trailhead is signed. There are nice views of McGregor Peak to the east from the first portion of the trail, and a spectacular view of Agnes Mountain to the west at about 2 miles. Wildflowers are impressive, as are blooming dogwoods in season. Trail distance is 2.5 miles to the gorge; walking time is approximately 1 hour in each direction, and elevation gain is minimal either way.

The trail enters the Glacier Peak Wilderness and leaves the national park at 1.3 miles. Just beyond 2 miles, there is an impressive view of the Agnes River running swiftly below. There are many wildflowers in this area. Just before the end of the trail, multiple trilliums bloom in late May, and an occasional calypso orchid can be found.

The main trail terminates at the chasm of Agnes Gorge. Thirty years ago, the Forest Service had a suspension bridge at this location. It gradually became hazardous due to heavy winter snowfall and was eventually destroyed. An old metal chair seat from the bridge is still there.

Hikers should stay on a way trail leaving the main trail a few feet before the gorge and follow it 0.1 mile west and down. The head of the gorge can be reached with reasonable safety in this manner, and it is possible (with care) to climb a great pile of driftwood and actually stand on top of the precipice above the major falls within the gorge. The place is hypnotically beautiful. A waterfall coming from the south side makes the area even more impressive. There is a good campsite for two tents here. Note the footlog across the creek above the cataract. It would probably be possible to inch across with reasonable safety. A fall here, however, might well be fatal if one were swept into the torrent below. Great care should be exercised in this area.

This is a splendid trail for mountain views, wildflowers, and views of the river and the impressive chasm and cataracts. There are reasonable amounts of water en route (at least in late May), but no other obvious campsites. Beware of ticks; use repellent and check one another after coming off the trail.

(May 1978)

LAKESHORE
Elevations
Trailhead:	1,100 feet
Destination:	1,100 feet
High Point:	2,000 feet

Altitude Gain	3,000 feet (including ups and downs)
Walking Time	2 days
Trail Length	17 miles one-way
Accessibility	April to November
Difficulty	Moderately strenuous
Pack	Full
Topographic Sheets	USGS: Stehekin, Sun Mountain, Lucerne, Prince Creek
	Green Trails: Stehekin, Lucerne, Prince Creek

The boat disembarkation point is 0.2 mile north of the mouth of Prince Creek. Walk southeast to the creek and cross it on a narrow but serviceable log bridge. There are a number of satisfactory campsites near the creek mouth. From the Prince Creek trail junction, it is 6 miles to Meadow Creek, 11 miles to Fish Creek, and 17 miles to Stehekin. Less than 1 mile to the south is the official Prince Creek Campground.

In the first mile to the north, the trail gains 500 feet and reaches a good viewpoint at the 16-mile point. There is another corner with a good view 0.5 mile beyond.

At about 14 miles, there is another substantial altitude gain. (Mile marker signs have been removed.) Shortly thereafter, Rex Creek is forded. At about 11 miles from Stehekin, cross Cascade Creek. There is one poor campsite near the creek.

At 10 miles is Meadow Creek, where there is another unattractive shelter (in good condition) in the deep forest. If you walk down toward the lake, you will reach private property, liberally marked with No Trespassing signs.

In this vicinity, the tread enters the 1985 burn. The character of the next

0.5 mile of the trail has been impacted by this fire. Burned-out trees continue to fall. Access to sunlight has changed the character of the understory of the forest.

Seven-tenths of a mile beyond the shelter, leave the trail to the left, lose about 150 feet of elevation, and find two lovely campsites in the ponderosa pines just above the lake. A short scramble over class 2 rock gives access to the lakeshore for bathing, drinking, and cooking water. There are great views from this point to the north and south. Directly across the lake from this campsite is Lucerne. There are no other satisfactory camping areas from here to Moore Point, 3 miles to the north.

The first 7.7 miles are hot, even in the spring; have lots of ups and downs; and are fatiguing. Watch for ticks and, more importantly, look out for rattlesnakes.

At 9.8 miles, the trail loses several hundred feet of elevation as it switchbacks down to a pasture east of Moore. Four-tenths of a mile farther, the Fish Creek bridge is reached. At this point, there are two important junctions; it is 0.5 mile downstream to the lakeshore and the established campsite and trail shelter at Moore Point. Lilacs of the old Moore Hotel still bloom in season near the campground. Upstream, the Fish Creek trail leads to the high meadows. Two-tenths of a mile beyond the bridge is the junction of several roads.

The route now gains 1,000 feet in the next 1.5 miles to reach the high point on Hunt's Bluff at the 5-mile marker. This is an excellent place to eat lunch.

After descending the bluff, cross Hunt's Creek. After an additional mile, the boundary of the Lake Chelan National Recreation Area is reached, and shortly beyond this point is the Flick Creek shelter, located on the lakeshore with a delightful view to the south. There are few flat spots around the shelter. This area probably could not handle more than 5 or 6 overnight campers simultaneously, and it is the only designated campsite between the national recreation area boundary and Stehekin.

Cross pretty Flick Creek 1 mile north of the shelter. Fourmile Creek is 0.9 mile farther. One mile from the Stehekin Landing, the footpath drops down to the lakeshore; there are good views at this point. Shortly thereafter, Hazard Creek is crossed. One-tenth of a mile from the north trailhead, a rocky promontory alongside the trail offers great downlake views.

To access the north trailhead from the Stehekin Landing, following the road past the Golden West Visitor Center and cabin #11. Continue between buildings and above the parking lot east to the start of the trail.

Although called the Lakeshore trail, most of the time it is 200 to 500 feet above the lake, making it difficult to reach the lake for water, campsites, and so forth. The elevation gain in the entire 17 miles is 3,000 feet. Water is available from the creeks mentioned or at the lake, if reachable. Good campsites are scarce. Perhaps 5 of the 17 miles are in forest, without views, but the other 12 miles are relatively open and provide panoramas up, down, and across the lake. This hike is best done in the spring or fall and should be avoided during the heat of the summer.

High boots and long pants are recommended, since almost everyone walking this 17-mile distance will meet at least one rattlesnake. Check carefully when reaching Stehekin to remove any ticks that have been accumulated during the trip.

Note: The southern half of this trail is within the Lake Chelan–Sawtooth Wilderness Area.

(May 1979; north 4 miles, April 1995)

MCALESTER PASS AND LAKE
Elevations
Trailhead:	1,200 feet (Stehekin Road)
Destination:	6,017 feet (McAlester Pass)
High Point:	6,017 feet

Other Significant Locations: Bench Camp, 3,800 feet; Fireweed Camp, 3,900 feet; North Cascades Highway, 4,400 feet

Altitude Gain 2,200 feet

Walking Time 2 days

Trail Length 20 miles from Stehekin Road, 17 miles from North Cascades Highway (round-trip)

Accessibility July to September

Difficulty Strenuous

Pack Full

Topographic Sheets USGS: McAlester Mountain
Green Trails: Stehekin

From Bench Camp (see Rainbow Creek and Lake), continue up in forest 2.5 miles. Cross Rainbow Creek at this point. Bowman Campsite is near this crossing. McAlester Pass is another 2.5 miles. The last 0.5 mile is fairly steep. Although the trail is not too scenic, the views from the McAlester Pass area are impressive. The "pass" is really a meadow about 0.5 mile long with a small tarn at the southern end. It is a splendid area in which to ramble. A camping area, High campsite, has been established at the pass itself.

McAlester Pass is 6,017 feet high and is 10 miles from Stehekin Road and 8.5 miles from the North Cascades Highway.

Near the center of the meadow is the trail junction to South Pass. It takes about 30 minutes to walk the 1.2 miles to South Pass. The trail switchbacks moderately steeply for about 0.3 mile, reaches a bench, and then contours without much altitude gain to the pass, which is the boundary between the recreation area and the national forest. Views are spectacular, and the meadow is superb throughout this entire 1.2-mile distance.

From South Pass, it is about a 30-minute bushwhack over heather, meadow, and talus for 0.4 mile to two unnamed lakes nestled under McAlester Mountain. There are camping areas at both lakes. Fish can be found in the larger lake. This faint scrabble trail is for experienced cross-country hikers only, since it is a steep traverse and is particularly dangerous when wet and slippery.

On the east side of South Pass, burn scars from a recent forest fire are still evident.

It is 7 miles from South Pass to the trailhead in the Okanogan National Forest. The altitude gain is 2,200 feet. The trail is open to motorbikes, but they are prohibited in the recreation area. The trailhead begins in the South Creek Campground, 22 miles up the Twisp River Road. The approximate up-hiking time is 5 hours; down-time is 3 hours. Water and campsites are scarce along the South Creek trail.

It is 1 mile from the trail junction at McAlester Pass to McAlester Lake, the primary established campsite in the area. Altitude loss in this mile is about 500 feet. Wood supplies were adequate at the lake in 1976. The campsite is now located at the north side of the lake, accessed by crossing the outlet stream.

Below McAlester Lake, the trail to Fireweed and the North Cascades Highway is in timber most of the way. It is 4 miles from the lake to the junction with the Twisp Pass trail. Halfway Camp is 2 miles from both the lake and the trail junction. Fifty yards from the junction with the Twisp Pass trail is the junction with the Stiletto trail, the shortest and quickest route northward to reach the North Cascades Highway. Three-tenths of a mile westward is Fireweed Camp and a crossing of Bridge Creek. From this point, it is 3.3 miles via the Crest trail to the North Cascades Highway.

The altitude loss from the lake to Fireweed is 1,900 feet; from Fireweed to the highway, the altitude gain is 400 feet.

At Fireweed Camp, there are six to eight campsites with tables and adequate supplies of wood and water, although the area is not particularly attractive.

(September 1976)

MCGREGOR MOUNTAIN

Elevations

Trailhead:	1,700 (High Bridge)
Destination:	7,000 feet (Heaton Camp)
High Point:	8,122 feet (summit)

Altitude Gain   6,500 feet (summit); 5,200 feet (Heaton Camp)
Walking Time   2 days
Trail Length   16 miles to summit; 14 miles to Heaton Camp (round-trip)
Accessibility   July 15 to early October
Difficulty   Strenuous
Pack   Full to Heaton Camp; light from camp to summit
Topographic Sheets   USGS: McGregor Mountain (trail not shown)
Green Trails: McGregor Mountain

The trail starts at the ranger cabin at High Bridge on the Stehekin Road 10.5 miles from Stehekin. Switchbacks start almost immediately. Six-tenths of a mile from the trailhead, there is a signed junction as the old Stehekin Wagon Road joins the trail from the right. A 30-minute walk with a 550-vertical-foot gain brings you to Coon Lake, 1.2 miles from the trailhead. Agnes Mountain can be seen at two or three places along the trail to the lake. Coon Lake can be described as either a deep swamp or a shallow lake; it does not contain fish and is not particularly scenic. Beavers frequent the area; it is also a good place to observe waterfowl, particularly in the spring, when several species of ducks are engaged in mating rituals.

The trail continues to the northwest end of the lake, where there is a signed junction. From there, the old Wagon Road continues 1 mile to its junction with the Stehekin Road above the Tumwater Bridge and then 3 additional miles, almost to the Bridge Creek Campground. The trail to McGregor Mountain turns east, drops down slightly, and follows the north side of the lake; seemingly unending switchbacks are then encountered as the trail begins its climb from the east side of the lake.

One mile from the Coon Lake junction, the trail passes a waterfall on the right. You can obtain water via a steep scrabble trail at this point. Drink deeply and fill canteens, since the next easily accessible water is several miles away. Just below this waterfall is a bluff with views of Coon Lake below and the Agnes Valley to the west; day hikers may find this point an attractive place to eat lunch.

From the end of Coon Lake, the trail switchbacks upward remorselessly, initially in ponderosa pine forest. At about 3.5 miles, there is another bluff for sitting and viewing; Coon Lake is appreciably smaller now below. More mountains are visible, including Dome, Boston, Goode, and Buckner. The ponderosa forest is left behind; now the trail passes through the Canadian or Douglas fir zone. Between miles 4 and 5, scrambles over rather difficult terrain allow the desperate to reach water at several locations, but the first easy water is available at 5.5 miles, where it can be obtained a few feet to the right of the trail. At 6 miles, an unofficial campsite is located below the trail, with water from a stream nearby. The first larch trees are seen at about this point, which marks the transition to the Hudsonian or alpine fir zone. At 6.3 miles, the trail, which has been going up a fairly open valley for the past 2 miles, suddenly enters a talus bowl.

After switchbacking up through the talus bowl, Heaton Camp, located at a cliff on the left (north side) of the talus bowl, is reached. Look carefully for the 150-foot side trail to the left (west). There is a sign at 100 feet, but none at the junction. This is the only designated camping area and is at about 7,000 feet.

Heaton Camp has two fire pits, a moderate wood supply, a toilet 300 feet to the north behind a granite outcrop, water from a small spring 100 feet below and northwest of the camp, and water from a larger spring 0.1 mile down the trail. Water from this source can be sporadic. There are five small tent sites. The area is almost bug free. There is evidence of horses throughout most of the camp area.

Note an interesting, faint trail up the ridge to the southeast; this was probably made by mountain goats. The view from the campsite to the west is splendid, but views to the south and north are limited by ridges, and the main bulk of McGregor is to the east.

An additional fairly steep 0.4-mile trail leads to the base of the talus slope beneath the summit of the peak. Here are two standing timbers of the A-frame used to winch materials for the lookout from this point to the summit. The summit can be identified by the radio aerial of the Park Service repeater station clearly visible from below.

From this point, the route to the summit looks formidable. However, if the proper route is located and followed, the ascent, though exposed, is not technical (class 2). From the base of the talus slope, the best route is between two large rocks near the top of the rocky incline; both are marked with hard-to-spot red paint (a cairn was built on the left rock in 1980). Continue to the end of the highest left talus slope. Turn right at this point, and follow a ledge approximately 200 feet to the gully on the right (look for red marker arrows). Just before reaching the gully, turn left and go above a 20-foot rock block in the chute above the original talus slope. From here, the route is more obvious and better marked. It goes up the ridge to the left, and near the top, it cuts right and goes through a notch to the left of the first tor left of the summit. From here, there are magnificent views of peaks to the north and east. Cross snow (or talus, later in the year) on a faint trail east of this spire and then proceed upward on trail, snow, or talus 150 yards to the summit. Red arrows and dots are helpful route markers but are not always easily seen. There is no other simple, safe route to the summit; it is most important not to go to the right at the base of the talus slope.

The flat 10-by-12-foot summit block was the site of the old McGregor Lookout. Even today, metal, fused glass, and other remnants of this structure can be found. Twenty feet below is the solar-powered Park Service repeater station and aerial.

From the summit, views in every direction provide a panorama of practically every significant peak in the North Cascades, except Baker and Shuksan, which are obscured by the peaks to the northwest. Immediately below is the ice and snow of the Sandalee Glacier. The whole Stehekin Valley is spread out below, and Lake Chelan curves out of sight near Round and Domke Mountains. The hiker is now in the Arctic-alpine zone, where only shrubs and flowers flourish briefly during the summer.

Almost everyone leaves this splendid viewpoint reluctantly. Descent, although easier on the lungs, is at best only a little faster, since one misstep can have severe consequences.

On the way down, less heavily laden and less fatigued, the hiker can appreciate the creek flowers more and be more sensitive to the life zone changes. Only 35 minutes of walking separate the last larch (at about 5.5 miles) from the first ponderosa pine (at about 4 miles from High Bridge).

Allow 5 hours up fully packed to Heaton Camp. Round-trip from Heaton Camp to the summit takes another 2 hours and 30 minutes. It is 3 hours down to the trailhead from Heaton Camp.

Watch for rattlesnakes on the lower portions of the trail. An early start is advisable to avoid the heat of the day while still at low altitude. One quart of water is mandatory; an extra quart and several salt tablets are advisable.*

This trail is without question strenuous even to Heaton Camp; however, if pursued to the summit, this is probably the most scenic and splendid trail in the Stehekin area. Experienced climbers with appropriate equipment can continue cross-country over ice and rock from the summit to Rainbow Lake; this mountaineering traverse takes about 8 hours

(August 1980)

---

*If you are sweating profusely on a hot day, dissolve one 0.5-gram salt tablet (or one Thermotab) in 1 quart or 1 liter of water and drink as thirst dictates; swallowing the tablet whole may cause abdominal discomfort.

PURPLE CREEK (PURPLE PASS)
Elevations
    Trailhead: 1,100 feet
    Destination: 6,884 feet (Purple Pass)
    High Point: 7,372 feet (Boulder Butte)
    Other Significant Locations: 6,550 feet (Juanita Lake Camp)
Altitude Gain   5,800 feet
Walking Time   1 day
Trail Length   7.8 miles
Accessibility   July to September
Difficulty   Strenuous
Pack   Light
Topographic Sheets   USGS: Stehekin, Sun Mountain
                      Green Trails: Stehekin

From the southeast end of the visitors' center, follow the primitive road upward 0.2 mile, passing a cement cistern and redwood tank; turn left and cross Purple Creek* on a bridge. Turn right (east) 0.1 mile farther at the junction with the Imus Creek Nature Trail.

The trail switchbacks both steeply and consistently upward until Purple Pass (6,884 feet) is reached at 7.8 miles. The trail crosses Purple Creek at 1.8 miles; in the spring, this can be a difficult crossing.

Drink deeply and fill water bottles here; water is scarce beyond this point. The next water is at Cougar Springs at 4.5 miles (unless the spring is dry), and at 4.7 miles via a scrabble trail going 200 feet south to a creek. In the spring and early summer, water is available from melting snowfields near the summit, but later in the year, this is a dry, hot trail. A minimum of two water bottles is suggested. It is also desirable to start early in the day in the summer to avoid problems with overheating. It is a full day's walk for a strong hiker to reach Purple Pass and descend the additional 0.5 mile to the formal campsite near Juanita Lake. Lightly packed, the walking time to the pass is about 5 hours. Add 1 to 2 hours if carrying a heavy pack. Down-time is about 3 hours. Beyond 2.2 miles, there are a number of grassy knolls slightly off the trail where you can sit at leisure and watch the clouds and peaks reflected in the great trough of Lake Chelan. The 1,500-foot gain to the view areas is not too difficult and takes the average day hiker about 2 hours. Views improve as you go higher; at the pass, the spectacle of the North Cascades is stirring. Larch,

---

*The Purples were originally homesteaders in the Stehekin area. The creek, pass, and campground are named after them. There is nothing purple-colored in the area.

the only deciduous conifer, is first seen at about 6.5 miles. A larch forest graces the area between Purple and War Creek Passes. The altitude gain is 5,800 feet to the pass. There are reasonable amounts of wood near Juanita Camp. Wildflowers are impressive in June. Deer are commonly seen on the trail, as well as an occasional bear. Carry an ice ax during ascents in May and June, since snow can be anticipated on the last 1 to 2 miles of the trail during these months.

From Purple Pass, the trail drops down 0.7 mile to reach Juanita Camp. At 0.2 mile is the junction with the Boulder Butte trail. This side trail to the site of an old demolished lookout is 0.5 mile long and gains 450 feet. Enjoy an incredible 360-degree panorama from an elevation of 7,372 feet. This is one of the most beautiful places in the North Cascades. This side trip must not be missed under any circumstances. Ideally, the area should be visited in the late afternoon, at sunset, and the following morning to appreciate the different lighting at these times of day.

Juanita Camp is pleasant except for the mosquitoes. It has widely scattered camping areas over a distance of 0.3 mile. Juanita Lake is shallow and could be considered simply a high tarn; it does not contain fish. Walk above Juanita Lake to the junction with the Summit trail and a bit above that to War Creek Pass.

(July 1979)

LYMAN LAKE (RAILROAD CREEK)
Elevations

Trailhead:	3,100 feet
Destination:	5,600 feet (Lyman Lake)
High Point:	6,450 feet (Cloudy Pass)

Other Significant Locations: Suiattle Pass, 6,000 feet; Phelps Creek (Spider) Pass, 7,050 feet

Altitude Gain	2,600 feet (including ups and downs)
Walking Time	In: 6 hours Out: 4 hours 20 minutes
Trail Length	9 miles one-way
Accessibility	August 1 to October 15
Difficulty	Moderately strenuous
Pack	Full
Topographic Sheets	USGS: Holden
	Green Trails: Holden

The trailhead is 0.75 mile west of Holden Village, just outside the boundary of the Glacier Peak Wilderness Area. There is a road from the village to the trailhead. From the trailhead, it is about 8.3 miles to Lyman Lake. The 9 miles given above is from the center of Holden Village. Nine-tenths of a mile up the trail is the junction with the Holden Lake trail. About 3 miles farther is Hart Lake, elevation 3,956 feet, where there is a good campsite; 0.9 mile farther, there is another campsite near a stream. Shortly thereafter, the trail begins switchbacking upward, gaining over 800 feet in altitude before it again levels out; from here, the trail gains altitude gradually until it reaches the north end of Lyman Lake. The switchback section is very brushy. It is advisable to check whether this trail has recently been brushed out before planning a trip, since this section can be quite difficult before the annual visitation of the trail crew, particularly during or following rain.

Between Holden and Hart Lake, the trail is uninspiring. Westward from Hart Lake, scenery improves. The trail thereafter can be described as a vista of magnificent waterfalls. There are a number of spectacular cascades coming off Bonanza Peak and terminating in the Hart Lake area. Crown Point Falls, just below Lyman Lake, is gorgeous and can be seen well from the trail.

Lyman Lake is splendid. There is a way trail along the west side of the lake. A more recently constructed trail accesses the three smaller lakes higher in the basin to the southeast. Experienced backcountry travelers equipped with ice axes can ascend to the Phelps Creek Pass area for even better views. There are good campsites at all three lakes. (My favorite is by a small tarn just west of Lyman Lake about 0.25 mile from the Railroad Creek trail.) Fishing is generally good in Lyman Lake. Water is not a problem, but wood is scarce. A backpacker's stove is a virtual necessity. The area is buggy, and insect repellent should be carried. Much of the area around Lyman Lake is relatively wet and marshy.

From the lake, you can follow the Railroad Creek trail farther to Cloudy Pass. At this location, there is an unbelievably scenic view down into the Lyman Lake basin and its backdrop of Chiwawa Mountain, Lyman Glacier, Phelps Creek Pass, and Dumbbell Mountain. The distance from the lake to the pass is about 2 miles, with an altitude gain of roughly 1,000 vertical feet. From Cloudy Pass, there are a hiker's high route and a horseman's low route to Suiattle Pass, about a mile to the west. From this point, there are connections via the Pacific Crest Trail with the Stehekin Road to the northeast and with various routes to the west (described under Image Lake elsewhere in this book). Lyman Lake can also be reached by the Phelps Creek trail and high route (described elsewhere).

The country between Lyman Lake and Image Lake is one of the most splendid areas in the North Cascades. In spite of its difficult access, the area is fairly heavily utilized, and the lakeshore has been significantly impacted. Camping is presently prohibited within 200 feet of Lyman Lake. Alternative tent sites can be found in the vicinity of Cloudy Pass. Additional regulations to protect the fragile alpine environment may be promulgated in the future.

Although not highly hazardous, Lyman Glacier is crevassed. The area is dangerous and should be avoided by all except for roped-up and experienced climbers.

The eastern trailhead at Holden can be reached by boat from Chelan to Lucerne, and by Holden Village bus from Lucerne to Holden.

Very strong hikers with day packs can make the round-trip from the trailhead to Lyman Lake or Cloudy Pass in one long summer day. I recommend, however, that you allow a minimum of two days and one night. In spite of the bugs, the area is so scenic and enjoyable that departing back down the trail a few minutes after arrival would be heartbreaking.

(August 1975)

RAINBOW CREEK AND LAKE

Elevations

Trailhead:	1,200 feet (Stehekin Road)	
Destination:	5,630 feet (Rainbow Lake)	
High Point:	6,230	

Other Significant Locations: Bench Creek Camp, 3,800 feet

Altitude Gain	5,000 feet (including ups and downs)
Walking Time	5 hours 30 minutes to lake, 3 hours from lake down to Bridge Creek
Trail Length	11 miles to Rainbow Lake; 17 miles to Bridge Creek (one-way)
Accessibility	July to September
Difficulty	Strenuous
Pack	Full
Topographic Sheets	USGS: Stehekin, McAlester Mountain, McGregor Mountain
	Green Trails: Stehekin, McGregor Mountain

The trailhead is about 3 miles from Stehekin on the east side of the Stehekin–Cottonwood Camp Road. It is well signed. The trail goes up through typically dry east-side slopes. At 0.2 mile, the abandoned water reservoir and wooden pipes of the system to supply water to property owners below are passed. A steep off-trail side trip down to Boulder Creek to fill water bottles may be appropriate here; the next water is 2.3 miles away.

From here, the trail switchbacks up moderately steeply. At 1 mile, there is a nice view from the trail of Lake Chelan, the south end of the Stehekin valley, and the mountains to the west. From knolls off the trail beyond this area, there are fine viewpoints and picnic spots.

At 2 miles, reach the junction with the Boulder Creek trail. The Rainbow Creek trail continues to the left for a few hundred yards (a scramble of 0.4 mile to the west from this point brings you to the top of Rainbow Falls) and then drops down into the Rainbow Creek valley to a bridge crossing Rainbow Creek. This is a nice picnic spot, particularly in the spring, when the entire valley is filled with blooming dogwood. Refill water bottles here, for this is the last water for a substantial distance.

A designated campsite is located here; two tent sites are near the bridge; two additional, less pleasant sites are located 100 feet below and west of the footpath.

The trail then switchbacks up moderately steeply onto the side hill on the north side of the valley and follows the Rainbow valley upward. The Rainbow Loop trail continues northward 0.3 mile beyond the bridge. At 3.2 miles, there is an incredible vista from a grassy knoll, particularly impressive when the yellow balsam is blooming in the late spring. It takes about 1.25 hours to reach this viewing area. From this point, there is a fairly level traverse for 1.4 miles. There are many wildflowers along this section of the trail in the spring.

Cross Rainbow Creek on a cable suspension bridge. One mile above the crossing is Bench Camp, with five campsites in a not too scenic area. At this point, the trail forks; the left path leads to Rainbow Lake 5.5 miles farther; the right trail heads to McAlester Pass.

The Rainbow Lake trail drops down to reach Rainbow Creek, which can be forded or crossed on a crude bridge. The elevation at the ford is 3,600 feet, so 2,400 feet have been gained since leaving the road. Drink deeply and stock up on water at this point, as the next water is 2 miles, 1,200 feet, and 1 hour and 30 minutes away via hot, steep, dusty, dry switchbacks.

After water is reached, the trail begins to level out. Three miles from the junction (2 hours), there is a fine view of peaks from a meadow and a good campsite (Rainbow Meadows) nestled in the trees. Beware of mosquitoes.

On this trail, the best is saved for last. There is 600 feet to be gained over the last 0.7 mile of trail. Beautiful Sierra-type waterfalls nearby lessen the pain of trudging upward again, and soon the path tops out and drops to reach Rainbow Lake, nestled under the peaks and ridges at an altitude of 5,630 feet. The distance covered from Stehekin Road is 11 miles; the total altitude gained (including ups and downs) is about 5,000 feet. Ascent time fully packed is 5 hours and 30 minutes; estimated descent time is 4 hours.

The lake is very scenic, an emerald gem set in a horseshoe ring of crags and spires. There are fish in the lake. Four or five campsites are by the lake, but none of them are really comfortable for one reason or another. Mosquitoes are ubiquitous. Two lakes west of Rainbow Lake can be reached without too much difficulty by traveling cross-country. However, these lakes often retain ice much of the summer.

The trail northward climbs 0.9 mile from this point to an unnamed pass at

6,230 feet. Just before the pass is reached, there is an interesting geologic transformation from granitic to much darker colored rock.

The trail drops steeply from larch forest at the top of the pass, losing 1,000 feet in the next mile. The trail is difficult to locate in the meadow below the pass; it goes almost due north and can be found most easily by looking down when midway in the slope above the meadow, or by looking for cut ends of avalanche-fallen trees while in the meadow. Note the splendid waterfall coming from Bowan Mountain at this point.

The trail descends through forest for a few miles and then goes through avalanche slopes with views of the surrounding mountains. The national park boundary is 3 miles from the pass. Dan's campsite is located midway between the pass and the Bridge Creek trail. At 5 miles, cross Bridge Creek on a footlog. There is a 3,000-foot loss from the pass to the junction with Bridge Creek–Pacific Crest Trail. It is 6.2 miles from the lake to Bridge Creek. There is a designated campsite (South Fork Camp at 3,200 feet) on the north side of Bridge Creek 0.2 mile from the Bridge Creek trail.

From Rainbow Lake, it is a 5-hour-and-30-minute walk to the North Cascades Highway. Watch carefully for rattlesnakes between the trailhead and Bench Camp.

(September 1981)

STEHEKIN RIVER

Elevations

Trailhead:	1,200 feet (Stehekin Road)
Destination:	1,100 feet (Lakeshore; Weaver Point Campground)
High Point:	1,280 feet
Altitude Gain	200 feet
Walking Time	3 hours
Trail Length	8 miles
Accessibility	Mid-April to Mid-November
Difficulty	Moderate
Pack	Light
Topographic Sheets	USGS: Stehekin
	Green Trails: Stehekin

The trail starts at the Harlequin Campground.* It is 3.5 miles to the Devore Creek trail and 4 miles to Weaver Point. Follow the Harlequin Camp-

---

*Future development plans call for the placement of a pedestrian suspension bridge over the Stehekin River about 2.5 miles from the landing; if and when this happens, an alternative access to this footpath will be available.

ground Road from its junction with the Company Creek Road 0.2 mile. Turn right at the signed trailhead (the road continues beyond this point). This portion of the trail is for hikers only; horse access is via a road west of the airstrip.

The trail crosses streams, swamps, and ponds on interesting bridges and also passes through occasional grassy, meadowlike areas. The trail mood is pastoral and tranquil. This section of the trail is 0.6 mile long and joins the horse trail at the end of the airstrip.

The trail enters the woods south of the airstrip after crossing a creek on a footlog. There are bridges across all streams. In one place, the trail runs alongside a lazy, quiet, deep, meandering side channel of the Stehekin River; this is a forest dell of substantial beauty.

Watch for beaver dams in this area. In the open areas south of the airstrip, note the blooming dogwoods in the spring, and enjoy the reds and yellows of the leaves in the fall. Calypso orchids bloom alongside the footpath in May.

At 1.5 miles, a short scramble east of the footpath down to a grassy bluff offers a fine view of Rainbow Falls, with the Stehekin River in the foreground. Tread gently here to protect the wildflowers and maintain the turf.

Harlequin ducks are often seen in this part of the river. Cross Devore Creek on a bridge upstream. The trail ends slightly northwest of the Weaver Point Campground. Walking time is about 1 hour and 30 minutes.

By prearrangement with the people at the North Cascades Lodge, it is possible to obtain boat transportation from the Weaver Point dock back to Stehekin. Otherwise, steps must be retraced.

There is ample time to make this walk, in both directions, between the morning and afternoon shuttle-bus trips. This lowland trail is generally open from late March until late November. Altitude gain is negligible downstream and 200 feet upstream. Watch out for yellow jackets

(May 1993)

Mount Baker National Recreation Area

PARK BUTTE LOOKOUT
Elevations
Trailhead:	3,350 feet
Destination:	5,450 feet (Park Butte Lookout)
Altitude Gain	2,200 feet (including ups and downs)
Walking Time	In: 2 hours 30 minutes Out: 1 hour 30 minutes
Trail Length	4 miles one-way
Accessibility	July 15 to October 15
Difficulty	Moderate
Pack	Full
Topographic Sheets	USGS: Hamilton
	Green Trails: Hamilton

This trail is now the primary access to the recently created Mount Baker National Recreation Area (MBNRA), one of the few administered by the U.S. Forest Service. As such, it receives much greater visitation than previously, necessitating a number of changes: a larger parking area, upgrade of the trailhead privy, tread upgrade, construction of new trails, placement of a shelter in Mazama Park, meadow rehabilitation, closure of hiker-caused way trails, limiting camping to hardened designated campsites, continuing the ban on trail machines and mountain bikes, limiting horse use in early summer (the tread cannot withstand hooves when wet), restricting snowmobile use in the winter and spring, and establishment of regular patrols of the area by wilderness rangers.

To access the trailhead, drive up the Baker Lake Road from State Route 20. Turn west just past the concrete bridge 0.4 mile inside the national forest boundary. At 3.6 miles, turn right and continue an additional 5.4 miles to the trailhead. There is parking for about fifty cars plus several overnight drive-in campsites. There is a large bulletin board at the trailhead. The trail follows a side road for about 200 feet, then turns right. About 100 feet farther on the right is the Scott Paul trailhead. A few feet farther, the Park Butte trail crosses Sulfur Creek on a sturdy bridge and then traverses Schrieber's Meadows for about a mile. This section of trail is a good place to pick blueberries and huckleberries in September. Three devastated areas follow, where volcanic mudflows have destroyed substantial sections of the forest and left boulder-strewn denuded areas. One of these flows occurred in 1911, when enormous amounts of debris were released from the terminus of the Easton Glacier, which at that time was substantially longer and ended lower than it does at present. One of the channels is spanned by a bouncy cable bridge; unfortunately, the creek issuing from

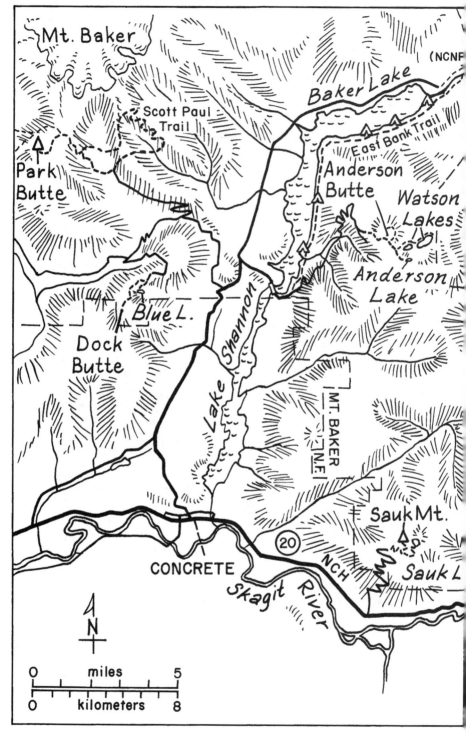

Mount Baker National Recreation Area

the mouth of the glacier changes its channel frequently, so passage can be difficult, especially on hot afternoons when the creek flow is maximal. A ford may be required. Put another way, in any given year, most of the water may not be flowing under the bridge. After these three areas have been crossed and a bit of altitude has been gained, a small, usually clear creek is crossed; this is the last water until the upper Morovits Meadow is reached. The gradient of the footpath steepens after the creek has been crossed. About 800 vertical feet in altitude are gained over the next mile. Two-thirds of the way up the switchbacks, the upper terminus of the Scott Paul trail is passed. The footpath breaks out into the lower Morovits Meadow 2.4 miles from the trailhead. Mount Baker and the Black Buttes can easily be seen from this point onward. The trail goes northwest through splendid open meadowland, reaching a signed trail junction at 2.6 miles.

The right fork climbs steeply on rock steps for 0.15 mile and then follows the ridge crest northward, passing several designated campsites en route. The footpath then drops a bit and reascends to the crest of the Railroad Grade (so named because the gradual ascent of the lateral moraine of the Easton Glacier is similar to the inclines required by trains). About 1,000 vertical feet are gained on the 1-mile ascent to timberline along the crest of the Railroad Grade. High camps for climbers (and hikers) are located near or at timberline. The snout of the glacier is directly below the last trees. Ascend the steep rough slopes of the Railroad Grade and gaze downward into the great cleft gouged by the Easton Glacier. In the early 1900s, this glacier extended almost a mile farther than it does at present. The recession of the ice was substantial until the late 1960s; however, over the past two decades, the glacier has again been growing rather than receding.

From timberline, another option for experienced hikers is to proceed to the northwest cross-country through trailless meadow. After about a mile, it is possible to look down into the Deming Glacier far below and up to the summit of Mount Baker to the northeast. Across this chasm are the Black Buttes. Those with good eyes can usually find mountain goats foraging on the steep slopes of the buttes. Binoculars help distinguish goats from snow patches. This is another splendid vista point. A short distance to the west, with the loss of several hundred vertical feet in altitude, is Mazama Lake, a splendid alpine campsite. From here, it is a short scramble to the top of Meadow Point, where mountain goats are often seen. Deer and bears also inhabit the meadow areas.

From timberline, a scrabble trail continues upward, allowing climbers to access the mountain and photographers to reach more scenic viewpoints. (A word of caution: Hikers should keep off the glaciers and steep snowfields. They are dangerous places. Only roped-up and properly equipped climbers can safely traverse the icefields of Mount Baker.) The experienced can also ascend

Mount Baker, monarch of the North Cascades, as seen from Three Tree Tarn adjacent to the Park Butte Trail.

the ridge above the last trees to about the 7,500-foot level on Mount Baker without venturing onto the glacier, although snow slopes must be crossed; some require an ice ax. From this point, there are better views of Puget Sound, the San Juan Islands, and the surrounding peaks.

Returning to the junction, the left fork continues through the lower meadow, contours above a streambed, eventually crosses the stream, and enters the upper Morovits Meadow. The footpath continues westward across this meadow and then turns south and climbs a ridge. At the ridge top, a trail to the right leads to another designated campsite beneath the Cathedral Crags. After the campsite turnoff, this path switchbacks downward to reach the Mazama Park shelter after about 0.6 mile. Mazama Park was named by the Mazama Climbing Club in Portland at an outing in this location in the early 1900s. Many years ago, the club maintained a cabin in this meadow; the remnants of its foundation can still be seen. There are good campsites in the Mazama Park area, and water is available nearby.

Returning to the last junction, the Park Butte trail turns left and then climbs to reach a bench. To the left (east) of this level area are two of the most beautiful tarns in the North Cascades. This area is closed to camping. Tread gently in this fragile place; try to stay on the footpaths that previous hikers have made. Avoid stepping on heather. (Be aware that above 4,500 feet, snow patches over the tread may persist well into August.)

The trail to Park Butte continues southward and then curves to the west above Pocket Lake, 400 or so feet below to the southeast. The final half-mile ascent to the Park Butte Lookout follows. The lookout is currently leased and maintained by the Skagit Alpine Club of Mount Vernon. The structure is available for public use when it is not occupied by a Skagit Alpine Club work party.

The view from Park Butte is one of the best in the North Cascades and may be one of the most beautiful places in the entire world. Dominating the scene is the ice-clad cone of Mount Baker with its satellite peaks, the Black Buttes. The tip of Mount Shuksan is barely visible. To the west is the valley of the middle fork of the Nooksack, and to the southwest is the orange-tinted, snow-clad Sisters range. To the south are Loomis Mountain, Dock Butte, and in the far distance, the ice-clad tip of Mount Rainier. To the east and southeast rear the spires of the great peaks of the North Cascades, including Blum, Hagen, Sauk, and Glacier Peak in the distance. On clear days, Puget Sound can be seen to the west. The comments in the Park Butte Lookout register reveal that reverence, awe, and a sense of closeness to the Creator are engendered in visitors to this outdoor cathedral.

The Park Butte trail is also interesting from a geological viewpoint. About 2.5 miles from the paved Baker Lake Highway turnoff, the Park Butte Road passes through vesicular andesite lava, known as the Sulfur Creek flow.

The rounded, forested hill to the left just before the clear-cut, about 8 miles from the turnoff and near the 4-mile road marker, is a cinder cone. The orange material through which the road passes from roughly 3 to 4.2 miles is volcanic cinders, deposited downwind from the cone by the prevailing southwest winds.

West of Rocky Creek and Schrieber's Meadow is a shear-walled ridge composed of Yellow Aster Complex rocks, which are 460 to 1,100 million years in age.

Volcanic mudflows, discussed in the trail description, are called lahars. Lahar deposits from Mount Baker are crossed in several locations between 1 and 1.4 miles on the trail.

West of the second Morovits Meadow is a ridge composed of volcanic rock. This rock is believed to be part of a flow that originated from the Black Buttes.

At the southwestern end of the Second Morovits Meadow, perhaps 50 yards from the trail toward the Cathedral Crags, clay-rich lake sediments form a 25-foot-wide, 8-foot-thick sequence of horizontal strata. This deposit was presumably formed by glacial outwash debris.

In the saddle between the South Cathedral Crag and Park Butte, ancient Yellow Aster basement Complex rock is exposed.

Lighter-colored rocks farther along the trail west of the tarns are probably part of the older Park Butte phase of the Mount Baker volcanic center; this rock is either olivine-bearing basaltic andesite or an olivine basalt.

The Morovits Meadows themselves are composed of quaternary alluvium. The Chilliwack Formation is exposed at Pocket Lake and Survey Point. The Cathedral Crags are composed of porphyritic olivine andesite, and Park Butte itself is sculpted from Yellow Aster Complex rock. (I am indebted to graduate student Doug McKeever of the Department of Geology, Western Washington University, from whose master's thesis this geological information was abstracted.)

MBNRA regulations follow: (1) campfires are prohibited within 1 mile of designated trails; (2) camping or being in a closed-for-restoration area is prohibited; (3) the Railroad Grade and Scott Paul trails are for hikers only (no stock); (4) motorized vehicles and bicycles are prohibited on all trails; (5) short-cutting switchbacks is not allowed; (6) backpackers must camp at designated areas identified by tent pads; (7) groups may not exceed twelve in number (total consists of both persons and pack and saddle animals); and (8) dogs must be leashed or under voice control at all times.

(July 1997)

SCOTT PAUL TRAIL
Elevations

Trailhead:	3,300 feet
Destination:	4,500 feet (Park Butte Trail)
High Point:	5,400 feet (south slope of Mount Baker)
Altitude Gain	2,900 feet up, 1,000 feet down (including ups and downs)
Walking Time	In: 3 hours 45 minutes Out: 3 hours
Trail Length	7 miles one-way
Accessibility	Late July to mid-October
Difficulty	Up, moderately strenuous; down, moderate
Pack	Light
Topographic Sheets	USGS: Hamilton
	Green Trails: Hamilton

This trail, named after a deceased trail crew foreman, offers a longer but scenic route to the elegant meadows south of Mount Baker. To reach the trailhead, follow the directions for accessing the Park Butte trail.

The footpath circles around the clear-cut above the parking lot and gains altitude steadily through old-growth forest. It is 2 miles, with an altitude gain of 1,400 feet, to reach the meadowed ridge crest; the ascent takes about 1 hour and 20 minutes. The first views are found here. From the ridge crest, a climber's trail ascends steeply to the northwest for about 1 mile; views improve as altitude is gained. Hikers who elect this option should make an aggressive effort to stay on the tread to avoid damage to the fragile meadows.

The Scott Paul trail turns westward (initially going through forest) from the ridge crest and gradually gains altitude. After about 40 minutes, a creek is crossed, and the footpath has reached its high point; from here until the path reaches the Railroad Grade, little altitude is gained or lost as the tread winds in and out of multiple gullies. Following rain, or during snowmelt, the tread is quite muddy. About 45 minutes later, the highest point adjacent to the Railroad Grade is reached. Fifteen minutes later, a small creek is boulder-hopped during the descent to the crossing of the stream issuing from the snout of the Easton Glacier. After a switchbacking descent, the stream is crossed on a hanging bridge (early or late in the year, the bridge may not be in place; at most water levels, the crossing can be made by boulder-hopping 50 feet downstream from the bridge site). From the bridge, the trail climbs to the top of the west lateral moraine of the Easton Glacier. In mid-July, there is a profusion of wildflowers alongside this section of the footpath. From the top, there is an impressive view of the excavation carved out by the glacier and of Mount Baker in the background. Ten minutes later, a small creek is crossed; 5 minutes past the crossing, the trail joins the Park Butte trail.

There are no designated campsites along the Scott Paul trail. Camping is prohibited within 1 mile of the footpath. If camping is desired, it is best to ascend the Park Butte trail, camp in a designated campsite in the Morovits Meadows, and descend via the Scott Paul trail.

(July 1994)

DOCK BUTTE (BLUE LAKE)
Elevations
Trailhead:	3,900 feet
Destination:	5,210 feet (Dock Butte)

Other Significant Locations: Blue Lake, 4,000 feet
Altitude Gain   1,500 feet (including ups and downs)
Walking Time   In: 1 hour   Out: 40 minutes
Trail Length   1.8 miles one-way
Accessibility   Butte, July 15 to October 15; lake, July 1 to November 1
Difficulty   Butte, moderate; lake, moderately easy
Pack   Light
Topographic Sheets   USGS: Hamilton, Lake Shannon
Green Trails: Hamilton

Drive eastward from Burlington on State Highway 20; turn north 6 miles east of Hamilton, and follow Baker Lake Road to the national forest boundary. Half a mile beyond the boundary, immediately after crossing a bridge, turn sharply left to the west. Note the odometer reading at this point. Make a left turn at 3.6 miles onto the Loomis Mountain Road. Again, turn left at 7 miles at the Wanlick Creek saddle. One mile farther, make another left turn. The trailhead is 10.9 miles from the Baker Lake Road turnoff. There is parking for approximately ten cars at the trailhead and a reasonable amount of room for turning around.

From the signed trailhead, a way trail has been constructed through logging debris for 0.1 mile, where it connects with the old trail, which originally started just inside the forest boundary near the Baker Lake Road. Turn right, or westward, and follow the old trail; 0.3 mile from the trailhead is a junction. The upgraded and rerouted Blue Lake trail turns to the left; the old trail to Dock Butte continues to the right.

The trail to the lake is about 0.6 mile in length. There is negligible altitude gain from the junction to the lake. The trail is generally muddy and slippery. There are several excellent campsites at the east end of the lake. The area is fairly heavily used; wood for campfires is becoming difficult to obtain. Fishing in the lake is unpredictable but sometimes good. A small peninsula extends into the lake near the camping areas; the water is sufficiently deep at this point to permit both bait- and fly-fishing. There are sharp, rocky walls above the lake to the south and west. Unfortunately, the area is frequently littered; the impact on the lake area since the access was improved has been substantial. Youth groups frequently use the area for overnight campouts. The walking time to the lake from the trailhead is about 20 minutes. Parents with small children may find that Blue Lake offers a pleasant one-day family outing.

Returning to the trail junction, the hiker should continue upward on the poorly maintained trail to Dock Butte. On the ridge above Blue Lake, the tread is difficult to locate in places, but if the trail cannot be found, follow the ridge crest southward, and the tread will become apparent again. About 0.2 mile from the top of the butte, the easier-appearing trail to the right (west) dead-ends and is not the correct route. Take the fairly steep ascent to the left; if necessary, use the telephone wire beside the trail to pull yourself up hand over hand to reach the summit ridge; follow the scrabble trail on the ridge to the top. There is one minor class 2 rock move; it is not difficult under normal circumstances but can be a bit sticky if the rock is wet or icy.

The view from the top is nice but is marred by patch cuts in every direction. Glass and metal debris, the residuals of the Dock Butte lookout burned by the Forest Service in the early 1960s, also detracts from the appearance at the summit. In spite of these liabilities, it is a pleasant place. The valley of the Baker River lies below and to the east. Loomis Mountain, Park Butte, and the Mount Baker–Black Buttes massif lie to the north. To the west are the multiple summits of the Twin Sisters range. To the south is the Skagit valley.

The Nooksack elk herd often frequents this area and can sometimes be seen along the approach ridge or from the summit. Binoculars may help in locating and viewing the animals, which are uncommon in the North Cascades. On the ridge above Blue Lake, there are several tarns and level areas that provide nice campsites. Although Blue Lake is often crowded, the Dock Butte area receives surprisingly little visitation.

(Lake, October 1974; butte, September 1977)

ANDERSON LAKE, WATSON LAKES, AND ANDERSON BUTTE

Elevations

Trailhead:	4,300 feet
Destination:	5,420 feet

Other Significant Locations: Watson Lakes, 4,550 feet; Anderson Lake, 4,450 feet

Altitude Gain	1,200 feet (including ups and downs)
Walking Time	In: 1 hour Out: 40 minutes
Trail Length	Anderson Butte, 1.6 miles; Anderson Lake, 2.3 miles; Watson Lake, 2.5 miles one-way
Accessibility	Early June to late October
Difficulty	Moderate
Pack	Light
Topographic Sheets	USGS: Lake Shannon
	Green Trails: Lake Shannon

Take Highway 20 eastward; about 6 miles east of the overpass at Hamilton, turn north and follow the county road past Grandy Lake to intersect Baker Lake Road about 4 miles north of Concrete (if coming from the east, turn north a few blocks west of Concrete and follow a steep road to this point). The national forest boundary is about 5 miles from where these roads join; from the forest boundary, drive the main road 2.1 miles farther, turn right just before the ranger station, and cross upper Baker Dam. Turn left 0.5 mile after crossing the dam. Impressive views of Mount Baker and Mount Shuksan are available at several locations along the access road.

Continue upward on Road 1107. About 9.7 miles from the south end of the dam, turn left onto Road 022, and follow this steep, narrow road to the trailhead 1.2 miles from the turnoff; about thirty cars can park here. This trail is a hiker-only footpath. The Watson Lakes are within the Noisy-Diobsud Wilderness; campfires are prohibited within a mile of the lakes, and other wilderness restrictions apply. Anderson Lake is not within the wilderness. This intermittently muddy and moderately buggy trail ascends moderately steeply through virgin timber for about 0.6 mile before entering an open meadow. The trail divides here. To ascend Anderson Butte, go eastward about 200 feet, and locate the Anderson Butte sign. Follow this footpath about 100 yards upward to the east and then to the north. Watch for a planklike scored footlog across a bog about 25 feet east of the tread. The east end of the footlog accesses the deteriorating footpath to the summit of Anderson Butte. Moderately steep switchbacks reach the ridge crest and the boundary of the Noisy-Diobsud Wilderness (0.6 miles; 25 minutes); the trail then follows the crest to the north an additional 0.1 mile to the summit of the butte, where fine views of the surrounding areas may be had (Mounts Shuksan and Baker dominate the summits of Mounts Watson, Hagen, Bacon, and the Pickett Range).

Return to where the trail divided; the right fork of the trail drops down a bit and then ascends about 0.5 mile through a long meadow featuring spectacular views of Mount Baker from the upper meadow. The path then plunges through a notch and drops steeply down a wooded ridge for about 0.5 mile, finally opening up into a small meadow. At this point, the trail again forks; the right fork becomes a scrabble trail and progresses downward through timber and talus about 0.5 mile, finally breaking into the meadowland around Anderson Lake. This is a nice campsite with an excellent view of Mount Baker. Bears and deer are often seen in the area. The lake is relatively shallow, limiting fishing somewhat.

From the signed junction, the left fork of the trail goes steeply upward, gaining 200 vertical feet to surmount a rocky knoll; it then loses about 400 feet in altitude as it descends via switchbacks to reach Lower Watson Lake, about 0.6 mile from the junction. The footpath, now a scrabble trail, contours along the north side of the lower lake, crosses the relatively flat area between the lakes, and continues around the north side of the upper lake until it terminates east of Upper Watson Lake. Camping at both Watson Lakes is allowed only at nine designated locations—four around the lower lake and five around the upper lake. Both lakes are a beautiful deep blue color; there are fine views of Bacon Peak in the background to the east.

From the Anderson Butte junction, it is about 1.5 miles to Lower Watson Lake and a bit less to Anderson Lake. Wood is plentiful at the lakes. The first 0.6 mile from the logging road is fairly monotonous hiking in deep timber, without access to water. Little springs and creeks in the meadows do provide water thereafter. Hikers in good condition may visit both Anderson Butte and all the lakes in a one-day trip. Fishing in the Watson Lakes remains good in spite of the improved access since the advent of the logging road.

The relatively easy access makes this a good trip for families. This scenic and enjoyable area can be visited without a great expenditure of energy.

(Anderson Butte, July 1997; Anderson and Watson Lakes, August 1989)

EAST BANK–UPPER BAKER LAKE
Elevations
Trailhead:	1,000 feet
Destination:	700 feet (Maple Grove Camp)

Altitude Gain 500 feet both directions (including ups and downs)
Walking Time In: 1 hour 30 minutes   Out: 1 hour 30 minutes
Trail Length 3.8 miles one-way
Accessibility Mid-March to November
Difficulty Moderately easy
Pack Light
Topographic Sheets USGS: Lake Shannon
Green Trails: Lake Shannon

This pleasant lowland walk, snow free most of the year, traverses deep forest much of the time, but in places there are views across the lake of both Mount Baker and Mount Shuksan.

Drive Baker Lake Road from Highway 20. Turn right onto the Baker Lake Dam Road just before the Koma Kulshan guard station. Cross the dam and take the first left thereafter; the signed trailhead is about 1 mile farther, where there is parking for about ten cars.

A 35-minute walk brings the hiker to a way trail to the left just before a bridge. Drop down 0.1 mile to the lakeshore. There are one or two campsites here, views of Mount Baker (Koma Kulshan), places to fish, and a scenic place to eat lunch. Five minutes farther (1.8 miles), a way footpath leads to a point projecting into Baker Lake; after 0.2 mile it dead-ends at the lakeshore.

The main trail continues north from this junction. About 1.3 miles farther, the trail forks. The left fork is signed Maple Camp, but the tread looks little used and I did not walk it. The right fork accesses Maple Camp by a short way trail 25 minutes later. At the camp, there are several campsites, two privies, and views of both mountains from the pleasant beach. This camp is also used by boaters. Drawdown at the dam causes the water level at the lakeshore to vary.

Alongside the East Bank trail, notice the deep splendid moss, yellow violets, and blooming trillium. Enjoy the ancient forest.

From Maple Camp, the footpath continues north and then east to reach Baker River. Bridges across Blum Creek and Baker River are under construction and should be completed by May 31, 1998. At that time, the footpath may be renamed the Baker Lake trail.

I have not walked the newly constructed section between Maple Camp and Baker River, but I plan to do so when the bridges have been completed.

SAUK MOUNTAIN
Elevations
    Trailhead: 4,350 feet
    Destination: 5,537 feet (Sauk Lookout site)
    Other Significant Locations: Sauk Lake, 4,100 feet
Altitude Gain   1,300 feet (including ups and downs)
Walking Time   In: 1 hour 10 minutes   Out: 50 minutes
Trail Length   2 miles one-way
Accessibility   July 1 to November 1
Difficulty   To summit, moderate; one-day round trip to Sauk Lake, moderately strenuous
Pack   Light
Topographic Sheets   USGS: Lake Shannon
                            Green Trails: Lake Shannon

About 7 miles east of Concrete on State Highway 20 (just before entering Rockport State Park), turn left and take a fairly rough logging road to the north. At about 6 miles, take the right fork in the road. At 6.8 miles, make a very sharp turn to the right and drive an additional 0.2 mile up a fairly steep road to the parking and picnic area on top of a bluff. The trail leaves from the east side of this parking area and immediately passes an A-frame toilet on the right. Snow hangs late on the last two switchbacks on the road; it may not be possible to reach the parking area until mid-July.

A series of gentle switchbacks go up the southwest side of the mountain, mostly in meadow, but occasionally in forest. If there are people on the trail above, use great caution where the trail crosses a slide area; rockfalls in this area can be dangerous. Also, do not shortcut the switchbacks; substantial erosion is occurring because of this practice. The trail tops out on the southwest portion of the mountain and then follows the east side of the ridge almost to the lookout, where it crosses again to the west side for the last 100 yards of the trail. It is often possible to climb to the ridge crest on Sauk in late June, encountering little or no snow; the trail from the crest to the lookout site, however, is not snow free until late July. The lookout was removed by the Forest Service in 1991.

Views from the lookout site are impressive in all directions. The Skagit Valley lies directly below to the west. In the late-afternoon sun, the Skagit River shimmers and gleams as it meanders toward its junction with Puget Sound. To the northwest, the Twin Sisters range is dwarfed by the Mount Baker massif. To the north is Mount Shuksan, and to the northeast, the spires of the Picket Range can be seen. To the east are Hidden Lake Peak and, beyond that, the peaks of the Cascade Pass area. To the southeast, the snow cone of

Glacier Peak is visible. To the south is the Sauk valley with its associated mountains, White Chuck and White Horse.

From afar, the meadow through which the trail ascends is a restful, deep green. Early in the season, glacier lilies and alpine phlox are very attractive. Later in the summer, most of the wildflowers found in the North Cascades bloom alongside the trail.

At about the 1.7-mile mark, 0.1 mile after reaching the ridge crest, a fairly steep trail drops down to the southeast and then back to the northeast, passes through a notch, and again descends via switchbacks, eventually reaching the east side of Sauk Lake. This trail is about 1.5 miles in length and loses about 1,300 vertical feet. The down-time to the lake is only 35 minutes, but the up-time back to the junction is close to 1 hour. There are fish in Sauk Lake. The nicest campsites in the area are at the lake or on a bench above the lake. There are also campsites at about the 1.8-mile mark on the trail along the ridge crest, extending toward the east. After the snow has melted, acquiring water can be a problem at this area. There are no other suitable camping areas.

The trail is fairly heavily used, but crowding is uncommon. Active logging is still taking place in the surrounding area, so those using the access road during the week must use caution with regard to logging trucks. The extensive patch-cutting around the mountain is a scenic liability. Because of easy accessibility by vehicle and the relatively short and gentle trail, this is a good hike for families. In fact, the view is sufficiently good from the trailhead that one need not even get out of the car to enjoy the vistas to the south and west.

Two other words of caution: Until the snow has completely melted, carry an ice ax. Also, look upward before crossing the chutes. Falls on steep snow and head injuries from falling rock in the slide areas have claimed several lives on this mountain in the past.

(June 1997)

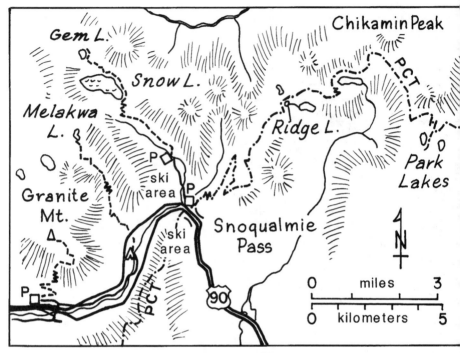

Snoqualmie Pass

Snoqualmie Pass

The four described footpaths on the north side of Snoqualmie Pass are within the Alpine Lakes Wilderness (ALW). Permits are required for entry. Day-use permits are obtainable by self-registration at the trailheads. Preregistration for overnight camping is required. Toll-free information about obtaining overnight permits can be obtained by phoning 800-627-0062. Information is also available from the North Bend Ranger Station, 42404 SE North Bend Way, North Bend, WA 98045; phone 425-888-1421.

Other current ALW rules are as follows: (1) Except for the Pacific Crest Trail, where horses are allowed, only hikers and llamas are allowed entry; (2) dogs must be leashed on all trails; (3) camping is limited to designated sites within half a mile of the following lakes: Ridge, Gravel, Snow, Gem, and Melakwa; (4) campfires are prohibited above 4,000 feet west of the Cascade Crest and 5,000 feet east of the crest; and (5) group size is limited to twelve (any combination of people and stock).

The MBSNF is considering constructing a nonwilderness alpine loop footpath in the vicinity of Source Lake to be known as the Alpental Interpretive trail. Facilities for wilderness-use education would be an integral part of the new trail.

GRANITE MOUNTAIN
Elevations
Trailhead:	1,800 feet
Destination:	5,629 feet (Granite Mountain Lookout)
Altitude Gain	3,800 feet (including ups and downs)
Walking Time	In: 2 hours 15 minutes Out: 1 hour 45 minutes
Trail Length	4.6 miles one-way
Accessibility	July 15 to October 15
Difficulty	Moderately strenuous
Pack	Light
Topographic Sheets	USGS: Snoqualmie Pass
	Green Trails: Snoqualmie Pass

To reach the trailhead from the west, take Exit 47 off I-90. Turn left and cross over I-90. Continue about 100 feet north to the Pratt Lake–Granite Mountain sign; turn left (west) and drive 0.4 mile to the fifty-car parking area at the trailhead. From the east, take Exit 47, turn right, and go 100 feet; then turn left as above.

Both a bulletin board and a privy are located at the trailhead. A loop footpath for backpackers is described on the board (as of July 1996). This trail is heavily used; if at all possible, come on a weekday.

After 22 minutes (about 0.9 mile), the Granite Mountain trail junction is reached; turn right. Water is available along this section of the footpath. The tread is excellent to this junction; thereafter, it is steep, rocky, and difficult. The trail ascends in timber, except for one brief breakout for about 30 minutes (2.1 miles); at this point, the forest is left behind. Views improve as altitude is gained. At about 3.6 miles, several small tarns are reached; there are several campsites here about 50 feet to the right of the footpath. The tread forks 0.1 mile farther; the right fork into the col is the preferred and easier route. After ascending through meadow 0.3 mile farther, there are several small tarns to the right of the trail and several good tent sites around the tarn area. Thereafter, there are views to the east as the trail makes a long traverse across an avalanche slope and then turns back to the west again. The path passes under the fire lookout on the east and makes a final ascent to the structure via switchbacks from the north. The lookout is on top of granite talus. It is elevated about 20 feet on a stout timber platform and is the standard 14-by-14-foot box design.

Views from the top are impressive, except to the south, where the highway, railroad, power lines, and extensive clear-cuts mar the scenery. Mounts Baker, Adams, and Rainier are in view on a clear day. The Tooth and Denny Mountains are visible nearby, as are Crystal, Cad, and Tuscohatchie Lakes. Deer and bears frequent the area.

When I visited, the trail had been brushed recently. The lower sections would be difficult if overgrown, particularly if wet.

(August 1980)

MELAKWA LAKE

Elevations

Trailhead:	2,300 feet
Destination:	4,500 feet (Melakwa Lake)
Altitude Gain	2,500 feet in; 300 feet out (including ups and downs)
Walking Time	In: 2 hours 15 minutes Out: 2 hours
Trail Length	4.5 miles one-way
Accessibility	July to October
Difficulty	Moderate
Pack	Light
Topographic Sheets	USGS: Snoqualmie Pass
	Green Trails: Snoqualmie Pass

To access the trailhead from I-90, from the west, take Exit 47; cross the overpass to a T 0.1 mile; turn right (east). Go left at 0.3 mile on the chuckholed, poorly maintained Denny Creek Road. Two-tenths of a mile past the Denny

Creek Campground, turn left at the Denny Creek trailhead sign and cross the bridge; the trailhead is 0.3 mile farther. The road loops at the trailhead. There is parking space for about twenty-five cars.

From the east, take West Summit Exit 52. Cross under I-90 after passing the commercial area at the summit. Continue down Denny Creek Road 2.5 miles past the Alpental junction; turn right, cross the bridge, and continue 0.3 mile to the road end.

This footpath is heavily used. If possible, come on a weekday when it is less crowded. However, even on weekends, it is an enjoyable walk.

At 0.4 mile, cross Denny Creek on a bridge. At 0.5 mile, the trail goes under the north I-90 overpass, an impressive structure. At 0.8 mile (20 minutes), the Alpine Lakes Wilderness is entered. At 1 mile, Denny Creek is again crossed by jumping, rock-hopping, or fording.

There is a pleasant cascade, as the creek flows over the granite bedrock, at this point. Many stop here for a picnic, to soak their feet in the water, or simply to watch the water flowing on its way to the everlasting ocean. At 1.6 miles, the trail passes through a slide alder area; the low vegetation allows views of Denny Mountain to the north. At 1.9 miles, the trail passes Keekwulee Falls; this elegant waterfall, to the right of the trail, is impressive. This is another potential stopping point, approximately 55 minutes from the trailhead.

Above the falls, the trail gradient steepens; switchbacks must be surmounted. At 2.8 miles, Denny Creek, now considerably smaller, is crossed on a footlog. At 3.6 miles, a creek is crossed. Following that, there are switchbacks for about 0.5 mile, topping out at Hemlock Pass, 2 hours and slightly over 4 miles from the trailhead. From here the trail descends gradually; tread quality deteriorates, with mud and roots predominating underfoot. At 4.4 miles, trail 1011 drops down to the west. Follow the main trail another 0.1 mile to reach the south end of the lower lake. Cross a footlog to reach the lakeshore; one of the designated campsites, often damp, is located here.

A scrabble trail, which crosses several talus slopes on the west side of the lake, can be followed; it takes about 10 minutes to reach the north, or upper, lake. From here, there are good views of Chair and Kaleetan Peaks. It is about 0.5 mile farther cross-country to the north to Melakwa Pass. There are designated campsites around both lakes. A wilderness ranger patrols the area in the summertime.

There are no campsites whatsoever from the trailhead to the lower lake. Both lakes are quite scenic. Bunchberries and bead lilies are seen on the lower trail; small, blue alpine flowers bloom at the lakes. In mid-July, the area around the lakes was 90 percent snow free. From the trailhead to Hemlock Pass, the tread was in good condition.

(July 1988)

SNOW AND GEM LAKES
Elevations
>   Trailhead: 3,100 feet
>   Destination: 4,900 feet (Gem Lake)
>   Other Significant Locations: Snow Lake, 4,016 feet

Altitude Gain   In, 2,100 feet; out, 400 feet (including ups and downs)
                      Snow Lake: in, 1,300 feet; out, 400 feet (including ups and downs)
Walking Time   Gem Lake

In: 3 hours 10 minutes	Out: 2 hours 30 minutes

Snow Lake

In: 1 hour 35 minutes	Out: 1 hour 25 minutes

Trail Length   Snow Lake, 3 miles; Gem Lake, 5.5 miles (one-way)
Accessibility   Early July to late October
Difficulty   Gem Lake, moderately strenuous; Snow Lake, moderate
Pack   Light
Topographic Sheets   USGS: Snoqualmie Pass
                         Green Trails: Snoqualmie Pass

To access the trailhead from I-90, take West Summit Exit 52; cross under I-90. Take the second right and drive 1.3 miles past the Alpental complex. Park in the large lot to the left of the gate. Walk up the road behind the gate about 200 feet to reach the signed trailhead on the right.

At 0.2 mile (8 minutes), the trail crosses an avalanche slope from a cliff on the right; chest-high brush here is no problem if dry but unpleasant if wet. There are views of Tooth, Bryant, and Chair Peaks. The trail alternates between timbered and open areas from here to the pass above Snow Lake. At 0.7 mile, there is a 40-foot-wide rocky crossing of a small creek. The trail junction to the Source Lake Overlook is reached at 1.5 miles (52 minutes); the Snow Lake footpath turns right here (a 0.25-mile hike with a 150-foot altitude gain over difficult tread leads to a waterfall area with a view of Source Lake below). At 1.7 miles, the trail reaches a rock cliff; the tread worsens, and the switchback gradient steepens. Note blooming bear grass adjacent to the trail as altitude is gained. A view of Alpental below follows. At 2 miles (1 hour 20 minutes), the Alpine Lakes Wilderness is entered, and the pass above Snow Lake is crested. There is a view of Snow Lake about 375 feet below from the pass. The descent to the lake takes about 15 minutes. An instruction sign above the lake shows the location of the nine designated campsites and urges hikers to keep off the revegetated areas around the lake. One-tenth of a mile beyond the sign, the trail crosses a stream on rocks below a waterfall and pool. A way trail before the crossing leads to the ruins of the Snow Lake cabin, built in 1932, and to the east lakeshore. This scenic area is a good place to eat lunch. Twenty minutes from the stream crossing is the junction of the Gem Lake and Middle Fork of the Snoqualmie River trails; turn left here. Half a mile farther, cross Rock Creek on a wide footlog. Soon after the crossing, there are good views of the peaks to the east. Four-tenths of a mile farther, there is a scenic tarn below the footpath, with Chair Peak in the background. Ten minutes farther, the tread worsens and the upward gradient steepens. After passing several small tarns, the east shore of Gem Lake is reached, 1 hour and 15 minutes and 2 miles from the junction. There are several tent sites on the east side and one about 75 feet above the north side of the lake. Designated campsites are being established around Gem Lake and should be in place by 1998. Snow patches about the lake were still present in late July 1996. The lake is pleasant, but not spectacular.

The footpath to Snow Lake is heavily used. Go on a weekday if at all possible.

(July 1996)

SNOQUALMIE PASS TO PARK LAKES (PACIFIC CREST TRAIL)

Elevations

Trailhead:	3,000 feet
Destination:	4,800 feet (Park Lakes)
High Point:	5,800 feet (below Chikamin Peak)

Other Significant Locations: Ridge Lake, 5,300 feet

Altitude Gain   4,200 feet going north, 2,800 feet going south (including ups and downs)

Walking Times   Snoqualmie Pass to Ridge Lake, 4 hours 25 minutes (full pack; includes lunch stop); Ridge Lake to campsite on Chikamin Ridge, 5 hours 25 minutes (includes lunch stop); campsite to Park Lake, 35 minutes (light pack); return, 45 minutes. Campsite to Ridge Lake, 5 hours 15 minutes (includes lunch stop, photography, and some exploration); Ridge Lake to Snoqualmie Pass, 3 hours 15 minutes

Trail Length   15.7 miles one-way

Accessibility   July 15 to October 15

Difficulty   Moderately strenuous

Pack   Full to campsites, light for exploration beyond camp

Topographic Sheets   USGS: Snoqualmie Pass
Green Trails: Snoqualmie Pass

To reach the trailhead from I-90, take West Summit Exit 52; cross under I-90. After 0.1 mile, take the first right turn (signed if coming from the east, but not from the west). Drive 0.2 mile to a junction. Horse trailers turn left here;

cars containing hikers continue an additional 100 yards to the large parking lot at the trailhead. A privy is adjacent to the trailhead. The sign at the trailhead says that Stevens Pass is 67 miles away. Trail users should consult the signboard for other important information and regulations.

The Pacific Crest Trail (PCT) switchbacks up moderately through timber, gaining altitude but not distance from the highway for the first 1.5 miles. At 2.5 miles is the junction with the Commonwealth Basin trail. The PCT then goes northward about half a mile, then southward, gaining altitude for another mile to the ridge crest; it then contours the ridge crest northward. At about 2 hours and 15 minutes (5.3 miles), it breaks out into meadow. At about 3 miles, there is one forested campsite; a nearby creek provides water. There are several other campsites without water along the high ridge (there is also a campsite in the Commonwealth Basin, perhaps half a mile from the junction).

At the breakout point, there is a splendid view southward of Mount Rainier, with a nearby ridge obscuring the scars of the Snoqualmie Pass clearcuts and ski developments. The trail contours upward through delightful meadow, with excellent views of Guye Peak, Red Mountain, and Snoqualmie Mountain. At about 6.3 miles, a 0.1-mile stretch has been blasted out of the granite for an elegant high traverse. From this point, there are views of Kendall Peak, Alta Mountain, and Chikamin Ridge. About 0.4 mile before Gravel and Ridge Lakes, the trail begins its descent to the saddle between the lakes.

Turning west, a scrabble trail descends gently at first, then drops abruptly downward about 200 feet to reach Gravel Lake, where several designated campsites are located. However, the preferred campsites are on the east side of scenic Ridge Lake, most easily reached by proceeding on the PCT through a talus slope for 100 yards and then taking a way trail that leads to several designated campsites on both the north and south sides of the Ridge Lake outflow stream.

Camping with stock is prohibited between Snoqualmie Pass and Park Lake. No fires are allowed anywhere between Ridge Lake and Park Lake. A number of pikas live in the talus slope on the north side of Ridge Lake and can be observed by sitting quietly in this area. Marmots abound throughout the entire walk. Observing a marmot emit its high-pitched whistle is of interest; their large incisors can be seen when they whistle, clearly identifying them as rodents. Fish circles can be seen in both lakes. The area is quite buggy with gnats, an occasional horsefly, and lots of mosquitoes. Insect netting and repellent are musts when the wind stops blowing.

The next day's walk is one of the more elegant ones in the entire North Cascades. The trail drops down a bit, then regains altitude to reach a high ridge on the east flank of Alaska Mountain. It then switchbacks downward, losing about 500 vertical feet. Steps must be kicked across an occasional snow slope. About 100 yards before the saddle between Edds and Joe Lakes, there is a spring located in a hole at foot level along the trail; the flow is sufficient to fill a water bottle in about 60 seconds (but the Cle Elum ranger advises that this spring dries up in late summer). The trail enters timber at the saddle. There are several dry campsites along the saddle (and a small remaining snowbank in August 1988). A better campsite is located northeast of the saddle in a meadow, where a little poor-quality water was available. From that campsite, the trail gains altitude, ascending around Huckleberry Mountain. An elegant campsite, with two tarns to supply water, is in the saddle between Huckleberry and Chikamin, but the Forest Service prefers that no one camp in this vicinity in order to preserve its quality. There are one or two footpaths and several reasonably good campsites on sedge in this area, and it is quite scenic (and has water). The trail gains another several hundred vertical feet in altitude, reaching a notch before making the traverse eastward along Chikamin Ridge. This notch is a great place to have lunch, since one can see Glacier Peak to the north, Mount Rainier to the south, and mountains upon mountains in all other directions. One-tenth of a mile east of this notch, the trail reaches its high point. It then drops, losing several hundred vertical feet in altitude, and reascends to the point of the mountain (a southward projection of Chikamin Ridge). About a mile before reaching the point on Chikamin Ridge, a second spring is located at foot level (but also dries up in late summer). Several snowfields are also crossed in this area. No other water is available.

At the ridge high point, there are great views below of Park Lake. After descending about half a mile, a way trail leads northwestward to a flat vista area, which offers a splendid campsite and viewpoint; a scrabble trail descends from here to Glacier Lake, half a mile to the north. Unfortunately, the insects in this area are dreadful, but the views are worth it. Ascend a granite knoll 0.15 mile to the northeast. Two elegant tarns are located on either side of this knoll. Deer frequent the area in the early morning and late evening.

The designated camping area for hikers and stock is about 0.2 mile below the junction; this way trail is well marked. Another 0.3 mile downward is the trail junction to Park Lake. There is also a way trail leading northward to an unnamed small lake or large tarn about 0.15 mile away. There are good campsites on the south end and a fair campsite on the north end of this tarn. The PCT gains altitude after leaving the junction, reaches a forested ridge crest, and then descends via switchbacks to Spectacle Lake (an excellent view of Spectacle Lake and Mount Stuart can be had from the vista campsite described earlier). The trail to Park Lake descends several hundred vertical feet in slightly over half a mile to about 0.15 mile east of the lake, where a way trail goes westward to reach the lake itself. A number of trails in this area are being rehabilitated. There are at least two good campsites at the east end of Park Lake. Both the unnamed lake and Park Lake are green gems.

During the Chikamin traverse, Mount Rainier is in view much of the time. The trail to Park Lake is for hikers only. No fires are allowed anywhere in the Park Lake basin. Flowers are plentiful. Bumblebee noises are almost continuously audible, and hummingbirds are often attracted to those wearing red clothing or hats.

I did not descend to Spectacle Lake, but from above, it was apparent that forest rather than meadow surrounds the lake.

From Park Lake, it is 5.4 miles to forest road 46, or 9.7 miles to the Kachess Lake Campground via the Mineral Creek trail. If a car is left at one of these locations, steps back to Snoqualmie Pass need not be retraced.

The section of the PCT between Ridge and Park Lakes is scenically spectacular. The engineering of the PCT along this high ridge engenders respect for the trail-building capacities of those who constructed it.

Be aware that military jet aircraft fly near the ground up the Gold Creek valley. The sudden impact of the loud jet noise on the wilderness experience is substantial and unfavorable. Another annoyance is the I-90 traffic noise, which is intermittently audible for the first 5 miles (3 hours) after leaving Snoqualmie Pass.

(August 1988)

Mount Baker–Snoqualmie National Forest

BIG FOUR ICE CAVES

Elevations

Trailhead:	1,700 feet
Destination:	1,900 feet (Big Four Ice Caves)

Altitude Gain   250 feet (including ups and downs)

Walking Time   In: 35 minutes   Out: 30 minutes

Trail Length   1.1 miles one-way

Accessibility   May to November

Difficulty   Moderately easy

Pack   Light

Topographic Sheets   USGS: Silverton
Green Trails: Silverton

This is a popular trail best visited on weekdays to avoid the crowds. Drive east from Granite Falls on the Mountain Loop Highway. Continue 14.9 miles east of the Verlot Public Service Center. Turn right and drive into the new parking area. There are toilets there, and a blacktop path to the trailhead 0.2 mile to the west. Halfway there, the walkway passes a scenic wetland with good views of Big Four Mountain in the background.

All that remains of the historic Big Four Inn is the fireplace. Four picnic tables are scattered in the meadow between the fireplace and the trailhead. A double privy is also adjacent to the trailhead.

The trail for the first 0.1 mile crosses wetlands on a boardwalk; marsh flowers bloom here in season. It then becomes a wide gravel footpath for the next 0.2 mile. Note the large tree on the right with air spaces beneath the roots. This tree originally rooted on a fallen tree and had the advantage of getting more sunlight than ground-rooted trees; as the dead nurse tree below rotted, the growing tree sent roots downward to reach the ground. Eventually, the tree below completely disappeared, leaving a tree that appears to be supported by multiple "stilt" roots.

The south fork of the Stillaguamish River is crossed on a bridge. The riverbank may be accessed via a way trail after the bridge crossing. A second, smaller bridge over a creek offers a good view of Big Four Mountain. The upgraded, well-maintained footpath then ascends through a dense forest of western hemlock, western red cedar, and Pacific silver fir. The tread becomes rocky where the trail breaks out of the forest. Note the multiple waterfalls descending from Big Four. Cross 0.1 mile of rocky rubble to reach the opening of the east ice cave. The caves are located beneath massive snow slides that

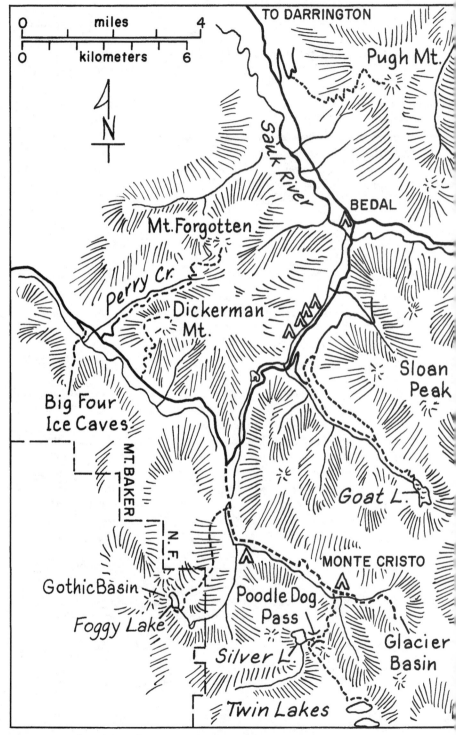

Mount Baker–Snoqualmie National Forest

have descended from the 4,000-foot-high cliff of Big Four Mountain during the preceding winter. Over the years, cascading avalanches have formed a small, stagnant glacier at the base of the mountain. When temperatures rise in the spring, meltwater trickles down the rocks, gradually creating small channels within the ice. Warm air follows, and eventually, large tunnels are eroded. Two to three ice caves are usually exposed between late July and October each year.

It is dangerous to enter the caves or to climb on the snow or ice slopes above them. This is particularly true in hot weather, when icefalls are more likely to occur. Truck-sized chunks of ice may come crashing down at any time. In the winter and early spring, avalanches are also a constant threat to hikers and cross-country skiers. If you elect to take the risk, be aware that because of a constant ice-water drip from the ceiling, it is wise to wear raingear if the caves are to be explored. A flashlight is also desirable for penetrating the far reaches of the ice caverns. It is cold inside the caves, and a cold breeze issues from them.

Fireweed, columbine, red monkey flower, and other wildflowers grow near the caves below a bare area that marks the zone of intermittent growth and retreat of the ice and snow. The cool microclimate in this area allows subalpine wildflowers to grow here; many of these flowers are rarely found at such low elevations. (Do not pick these flowers; photograph them, but leave them for the enjoyment of others.)

Do not leave the area until you have scrambled up the rocky slope to the west. The bases of several spectacular waterfalls are located here; these are at their most impressive when viewed on a hot day early in the season, when the volume of tumbling water is highest. On warm days, many folks play in the pools below the cataracts. Allow 2 to 3 hours to explore below the falls and near the caves. Eat lunch there. Take photographs. This is a great trip for everyone, including children and the elderly. Overnight camping is not permitted in the area.

Forest Service staff lead guided tours here. Check at the Public Service Center for tour schedules.

(July 1996)

DICKERMAN MOUNTAIN
Elevations

Trailhead:	2,000 feet
Destination:	5,723 feet (summit)

Altitude Gain   3,800 feet (including ups and downs)
Walking Time   In: 2 hours 10 minutes   Out: 1 hour 30 minutes
Trail Length   4.2 miles one-way
Accessibility   July 15 to October 15
Difficulty   Strenuous
Pack   Light
Topographic Sheets   USGS: Bedal 7.5
                          Green Trails: Sloan Peak

The trailhead is 16.4 miles from the Verlot Ranger Station on the Mountain Loop Highway east of Granite Falls. There is parking space for about five cars at the signed trailhead. A few feet up the trail, there is a spectacular view of Big Four Mountain. The trail switchbacks up moderately steeply and constantly through deep forest for about 2.7 miles. Occasional breaks in the forest cover allow views to the south. At about 2.7 miles, an impressive waterfall comes down a rock cliff to the north. Meadow is entered at about 2.9 miles, and at 3.1 miles, the trail forks. The left fork goes to a rather large tarn and pleasant campsite; this trail rejoins the main trail about 0.2 mile farther on. Although there is not much of a view from the tarn itself, there is a nice view of the mountains to the south from a ridge a few hundred feet above the tarn.

The main trail goes upward east of the tarn; at about 3.4 miles, the trail forks, with the left fork being a dead end. The right fork is the main trail leading to the summit. From 3 miles on, the trail passes through blueberry meadows, except for a short stretch of about 0.1 mile where it reenters woods on the ridge. Spectacular vine maple and mountain ash add to the color of the blueberries, providing vivid yellow and red colors in late September and early October. Blueberries and huckleberries are available throughout the meadow. The trail ends rather abruptly at the summit of the twin peaks of Dickerman Mountain. A sharp drop-off to the west makes the summit a scenic spot for lunch in good weather. A second peak (slightly lower and 0.1 mile to the north) contains small seams of agate; it is possible that further inspection might reveal larger deposits in the immediate area. This is a steep climb, but the lovely meadow for the last 1.2 miles is well worth the effort. The views from the summit are outstanding, with Baker, Shuksan, Glacier Peak, Three Fingers, White Horse, White Chuck, Pugh, Sloan, the Monte Cristo group, Del Campo, Big Four, Pilchuck, Puget Sound, and the Olympics all visible on a clear day. The west face of Dickerman is a straight drop of almost 500 feet and is an ideal location for those interested in spectacular rock climbs. Water is available without difficulty en route except on the summit ridge. Moderate wood supplies are available at the tarn, the only good camping area on this trail. Store food high if camping; there is abundant bear sign in the meadows.

As of 1994, the Forest Service reports that the tread is in good condition and that water is scarce to nonexistent from late July until early September.

(Fall 1969)

GOAT LAKE
Elevations

Trailhead:	1,900 feet
Destination:	3,161 feet (Goat Lake)
High Point:	3,200 feet
Altitude Gain	1,500 feet (including ups and downs)
Walking Time	In: 3 hours　　　Out: 2 hours 30 minutes
Trail Length	4.7 miles by trail; 5.5 miles by road (one-way)
Accessibility	June 1 to November 1
Difficulty	Moderate
Pack	Light
Topographic Sheets	USGS: Bedal, Sloan Peak
	Green Trails: Sloan Peak

Take the Mountain Loop Highway eastward from Granite Falls to Barlow Pass (elevation 2,349 feet), where the pavement ends. Turn left (north) here onto the graveled, potholed, one-lane-in-places road; drive carefully 3.4 miles, and then turn right (east) on the Elliott Creek Road, also rough and potholed. (The road to the turnoff may be paved in the not-too-distant future.) Continue 0.8 mile to the road end, where there is parking for about fifteen cars. A bulletin board is located at the trailheads. The footpath, seldom used presently, is about 15 feet from the instruction board and is not signed. Tread over the first 100 feet is in poor condition and presumably difficult to walk throughout. The footpath enters dense forest and drops down beside Elliot Creek. One-tenth of a mile from the trailhead, there is an impressive tree growing from a large, mossy rock at creekside. Unfortunately, even in midsummer, the first 2 miles of the trail are a quagmire; ankle- and occasionally knee-deep mud is the rule rather than the exception. Recent work on this trail may have improved drainage.

The trail follows the creek upstream. At 0.9 mile, it reaches a portion of the 7-mile-long Puncheon Wagon Road, built in 1896 to reach the mining claims at Goat Lake. There is a footbridge at 1 mile. The trail continues its gradual ascent through the forest. There are some campsites available at 2 miles. At 2.4

miles, the trail breaks out into an area that was clear-cut in 1960 and meanders through that area before joining the logging road at 3 miles. (There are good views from the clear-cut area and spectacular fireweed blooms.) It continues on the logging road for an additional 0.3 mile. From the road end, the trail plunges back into the forest, again following the historic Puncheon Road. The rate of ascent steepens at 3.9 miles, and the last half mile to the lake is a moderately vigorous ascent up multiple switchbacks. A faint way path to the right descends to Elliot Creek and the site of the 1896 Penn mining camp. Near the end of the trail, a waterfall is passed, and at 4.7 miles, the trail arrives at the shores of Goat Lake. This is a deep, fairly large lake. It is quite scenic, with the northwest face of Cadet Peak rising to 7,197 feet at the east end of the lake.

Camping is prohibited within 200 feet of the lakeshore, but there is a designated camping area on the knoll at the northeast side of the lake outlet. In 1964, there were remnants of the historic buildings that occupied this knoll, which included the original headquarters of the Penn Mining Company, Coffin's Cabin, and a rustic hotel operated by the McIntosh family between 1927 and 1936. Campfires are prohibited in the lake basin.

There is a way trail that continues around the north side of the lake, originally built by miners to reach the claims at the head of Goat Lake. After about half a mile, the footpath reaches the base of a spectacular waterfall. There is a wonderful wildflower display beneath the waterfall. The water is deep here, and it is a good place to fish, eat lunch, and contemplate the upsweep of Cadet Peak at the southeast end of the lake. Views of the peaks improve as this trail is followed, but trail quality deteriorates, and the trail gradually peters out in the vine maple and slide alder at the northeast end of the lake.

The preferred route to Goat Lake follows an abandoned road. Although overgrown by brush in places, and a half mile longer than the trail, it is easier and faster than the footpath. Tread is firm 95 percent of the time; slides and stream erosion have impacted the tread adversely intermittently. Trail machines, mountain bikes, and horses are allowed on the first 3.6 miles of this route, but hikers only may proceed further on the last 1.6 miles to the lake. Large rocks at the end of the road mark the trailhead.

At 0.4 mile, a 250-foot slide area is crossed; this is the worst of the slide areas. One mile from the trailhead, the trail curves to the southeast; there are about 200 feet of creek erosion in the tread here. At 2.5 to 2.6 miles, there are three view areas where the mountains to the southeast can be seen. Several creeks must be rock-hopped from 2.7 to 3.4 miles; waterfalls feed two of these streams. Dripping springs over a grotto where there are maidenhair ferns are impressive north of the trail. After about 1.5 hours at 3.6 miles, hikers reach the flat area where the dedication of the 1984 Washington Wilderness Bill took place. A campsite is located here. A creek is located 125 feet to the east of the flats; only hikers may proceed further. Tread on the east side of the creek is difficult to locate; cross the creek and go southeast, bypassing washed-out areas. Tread will soon become apparent; water runs in the tread for about 150 feet, further complicating route finding. Tread quality deteriorates from the creek to the lake. The trail now enters old-growth timber. The Henry Jackson Wilderness (HJW) boundary is reached at about 4 miles. Blooming trillium are impressive from the deep woods to the meadow areas around Goat Lake. Twenty-five minutes past the dedication flat area, the upward gradient of the footpath steepens. Switchbacks up the old mining road begin here; it takes about 25 minutes to surmount this ascent. Goat Lake is but 50 yards from the top-out point.

This alternative is less tiring, takes less time, and offers better views, although the route is slightly longer. Only if the weather has been very dry for several weeks should the boggy trail be considered. A loop trip—road one way and trail the other—is another alternative after a spell of good weather.

Although strong hikers can make the round-trip in a day, with present access, most visitors will prefer an overnight backpack when visiting the area. This hike is particularly recommended for a June conditioning walk before the higher country is snow free.

Readers interested in the mining history of Goat Lake should obtain *Monte Cristo Area*, by H. M. Majors and R. C. McCollum.

The Darrington ranger reports that current use is heavy and that the lake is often crowded on weekends, in spite of the muddy footpath.

(June 1997)

MONTE CRISTO
Elevations

Trailhead:	2,351 feet
Destination:	2,756 feet (Monte Cristo Ghost Town)
Altitude Gain	450 feet (including ups and downs)
Walking Time	In: 1 hour 45 minutes Out: 1 hour 30 minutes
Trail Length	4.1 miles one-way
Accessibility	Mid-May to mid-November
Difficulty	Moderate (round-trip)
Pack	Light
Topographic Sheets	USGS: Bedal, Monte Cristo
	Green Trails: Sloan Peak, Monte Cristo

Hikers and mountain bikers can explore the ghost town of Monte Cristo, an active mining town 100 years ago served by a no-longer-existing railroad, via a road damaged in the floods of 1980 and thereafter. The road is closed to car travel except for use in emergencies and by those owning private property in Monte Cristo. Three trails to the high country are also accessed by this road; space does not permit descriptions of these footpaths.

Drive east on the Mountain Loop Highway from Granite Falls to Barlow Pass, elevation 2,351 feet. Just before the pavement ends, there is parking space for ten to twelve cars on the right. Walk eastward 100 yards to the gated road.

At 0.5 miles, there is a scenic view of the south fork of the Sauk River in the foreground and one of the Twin Peaks in the distance. On the right 0.2 mile farther, there is a plank bridge, with tread thereafter; this is not the Weden Creek trailhead. A jeep road 0.1 mile farther bypasses a washout; the roadbed is rough and muddy for about 250 feet. At 1.1 miles, the Weden Creek trailhead is passed on the right; a privy is located nearby. Gothic Basin is 3 miles away. Rickety bridges cross the river immediately after the trailhead sign is passed. A washout 0.2 mile farther is bypassed by a muddy trail. Weden House signs are noted on the left at 1.6 miles. There are good views of Wilmon Peak at 1.7 miles. Another washout is bypassed at 1.8 miles. A junction with the signed Haps Hill campsite is located on the right at 2.2 miles. A small but nice tent site by the river below the roadbed is noted at 2.9 miles. At 3.3 miles, you enter private land. At cabins below the road on the right at 3.4 miles, you can access the sheriff by radio in an emergency. At 3.6 miles, the road passes through a timber-free area. Fall color is impressive here, as are the views of the surrounding peaks. At 3.9 miles, the road forks; left goes 0.1 mile to the Monte Cristo Campground. Go straight ahead to the Monte Cristo Townsite sign and a bridge crossing the river at 4 miles. There are nice views of the peaks upstream from the bridge. At 4.1 miles, reach the trailhead to Silver and Twin Lakes. The elevation here is 2,756 feet; Silver Lake is about 1,500 feet higher. The footpath to Glacier Basin passes a Pelton wheel generator and the railroad turntable, then a bulletin board, and after 0.1 mile reaches a sign before two plank bridges. Cross 76 Creek, turn right just past the bridge, pass through the old town after an eighth of a mile, and then proceed upward to Glacier Falls 1.5 miles from the bridge and Glacier Basin 2.5 miles from the bridge.

The Monte Cristo Campground has five to six tent sites, a privy, a shelter in excellent condition with a stove, and space inside to sleep up to eight people if the weather deteriorates. There is also an interesting historical sign here with a photograph and diagram of Monte Cristo circa 1900. Peaks seen from the sign from left to right are Foggy Peak, Mystery Ridge, Wilmon Peak, and Columbia Peak.

Much of the land in Monte Cristo is still privately owned. The antiquities here are also protected by federal law.

(October 1996)

PERRY CREEK (MOUNT FORGOTTEN)
Elevations
   Trailhead: 2,100 feet
   Destination: 5,000 feet (trail end)
   Other Significant Locations: Perry Creek Falls, 3,200 feet
Altitude Gain   3,000 feet (including ups and downs)
Walking Time   In: 2 hours   Out: 1 hour 20 minutes
Trail Length   4 miles one-way
Accessibility   July 15 to October 15
Difficulty   Moderately difficult
Pack   Light
Topographic Sheets   USGS: Bedal 7.5'
                 Green Trails: Sloan Peak

   The trailhead is 15.2 miles east of the Verlot Ranger Station on Highway 92 (Mountain Loop). Turn left (north) about 0.1 mile east of the Perry Creek bridge and drive up the logging road 1.1 miles to its end. There is cramped parking space for four to five cars here; the turnaround is not for the timid driver. The trail goes moderately upward, primarily through talus slopes, for about 1.9 miles. At about 1 mile, there is a spectacular waterfall on the left, as well as maidenhair fern along the trail. Fall color of the numerous vine maple and big-leaf maple en route is notable. At 1.9 miles, Perry Creek Falls, a beautiful mossy waterfall, is reached. There is a fair campsite at the pool just above the falls. In the timber for the next 0.1 mile, there are a number of pleasant campsites. From here, the trail switchbacks up moderately steeply through deep timber, with only occasional views of the surrounding peaks until it breaks out in meadow at approximately 3.5 miles. The up-time to this point (entering meadow) is approximately 2 hours, and the altitude gain is about 3,000 feet. Here the trail forks, and the left fork almost immediately forks again. The left fork of the left fork continues along the ridge approximately 0.3 mile and then divides again, with the lower fork dropping downward and probably contouring to the southwest to gain access to a plateau and meadow seen in that area (I did not explore beyond this point). The right fork gradually peters out on a rocky ridge that can be traversed with moderate difficulty by those with climbing experience. A class 2 to class 3 rock scramble also gives access to the plateau meadow to the southwest.

   The right fork of the left fork brings you to a campsite and viewpoint overlooking a deep valley with impressive views of White Chuck, Shuksan, and Baker. From this point, you can progress north and rejoin the original right fork of the trail, which goes moderately steeply upward an additional 0.5 mile, terminating at a saddle beneath Forgotten Mountain. A short scramble immediately to the south gains about 200 feet in altitude and gives you a magnificent 360-degree view of surrounding peaks. A fine campsite by a tarn is located at about the 3.9-mile mark; from this location, there is an exceptional view of Glacier Peak to the north.

Water is available at about 1.5 miles, at 1.9 miles, at one or two sites on the switchbacks, and at the tarn. The up-time to Perry Creek waterfall is 50 minutes; this alone is a fine hike, since there are lovely views down the valley, and the altitude gain to this point is not too great (1,000 feet). The climb of Forgotten Peak requires a hands-on scramble, dropping down several hundred feet and then traversing scree and talus over quite difficult terrain to reach the skyline ridge on the right. It is not recommended for inexperienced climbers. Mountain goats are often seen on Mount Forgotten. Gray jays frequent the meadows. Fine views of Mount Dickerman and Big Four can also be had from this meadow. Down-time from the trail end is 1 hour and 20 minutes; from the waterfall, it is 40 minutes. Wood supply is adequate everywhere en route. The 1.5 miles of switchbacks in the woods gain 2,000 feet in altitude and make the footpath moderately strenuous.

The MBSNF is considering the establishment of a research natural area in the vicinity of Perry Creek.

(October 1969)

PUGH MOUNTAIN
Elevations
Trailhead:	1,900 feet
Destination:	7,201 feet (summit–lookout site)

Other Significant Locations: Stujack Pass, 5,750 feet; Metan Lake, 3,250 feet

Altitude Gain	5,500 feet (including ups and downs)
Walking Time	In: 5 hours Out: 3 hours
Trail Length	5.5 miles; Stujack Pass, 3.8 miles
Accessibility	August 1 to September 30
Difficulty	Strenuous
Pack	Light
Topographic Sheets	USGS: White Chuck and Pugh Mountains
	Green Trails: Sloan Peak

The access road to the trailhead is the Mountain Loop Highway. About 2 miles south of the White Chuck bridge, take Pugh Mountain Road 2095 and drive 1 mile to the signed trailhead. The parking area is limited. The footpath ascends through deep forest. At about 1.5 miles, the trail passes Metan Lake, which covers about an acre and is surrounded by dense woods. In spite of the forest cover, there is a fine view of Pugh Mountain from this point. The lake probably does not contain fish. The trail turns left at the lake and ascends in gradual, long switchbacks for about another 2 miles (watch out for yellow jacket nests in this area). At the 3.5-mile mark, the footpath enters meadow. A herd of mountain goats often frequents this area; keep an eye out for them. From here, the gradient steepens; switchbacks top out at Stujack Pass. There are good views from this point. Hikers averse to exposure and without climbing experience should turn back here.

The footpath now threads over the top of a razorback ridge until it reaches the main bulk of Pugh Mountain. In places, the trail has been blasted out of solid rock. In 1961, one pitch had fixed rope in place at the site of a 40-foot class 3 rock climb. The ascents in the next 300 to 400 yards are more benign but require the use of hands. After these several scrambles, the trail goes up steeply through heather and rock slopes to the knifelike summit ridge. The two-story lookout burned down in 1966. Views from the summit are magnificent; for practical purposes, all of the Cascades can be seen. The three great volcanoes, Rainier, Glacier Peak, and Mount Baker, are visible on clear days. The view is a bit marred by the multiple patch-cuts clearly evident along the White Chuck River. Other visible peaks are White Chuck Mountain, Meadow Mountain, Bedal Peak, and Mount Forgotten. On a clear day, the hiker can see forever!

From Metan Lake upward, water is very scarce, and adequate supplies should be carried. Of interest are the residual A-frames below the summit, from which the material to construct the lookout was winched to bypass terrain too exposed and too dangerous for packhorses. There are few good places for camping anywhere en route. Since this is a long and arduous one-day trip, an early start is essential for those planning to reach the summit.

(September 1961)

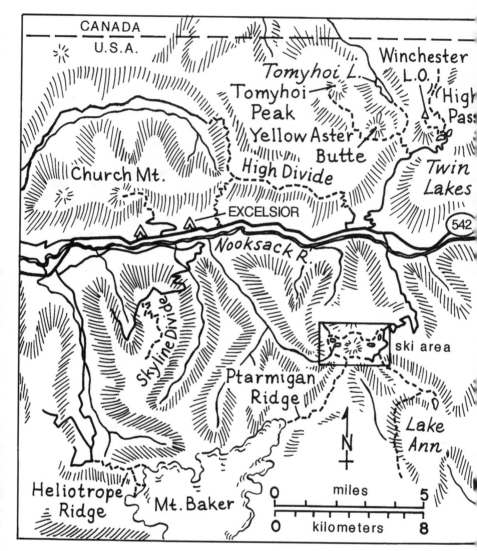

Mount Baker Wilderness

Mount Baker Wilderness

CHURCH MOUNTAIN

Elevations

Trailhead:	2,600 feet
Destination:	6,100 feet (Church Mountain lookout site)

Altitude Gain 3,500 feet (including ups and downs)
Walking Time In: 3 hours   Out: 1 hour 45 minutes
Trail Length 4.5 miles one-way
Accessibility July 15 to early October
Difficulty Moderately strenuous
Pack Light
Topographic Sheets USGS: Mount Baker
Green Trails: Mount Baker

To reach the trailhead, drive up State Highway 542 5.6 miles east of the town of Glacier. Turn north and drive up the logging road 2.5 miles to the trailhead. There is parking for about twelve to fifteen cars at the road end. The last half mile of logging road is blocked off and must be walked. One creek en route to the trailhead cascades over the road and might pose difficulty during the spring high-water runoff. After leaving the roadbed, the trail switchbacks up moderately steeply, initially through a patch-cut, and then through deep woods. At about 2 miles, it begins contouring northward, still through deep forest but with a diminished upward gradient. At about 3 miles, it breaks out into subalpine meadow. From here to the old lookout site, the trail passes through 1.5 miles of alpine gardens in the sky. After entering the meadow, the trail turns westward, gradually climbing onto a ridge and eventually switchbacking up the ridge to the old lookout site, about 4.5 miles from the current trailhead. The lookout was destroyed by the Forest Service in 1966.

From this point, there are spectacular views of Mount Baker, Shuksan, and the Picket Range. Unfortunately, the views of Mount Baker are marred by extensive patch-cutting on its north flanks. There are nice camping areas in the meadow below the lookout; in addition, there is a level campsite just east of the last switchback turn below the top-out point.

Two small pockets lakes lie about half a mile northwest of the trail end; reaching them is not difficult, particularly if there is sufficient snow present to glissade. The true summit of Church Mountain is almost directly to the west.

Experienced hikers may wish to contour to the right immediately upon entering the meadow, a bit before the meadow, or in the middle of the meadow and then climb steeply upward to the east to reach the ridge. Do not attempt to climb the steep rock to the north. The ridge crest leads eastward; it is possible to walk the ridge with only minor losses and gains of altitude for approximately 10 miles to Yellow Aster Butte. You can descend either of the Excelsior trails, the Welcome Pass trail, or the Yellow Aster Butte trail built in 1997. There is a trail between Excelsior and Welcome Passes. The remainder of the ridge has no trail but is not difficult.

Vast fields of glacier lilies turn the upper meadows a golden yellow as the snows recede from the area. Other wildflowers often seen along the trail are the yellow violet, calypso orchid, and trillium. In early autumn, fall color is impressive. Vine maples, big-leaf maples, mountain ash, and blueberries are some of the trees and shrubs that put on colorful displays. Marmots are commonly seen in the meadows.

(October 1981)

GOLD RUN PASS (TOMYHOI LAKE)
Elevations

Trailhead:	3,700 feet	
Destination:	3,700 feet (Tomyhoi Lake)	
High Point:	5,400 feet	

Altitude Gain 1,800 feet in both directions (including ups and downs)

Walking Time In: 2 hours 10 minutes   Out: 2 hours 10 minutes

Trail Length 4 miles one-way

Accessibility July 15 to October 15

Difficulty Moderately strenuous

Pack Light

Topographic Sheets USGS: Mount Shuksan
Green Trails: Mount Shuksan

At 13.1 miles past the store at Glacier on State Route 542, turn off to the north just beyond the highway maintenance shops. Travel up this narrow, rough road 4.6 miles to the trailhead. There is parking space for six or seven cars in the trailhead area and additional parking at the road switchback below the trailhead. By the 1998 hiking season, this trail will also access Yellow Aster Meadows and Butte and Tomyhoi Peak. Trailhead parking will also be upgraded. See Yellow Aster Butte for more information. A hundred yards up the road from the trailhead, there is a nice view of Mount Baker.

The path ascends about 400 vertical feet in switchbacks through a pleasant meadow and then plunges into the forest. It runs fairly level to the west for about half a mile and then ascends out of the deep woods into meadow below Gold Run Pass. Take the well-used trail to the crest of the pass; an overgrown way trail also rambles through the upper meadow and may be followed to abandoned mining claims. It is 2 miles from the trailhead to Gold Run Pass.

The up-time is 1 hour, the down-time is 40 minutes, and the altitude gain is about 1,700 feet. From the pass, there are impressive views of Mount Baker to the south and of Larrabee, American Border, and Canadian Border Peaks to the north. A brief side trip 0.1 mile to the west of the pass brings the hiker to a knob; from there, Tomyhoi Lake is easily seen below. This location is the best viewpoint and lunch stop on the trail.

From the pass, it is 2 miles to the lake. The down-time is roughly 55 minutes, and the up-time is about 1 hour and 15 minutes. The trail drops down steeply on switchbacks, passing a campsite at about 0.5 mile. It then parallels a stream and crosses a meadow. There are several campsites in this area. The path leaves the southwest end of the meadow, drops underneath a moss-covered, tree-bedecked rock, and descends through forest 0.4 mile. The trail then breaks out into the open and crosses a creek several times. One-tenth of a mile before the lake, beside a creek, there are two campsites. The trail bears left at this point, and the tread quality deteriorates. A scrabble trail reaches the lakeshore, where there are perhaps six or seven additional campsites. A rough way trail continues around the south side of the lake. In the late fall, the lake level may be as low as 20 feet below the high-water mark. Although Larrabee, American, and Canadian Border Peaks are visible, the lake is not particularly scenic; clear-cuts at the west end of the lake are unattractive. Wood and water are not a problem at any of the campsites. Fires are prohibited within 1 mile of Gold Run Pass.

The 1,800 vertical feet descended must be regained en route back to the car; this is one of the few North Cascades trails where the walking time is the same in both directions. The lake area is used primarily by fishermen.

Experienced wilderness travelers can cut off the trail about 0.6 mile north of the pass and proceed cross-country to the Low Pass area. From that point, they can return via Twin Lakes.

(October 1978)

HELIOTROPE RIDGE
Elevations
> Trailhead: 3,700 feet
> Destination: 6,000 feet (Heliotrope Ridge)
> Other Significant Locations: Coleman Glacier snout, 4,700 feet

Altitude Gain   2,300 feet (including ups and downs)
Walking Time   In: 2 hours   Out: 1 hour 45 minutes
Trail Length   3 miles one-way
Accessibility   July 25 to October 1
Difficulty   Moderately strenuous
Pack   Light
Topographic Sheets   USGS: Mount Baker
>   Green Trails: Mount Baker

Drive State Highway 542 to the village of Glacier. Turn south about 1 mile east of Glacier, and drive the initially paved one-lane road with turnouts 8.1 miles to the trailhead. Use great caution on the road, since traffic is substantial, particularly on weekends, and head-on collisions are a threat. Substantial parking space is available, but space may be at a premium, since this trail is heavily used. There is a picnic area and viewpoint 1.5 miles farther up this road. The view of Mount Baker from the road end is awesome.

The footpath ascends gradually through deep forest. A mossy cliff on the right is scenic at about 1.4 miles. At 1.5 miles, Kulshan Creek must be crossed; there is no bridge. In the late spring and early summer, especially on warm afternoons, this crossing is difficult, potentially hazardous, and perhaps impossible. Even in the fall, getting across is not easy. At 1.9 miles, note the waterfall on the right. At 2 miles, the site of Kulshan Cabin is reached; the structure was removed some years ago. There are campsites in this vicinity. The trail to the snout of the Coleman Glacier has been closed.

The tread continues upward. One-tenth of a mile farther, a shallow creek is crossed, and 0.3 mile after the crossing, a junction is reached. The right fork leads to the climbers' scrabble trail up the Heliotrope Ridge hogback. This route, for the surefooted only, goes up steeply to the south until it terminates at the Coleman Glacier at an altitude of about 6,000 feet. A number of climbers' camps are located just below the glacier. There are views from this location to the north. The average hiker should not proceed further. The experienced cross-country traveler with an ice ax can contour upward and westward to reach a green knoll 0.9 mile from the top of the hogback. In late July, there are splendid wildflower displays here. It is an ideal place to eat lunch and to view the impressive surrounding vistas. The ability to kick steps in snow is a required skill to safely visit this area.

The experienced can also turn eastward at the top of the hogback for about 0.5 mile; creeks must be crossed. A scrabble descent route leads downward to connect with the Coleman Glacier Overlook trail.

Returning to the trail junction, the left fork leads to the Glacier Overlook viewpoint mentioned above. This footpath leads to a rocky knob above the Coleman Glacier about 0.5 mile from the junction. Unfortunately, two streams must be crossed en route; both are difficult even early in the morning. The steep scrabble descent route mentioned above joins this trail on the west side of the second creek. The spectacle from the overlook of the broken ice of the glacier below and the great bulk of ice-clad Mount Baker above is noteworthy.

Individuals without mountaineering experience, equipment, and trained companions should NEVER venture onto the Coleman (or any other) Glacier. To do so is to invite serious injury or loss of life; many have died in the Northwest who have not heeded this warning.

It is suggested that hikers carry binoculars. Mountain goats can often be seen on Bastile Ridge. Magnification is also helpful for observing climbers on the slopes of Koma Kulshan, the Native American name for Mount Baker.

This area is the most common route for the ascent of Mount Baker. Campers should be aware that most climbers arise between 1 and 2 A.M. to begin their climb. These departures often disturb the sleep of campers in nearby areas. The climbers' tent sites adjacent to the glacier are bleak, barren, and cold. Most hikers will want to find a location near the cabin site to overnight. Fires are not allowed within 1 mile of the trail.

(August 1996)

HIGH DIVIDE (EXCELSIOR RIDGE)

Elevations

Trailhead:	4,150 feet (Canyon Creek)
Destination:	5,350 feet (Excelsior Pass)
High Point:	5,800 feet (Excelsior Ridge)
Altitude Gain	1,300 feet to Excelsior (including ups and downs)
Walking Time	In: 1 hour 15 minutes Out: 1 hour
Trail Length	2.6 miles one-way
Accessibility	July 15 to late October
Difficulty	Moderate
Pack	Light
Topographic Sheets	USGS: Mount Baker
	Green Trails: Mount Baker

There are two access routes to this area; both start by taking Highway 542 from Bellingham. One trailhead is on the Mount Baker Highway 7.7 miles east of the gas station in Glacier. This trail switchbacks up steeply with no view for over 2 miles, breaks out briefly into semimeadow at that point, then goes back into forest with only glimpses of the surrounding mountains until it breaks out again at 3.5 miles. About 100 feet of trail is obliterated at this point, and one must go north-northeast to locate it.

It is 4.1 miles from the trailhead to the crest of Excelsior Pass. The site of the Excelsior lookout, burned down by the Forest Service in 1968, is a steep additional 0.25 mile to the east of the pass, accessed by a scrabble trail. (The west end of the High Divide footpath to Welcome Pass starts at the same location and contours eastward on the south side of the hump beneath the site where the lookout previously stood.) The up-time by this route to the pass is 3 hours; down-time is 1 hour and 30 minutes. Altitude gain is 3,500 feet.

Camping in Excelsior Pass is pleasant, with splendid views of Shuksan and Baker. There are lovely wildflowers in July and August and brilliant fall color in late September and early October. Water is scarce on the ridge crest. Fires are prohibited here and within 1 mile of the High Divide trail.

The easier access route is to take the Canyon Creek Road 2.2 miles past Glacier and drive 14 miles from the highway to a parking lot on the right, where there is space for about fifteen to twenty cars. The trail starts immediately east of this round parking area, cutting across slash until it enters the woods after about 200 yards.

From the trailhead, it is roughly 0.7 mile to the junction of the Canyon Ridge trail, 0.8 mile to Damfino Lakes, and 2.6 miles to Excelsior Pass. The Damfino Lakes are too shallow to support fish; there are, however, nice scenic campsites at the lakes, as well as lots of bugs in season. From the lakes, the trail switchbacks upward through forest to break out into meadow below Excelsior Pass about 1.5 miles beyond the lakes; an additional 0.5-mile walk brings you to the pass with substantially less altitude gain and with a saving of approximately 1.5 miles over the other access route. A stream is crossed 0.5 mile below Excelsior Pass; fill water bottles here. There is no water along the last half mile of trail or along the ridge crest (except for snow patches). A tarn 0.1 mile west of the footpath, and about 0.3 mile below Excelsior Pass, offers both tent sites and access to water. The lower portions of this trail can be muddy at times. Deer, bears, and mountain goats are seen in this area occasionally.

The High Divide trail between Excelsior Pass and Welcome Pass is approximately 5 miles long, with an approximate altitude gain and loss in each direction of 1,000 feet. The only water sources available on this rather dry trail are a spring approximately 1 mile west of Welcome Pass; about 0.3 mile from Welcome Pass, a large tarn on the south side of the trail fed by a spring, which is probably drinkable; and a shallow tarn 0.4 mile from Welcome Pass. There are several level areas for camping, but they are waterless after snowfields have melted in the summer. The approximate walking time one-way is 2.5 hours in either direction. The trail is in excellent condition and marked by tree-trunk cairns in areas where it may be slightly difficult to find. This is a magnificent trail, particularly lovely around October 1, at the height of fall color. Although largely exterminated by hunters, occasional bears are still seen in this area. There are a number of areas along the route where you can sit and picnic and enjoy the splendid panorama of mountains in every direction. From the Welcome Pass end, there are splendid views of the Nooksack Cirque under Mount Shuksan and of the crests of Icy and Ruth Mountains. Fires are not allowed within 1 mile of the High Divide trail.

From Excelsior Pass, it is also possible to walk the ridge westward, following scrabble trail tread that fades out after a mile or so. Experienced hikers can continue cross-country all the way to Church Mountain without undue difficulty or significant loss of altitude.

The access road was washed out several years ago and was reopened in 1996. Pavement has been lost in places, and the roadbed is rough intermittently. The road is one lane with turnouts. Use of the area is substantial, so watch carefully for oncoming traffic.

Do not be concerned that the trail is open to horses, mountain bikes, and trail machines. After 0.7 mile, horses are allowed only after August 1. Trail machines and bikes are prohibited after 0.7 mile; their trail turns off at that point to the north.

The tread has been upgraded over the past several years. Mud holes are far less common. Steps are present in several areas of the ridge. One rock step contains two nice fossils, probably an oyster and a clam.

In season, there are elegant flowers in bloom along the first half mile of High Divide trail. Mount Baker looms in the distance above the blossoms. Unfortunately, during hot weather, insects can be annoying.

(South approach, October 1966; north approach, August 1996)

HIGH PASS (TWIN LAKES)

Elevations

Trailhead:	5,200 feet (Twin Lakes)
Destination:	5,800 feet (Gargett Mine)
High Point:	6,000 feet (High Pass)

Other Significant Locations: Ridge at the end of trail, 6,700 feet

Altitude Gain   1,000 feet (including ups and downs)

Walking Time   In: 1 hour 40 minutes   Out: 1 hour

Trail Length   2 miles one-way

Accessibility   July 15 to October 15

Difficulty   Moderate

Pack   Light

Topographic Sheets   USGS: Mount Shuksan
                     Green Trails: Mount Shuksan

See Winchester Mountain for information on reaching the trailhead and for other pertinent data about the Twin Lakes area.

After the junction 0.1 mile from the combined trailhead, turn right (north). The footpath contours under Winchester Peak, reaching Low Pass 1.5 miles from the trailhead and then proceeding upward to High Pass at 2.3 miles. The trail forks in the High Pass area. The left fork descends about 200 vertical feet to the Gargett Mine, about 0.2 mile from the junction. The trail to the right ascends the ridge; the tread becomes progressively less apparent and ultimately disappears at the ridge top, about 0.8 mile from the junction, having gained about 750 vertical feet in altitude after leaving High Pass. An additional 45 minutes is required to reach the trail end on the ridge crest. There is evidence of mining activity throughout the area; old pipes and timbers mark the site of an abortive glory hole on the shoulder of the Pleiades, a seven-spired peak near Mount Larrabee. Beyond the ridge crest, a not too difficult rock scramble (but requiring rock climbing experience) allows the hiker-climber to reach the summit of Mount Larrabee (Red Mountain). There are many blueberries in the area. The alpine floral display is splendid in season and includes many dwarf fireweed.

There are a few springs along the trail, and water is generally available from permanent snowfields. Wood is scarce. There are fair campsites at High Pass. Grouse and ptarmigan are seen frequently. Bears, mountain goats, and deer are observed occasionally. Fires are not allowed within 1 mile of the trail.

All trails in the Twin Lakes area are closed to motorized vehicles. Current logging on patented mine claims in the area may well leave scars visible for many years. The mines in the area have been reactivated and presumably will continue to operate as long as they are profitable. When the timber is cut and/or the ore depleted, the miners will no longer maintain the last 2 miles of the access road to the lakes. At that time, the MBSNF will have to decide whether to maintain the road (perhaps with help from Whatcom County) or to allow the road past the Tomyhoi Lake–Yellow Aster Butte trailhead to revert to trail status.

(September 1970)

LAKE ANN (MOUNT SHUKSAN VICINITY)

Elevations

Trailhead:	4,700 feet
Destination:	4,900 feet (Lake Ann)
Altitude Gain	1,000 feet (including ups and downs, both in and out)
Walking Time	In: 2 hours Out: 2 hours
Trail Length	4 miles one-way
Accessibility	Early June to mid-October
Difficulty	Moderate
Pack	Full
Topographic Sheets	USGS: Mount Shuksan
	Green Trails: Mount Shuksan

Drive State Highway 542 1.6 miles beyond the Mount Baker ski facilities. There is parking for about ten cars at the Austin Pass trailhead. The trail loses 500 vertical feet in the first half mile in a series of switchbacks. After reaching the valley floor, it then follows the headwaters of Swift Creek southeastward, losing altitude gradually. After about 1.5 miles, the recreation area boundary is passed. The portion of the trail within the recreation area is closed to overnight camping. After traversing lovely meadow beneath Shuksan Arm to the northeast and Kulshan Ridge to the southwest, the hiker reaches a trail junction at the 3-mile mark. The right fork descends the poorly maintained Swift Creek trail. The more easily seen left fork switchbacks upward to the east, gaining 1,000 vertical feet in altitude and topping out on a ridge crest above Lake Ann; a short descent brings you to the lake, some 4 miles from the trailhead. From the trailhead to the junction, 800 feet in altitude are lost; then 1,000 feet are gained; thereafter, 200 feet are lost. There are a number of campsites scattered around the lake, which is quite deep and serves as a water source. Campfires are prohibited, so a stove should be carried for cooking. Lake Ann is the base camp for mountaineers who intend to climb Mount Shuksan by the standard route. Particularly on weekends and holidays, the Lake Ann area is usually overflowing with mountain climbers, and campsites are at a premium.

For the more adventurous and more experienced, it is possible to follow the scrabble trail from Lake Ann a reasonable distance up toward Fisher's

Chimneys; those without climbing experience should not go too far, since the trail narrows and becomes significantly exposed a mile or so beyond the lake. Views from the lake eastward to Mount Shuksan are impressive. Avalanches from the Upper Curtis Glacier occur frequently; the noise produced by the falling ice suggests distant thunder. From the ridge above the lake, there are also impressive views of the Mount Baker massif to the west.

The national park boundary is about half a mile east of Lake Ann. The entire Lake Ann trail lies within a game reserve. Pets are prohibited, and firearms may not be discharged anywhere along the trail between Austin Pass and Mount Shuksan.

The geological formations that can be viewed from the Lake Ann trail are interesting. Volcanic flows, presumably from Mount Baker, displaying columnar jointing and horizontal flow banding can be seen at Austin Pass. The rock is a porphyritic andesite and contains large phenocrysts of white plagioclase.

At the 4,400-foot contour, in one of the many stream channels that cross the trail, there is an outcrop of Chilliwack metavolcanic rock. The Chilliwack can also be seen as dark, fairly massive rocks forming the northeastern wall of the valley along Shuksan Arm. The Chilliwack consists mostly of fine-grained greenstone, probably derived from the metamorphism of an andesite flow.

Beginning at the Swift Creek log bridge is the first observed outcrop of the granodiorite Lake Ann stock (a stock is a batholith of which less than 40 square miles have been exposed by erosion). This rock can be seen in outcrops along the trail from this point all the way to Lake Ann. Recent studies indicate an age of 2.5 to 2.7 million years, making it one of the youngest exposed igneous intrusive rock anywhere in the world.

The reddish brown rock exposed on the Shuksan Arm ridge has been thermally altered by the intrusion of the Lake Ann stock. This formation contains sulfide minerals; old-time prospectors sank several mine shafts in the area.

The Shuksan metamorphic suite is exposed northeast of Lake Ann. The Darrington Phyllite and Shuksan Greenschist together form the Shuksan Metamorphic Suite; both are unlike any other rock in the Northwest. The upper portion of Mount Shuksan (the greenschist) may represent a segment of seafloor basalt that has been metamorphosed in a subduction zone along the boundary between two colliding plates. This is presumably what is happening to rocks of the Juan de Fuca plate, which are being forced beneath the western edge of North America. (I am indebted to graduate student Eric James of the Department of Geology, Western Washington University, from whose master's thesis this geological information was obtained.)

(August 1964)

PTARMIGAN RIDGE

Elevations
Trailhead: 5,100 feet
Destination: 6,500 feet (The Portals)
Other Significant Locations: Coleman Pinnacle, 6,414 feet

Altitude Gain   1,700 feet (including ups and downs)
Walking Time   In: 2 hours 30 minutes   Out: 2 hours 15 minutes
Trail Length   6.5 miles one-way
Accessibility   Late July to late September
Difficulty   Moderately strenuous
Pack   Light
Topographic Sheets   USGS: Mount Shuksan, Mount Baker
                         Green Trails: Mount Shuksan, Mount Baker

To reach the trailhead, drive past the Mount Baker ski development on State Route 542 to the road termination at the Artist Point parking area, where there is space for perhaps eighty cars. The trailhead is at the west end of the parking lot. The footpath then traverses the south side of Table Mountain, losing a few feet in altitude initially and then regaining it by the time the Chain Lakes trail junction is reached 1.1 miles from the trailhead. This section of trail is understandably popular and heavily used; however, most people either terminate at this point or turn northward to Chain Lakes or the Table Mountain Loop.

The less apparent trail to Coleman Pinnacle, Camp Kiser (a misnomer, since there is no formal camp in this general area of subalpine meadow), and the Portals (the rock and ice gateway to the slopes of Mount Baker itself) drops down to the left. The footpath contours underneath the rock ridge to the south for about half a mile and then climbs up to the crest of a broad ridge. This portion of the trail commonly cannot be located due to the presence of persistent snow; those without Vibram lug boots, or other traction-improving footwear, and an ice ax should turn back at this point. Those experienced in self-arrest and in kicking steps in snow can ascend this ridge and proceed westward along the south side of Ptarmigan Ridge. At about 2.4 miles, the tread is usually buried by a steep snow slope for about 100 yards. This dangerous snow slope can sometimes be bypassed on scree and gravel above the trail location but must usually be traversed to continue. Again, boots with lug soles, an ice ax, and experience in kicking steps are mandatory to proceed safely across. About 3 miles from the trailhead, the footpath reaches the south side of Coleman Pinnacle. From here, after the winter snows have melted, a very high lake with a brilliant blue-green color is apparent half a mile to the south. Depending on snow conditions, this lake can be inspected either by a snow traverse or by cross-country travel on a nonformal way trail. The area around the lake is exceptionally beautiful, and there are several good campsites here.

Just beyond Coleman Pinnacle, the trail passes above a pleasant campsite in the subalpine meadows below the trail. Another good campsite with adjacent water is passed at about 6 miles. In heavy snow years the tread is snow covered beyond the crossing of Sholes Creek. In low snow pack years, the tread continues upward on a ridge between the Mazama and Sholes Glaciers; tread quality deteriorates as altitude is gained. After a gain of about 500 vertical feet over a 0.7-mile distance, a rocky promontory is reached. There are several camping areas on this exposed ridge; melting snow provides water. If this section of the trail is free of snow, the distance to the promontory is about 7.2 miles from the trailhead.

This is one of the most splendid walks in the North Cascades cordillera. Views are splendid in all directions for the entire length of the trail. Unlike most trails in the range, this one has no forest approach prior to the splendid scenery. Surprisingly, in view of the crowds at the trailhead, people are seldom seen beyond 1.5 miles. Mount Shuksan is in view throughout the walk. During the height of the heather season, the view at the Chain Lake junction is magnificent. Views in late September and early October, when the fall color is at its height, are also impressive. Mount Baker is also in view throughout. If Coleman Pinnacle is ascended, most of the great peaks of the North Cascades are in view. To the north is Excelsior Ridge, Yellow Aster Butte, Winchester Mountain, Mount Larrabee, and American and Canadian Border Peaks. To the east are Ruth Mountain and, beyond it, the Pickets. To the south are Blum and Hagen Mountains and, in the far distance, Glacier Peak. Pikas, marmots, and ptarmigan are common. Occasionally, mountain goats and deer are seen in the area.

The one disadvantage of this hike is that overnight campsites are limited. No campfires are allowed, and there is no camping within 1 mile of the Chain Lakes trail junction. The eastern section of Ptarmigan Ridge is flat but is within a mile of that junction. Just past the 1-mile mark, there is a campsite to the left of the trail in the trees. All other places to pitch a tent are listed in the trail description. Since most sites are exposed, protection from wind and cold is essential for campers. Even day hikers should be prepared to cope with the sudden onset of inclement weather.

For those properly prepared, the main trail is splendid, and side trips to lofty vistas beckon in many directions. Access is easy, assuming that the road from the ski area to the trailhead is snowfree. Be sure to carry an ice ax and take lots of extra clothes. Allow a full day to contemplate the fabulous scenery and to take walks off the main trail.

(September 1995)

SKYLINE

Elevations

Trailhead:	4,400 feet
Destination:	5,900 feet
High Point:	6,563 feet (knob, south end of Skyline Divide)

Altitude Gain 2,000 feet (including ups and downs)

Walking Time In: 1 hour 45 minutes   Out: 1 hour 15 minutes

Trail Length 3.5 miles one-way

Accessibility July 15 to October 15

Difficulty Moderate

Pack Light

Topographic Sheets USGS: Mount Baker
Green Trails: Mount Baker

To reach the trailhead, drive 1.1 miles on Mount Baker Highway past the store in Glacier, turn right on Glacier Creek Road, and immediately thereafter turn left on Dead Horse Road. Drive 12.9 miles up this moderately rough back road to the trailhead, where there is a large parking lot.

The trail switchbacks up moderately steeply through deep hemlock forest and remains in the woods for about 1 mile. Over the next mile, there is a gradual transition from timbered ridge to open meadow. At about 1.8 miles, a short side trip to the northeast brings the hiker to a scenic overlook above the Nooksack valley. Two miles from the trailhead, the footpath tops out on the ridge crest, having gained 1,500 feet in the process. The walk to this point takes an hour. From here, a short quarter-mile stroll toward the east along the ridge top (no trail) provides excellent views of the surrounding area. The trail itself goes south toward Mount Baker. It meanders up and down for about an additional 1.5 miles over several ridges, bluffs, and knolls, gaining (and losing) an additional 500 vertical feet in the process. The trail gradually peters out at about the 3.5-mile mark, where it terminates in a small col or notch, marked with a cairn.

Although most hikers will probably stop at this point and retrace their steps to the car, experienced hikers have three options: (1) descend slightly to the southeast, continue around the point descending from Skyline Divide, and follow a scrabble footpath through the meadow to the south for about another mile until blocked by Chowder Ridge; (2) turn westward and follow a scrabble trail downward for about 1 mile to reach a lovely level meadow with a small stream, an ideal isolated camping spot; or (3) follow a scrabble footpath upward along Skyline Divide to the south, passing several viewpoints as altitude is gained. After about 1 mile and a gain of 750 vertical feet, the ridge levels out, allowing an additional mile of hiking to the south, ending at the cliffs of

Chowder Ridge. The scenery visible during this ridge stroll is magnificent. A steep cross-country descent from the divide connects at the end of the option-one trail, allowing an elective loop to return to the notch at 3.5 miles. Note: The statistics listed for this hike are for the maintained portion of the trail and do not include the walking time and altitude gains for cross-country options.

Trail damage due to shortcutting switchbacks is becoming substantial in the meadows. Please stay on the trail.

From the high open meadowland, the views in all directions are breathtaking. To the north is the high ridge extending from Church Mountain on the west to Winchester Mountain on the east. To the east are the rugged contours of Mount Shuksan, one of the most beautiful mountains in the world. Looming to the south is the heavily glaciated massif of Mount Baker.

There are campsites in the option-one meadow and at a number of locations along the Skyline Drive ridge. After the snow completely melts, the ridge-crest sites are dry, and water must be carried a considerable distance. The ridge-crest sites have spectacular views but are exposed to the elements if the weather deteriorates. Campfires are prohibited within 1 mile of the trail.

Wildflower displays are excellent about August 1. Fall color is impressive about October 1. Biting insects (mosquitoes and deer- and horseflies) and yellow jackets are prevalent intermittently in these areas. Be prepared to cope with these pests.

(August 1994)

WINCHESTER MOUNTAIN
Elevations

Trailhead:	5,200 feet (Twin Lakes)
Destination:	6,521 feet (Winchester Lookout)
Altitude Gain	1,600 feet (including ups and downs)
Walking Time	In: 1 hour Out: 40 minutes
Trail Length	1.6 miles one-way
Accessibility	July 15 to October 15
Difficulty	Moderate (after snowmelt)
Pack	Light
Topographic Sheets	USGS: Mount Shuksan
	Green Trails: Mount Shuksan

To reach the trailhead, turn left immediately past the highway maintenance buildings on State Highway 542 and proceed up forest road 3065. This one-way road is usually passable by standard cars to the Tomyhoi Lake trailhead, although it is rough in places. Beyond there, it may be impassable or require a four-wheel-drive, high-clearance vehicle to reach the Twin Lakes early in the summer. After all the snow melts, miners with private claims have been opening the road to access their mines, so in August and September, experienced back-road drivers can drive passenger cars to the road end between the Twin Lakes, where there is parking for twenty-five to thirty cars. Alternatively, park at the Tomyhoi trailhead; walking up the last 2 miles of road gains 1,500 feet in altitude and takes an hour. There are many quality places to camp around the two lakes; a privy is located at the south end of the south lake.

The trailhead for both Winchester Mountain and High Pass starts at the west end of the isthmus between the lakes. The trail enters the Mount Baker Wilderness almost immediately. One-tenth of a mile beyond the trailhead, the trail forks, with the right fork leading to High and Low Passes, the Gargett Mine, and Mount Larrabee, and the left fork leading to Winchester Mountain. The latter trail goes up moderately steeply through enjoyable subalpine meadows. Well into August in an average year, steep snow slopes block the trail in several places; there is no runout below the most dangerous one. Hikers should look for and use the safer scrabble footpaths below these snow accumulations. Less desirably, those with climbing skills and an ice ax to use for self-arrest may choose to kick steps across the obstructing snowfields. After the snow melts, the only mildly hazardous area is the 150-foot traverse of the "red band," located on the south end of the last switchback before the ridge crest is reached.

The Winchester fire lookout has been restored and is maintained by the Mount Baker Club of Bellingham. The building is open for public use when club members are not working on the structure. The door is left open, and the shutters are left up until sometime in September. Inside, there are two single bunks and a propane stove; outside, there is a new metal flagpole.

Views improve progressively as altitude is gained. From the summit, there are fine views in all directions. The 360-degree panorama includes the following mountains: American and Canadian Border Peaks, Mount Larrabee, the Pleiades, the Pickets, the two peaks of Goat Mountain, Mount Shuksan, and Mount Baker. Tomyhoi Lake lies below to the west. Twin Lakes are azure pools to the east, Silesia Valley is to the north, and Swamp Creek is to the south.

The Twin Lakes area is a splendid location for family camping, although it is often crowded on weekends after car access to the lakes is possible. The sunrise and sunset views of Mount Baker reflected in the southern lake, and similar views of the Canadian Mountains reflected in the northern lake, are elegant and well worth recording in photographs and memories.

Another option for hikers is to take the gated road east of the north lake and follow the Silesia Creek trail down into the valley below. Cross-country hikers can head upward to the southeast to an unnamed knob at 6,100 feet above the picnic area and to a somewhat more scenic knob 400 feet higher and half a mile to the southeast. Climbers can also approach the north peak of Goat Mountain at 6,508 feet via this route.

Early in the year, when snow fills the gullies on the west side of Winchester Mountain, experienced cross-country travelers can descend from the ridge crest (before the lookout is reached) to the area below Low Pass, cross-country to the trail to Tomyhoi Lake, ascend Gold Run Pass, and return to Swamp Creek Road 3065.

After the snow melts, there is no water on Winchester Mountain. Those planning to stay on top for the sunset or sunrise should carry water and a good-quality tent in case the lookout shelter is already occupied. Fires are prohibited within 1 mile of this trail.

(July 1996)

YELLOW ASTER BUTTE
Elevations

Trailhead:	3,600 feet
Destination:	6,145 feet (Yellow Aster Butte)
High Point:	7,451 feet (Tomyhoi Peak)
Altitude Gain	2,600 feet (including ups and downs)
Walking Time	In: 2 hours 30 minutes Out: 2 hours
Trail Length	3.5 miles one-way
Accessibility	July 15 to October 15
Difficulty	Moderately strenuous (to the butte); strenuous (to Tomyhoi Peak)
Pack	Light
Topographic Sheets	USGS: Mount Shuksan
	Green Trails: Mount Shuksan

Work was scheduled to start in the summer of 1997, with an estimated completion time in the late fall of 1997 or early summer of 1998, to construct a new trail access to the Yellow Aster Butte area. When this is completed, the lower section of the current Keep Kool trail will be closed. The parking area at the Tomyhoi Lake (Gold Run Pass) trailhead will also be enlarged and improved. The tread of the first 1.5 miles of the Gold Run Pass trail will be upgraded.

Visitors to Yellow Aster Butte and Tomyhoi Peak will walk about 1.5 miles on the Tomyhoi Lake trail and turn off on the new tread leading to Yellow Aster Butte or connect with the distal portion of the Keep Kool trail to access Tomyhoi Peak. This connecting trail will be about 2 miles long.

The connection with the remainder of the Keep Cool trail will probably be on the saddle between Yellow Aster Butte to the north and the unnamed hump to the south. In this saddle, there are six or seven tarns with level areas nearby serving as pleasant campsites. Fires are prohibited within 1 mile of the trail. From here or nearby, new tread will gain about 800 vertical feet to the top of Yellow Aster Butte. In season, wildflowers in this area are profuse and splendid. From Yellow Aster Butte, it is not difficult to climb an unnamed butte to the north. An unnamed butte to the south can also be ascended without difficulty, and it is possible to follow this trailless ridge to intersect the Welcome Pass trail and descend by that route; alternatively, the hiker can proceed westward as far as desired on the High Divide trail.

Another alternative is to continue to the northwest, ascending progressively higher ridges. Tomyhoi Peak can be surmounted by those with climbing experience. The ascent is technical only for the last several hundred feet; a steep snow and ice field with exposure must be crossed, after which a class 3 rock climb brings the hiker to the narrow summit. Two additional hours are required from the Yellow Aster saddle to reach the summit of Tomyhoi.

In the upper Yellow Aster meadows, several mining excavations and the remant of abandoned mining equipment are reminders of the gold searchers that were here long ago. Ptarmigan are commonly seen in the area, and mountain goats frequent the high ridges.

Views from any of the high places are extraordinary. Mount Larrabee, American Border Peak, and Canadian Border Peak can be seen to the north. Winchester Mountain lies to the immediate east; beyond are the high peaks of the Pickett Range in North Cascades National Park. The twin summits of Goat Mountain can be seen to the southeast. Beyond Goat Mountain, Mount Shuksan rears its splendid head. To the south is the snow cone of Mount Baker. Below, to the north, is Tomyhoi Lake. It is hard to keep one's cool in so breathtaking a place!

(1982)

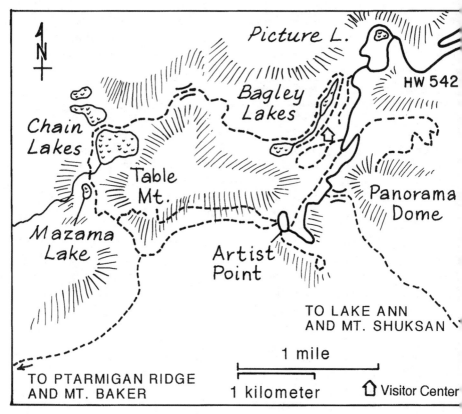

Heather Meadows–Artist Point Area

Heather Meadows–Artist Point Area

Six short trails have been constructed or upgraded in the Heather Meadows–Artist Point area in recent years. These are described below. Trailhead elevations range from 3,850 feet at Picture Lake to 5,100 feet at Artist Point. The Forest Service publication *Discover Heather Meadows—Self-Guided Tour and Map* is useful for locating trailheads and other important places. See also the USGS and Green Trails topographic sheets for Mount Shuksan. All dogs on these six trails must be leashed at all times. Separate trail information on the four longer footpaths originating in this area are listed under Table Mountain, Chain Lakes, Ptarmigan Ridge, and Lake Ann.

Picture Lake Path. Access is from State Route 542, the Mount Baker Scenic Byway. There is limited parking at the trailhead about 0.15 mile from the right turn on the one-way road around Picture Lake. It cannot be accessed by descending vehicles. The trail length is about 0.25 mile one-way; altitude gain is minimal. Average walking time is 20 minutes. Mount Shuksan is reflected in this scenic lake. The best times to photograph are from midafternoon to early evening. The best dates for photography are around August 1, when the wildflowers generally reach their blooming peak, and around October 1, the usual time for the best reds and yellows of autumn. A wide-angle lens is useful to capture both the mountain and its reflection in the lake (try not to include the bit of highway on the east side of the lake in your picture). If including people in the photo, have them dress in colors that contrast with the vegetation.

Bagley Lakes–Lower Wild Goose Loop. The Bagley Lakes and Lower Wild Goose footpaths both start at the lower large parking lot. Take the right fork not far from the lot and descend to near Lower Bagley Lake and its outlet dam; turn left (do not cross the dam). The trail follows the lakeshore, with good views of Table Mountain. At about 0.5 mile, note the basalt columns adjacent to the footpath. Soon thereafter, the trail follows Bagley Creek between the lakes and comes to a junction at Upper Bagley Lake. From here, there are three return options: (1) cross the Twin Arch bridge over Bagley Creek, walk to the east end of Chain Lake to the dam, cross it, and return to the parking lot; (2) return the way you came; or (3) go upward on the right fork of the Lower Wild Goose trail, gaining about 150 vertical feet. Note the tread on both sides of a small tarn while ascending. Reach another junction after 11 minutes; turn left. (The right fork ascends to the visitors' center.) After 0.1 mile, go right if you wish to connect with the Upper Wild Goose trail, which starts at the first Austin Pass parking lot. Of interest during the descent is the 75-foot traverse over the tops of an aggregation of basaltic columns as the parking lot is neared. In summary, this loop takes 45 to 50 minutes, is about 2 miles in length, and gains about 250 vertical feet. Scenic and pleasant throughout, it is worth the time and effort expended.

Panorama Dome. Trail length one-way is 1.5 miles. Altitude gain is 800 feet up, 250 feet down. Walking time up is 1 hour; down is 40 minutes. The trailhead is by a ski pylon between the first and second parking lots. There is no parking at the trailhead, but two or three cars can park on the north side of the paved road 0.1 mile below the trailhead. In summary, this footpath is not worth the effort; spend your time elsewhere.

Fire and Ice Trail. The trailhead is at the visitors' center, located at the second parking lot in the Austin Pass area. (Take time to explore the old building and exhibits; the staff can also answer questions about the surrounding areas.) The trail is a 0.5-mile loop; altitude gain is 150 feet. The first 0.2 mile is paved and wheelchair accessible. After 3 minutes, note basalt columns on the right. At 6 minutes, the pavement ends at a viewpoint with interpretive signs; the rest of the footpath is crushed rock. At 11 minutes, a scrabble trail goes downward to the south end of Upper Bagley Lake (not part of the loop). At 13 minutes, there is a tarn to the right of the trail. At 18 minutes, arrive back at the visitors' center.

Upper Wild Goose. The trail starts at the Austin Pass parking lot, goes steeply upward to the lower overflow parking area and then proceeds to the main Artist Point parking lot. Length is about 0.7 mile one way; altitude gain is 500 feet. Its major use is as a return route to Artist Point for those hiking the Chain Lakes trail from Artist Point to the Twin Arch bridge at Upper Bagley Lake.

Artist Ridge Trail. If you walk only one trail here, do this one. There are two access areas from the Artist Point parking lot. The eastern footpath is paved for 0.1 mile to the first viewpoint, where there are interpretive signs; it is wheelchair accessible. This is also the Mount Baker Wilderness boundary. The tread is graveled beyond this viewing area. The surroundings are spectacularly scenic. Mount Baker to the west and Mount Shuksan to the southeast are impressive; peaks to the north are also on display. The elevation gain is 250 to 300 feet. It is a 1-mile round-trip on the formal path. Average walking time is 1 hour, which allows you to read the many explanatory signs and photographs and to view and photograph the splendid surroundings. Mount Shuksan may be reflected in the first tarn passed on the left. After taking the right loop, a second tarn is passed on the right. From the farthest part of the loop, several nonformal (scrabble) footpaths can be walked; they lead around the tarn and to other viewpoints of Mount Baker. Hikers should make every effort to stay on the tread and to obey the No Boots signs. The surrounding meadow is fragile. Complete the formal graveled loop, and then retrace your steps to the parking lot.

(August 1996)

CHAIN LAKES

Elevations

Trailhead:	5,100 feet
Destination:	4,200 feet (Bagley Lakes)

Other Significant Locations: Iceberg Lake, 4,800 feet

Altitude Gain 800 feet (including ups and downs; 1,700 feet if walking back to Artist Point from Bagley Lakes)

Walking Time 3 hours (add 1 hour if walking back to Artist Point)

Trail Length 6.5 miles one-way (plus 1.2 miles if walking back to Artists Point)

Accessibility July 15 to October 15

Difficulty Moderate to moderately strenuous

Pack Light

Topographic Sheets USGS: Mount Shuksan
Green Trails: Mount Shuksan

Since there are three options on this loop trail, the three segments of the loop are described separately. For simplicity, a start at the Artist Point trailhead is assumed.

Drive to the end of State Highway 542 at Artist Point. The trail begins at the west end of the parking lot at 5,100 feet. The footpath proceeds westward along the south slope of Table Mountain. After half a mile, the Mount Baker Wilderness is entered. After an almost level 1.1 miles, the junction to the Chain Lakes is reached; turn right (north) at this point and descend about 400 vertical feet over half a mile to reach Mazama Lake. There are four designated campsites at this small lake. The trail descending from the west side of Table Mountain is passed during this descent. It is 0.6 mile farther to the isthmus between Iceberg and Galena Lakes. There are four additional designated campsites at Galena Lake. If these sites are all occupied, campers must find a site a mile or more away from the trail or return to their cars. There are three privy sites in the Chain Lakes vicinity. Campfires are not allowed at the Chain Lakes. Fishermen many wish to tempt the trout in the lakes with a well-placed fly. Iceberg Lake is about 4,750 feet in elevation; the isthmus is 2.2 miles from the trailhead. Campers and hikers may return the way they came or proceed with the second segment of the loop, as follows.

From the isthmus, the footpath goes eastward, gaining about 800 vertical feet to reach the pass north of Table Mountain at 3.7 miles. Two-tenths of a mile before reaching the pass, there is a delightful tarn at which to tarry a while and enjoy the view of Mount Baker and the reflections in Iceberg Lake below. From the pass, there are spectacular views of both Mount Baker and Mount Shuksan. The footpath descends steeply from the pass in switchbacks over talus in places, losing about 1,000 vertical feet by the time it reaches Upper Bagley Lake 5 miles from the trailhead. Keep an eye out for water ouzels (dippers) in the streams alongside the trail. The path then descends gently along the north side of the lakes until the dam at the east end of the lower lake is reached. A short ascent from the dam brings the hiker to the lower trailhead at the west end of a large parking lot 6.5 miles from the Artist Point trailhead.

The third segment starts here, or at the east end of Upper Bagley Lake, where the bridge over the outlet stream is crossed. Consult the Heather Meadows section for information on how to return to Artist Point via the Lower and Upper Wild Goose Trails from either of these locations. This segment can be avoided if two cars are available; park one at the lower trailhead, and use it to retrieve the car at the Artist Point trailhead.

This footpath is crowded, as are the lakes, on weekends and holidays; if possible, come on a weekday. Fall color is spectacular along this trail and usually reaches its peak during the first week in October. Marmots and pikas are often seen near the trail.

This is a very scenic footpath. It is one of the few trails in the North Cascades where the altitude gain to the trailhead is entirely by vehicle. It is therefore suitable for walkers of limited stamina, who can turn back at any point between the trailhead and Chain Lakes.

(October 1969)

TABLE MOUNTAIN
Elevations

Trailhead:	5,100 feet
Destination:	5,700 feet (Table Mountain)
Altitude Gain	700 feet (including ups and downs)
Walking Time	In: 1 hour 15 minutes Out: 45 minutes
Trail Length	1.1 miles to west end; 0.5 mile to east end (one-way)
Accessibility	July 15 to October 15
Difficulty	Moderate
Pack	Light
Topographic Sheets	USGS: Mount Shuksan
	Green Trails: Mount Shuksan

Follow State Route 542 to its end at the Artist Point parking lot. The trail begins on the north side of the parking lot, where there is an instructional sign. Dogs are prohibited on this footpath. Small children should be carefully supervised during the steep ascent.

The recently improved tread reaches the base of Table Mountain at 0.2 mile and then ascends steeply for an additional 0.3 mile, where it tops out on a plateau after an altitude gain of 500 feet from the trailhead. Views from anywhere on the top of Table Mountain are superlative. The trail then goes west-ward, intermittently gaining altitude until the west end of the mountain is reached after about another 0.7 mile. Two small tarns are present at the west end; from there, both Mount Baker and Mount Shuksan are spectacular. From the tarns, a scrabble trail goes north about 0.15 mile to the end at the top of a moderately steep snowfield. To continue, the snowy slope must be descended; alternatively, a class 2 rock climb downward about 150 feet leads to less steep snow. Hikers attempting either route should have snow- or rock-climbing experience; those without such skills should return the way they came. An ice ax is useful here.

After descending to the ridge below, there are several options: (1) Continue on the scrabble trail downward about 0.5 mile to join the Chain Lakes trail, and then return to one of the Chain Lakes trailheads (see Chain Lakes trail data). (2) Investigate the several tarns in the area. Late in the summer, there is an incredible view from the tarn on the right after the descent. The blue of the tarn and the white of the remaining snow in the foreground are highlighted by the view of Mount Shuksan in the background. (3) Proceed cross-country to the north until stopped by the cliff above the Chain Lakes trail pass (descent is not possible here; return to the parking lot the way you came or by the first route).

Neither camping nor fires are allowed on Table Mountain. It is a day-use area only from May 15 to November 15.

Remain on the footpaths as much as possible; the meadow is fragile. The Chain Lakes trail runs underneath the south side of Table Mountain. Use caution so that no rocks are dislodged that could injure hikers below. Patchy snow often blocks the trail until late in the summer; boots with lug soles are advisable.

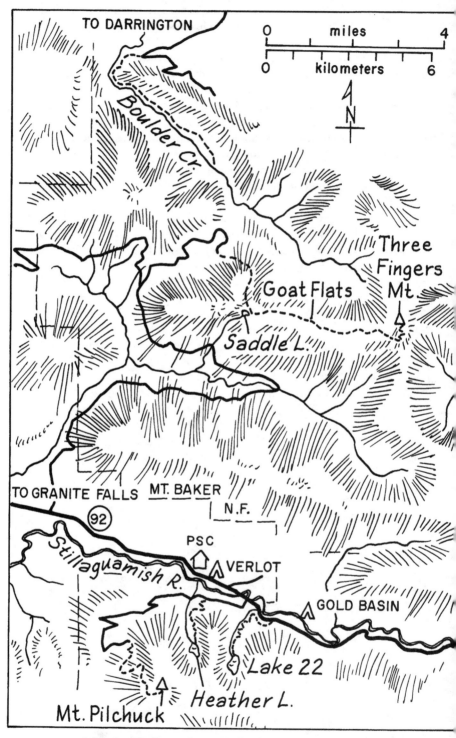

Mount Baker–Snoqualmie National Forest

Mount Baker–Snoqualmie National Forest

GOAT FLATS (THREE FINGERS LOOKOUT)

Elevations
Trailhead: 3,000 feet
Destination: 5,000 feet (Goat Flats)
High Point: 6,854 feet (Three Fingers Lookout)
Other Significant Locations: Saddle Lake, 3,800 feet; Camp Pass, 5,600 feet

Altitude Gain   2,250 feet (including ups and downs)
Walking Time   In: 2 hours 10 minutes   Out: 2 hours
Trail Length   5.3 miles one-way
Accessibility   August 1 to September 30
Difficulty   Strenuous to lookout
Pack   Light
Topographic Sheets   USGS: Granite Falls, Silverton
Green Trails: Granite Falls, Silverton

Take the Mountain Loop Highway east from Granite Falls 7.2 miles from the stoplight in the center of town. Turn left on Canyon Creek Road 41. Take left turns at 1.9, 8, and 8.9 miles. At 11 miles, the Meadow Mountain trail departs to the right; from this point, it is 4 miles to the summit, 5 miles to Saddle Lake, and 8 miles to Goat Flats. (The Forest Service advises that in the future, this trail may be upgraded and beome the main trail to Goat Flats and Three Fingers.) Turn right at 13.4 miles, and right again at 16.8 miles. The trailhead is 17.5 miles from the Mountain Loop Highway, poorly signed, on the left side of the road just past two large cedars also on the left. The last 0.7 mile is on Road 4160.

The first approximately 3 miles of the trail is difficult walking, since the trail is muddy, slick, and uneven and contains many large tree roots. Beyond that point, when meadow country is reached, the quality of the trail improves.

The trail initially goes up moderately through deep forest. After approximately 1 mile (30 minutes), the trail turns south, and from this point onward there are views of Three Fingers to the east through the forest cover. At about 2 miles, the trail loses 100 or so feet in altitude; crosses the floor of an open, rocky amphitheater; and regains the 100 feet of altitude on the other side. Emergency camps could be placed in this location. At about 2.3 miles, the trail passes by the east side of Saddle Lake. From this point, Saddle Lake Camp is 0.25 mile to the west, Goat Flats is 3 miles to the east, and the Three Fingers lookout on the south peak is a long 2 miles past the flats. Altitude gain to this point is 720 feet; walking time is 1 hour and 5 minutes.

About a mile past the lake, the trail begins to break out into subalpine meadow. A stream at roughly 3.3 miles provides water. Tarns and campsites are passed at about 3.5 and 3.7 miles.

Goat Flats is a wonderful camping area with multiple tarns, many good campsites, and splendid views of the Sisters, Baker, and Shuksan to the north and of Three Fingers to the east. Little wood is available; campers should carry stoves for cooking. Goat Flats is the base camp area for ascents of any of the three peaks of Three Fingers Mountain. In midsummer, the area is quite buggy; be sure to carry insect repellent. The Goat Flats shelter, functional in 1965, has succumbed to the elements. Most day hikers should consider Goat Flats their destination.

There are other options for the adventuous, however. From the shelter, the trail goes upward about 0.2 mile along a beautiful grassy knoll and then turns into the forest to the right (south) of a rock knob. When snow is present, this turnoff may not be obvious; the route to the left is exposed and hazardous and should not be attempted.

The trail goes through timber for perhaps 0.1 mile and then, losing 100 or so feet in altitude, goes eastward through a lovely meadow with fine views to the south and southeast. Turning a corner, the footpath goes considerably more steeply upward, crossing talus and scree slopes to the top of a pass about 1.4 miles from the Goat Flats shelter remains. The views from this pass are quite nice, and there are several level areas where tents can be pitched; water must be obtained from snowfields. There are no campsites beyond this point. The altitude at the pass is about 5,600 feet. (Beckey refers to this area as Camp Pass, presumably because this was the campsite for the construction of the lookout atop the south peak of Three Fingers in 1932. The Forest Service still refers to this area as Tin Pan Gap; Beckey, however, states that Tin Can Gap is farther west, presumably a notch bypassed by the trail.)

Only experienced and equipped mountaineers should proceed beyond this point. A scrabble trail goes upward along the ridge to the east; after 0.2 mile, a steep snowfield must be bypassed. Beyond the snow patch, there is a small notch. Moderately steep snow or rock, or the gully between the two, must be descended, losing 150 vertical feet in decending to another, larger notch. From here, the footpath again begins a remorseless ascent over talus and scree. The tread is sometimes difficult to locate. Below the summit snowfield, there is a reliable stream of water, the only water source from Goat Flats to the summit. The trail switchbacks up south of the lookout to a permanent snowfield. This is not steep and can be ascended easily when it is not frozen; if it is slick, the talus and scree slope to the left offers an alterative route. Use extreme caution at the top of the snowfield, since there is a steep drop-off to the west. Above the snow, climb class 2 rock perhaps 75 feet and then turn left, where a scrabble trail leads around the west side of the rock. An exposed but safe corner is passed, and from here the lookout can be seen approximately 50 feet above. It is reached by three ladders, followed by a minor rock scramble from the last ladder to a small level area of rock in front of the door.

Twelve boxes of dynamite were used to lower the south summit about 15 feet and level it sufficiently to place the lookout house on it in the summer of 1932. Since there is no place to stand on either the east or west side of the building, it must have been constructed totally from within. Whoever roofed the structure certainly had no fear of heights.

The historic fire lookout has been restored and is currently being maintained by volunteers affiliated with the Everett Mountaineers. The airy edifice does not contain a stove or lantern but does have a crude bed, shelves, and a register. The fire finder is still in place. The building is in good condition. To obtain access to the approximately 20 feet of summit to the north, it is necessary to go through the central north window. Safely inside, it is hard to believe how precarious an aerie this is.

The lookout on duty in 1937 reported the presence of St. Elmo's fire within the structure during electrical storms. With lightning striking nearby, the lookout house could accurately be called an eerie airy aerie.

The walking time with a light pack from Goat Flats to the lookout is 1 hour and 50 minutes. Descent is not a great deal faster than ascent, since caution must be used in high, exposed places, and the first 3 miles of the trail going down cannot be accomplished much faster than going up. Only strong hikers in good condition should attempt the round-trip in one day.

Views from the top are impressive. The north and middle peaks of Three Fingers, Mount Rainier, the Sisters, Mount Baker, Mount Shuksan, Mount Bullon, Jumbo Mountain, Whitehorse Mountain, and indeed, the entire North Cascade Range are spread out in a 360-degree panorama. Unfortunately, the view toward Mount Pilchuck is substandard, since most of the intervening ridge has been subjected to clear-cut logging. Extensive patch-cutting toward the Sound also mars the view in that direction to some degree. Mount Constitution in the San Juan Islands, Everett, Puget Sound, and the Olympic Range are clearly visible. It is a beautiful, isolated, and—undoubtedly for those who manned the lookout solo in the past—lonely place.

About half a mile below the flats to the south of the trail, there is a solitary magnificent specimen of mountain hemlock, perhaps the most splendid tree of this species I have observed anywhere.

No camping is allowed within 200 feet of Saddle Lake. Campfires are prohibited from the lake to the fire lookout. A functional shelter is present at the lake. Climbers may stay at the lookout overnight if a work party is not in residence. Four people can be accommodated comfortably. Elimination is challenging. Sunsets, sunrises, and the night sky are spectacular.

(August 1989)

HEATHER LAKE
Elevations

Trailhead:	1,400 feet
Destination:	2,500 feet (Heather Lake)

Altitude Gain   1,200 feet (including ups and downs)
Walking Time   In: 65 minutes   Out: 55 minutes
Trail Length   2.2 miles one-way
Accessibility   Late May to mid-November
Difficulty   Moderate
Pack   Light
Topographic Sheets   USGS: Granite Falls
                                        Green Trails: Granite Falls

Drive east on the Mountain Loop Highway from Granite Falls. One mile east of the Verlot Public Service Center, cross the bridge over the Stillaguamish River and turn south a few feet past the bridge. Drive 1.3 miles up the pot-holed, washboard gravel road to the trailhead on the left (south) side of the roadbed. Parking is available for about twenty-five cars on both sides of the road. There is a privy at the trailhead.

Much of the footpath to the lake was constructed recently, although the abandoned roadbed is still followed in places. The tread is intermittently muddy. The following observations were made during the ascent to Heather Lake:

14 minutes: Note the huge stump to the right of the trail; there are several of these in the second-growth areas, with young trees sprouting from the cut end of the nurse stump.

17–21 minutes: The tread follows a logging roadbed.

33 minutes: The trail enters ancient old-growth forest and goes upward less steeply.

41 minutes: Water is obtainable from small falls to the left of the trail.

57 minutes: Top out; descend about 100 vertical feet and then follow a level footpath to the lake. No viewpoints exist along the trail.

65 minutes: Arrive at the north end of the lake.

The lake nestles under the high cliffs of Mount Pilchuck; although at mid-altitude, it has the appearance of a high lake. Three to four fair campsites are scattered around the north side of the lake. There are scenic spots for eating lunch and gazing at the cliffs. Many ground dogwoods bloom near the lake-shore. Meadow flowers grace the southern end of the lake.

Volunteers, who upgraded the footpath, are still constructing a trail around the lake. About one-quarter is in place; a scrabble path, often on planks, allow access to the south side of the lake via the east side. The west half shows no signs of trail construction, so the entire trail will probably not be completed until 1998–99. The distance around the lake is approximately 0.6 mile. The lake contains fish; many fish rings may be seen.

Although the trail is not as scenic, the lake surpasses nearby Lake 22 in beauty, camp and eating sites, and access to the south end of the lake (in my opinion).

(June 1996)

MOUNT PILCHUCK LOOKOUT TRAIL

Elevations

Trailhead:	3,100 feet
Destination:	5,324 feet (lookout on summit)
Altitude Gain	2,300 feet (including ups and downs)
Walking Time	In: 2 hours Out: 1 hour 40 minutes
Trail Length	3 miles one-way
Accessibility	Mid-July to mid-October
Difficulty	Moderately strenuous
Pack	Light
Topographic Sheets	USGS: Granite Falls
	Green Trails: Granite Falls

This trail is still being reconstructed at the time of this writing (September 1997); however, new tread is in place from the trailhead to the summit. Depending on snowfall this fall, the upgrade may be completed in 1997. Certainly, the work should be done by early summer 1998.

Follow the Mountain Loop Highway eastward from Granite Falls. Turn south immediately east of the bridge 1 mile east of the Verlot Public Service Center. Anticipate 5.1 miles of potholes and washboard; curves prevent passing. There is pavement the last 1.9 miles, but several slumps mandate caution here also. The trailhead is 7 miles from the turnoff. (There is a gate just beyond the Heather Lake trailhead. The road is closed to all motorized vehicles from this point to the road end from early November to early April.)

Substantial parking spaces adjoin the trailhead; however, the footpath is popular on good-weather summer weekends, and parking for latecomers can be a problem. There are two privies 50 feet up the trail on the left. Camping and picnic areas are to the right of the trail.

Walk up the roadbed 0.2 mile; turn right and cross the shallow creek (this may be difficult when the early-summer runoff is flowing). The new tread starts shortly after the stream crossing. Turnpikes alternate with quite muddy areas as the switchbacks gain altitude; the old tread is intersected occasionally. The ridge crest adjacent to the clear-cut is reached in 20 minutes. After 37 minutes, the tread turns left and crosses talus. There is a good view of Mount Rainier from here, improved by the fall color in the foreground. The tread has been widened thereafter, and ballasted with a rock base along the north side of the peak. There are views of both Mount Baker and Three Fingers from this section of trail.

Near the remnants of the pylon and deck of a long-abandoned ski lift, the new footpath switchbacks upward through granite and heather slopes, ultimately reaching a ridge to the southwest. It follows the ridge crest upward and eastward, and then turns south. After about 0.25 mile, new tread has been blasted through large granite boulders for about 0.3 mile, directly accessing the 50-foot boulder climb to reach the restored fire lookout on the summit.

About 200 feet east of the summit, a short walk to the east brings the hiker to two scenic viewpoints of the mountains to the east. These two areas, and the lookout, are the preferred lunch stops along this trail.

Intermittent substantial mud, and the presence of rocks in the tread in many places, slows the walking pace both upward and downward.

There is a scrabble trail, marked with yellow paint, that descends steeply down a draw east of the lookout. This route allows experienced, adventurous hikers to access the ridge to the east of the summit. A tarn appears to offer a scenic campsite; it must be reached cross-country. There may be views of both Heather Lake and Lake 22 from this ridge.

The Everett Mountaineers have completely rebuilt the fire lookout on the summit. It is open to the public. Interpretive signs have been placed to educate visitors. Many hours of work and a substantial expenditure of funds were required to restore the structure. Visitors are urged to treat it with respect.

There are several tent sites adjacent to the summit, but after the snow has melted, the nearest water is a substantial distance below.

Views from the summit are impressive. To the south is Mount Rainier. In the evening, the lights of Everett and Seattle sparkle below. To the west, Puget Sound and the Olympic Mountains are seen. To the east, Glacier Peak, Big Four Mountain, Sloan Peak, and Dome Peak are impressive. To the north, Mount Baker, Mount Shuksan, and Three Fingers Mountain pierce the sky.

Mountain goats were transplanted to the Pilchuck area in 1975 and 1976. If the visitor is fortunate, one of these magnificent animals may be observed.

The drive from Seattle or Everett and the hike to the summit can comfortably be accomplished in 6 to 8 hours. Because of its accessibility, the footpath is popular. Therefore, it is best to come on a weekday if at all possible.

(September 1997)

Glacier Peak Wilderness–West

NORTH FORK SAUK RIVER (WHITE PASS)

Elevations

Trailhead: 2,100 feet
Destination: 5,904 feet (White Pass)
High Point: 6,000 feet (Pacific Crest Trail junction between Red and White Passes)

Other Significant Locations: Sauk shelter, 3,000 feet; Red Pass, 6,500 feet

Altitude Gain   4,000 feet (including ups and downs)
Walking Time   In: 6 hours   Out: 4 hours
Trail Length   9 miles one-way (White Pass)
Accessibility   July 15 to October 15
Difficulty   Strenuous
Pack   Full
Topographic Sheets   USGS: Sloan Peak 7.5', Glacier Peak 15'
Green Trails: Sloan Peak, Glacier Peak

Take the Mountain Loop Highway, preferably from Granite Falls, to Barlow Pass, turn north, and travel about 7 miles to the north fork of the Sauk River. Alternatively, drive the loop from Darrington about 17 miles to the same point. Drive 6.8 miles to the Sloan Creek Campground. The trail starts on the east side of the camp; the footpath goes up gradually through one of the most magnificent cedar forests in the entire Northwest. The Glacier Peak Wilderness is entered after half a mile. After 5 miles of walking and an altitude gain of 900 feet, the hiker reaches the Mackinaw shelter located immediately adjacent to the Sauk River; there is excellent stream fishing in this area. The shelter is watertight, has a bare floor, and sleeps four people. Deerflies are prevalent in the area when the temperature is warm.

Beyond the shelter, the trail gradient steepens substantially; switchbacks seem unending. Scenic vistas begin a mile or so beyond the shelter and improve progressively as altitude is gained. This ascent should be avoided during warm afternoons, both because of overheating and because the deerflies can be almost intolerable.

The footpath tops out at about 8.5 miles from the trailhead, where it joins the Pacific Crest Trail. Via the left fork, it is 1.5 miles to Red Pass; via the right fork, it is 0.7 mile to White Pass.

This is spectacular meadow country. For better viewing, cross-country upward to the ridge immediately above the trail between White and Red Passes. From the ridge crest, fine views of Glacier Peak and the White Chuck valley, with its obvious volcanic cinder cone, can be had.

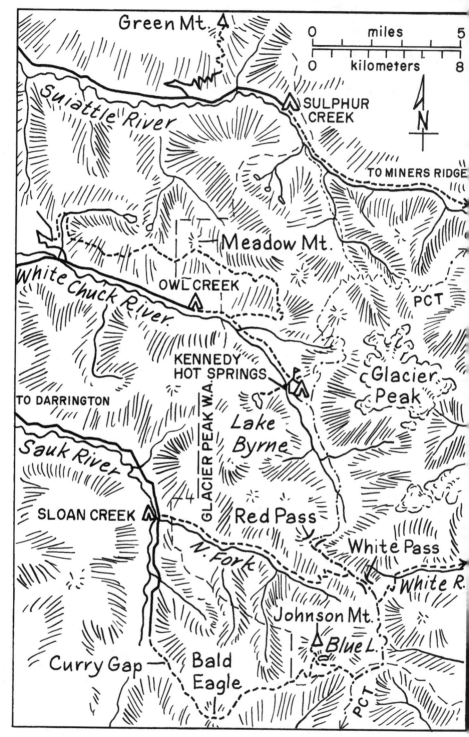

Glacier Peak Wilderness–West

Although very fit hikers can reach the ridge crest or White Pass and return in one day, two days is a more realistic minimum. Three days allows for a full day in the White Pass area to explore the surrounding meadowlands (see Pacific Crest Trail for additional data on the area). Hikers camping in the White Pass area are asked by the Forest Service to camp on the bench west of the pass rather than in the pass itself.

The footpath from the campground to the Mackinaw trail shelter should be open from May through November in average snow years. Firewood is available in the shelter area. Wood is scarce and campers should carry stoves for cooking. Water is obtainable without problems along the trail. Between the shelter and White Pass, camping spaces are nonexistent, due to the steepness of the terrain. There are places to camp roughly 3.5 and 4.5 miles from the Sloan Creek Campground in the deep woods.

(August 1974)

KENNEDY HOT SPRINGS (LAKE BYRNE)
Elevations
Trailhead: 2,300 feet
Destination: 3,300 feet (Kennedy Hot Springs Camp)
Other Significant Locations: Lake Byrne, 5,600 feet
Altitude Gain   1,000 feet (including ups and downs)
Walking Time   In: 2 hours 30 minutes   Out: 2 hours
Trail Length   5.2 miles one-way
Accessibility   Mid-May to mid-November
Difficulty   Moderate
Pack   Light
Topographic Sheets   USGS: Glacier Peak 15', Pugh Mountain 7.5'
    Green Trails: Sloan Peak, Glacier Peak

Kennedy Hot Springs has become very crowded. Limitations on the number of campers allowed in the Kennedy Campground were instituted over the past decade. If the campground is full, a sign at the trailhead says so. On summer weekends and holidays, the camping area is usually fully occupied fairly early in the day. Camping at Kennedy is restricted to locations designated for that purpose; users are asked to limit their stay to one night only.

Take State Route 530 to Darrington; drive 0.5 mile northeast to the Mountain Loop Highway just past the bridge over the Sauk River, and follow it slightly over 10 miles to the south. About 150 yards after crossing the bridge over the White Chuck River, turn left and drive 11 miles east to the end of White Chuck Road. There is a nice forest camp at the road end. The Glacier Peak Wilderness is entered about 0.3 mile from the start of the White Chuck trail. The junction with the easterly portion of the Meadow Mountain trail is about 1.5 miles, roughly 150 yards past a bridge over a beautiful, moss-lined stream with a spectacular waterfall some 75 yards upstream from the bridge (Fire Creek). The trail winds leisurely, with only occasional moderate upward pitches, above and along the White Chuck River, offering ample opportunity to descend to the stream for fishing. The trail intersects with the Kennedy Ridge trail at about the 4.5-mile mark, and an additional 0.75 mile puts the hiker at Kennedy Hot Springs. Avoid walking on the revegetation areas. Soap should not be used in the hot springs.

Firewood is scarce in the Kennedy vicinity; stoves should be used for cooking. Hikers who plan to visit Lake Byrne are encouraged to camp at Kennedy and day hike to the lake.

Both the guard station and shed are now locked and are not available for public use. The hot springs and bathhouse are 100 yards up the White Chuck River from the guard station. The springs are 5½ feet deep and are an excellent balm for tired muscles. Bathing suits and towels should be taken. Nude bathing, formerly acceptable when the area was remote, is impractical now that the area is heavily used, and the occasional skinny-dipper is subject to arrest and fine.

Climbers and PCT travelers are encouraged to use the Sitkum Creek Camp 1.8 miles beyond the hot springs to relieve the overcrowding at the Kennedy campsites.

Multiple side trips are available using Kennedy as a base camp: (1) It is possible to ascend Glacier Ridge connecting with Mica Lake (9.5 miles) and the Milk Creek trail. (2) Just before the 5-mile mark, you may connect with the Kennedy Ridge trail, or this can be approached from the campsite at the hot springs. A hike of about 2 miles—fairly steep initially, then gradually less so—brings you to the Cascade Crest trail, with access to Glacier Peak. (3) Connections to the south are with Red Pass and White Pass, the latter about 10 miles from Kennedy Hot Springs. (4) Also from Kennedy, you may switchback steeply upward, gaining about 2,300 feet in 2 miles to reach Lake Byrne. Camp Lake is an additional mile farther to the west. Several other lakes (Hardtack, Sun Up, and Round) lie along the ridge crest to the west. Although there is no trail between Hardtack and Sun Up Lakes, experienced outdoorsmen can "run" the ridge without great difficulty, exiting by the trail from Bingley Gap to the Sauk River Road 3 miles from the Mountain Loop Highway.

The route to Kennedy is notable for remarkable displays of ground cover, large cedar and Douglas-fir trees, quartz dikes twisted by immense geological pressures, two rockfalls from the cliffs that have decimated the forest beneath, pumice slides, and the vivid fall color of vine maples. As an added attraction, at about the 1.5-mile mark, there is a hanging garden of thick, green moss intermixed with maidenhair fern. Those who enjoy stream fishing should take rod and reel and probably hip boots. This hike is recommended as a one-day conditioning walk early or late in the season. When the meadows are open, nearby Meadow Mountain is far more attractive and scenic.

To reach Lake Byrne, take the Lost Creek Ridge trail, which begins at the bridge across the White Chuck River from the Kennedy guard station. The left fork leads to the hot springs; the right fork proceeds upward 2.5 miles to Lake Byrne, gaining 2,350 vertical feet in the process. The up-time with a full pack is 1 hour and 50 minutes; the down-time is 50 minutes.

After about 1.5 miles, the trail reaches a ridge crest and then contours without altitude change for about 0.2 mile southwestward. At this point, it makes a rather sharp turn to the right (north); if snow is present, the route of the trail may not be apparent at this point. Beyond the turn, switchbacks resume and continue all the way to the lake.

From Lake Byrne, the trail goes around the north end of the lake, gaining about 500 vertical feet, crosses near a tarn, and descends to Camp Lake from the highest knoll to the southwest from where the hiker reached the ridge crest. The walking time between the lakes is about 45 minutes.

Experienced wilderness travelers can walk the ridges around the entire circumference of Lake Byrne. The view from the high knob to the south of the lake is one of the best in the North Cascades. Below lies the azure blue of Lake Byrne. Below also are the Sauk and Kennedy valleys. The great peaks of the range are all visible, including Mount Baker, Mount Shuksan, and closer, Glacier Peak.

Insects are an annoyance in the Lake Byrne area. There are two reasonable campsites north of the lake outlet. (There may be other campsites I could not locate due to the presence of snow.) Water is available from the lake. When visited, the lake was 95 percent iced in, so it was impossible to determine whether there were fish in the lake. Impressive alpine flowers surround the lake. Directly west, there is a rocky ridge crest with views both to the west and to the east, a moderately easy 30-minute walk from the high camp by the lake.

Although there is some wood in the area, the high meadow is fragile, and it is best to use stoves to cook. Campfires are inappropriate here.

Snow remains late in this area; it is best visited after mid-August. The lake can be reached as a one-day trip by those camping in the Kennedy area. For hikers coming in from the trailhead, an overnight camp is strongly recommended. The area is beautiful and still relatively isolated, protected by the substantial altitude gain from the usually crowded Kennedy Hot Springs area. Those hikers desiring real isolation can move to lakes farther west to establish their overnight camps.

(August 1972)

GREEN MOUNTAIN
Elevations
Trailhead:	3,500 feet
Destination:	6,500 feet (Green Mountain Lookout)

Altitude Gain 3,200 feet (including ups and downs)
Walking Time In: 2 hours 30 minutes   Out: 1 hour 30 minutes
Trail Length 4 miles one-way
Accessibility July 15 to October 15
Difficulty Moderate
Pack Light
Topographic Sheets USGS: Downey Mountain 7.5'
Green Trails: Cascade Pass

Take either State Road 530 from Arlington or Highway 20 from Burlington; drive to the Suiattle River Road, midway between Rockport and Darrington. Turn east; the Green Mountain Road is 19.1 miles from the turnoff. Turn left (north) and drive 6.2 miles to the trailhead. The road ends 0.1 mile farther; there is a turnaround area where the road terminates. There are no formal parking spaces, but the road is wide enough to accommodate cars parked on one side of the road and still permit one-way traffic in the other direction. Do not park in the turnaround at the road end.

The trailhead is signed "Meadow 1 mile; Lookout 4 miles." Water is available from a creek 0.2 mile from the trailhead. At 1 mile, there is a campsite in the woods 50 feet to the right of the trail. At 1.1 miles, the trail breaks out of woods into meadow for 0.1 mile, then goes back into woods for an additional 0.1 mile, and thereafter is in open meadow. Note the old man's beard growing on the trees just before the footpath enters the meadow. The trail goes westward about 100 yards and then switchbacks upward and eastward to cut around the east curve of Green Mountain, at about the 1.8-mile mark. This portion of the meadow is overgrown and at least 3 feet high; rain pants are desirable if the trail is walked in the rain or within 12 to 24 hours afterward.

After another 0.5 mile, the trail drops downward, losing about 200 vertical feet, and passes by a large alpine tarn. There are excellent campsites with water, wood, and a Forest Service toilet below the lakes. From here, the trail goes northward. The last mile is steep switchbacks up the green meadow to the lookout (on July 13, 1980, there were snow patches on the trail, but it was 95 percent snow free). There are two campsites on the high ridge, both exposed but sufficiently level for a two-person tent. One is about 0.2 and the other about 0.1 mile from the lookout.

Green Mountain is aptly named. From the time the footpath breaks out of the woods, hikers traverse a fantastically green, thick meadow ablaze with wildflowers. This is one of the nicest and most impressive meadows in the entire North Cascades. Many marmots live on the high, grassy slopes between the tarn and the lookout. Their burrows can be seen in several locations along the trail, and their alarm whistles can be heard by almost every hiker in the area. This is one of the few places where marmots live in meadow without the protection of a talus slope. On occasion, grouse and bald eagles may also be seen along the trail. In the late evening and early morning, deer frequent the meadows. Copses of Alaska cedar are frequently seen in the upper meadows.

From the lookout, located almost on the boundary of the Glacier Peak Wilderness area, the hiker can look northward into the pristine North Cascades. To the north are Buckindy and Snow King Mountains. Glacier Peak dominates the southeastern skyline. Other visible peaks are Downey, Sulphur, Pugh, and Whitehorse. Views down into the Downey, Suiattle, and Milk Creek valleys are also impressive.

Appreciate the fire lookout house. It is listed on the National Register of Historic Places. Until recently, it was still operational when the risk of forest fires was high. Volunteers did restoration and maintenance work on the building for several years, but in spite of their efforts, the building was declared unsafe in 1995. The Green Mountain Lookout is scheduled for repairs in 1998, and it is hoped that funding and motivated volunteers can be found to help bring this historic structure back to usable status. Contact the Darrington Ranger Station.

One precaution: During midsummer, it is easy to lose the trail in the thick, overgrown meadow, particularly during or immediately after rain, when the vegetation tends to collapse over the footpath. Hikers will get soaked to the skin from the waist down if the lush meadow plants are wet. In good weather, however, this is one of the best one-day hikes in the entire "wilderness alps." Anticipate company, particularly on weekends and holidays.

The access road was impassable in 1997 due to washouts. The road has probably been cleared by this time, but a check stop at the Darrington Ranger Station to confirm this is advisable.

Help keep Green Mountain green. Use only existing tent sites. Stay off trampled sites and old trails being revegetated.

(July 1990)

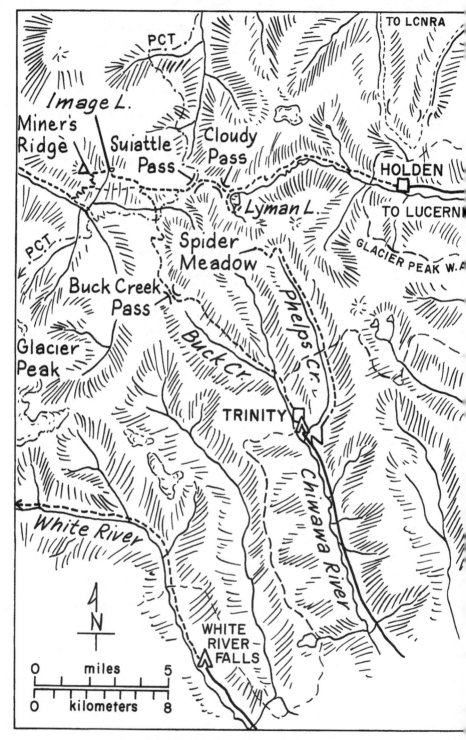

Glacier Peak Wilderness–East

Glacier Peak Wilderness–East

BUCK CREEK PASS (MIDDLE RIDGE)

Elevations

Trailhead:	2,772 feet
Destination:	5,900 feet (Buck Creek Pass)

Other Significant Locations: Flower Dome, 6,300 feet; Liberty Cap, 6,850 feet; Helmet Butte, 7,366 feet; Middle Ridge, 6,200 feet

Altitude Gain 3,550 feet (including ups and downs; Trinity to Buck Creek Pass)

Walking Time In: 6 hours   Out: 4 hours

Trail Length 10.5 miles one-way

Accessibility Late July to early October

Difficulty Strenuous

Pack Full

Topographic Sheets USGS: Holden
Green Trails: Holden

To reach the trailhead, turn northward off U.S. 2 toward Lake Wenatchee; 3.8 miles later, turn right onto Highway 209 and continue to Plain, 4.9 miles away. Turn left (north) at that intersection; 2.8 miles later, turn right. Seven miles from Plain, turn right on the Chiwawa Road. Ten miles from this turnoff, the road narrows; 1.4 miles later, the pavement ends. Twelve miles of rough, dusty, one-lane road with turnouts lie ahead. After 11.2 miles, the road forks (the right fork leads to the Phelps Creek trailhead). Take the left fork 0.8 mile farther, where the road ends at the gated bridge over Phelps Creek. There is parking space for about forty cars in the Phelps Creek Campground to the west of the road. The total distance from U.S. 2 to the trailhead is 39.1 miles. From the village of Plain, it is 31 miles. If coming from the east, Plain can be reached directly from Leavenworth.

Initially, the trail crosses Phelps Creek on a bridge. Since the old mining village of Trinity remains private property, the footpath has been rerouted around the no-longer-thriving town. Locate and follow the old country road-bed. Immediately past two large tanks on the left, take the left of the three roads; 0.2 mile farther, take the right fork at the junction.

The boundary of the Glacier Peak Wilderness is reached at 1.2 miles. Just beyond the boundary, there is a satisfactory campsite to the right of the trail. At 1.4 miles is the junction with the Red Mountain trail to the right; go left here. In the deep forest, note the profuse display of queen's cup (bead lily).

Open areas are often overgrown with dense vegetation. The footpath crosses the Chiwawa River on a sturdy bridge at 2.6 miles. There is a poor campsite at the bridge; a larger campsite is located 0.1 mile farther up the trail, on a bluff above the river. There are six switchbacks about 5 miles from the trailhead.

At times, the trail follows old sheep driveways or bypasses these routes. Years ago, the sheep reached the high meadows along these passage ways. Although this practice ceased many years ago, it is of interest that the driveways remain eroded and without vegetation to this day, evidence of the longstanding effect of this practice on the landscape.

At 6.9 miles on the left is a "granite throne." The new and old trails join at 7.1 miles. The old trail is no longer maintained.

There is no lack of campsites from 1.2 to 7.3 miles. A semiformal camping area is located at about 6 miles within the deep forest and has a Forest Service toilet. At 7.3 miles in the woods, to the right of the trail, there is another deep-forest campsite. Those who are fatigued should stop here, for there is no other place to camp until the campground at Buck Creek Pass is reached or until the junction of the Buck Creek Pass trail and the Flower Dome trail. In the last 3.2 miles to the pass, the altitude gain is roughly 1,500 vertical feet. Early in the season, one avalanche path (from Fortress Mountain) must be crossed. There is no dearth of water, at least in early July, anywhere along the trail. Four or five creeks must be crossed; some offer a bit of difficulty, particularly during the high spring runoff or when partially snow filled.

As the trail contours around the southwest shoulder of Helmet Butte, drop downward about 0.2 mile and 200 vertical feet to the southwest to reach the hikers' campground. The horse camp is located another quarter mile to the south from the hikers' camp. There are also four or five less formal campsites at the beginning of the Flower Dome trail. Except as mentioned, the main Buck Creek Pass area has been closed to camping and horse grazing.

Views from the area are impressive. Climb 400 vertical feet and 0.7 mile to the west to the flat crest of Flower Dome. Ogle Glacier Peak to the west, Miner's Ridge and Plummer Mountain to the north, Helmet Butte and Fortress Mountain to the northeast, and Liberty Cap to the south.

Spend a day in this area if at all possible. Helmet Butte is not a technically difficult climb. Perhaps easier and almost as scenic is to follow the trail southward from the campground up the north flanks of Liberty Cap. The trail contours underneath the west and south sides of this formation; the ascent through heather meadow and scree is not difficult, and views from the flat top are superb. Alternatively, continue on the High Pass trail to a high rock promontory where all the great peaks in the area are easily visible. Gaze downward into the Buck Creek and Suiattle valleys. (Experienced climbers with proper equipment can cross High Pass and drop down into the Napeequa valley below.)

For those continuing to the north, from Buck Creek Pass, the footpath to Middle Ridge drops down fairly steeply for about 1 mile; the descent begins just beyond Flower Dome trail. The footpath crosses Small Creek (5,125 feet) and then resumes an upward gradient until it reaches an altitude of about 6,200 feet on Middle Ridge. From here, the tread drops downward to where Miner's Creek is crossed on a footlog. The altitude loss in this segment of the trail is about 1,700 feet. After the crossing, a rather steep ascent brings the hiker to the Glacier Peak mines on the trail between Image Lake and Suiattle Pass (see Image Lake for further details beyond this trail junction).

The route up to Buck Creek Pass offers progressively improving views of Buck Mountain to the south, Liberty Cap, and Helmet Butte. Near the crest, Glacier Peak comes into view.

Wood is relatively scarce near the campground. There is more wood near the Flower Dome camping area. Rocks and fire pits are scarce in the area, and portable cooking stoves are strongly recommended. Wildflowers are fabulous. In July, the meadows are covered with glacier lilies and western pasque flowers. Deer are common in the area, and marmots are easily seen.

Those desiring to reach the Suiattle River can take the Triad trail, which descends on the south side of Flower Dome 3 miles to the Suiattle River trail.

For those traversing the high trail, an ice ax is suggested until at least August 1. At 7.2 miles on the trail, note the parallel fallen trees, mute evidence of the power of winter snow avalanches.

The trail is quite muddy in places. Water is available from melting snow at the pass area until late in the season.

The views from Flower Dome, Helmet Butte, and Liberty Cap on a clear day are among the most spectacular in the North Cascades.

(Trinity to Buck Creek Pass, High Pass trail, and Flower Dome, July 1981; Buck Creek Pass to Glacier Peak Mines, August 1966)

IMAGE LAKE (SUIATTLE PASS)
Elevations

Trailhead:	1,550 feet	
Destination:	6,100 feet (Image Lake)	

Other Significant Locations: Miner's Ridge Lookout, 6,210 feet; Suiattle Pass, 6,000 feet

Altitude Gain	4,600 feet (including ups and downs)
Walking Time	In: 9–10 hours Out: 6 hours 30 minutes
Trail Length	15 miles one-way
Accessibility	July 15 to October 15
Difficulty	Strenuous
Pack	Full
Topographic Sheets	USGS: Glacier Peak, Holden
	Green Trails: Glacier Peak, Holden

The western access route begins on either State Highway 20 or 530. Drive to the beginning of the Suiattle River Road, midway between Darrington and Rockport, and continue 23 miles to the road end, where ample parking is available. There is a horse unloading ramp and toilets in the parking area. The last mile of road has been closed to vehicles; therefore, the first mile beyond the parking lot follows the old roadbed before leaving the upper portion of the road loop and becoming a bona fide trail (trail mileages to follow are described from this point rather than from the parking lot).

The generally muddy trail winds gradually through the deep woods for the first 5 miles. Adequate drinking water is available. A few yards beyond the 5-mile marker is the Canyon Creek Bridge. Fishing in Canyon Creek is reputed to be good. The trail then continues approximately 2.5 miles farther, or just beyond benchmark 2,848, where a rough camp of tables and lean-tos has been established, although there is no formal shelter. There is water just before this camp. A quarter of a mile past the camp, the trail forks; the left fork goes to Image Lake, and the right continues to join the Pacific Crest Trail 1.4 miles distant. This junction is about 7.9 miles from the trailhead. The trail to Image Lake goes upward unremittingly for the next 5 miles, gaining about 4,000 vertical feet. Drink deeply and fill water bottles before starting up; water may be scarce until Image Lake is reached. At mile 11, the Image Lake and Miner's Cabin trails join. Here there is another campsite with lean-tos but without a formal shelter. A few hundred yards down the trail, there is water. The last 2 miles of the trail are steep, terminating on the crest of Miner's Ridge about 0.3 mile east of the lookout at mile 13. A fairly level walk over the last mile brings the hiker to Image Lake.

The fire lookout was built in 1938 and upgraded in 1952. Since it is no longer needed for fire detection, it is now occupied by the wilderness ranger stationed on Miner's Ridge during the summer months. The view from the lookout is elegant. The short side trip to the lookout is well worth the effort.

Camping at Image Lake is restricted to the designated camping area southeast of the lake. The memorial shelter has been removed. The lake basin and surrounding meadows are recovering from past overuse, and the Image Lake area has been completely closed to overnight camping. Overnight campers may wish to walk 1 mile past the lake to Lady Camp, another designated campsite. Only very fit and strong hikers can make the almost 16-mile walk from the present parking area to the designated campsite in one day. There are substantial restrictions on the use of horses in the Image Lake basin area. A wilderness guard is stationed in this area in the summer to be of assistance and to enforce regulations (no campfires on Miner's Ridge).

Miner's Ridge is one of the most beautiful places in the world. The sunrise views of Glacier Peak reflected in Image Lake are classic and are well worth

PHOTO BY FRED DARVILL

Image Lake and Glacier Peak

getting up at 4:00 in the morning to photograph. From the Miner's Ridge look-out to Suiattle Pass, hikers walk for 5 miles hip deep in wildflowers and are surrounded by incredible beauty.

From Suiattle Pass, Glacier Peak dominates the skyline to the southwest. Other visible peaks include Plummer Mountain to the north, North Star to the northeast, and Fortress Mountain to the southeast.

All persons visiting Miner's Ridge should be aware that a substantial area of the ridge is still privately owned. A half-mile-wide open-pit mine here was actively promoted by a mining company in 1967. Clearly, this plan was not compatible with wilderness. Intense opposition to this proposal caused the prior owner of the property to back off. However, at any time, the current owner could apply to the MBSNF and Snohomish County for the necessary permits to begin mining operations. There are few areas on planet Earth more scenic than Miner's Ridge. This ravagement of the Glacier Peak Wilderness must be prevented at all costs should the mining issue resurface in the future. Wilderness advocates should stay tuned for future developments and be prepared to vigorously oppose mining at this location.

From Suiattle Pass, hikers have the option of descending the Pacific Crest Trail through the Agnes Creek Valley. Another option is to take the higher hikers' scrabble trail or descend and take a considerably longer trail with better tread to reach Cloudy Pass (about a mile away by the high trail). From here, there is a fantastic view down into the Lyman Lake basin (for details of the trail beyond this point, see Lyman Lake). Walking time from Image Lake to Suiattle Pass is about 2 hours; from Suiattle to Cloudy Pass, it is an additional half an hour.

Other campsites in the area are at the Glacier Peak mines and below Suiattle Pass in the meadows of the upper Agnes Creek valley.

Three days are the minimum for a visit to this area, and four or more days are preferable. The high country between Lyman Lake and the Miner's Ridge lookout is perhaps the scenic climax of the North Cascades.

Of the four access routes to the Miner's Ridge, Suiattle Pass, and Lyman Lake areas, the most scenic are through Railroad Creek and Buck Creek Pass. The Agnes and Suiattle routes require long walks through deep woods; many people become bored with the long walk in deep forest before meadowland with its associated alpine scenery is reached. Hikers having access to two cars should consider making a loop trip through this area; car keys can be exchanged at a preplanned location and time. Cars can be left at 25 Mile Creek or at Trinity, as well as at the end of the Suiattle River Road.

(August 1985)

PHELPS CREEK (SPIDER MEADOW)
Elevations

Trailhead:	3,450 feet
Destination:	6,500 feet (Spider Glacier Camp)
High Point:	7,050 feet (Phelps Creek Pass)

Other Significant Locations: Spider Meadow, 5,000 feet

Altitude Gain	3,000 feet (including ups and downs)
Walking Time	In: 5 hours Out: 3 hours
Trail Length	7 miles one-way
Accessibility	August 1 to October 1
Difficulty	Strenuous
Pack	Full
Topographic Sheets	USGS: Holden
	Green Trails: Holden

To reach the trailhead, follow the directions for reaching Trinity as given in the Buck Creek Pass trail description. Turn right 11.2 miles from the end of the pavement (0.8 mile from Trinity). This side road, 2.4 miles long, goes uphill, makes two switchbacks, and ends at the trailhead, where there is a parking lot large enough to accommodate about fifteen cars.

The trail begins at the north end of the parking lot and initially follows the bed of an abandoned mining road. Two-tenths of a mile from the trailhead, the Carne Mountain trail junction is intersected. At about 2 miles, the trail forks just beyond a mining claim to the west of the trail; go right at this unsigned fork. The Glacier Peak Wilderness is entered after approximately 3 miles (1 hour and 20 minutes of walking); there is a campsite at the boundary. At 3.5 miles, there are a creek and a camp, and 100 yards beyond, there is a formal camp with toilets. The abandoned road ends at Leroy Creek; this stream must be forded or crossed on a footlog. At 3.9 miles, the Phelps Ridge trail junction is passed, leading 3 miles to the top of Phelps Ridge to the west.

It is roughly 5.5 miles to Spider Meadow. Hiking time is 2 hours and 45 minutes, and altitude gain is about 1,500 feet. There are a number of excellent campsites as the trail enters the south portion of the meadow. Eight-tenths of a mile farther, you must ford Phelps Creek or find a footlog crossing. Beyond this point, the trail gradient steepens. Four-tenths of a mile farther is an important junction. Nearby, there are several campsites. The trail to the right, or east, goes into Phelps Basin for approximately half a mile and dead-ends at about 5,500 feet elevation. The Spider Glacier–Lyman Lake trail goes to the left, makes a sharp left turn about 100 yards beyond the junction, and then goes up very steeply. The tread quality deteriorates. Hikers need to scramble up switchbacks, initially beneath the rock face to the southwest, and then up the meadow, topping out approximately 1 mile farther and 1,000 vertical feet higher in a magnificent high camp on a larch-covered knob. This is one of the most splendid campsites in the entire North Cascades. There are great views down into Spider Meadow and Phelps Creek valley, from which the hiker has just come. Across the valley to the east are Seven Fingered Jack and Mount Maude, both rearing into the sky a shade over 9,000 feet. To the southwest is Red Mountain. Behind the camp is the snow couloir leading to the pass 0.8 mile away between the Phelps Creek and Railroad Creek drainages.

Although there are campsites in Phelps Basin, the campsite at "Larch Knob" is so clearly superior that hikers should press on even though fatigued. There is space in this area for, at most, three parties or perhaps ten people. Water is easily available, but wood is very scarce; carry a stove for cooking. The distance to this campsite is approximately 7 miles, and the walking time is 5 hours with a full pack.

This is the point of deepest penetration for the average hiker, who should spend an enjoyable night at this campsite and then return to the trailhead. Those experienced in snow travel can proceed up the not-too-difficult snow slope to reach the Spider–Lyman or Phelps Creek Pass 35 minutes and 0.8 mile away. One cannot help but be impressed by the tenacity of the miners who dug shafts at the pass area. Even more impressive is the magnificent alpine scenery, a macrocosm of beauty. Below to the north lie the Lyman Lakes and Lyman

Glacier; in back of them are Cloudy Pass, Cloudy Peak, North Star Mountain, and Sitting Bull Mountain. To the rear are the mountains that the hiker became familiar with in camp the preceding night. Do not neglect the microcosm of splendid alpine flowers growing in the rock crevasses near the pass. In their small way, they are as beautiful as the great vistas in the distance. Spend time here, allowing the beauty and the peace of the mountains to seep into your soul.

With regret, descend back into Phelps Creek or, if you have an ice ax and climbing experience, descend to the north on nontechnical but fairly steep snow, staying to the right of the ice of Lyman Glacier. When off the snow, pick up trail 1256B and follow it downward. Note the splendid waterfall descending from the upper lakes basin. The footpath passes above the east side of Lyman Lake. Camping is prohibited within 200 feet of the lake; alternative campsites can be found in the vicinity of Cloudy Pass. Once the Railroad Creek trail is reached, there are several options for further travel. It is possible to return to Trinity, just 3 miles from the point of beginning, via Cloudy Pass, Suiattle Pass, Miner's Ridge, and Buck Creek Pass. The Suiattle River trail leads to a west side road. Another option is to descend to Holden via Railroad Creek. Stehekin can be reached via Suiattle Pass and the Pacific Crest Trail north. All options except the return to the Phelps Creek trailhead involve preplanning and the availability of two cars. See data elsewhere in this book with regard to these choices.

(July 1975)

Mount Baker–Snoqualmie National Forest/ Wenatchee National Forest

IRON GOAT
Elevations
Trailhead: 2,560 feet
Destination: 2,740 feet (east end Windy Point Tunnel)
Altitude Gain   200 feet (including ups and downs)
Walking Time   In: 2 hours   Out: 1 hour 30 minutes
Trail Length   3 miles one-way
Accessibility   May to November
Difficulty   Moderately easy
Pack   Light
Topographic Sheets   USGS: Stevens Pass
    Green Trails: Stevens Pass

From U.S. 2, turn left (north) 5 miles east of the Skykomish Ranger Station. The turnoff is signed; the 55-mile marker is close to the turnoff. Drive 2.2 miles on a paved, narrow, occasionally one-lane road with some potholes; turn left (signed) and drive 1.4 miles to the signed trailhead, where there is parking for about thirty cars, a toilet, and a trailhead exhibit. The access road continues past the trailhead and becomes a logging road. The map at the trailhead is confusing at first glance. Spend some time here, or pick up a trail map at the Skykomish Ranger Station beforehand.

Start down the 100-yard-long boardwalk. After 7 minutes (0.3 mile), ascend the Martin Creek Crossover to the upper level of the old railroad grade. Four minutes thereafter, pass the first of many rotting timbers; after another minute, there is a viewpoint to the southwest. This is a good lunch stop. Four minutes later, come to the mouth of the first of several tunnels (closed to entry because of rockfall hazards). Milepost 1716 is 3 minutes past the tunnel, as is the junction with the Corea Crossover. The first drinking water is 20 minutes east of milepost 1716; it is 8 more minutes to a concrete wall with a waterfall cascading over it. Two minutes farther is a viewpoint and the 1715 signpost. A minute farther is a junction with wood stairs going up 0.1 mile to a view of the spillway (for erosion control and a fire reservoir). This side trip takes about 15 minutes.

Walking farther eastward, it is 9 minutes to the entrance of another concrete tunnel to the left of the trail. Eight minutes farther, a 20-foot walk to the right allows viewing of a 50-foot-high rock wall below. Sixteen minutes later, pass a concrete wall and reach the west entrance of the Windy Point Tunnel (it

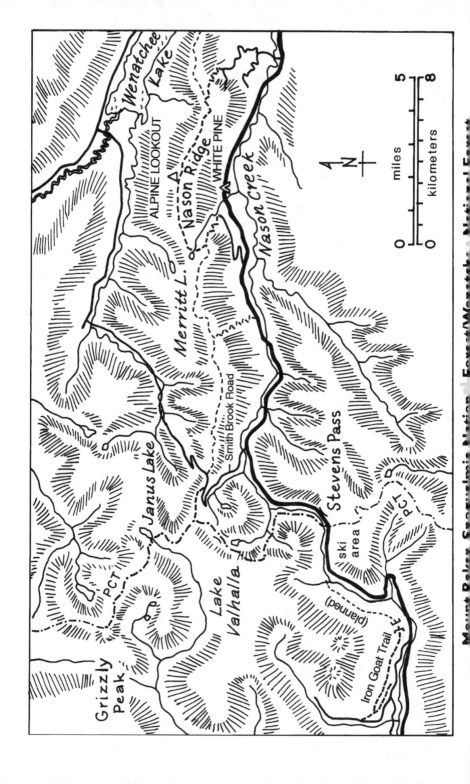

Mount Baker-Snoqualmie National Forest/Wenatchee National Forest

is windy here). The footpath goes around Windy Point. Ten minutes farther, there is a composting toilet about 75 feet below the trail. One minute farther, there is a viewpoint of Highway 2, the Great Northern Tunnel entrance, and surrounding peaks. Three minutes beyond the viewpoint, the maintained trail ends at the east end of the Windy Point tunnel.

With a 25-minute lunch stop, walking time to this point (including other stops, photos, and so forth) was 2 hours and 19 minutes. Return times with minimal stops are 52 minutes to Corea Crossover, 10 minutes on Corea Crossover to reach the lower railbed, and 13 minutes from lower Corea Crossover junction back to the trailhead, for a total of 1 hour and 15 minutes. Estimated altitude gain is 200 vertical feet. Round-trip mileage is about 6 miles. Pleasant greenery, nice flowers and ferns, and minimal mud make this an enjoyable spring or late-fall day hike. At a later date, the tread may be extended farther to the Wellington town site.

(June 1996)

JANUS LAKE (GRIZZLY PEAK)
Elevations
    Trailhead: 4,200 feet
    Destination: 5,600 feet (Grizzly Peak)
    Other Significant Locations: Union Gap, 4,700 feet; Janus Lake, 4,146 feet
Altitude Gain   2,700 feet (including ups and downs)
Walking Time   In: 4 hours   Out: 3 hours
Trail Length   7.5 miles one-way
Accessibility   July 15 to October 15
Difficulty   Moderately strenuous one-way; strenuous round trip
Pack   Light
Topographic Sheets   USGS: Labyrinth Mountain, Captain Point 7.5'
                        Green Trails: Benchmark Mountain

Drive 4.2 miles east of the crest of Stevens Pass; turn left (north) onto Smith Brook Road. Drive 3.3 miles to the signed trailhead, located about 0.3 mile beyond a hairpin curve. Since turnaround space at the trailhead is limited, it is best to drive an additional mile upward, turn around there, and then drive down to the trailhead and park on the left side of the road as available space permits; it is often crowded on weekends and holidays.

The first 20 feet of trail goes up steeply through the road cut. Fair-quality tread then contours upward above the road for about 0.3 mile in open meadow. There are views of Mount Lichtenberg to the south from this area. The Henry Jackson Wilderness is entered at 0.4 mile. From 0.3 to 0.5 mile, the footpath switchbacks up fairly steeply through deep woods. The grade then lessens; a nice meadow and potential campsite are passed on the left, about 0.2 mile from Union Gap. Walking time to Union Gap is 24 minutes; approximate distance is 0.85 mile. (All trail mileage through the rest of this description starts at Union Gap on the Pacific Crest Trail rather than at the Smith Brook trailhead.) From Union Gap, the trail goes downward at a moderate grade in a westward direction for approximately 1 mile. The trail is quite muddy. At about 0.3 mile, a nice meadow suitable for camping is passed on the left. The trail then turns northward. At 1.2 miles, it passes through a 0.1-mile section of slide alder, where there is a nice view to the southwest. At about 1.7 miles, there is a pleasant waterfall. It is approximately 2 miles to Lake Janus, taking about 35 minutes. Approximately 1,000 vertical feet are lost and 250 regained in the 2 miles between Union Gap and the lake. Except for the one view mentioned earlier, the trail is in timber the entire way. About 0.1 mile before reaching the lake, multiple trail forks are noted. The actual Crest trail bears left, or west, but all of the trails lead to the lake.

Janus Lake is about half a mile long. The forest comes down to the west side of the lakeshore, but there is meadow for 50 to 100 feet from the lakeshore on the east. The lake is fairly shallow, at least at the south end, with a number of lily pads present. Fall color in the area is quite spectacular. The area around the lake is boggy, and mosquitoes are present, even in late fall. There are multiple campsites at the south end of the lake. It appears possible (although not attempted) to walk fairly easily to the north end of the lake along the east shore.

The PCT crosses the outflow creek from Lake Janus, enters the forest, and then switchbacks up moderately steeply through the deep timber. There are no views of Lake Janus after entering the woods. At approximately 1.5 miles past the lake, an unmarked trail goes into a small meadow to the west. There is a small stream and campsite at this point. A walk of 0.1 mile to the south brings you to a nice view from the top of a burn area (a number of trees have been cut in this area, no doubt to control the fire). At approximately 3.8 miles, the trail goes through a pass, and from this point on, the views are magnificent and well worth the effort of reaching the ridge crest. Glacier Peak is impressive to the north. From 3.8 to 4.2 miles, the trail runs on the east side of the crest, then passes through a notch to the west side of the crest. At about 4.5 miles, the trail makes a U-shaped turn around a beautiful tarn and campsite. At 4.7 miles, a scrabble trail descends to Margaret Lake (4,840 feet), which can be seen with difficulty through the trees about 400 feet below. At 4.8 miles, Glasses Lake, lying approximately 400 vertical feet below and to the north, comes into view. An additional 0.1 mile brings you to a high camp where there is water available. From this site, a scrabble trail descends steeply to the lake below. There are also a number of nice campsites at the lake. The walking time to this point, from the road, is 2 hours and 40 minutes; the estimated altitude gain from Lake Janus is about 1,100 feet.

From the Glasses Lake overlook, the trail winds in and out and up and down following the ridge crest. Glacier Peak dominates the northern scenery. Grizzly Peak can be seen to the northwest. At about 5.7 miles, the trail begins switchbacking upward, gaining an additional 500 vertical feet and reaching the ridge crest at about 6.2 miles from Union Gap. Along this ridge crest, there are a number of rifts where the mountain appears to have partially slid away to the south; there may be caves at the bottom of some of these deep rifts. From 6.2 to 6.7 miles, the trail meanders along one of the loveliest ridges in the North Cascades, the Grizzly Meadows. The ridge terminates at Grizzly Peak, 5,593 feet in elevation. There is a sign about 75 feet east of the trail indicating the true location of Grizzly Peak. From this magnificent meadow (particularly impressive in the first weekend of October, when the fall color was incredible), there is a 360-degree view that defies description. Glacier Peak looms to the north; Mount Rainier can be seen to the south. High meadows, glaciated peaks, green forest, and deep valleys are spread out seemingly to infinity in every direction. Heather Lake is nestled in the Lake Creek Valley to the east. When I visited Grizzly Peak, there were places where fresh snow was 4 inches deep. The red blueberry leaves projecting above the gleaming white snow were lovely.

Although there is no water unless there are snowfields in Grizzly Meadows, this is a splendid place to camp or just spend time. Walking time from the Smith Brook trailhead to Grizzly Peak is 4 hours; the estimated altitude gain allowing for ups and downs is approximately 2,700 feet going in. The out-time is approximately 3 hours, and the estimated altitude gain out is approximately 1,200 feet.

Water is sparse to absent on the ridge top in the late summer and early fall, so an adequate supply should be carried from Lake Janus.

Although strenuous if done in one day, and although the first 4.6 miles of trail are relatively "blah," the high ridge from that point on more than makes up for the difficulty in getting there. This is truly one of the more spectacular walks in the high Cascades.

(Smith Brook trailhead to Curry Gap, August 1995; remainder of trail, October 1971)

LAKE VALHALLA (PCT)
Elevations

Trailhead:	4,000 feet (Stevens Pass)
Destination:	4,830 feet (Lake Valhalla)
High Point:	5,100 feet (ridge above lake)

Altitude Gain   1,500 feet (including ups and downs)
Walking Time   In: 2 hours 10 minutes   Out: 2 hours
Trail Length   5.5 miles one-way
Accessibility   July 15 to October 15
Difficulty   Moderate one-way; moderately strenuous round-trip
Pack   Light
Topographic Sheets   USGS: Stevens Pass, Labyrinth Mountain
Green Trails: Benchmark Mountain

The trail begins by the Chelan County power substation about 0.2 mile east of the summit of Stevens Pass. The first 1.5 miles or so follows the old Great Northern Railroad grade and loses about 400 vertical feet. This portion of the trail is not particularly scenic and simply parallels the highway on the west side of the canyon. (As an option, drive 1.7 miles east of the Stevens Pass summit and park by the chalets on the west. Bushwhack upward and westward, gaining about 200 vertical feet, to eliminate about 1.7 miles of low-quality trail en route to Lake Valhalla.) At about 1.5 miles, the trail turns westward and enters deep forest. Between 1 and 2 miles, the trail is poorly maintained, with lots of underbrush and downed timber. At about 2.2 miles, a stream is crossed; there is a rudimentary campsite at this point. At about 3.2 miles, a larger stream is crossed. There is a campsite at the creek and several adequate campsites in the basin 0.1 mile to the west. The walking time to this point is 1 hour and 15 minutes, and at this point, you have regained most of the 400 vertical feet lost in the first 1.5 miles. At about 3.4 miles, you enter a meadow with wildflowers. At 3.6 miles, there are a stream and a nice campsite. At the 5-mile mark (2 hours from the trailhead), there is a view down the valley, with U.S. 2 visible far below. At 5.2 miles, the 5,000-foot-high Lake Valhalla overlook is reached. A 0.3-mile descent from here brings the hiker to the shore of scenic Lake Valhalla. There is a small meadow bisected by a small stream west of the lake. A delightful sandy beach is located on the west shore of the lake; children will enjoy wading here. The steep, rocky cliff of Mount Lichtenberg to the east makes an impressive backdrop to the lake. There are fish in the lake.

The PCT then goes upward, reaching a pass above Lake Valhalla; the 0.4-mile ascent requires about 15 minutes and gains about 300 vertical feet. Just before the pass, stop and take in the sparkling lake below and the peaks in the background to the southeast.

An interesting side trip is to locate the scrabble trail about 50 feet north of the pass and proceed upward (gaining about 650 vertical feet) to the domelike summit of Mount McCausland (5,747 feet). The views from here are magnificent, particularly in late September and early October, when the fall color is at its height. Blueberries and huckleberries are found on this ridge. Follow a hard-to-find track northward, dip down a few feet near the ridge end, and contour onto the west side of the ridge and then north 50 feet. At this point, sit on the granite boulders on the ridge end and look northward to a fine view of Janus Lake, multiple ridges, and Glacier Peak and White Pass to the north. The ascent of this ridge is the high point of the trip to Lake Valhalla. The views from the south part of the ridge looking directly down on the lake and the impressive sheer face of Mount Lichtenberg, making up the eastern shore of the lake, are equally grand. Allow at least an hour for this side trip.

Several designated tent sites away from the lakeshore are found near Lake Valhalla. Campfires are prohibited here. Revegetation of affected areas around Lake Valhalla is being attempted; be sure to stay off the denuded areas being restored. If planning to camp overnight, it is best to come on weekdays, since crowding is likely on weekends, and solitude is improbable at any time. A shorter, easier route to Lake Valhalla is from Smith Brook Road; see the Janus Lake trail description for information on accessing the trailhead and Union Gap. From the trailhead, it is 3 miles to the lake; the altitude gain is 800 vertical feet. Hiking time up is 1 hour and 20 minutes; down is 1 hour. Most of the trail is in timber, but views are available to the east midway from the gap to the lake; Rock Mountain can be seen from the trail.

(Smith Brook Road to Lake Valhalla, August 1995; Stevens Pass to Lake Valhalla, August 1971)

NASON RIDGE (ALPINE LOOKOUT)
Elevations

Trailhead:	3,900 feet
Destination:	6,200 feet (Alpine Lookout)

Other Significant Locations: Merritt Lake, 5,000 feet; junction with U.S. 2, 2,600 feet

Altitude Gain	2,800 feet (including ups and downs)
Walking Time	In: 2 hours 35 minutes Out: 2 hours
Trail Length	5.3 miles; entire loop, 11 miles (one-way)
Accessibility	July to mid-October
Difficulty	Moderately strenuous
Pack	Light
Topographic Sheets	USGS: Wenatchee Lake
	Green Trails: Wenatchee Lake

The best access is via Butcher Creek Road 2717. This road, signed unobtrusively, is a few hundred yards east of the rest area on Highway 2, roughly 18
miles east of the Stevens Pass summit. The road crosses Nason Creek, then
goes underneath power lines and gains altitude. At 3.2 miles, there is a signed
junction; take the left fork. The trailhead is 4.5 miles from Highway 2 on the
north side of the road and is signed (Round Mountain trail). There is parking
for at most two to three cars at the trailhead. There is a turnaround about 200
feet to the west, with additional parking for several cars in that area. From the
trailhead, it is 1.5 miles to the junction with the Nason Ridge trail and roughly
5.3 miles to Alpine Lookout. This spur trail is closed to cycles. Some 10 minutes, or 0.4 mile, up the trail is Spring Camp, with water and one tent site. This
is the last water until Merritt Lake, at least in the fall. Forty-five minutes of brisk
uphill walking—mostly through forest, but with an occasional view—brings
the hiker to the junction with the Nason Ridge trail. From here it is 7 miles to
Merritt Lake and 4 miles to Alpine Lookout, both to the west; 6 miles to the
east is the road along the south shore of Lake Wenatchee.

One-tenth of a mile to the west of this junction, there are two splendid
views of the valley below, with Glacier Peak at the head of the valley. Lake
Wenatchee is also viewable slightly to the east. Twenty minutes of further
walking brings you out onto a grassy ridge with a good view to the south. An
additional 10 minutes are required to drop down into a saddle; at about 1 hour
and 35 minutes, the 8-mile marker is reached, and for the first time, Alpine
Lookout comes into view. Even high on the ridge, it is surprising how easily
truck and train noises are heard from the railroad and the highway below. After
approximately another 30 minutes, you drop down into a second saddle;
there is a cluster of yellow larch in the hollow to the north. In 2 hours and 20
minutes, the junction to the lookout (which is roughly 0.4 mile farther on) is
intersected, and the lookout itself is reached after 2 hours and 35 minutes, for a
total distance of roughly 5.3 miles. From the junction below the lookout, Merritt
Lake is 3 miles. Rock Lake is 9 miles, and Rock Mountain is 10 miles. Apparently,
the Nason Ridge trail is open to cycles, but the trail west of Alpine Lookout
is closed. From the lookout there are views in all directions, although the
views of Glacier Peak from this location are badly marred by extensive patch-
cutting in the foreground. Salt licks at the lookout undoubtedly attract deer
and mountain goats. The Nason Ridge trail is scenic from Round Mountain to
Merritt Lake.

Continuing the loop, the trail drops down, losing several hundred vertical
feet of altitude, on the south side of Nason Ridge under Alpine Lookout and
contours along the south side of the ridge for about 2 miles. It then comes near
the ridge crest again, where a short scramble brings you to inferior views of
Glacier Peak (compared with those from the lookout area). Roughly 50 feet past

the 12-mile sign, there is a junction above Merritt Lake. The only sign at the junction indicates that Alpine Lookout is 4 miles to the east. Neither the trail to the west nor the down trail are signed. Approximately 0.3 mile of downhill walking brings you to Merritt Lake, where there are a number of good campsites. The lake is pretty, but not spectacular. It takes about 10 minutes to descend from the junction to the lake. From the lake, it is approximately 2.8 miles to the trailhead at the end of Road 657. Views are minimal, and the downward tread is rough. Half a mile from the lake, the Nason Ridge trail junction is intersected. Rock Lake is 4 miles from this junction.

Trail distance for the Nason Ridge loop is estimated at 11.2 miles, including the side trip to the lookout. Including lunch and photo stops, the loop trip from east to west took 6 hours. There are dry campsites east of the lookout. Merritt Lake is the best overnight stopping place. The lookout is more easily accessed from the east than from the west. The views are enjoyable, but not spectacular; the exception is the view up the White River valley to Glacier Peak. Take a telephoto lens for shooting Glacier Peak from the lookout; with a standard lens, the clear-cuts in the foreground are distracting. Carry lots of water, because the ridge is a dry place. Two cars are required if the loop hike is planned.

(October 1978)

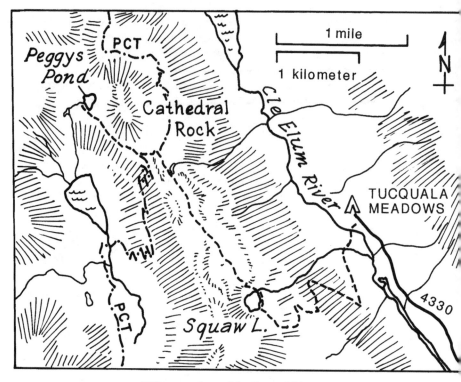

Wenatchee National Forest

Wenatchee National Forest

PEGGY'S PONDS
Elevations
Trailhead: 3,400 feet
Destination: 5,600 feet (Peggy's Ponds)
Other Significant Locations: East ridge of Mount Daniel, 6,600 feet
Altitude Gain   2,500 feet in; 300 feet out (including ups and downs)
Walking Time In: 3 hours   Out: 2 hours 30 minutes
Trail Length   5.5 miles one-way
Accessibility Mid-July to mid-October
Difficulty   Moderate (one-day round trip)
Pack   Full
Topographic Sheets USGS: The Cradle
                    Green Trails: Stevens Pass

Take I-90 exits to Roslyn and Salmon La Sac. Drive 20 miles to Salmon La Sac on paved road. Follow the poor-quality, often one-lane gravel road for 1.7 miles to the Davis Peak trailhead road; it is 11.4 miles to the Paddy Go Easy trailhead. At 12.5 miles, turn left (west); follow the road across the creek to a parking area suitable for twelve cars at the Cathedral Rock trailhead. (It is best to inspect this road on foot prior to entry. If the creek is deep or the road is deeply rutted through mud, it is best to park at the road junction or at the campground 0.1 mile north.) This area is heavily used by horsemen. There is an outhouse at the trailhead. If you keep going straight, you will reach the Tucquala Meadows Campground 0.1 mile past the junction.

The trail crosses a rickety bridge; 0.1 mile past the Cle Elum River crossing, the trail starts upward. After 0.2 mile, the Alpine Lakes Wilderness is entered. The trail continues upward steeply for about 1.5 miles. At 1.8 miles, the junction with trail 1332 is reached; stay right. Fifteen minutes of fairly level walking brings the hiker to Squaw Lake. There are campsites on the east and the north ends of the lake; campfires are allowed at this location. The trail starts gaining altitude at the north end of the lake. Forty minutes (1.5 miles) past the lake, a pond is passed on the right; 0.1 mile farther, there is a great view of a large mountain hemlock and of Cathedral Rock in the background. The trail for the next 0.4 mile passes tarns and lakes. There are probable campsites on the ridge to the east of the trail. At 2.7 miles and 1 hour and 10 minutes from the 1332 junction, the trail joins the Pacific Crest Trail in a pleasant meadow. There are lots of campsites to the north of this junction for 0.3 mile, both along the PCT and by a tarn visible from the junction.

Turn left at the PCT junction and follow it upward, over a pass, and down to the beginning of the first switchback. A sign at this point says, "Hiker trail—closed to stock." Follow the half-mile scrabble trail, which in places requires hands-on use, to the lowest of Peggy's Ponds. There are several campsites around the lower ponds but many nicer campsites in the half-mile climb to the higher ponds.

Beyond the upper pond, the trail crosses a creek filled with glacial till. There are two trails that leave from this vicinity and lead up the ridge to the west toward Mount Daniel. The tread is scrabble most of the way. The higher you go, the better the views of Cathedral Rock, Peggy's Ponds, and Mount Daniel.

Ptarmigan frequent the high ridge west of the ponds. Just before reaching the first pond, there are ruins of a log cabin, built long ago by miners in this avalanche-free location. From the upper pond, there is a scrabble trail leading eastward to the base of Cathedral Rock. Peggy's Ponds are quite scenic and are well worth the effort required to reach them.

Returning to the PCT, at the pass, there is a scrabble trail that follows the ridge crest south. There are a number of good, dry campsites along this ridge crest and some elegant views to the west, looking down into Deep Lake and across the valley into Circle Lake. There is a long cataract dropping down from Circle Lake into the valley below. Mount Rainier can also be viewed from this ridge crest.

The PCT begins to descend about 0.3 mile north of the Peggy's Ponds junction. From the trail, the Tucquala Meadows can be seen below and to the southeast. There is a warning sign about the hazards of attempting to cross the Mount Daniel Creek 2 miles north of the junction. Apparently, this is a difficult ford in high water. About 1 mile north of the junction, there is a good view of Mount Daniel.

The Tucquala Meadows are elegant, as is the lake of the same name. The splendid greenery of the meadows, with the spire of Cathedral Rock in the background, causes mountain photographers to expose substantial amounts of film. Another plus is the presence of several nice campgrounds in the vicinity of the meadows.

(July 1988)

Wenatchee National Forest

LARCH LAKES (COW CREEK MEADOWS)

Elevations

Trailhead:	3,100 feet
Destination:	5,800 feet (Upper Larch Lake)
Altitude Gain	2,700 feet (including ups and downs)
Walking Time	In: 3 hours 45 minutes Out: 3 hours
Trail Length	7.5 miles one-way
Accessibility	Early July to late October
Difficulty	Moderately strenuous
Pack	Full
Topographic Sheets	USGS: Lucerne
	Green Trails: Lucerne

Drive 38 miles from U.S. 97 to the end of the Entiat Road. There is a pleasant campground at Cottonwood at the end of the road, with sites above and below the side road alongside the Entiat River. The trailhead is a quarter mile farther, where there is parking for approximately forty cars. The area is used also by horses, mountain bikes, and trail machines, until it reaches the Glacier Peak Wilderness boundary.

Twenty minutes (0.8 mile) in, there is a pleasant streamside campsite below and to the west of the trail. It is 2.2 miles (45 minutes) to the junction with the Anthem Creek trail. The first water on the trail is at 55 minutes. Water is not difficult to find thereafter. There are several fair to good campsites around the stream and an additional one about 100 yards to the west. It is about 3.6 miles to the junction with the Cow Creek trail (1 hour and 22 minutes). Trail signs here indicate that the hiker's route to Larch Lake is now via this trail, in order to eliminate the ford of the Entiat a mile farther upstream. This trail drops down a bit, crosses a bridge, goes upward, turns right at the junction at Myrtle Lake, and crosses the outlet stream, which is somewhat difficult. About 200 yards after passing the outlet stream, a newly constructed scrabble trail runs northward to intersect with the Larch Lake trail about 0.25 mile west of the river crossing. This segment of the route is about 1.2 miles in length. The scrabble trail crosses two streams that must be forded or boulder-hopped. From the junction, it takes 1 hour and 20 minutes to do the approximately 2.4 miles to Lower Larch Lake. The trail is steep in places. There is a splendid waterfall cascading to the left of the trail (this is the outlet stream from Larch Lake). A hundred yards after reaching the lake, the trail drops slightly into an elegant and large meadow, containing multiple campsites. The best site is at the base of a large, four-trunked larch tree.

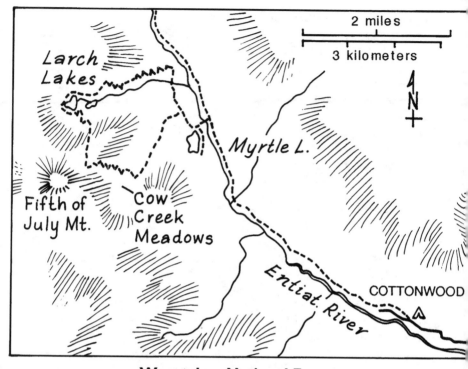

Wenatchee National Forest

Mosquitoes were a minor annoyance in 1990 but a horrendous problem in 1991 at both of the Larch Lakes, at Cow Creek Meadows, and on the connecting trail between these locations. This difference may have been due to the three- to four-week-late snowmelt in 1991. Visits in late August or September may avoid the intermittent swarms of bloodsucking insects. At any time, it is wise to take along repellents, mosquito netting, a tent with an insect screen, and to pretreat clothes with permethrin.

There is a wilderness toilet near the inlet stream. A 10-minute walk, gaining perhaps 150 feet in altitude, brings you to Upper Larch Lake, an equally picturesque high alpine lake, surrounded by extensive meadow and with multiple high-quality campsites. There is a trail junction at the north end of the upper lake. The left fork leads to Fifth of July Mountain; the right fork goes to Pomas Pass. The Pomas Pass trail gains altitude, then reaches a ridge crest from which there are scenic views into Rock Creek valley below and of the multiple peaks to the west. There is also a good view of both lakes below at this point. The trail continues to gain altitude for the next 45 minutes, reaching a high point on the ridge crest of about 6,700 feet. This is perhaps the most scenic location on the entire trail.

Hikers wishing to make a loop trip can do the 2-mile segment (gaining 700 vertical feet) to the junction with the Cow Creek Meadow trail beneath the summit of Fifth of July Mountain. Descend here about 1.8 miles to this pleasant meadow at 5,100 feet elevation, where there are several campsites on the north side. Deer frequent the meadow early and late in the day. Just below the meadow, the footpath crosses a stream. A downstream footlog was present in 1991; if it is no longer in place, the creek may need to be forded. From the meadows to the junction with the Entiat River trail is about 2.2 miles, losing about 1,400 feet of elevation.

(Larch Lakes, August 1990; Cow Creek Meadows, August 1991)

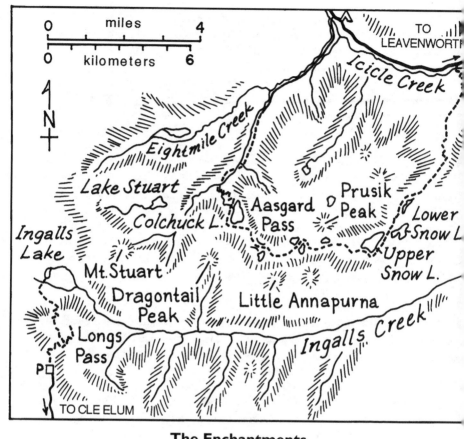

The Enchantments

The Enchantments

COLCHUCK LAKE (AASGARD PASS)

Elevations
Trailhead: 3,400 feet
Destination: 7,800 feet (Aasgard Pass)
High Point: 8,436 feet (Little Annapurna)
Other Significant Locations: Colchuck Lake, 5,570 feet
Altitude Gain   4,400 feet (including ups and downs)
Walking Time   In: 5 hours 15 minutes   Out: 3 hours 45 minutes
Trail Length   6.6 miles one-way
Accessibility   Late July to early October
Difficulty   Strenuous
Pack   Full
Topographic Sheets   USGS: Chiwaukum Mountains, Mount Stuart
    Green Trails: The Enchantments, Washington

See the first paragraph of the Enchantment Lakes trail description for important information.

Accessing Aasgard Pass via Colchuck Lake saves 2,100 feet of altitude gain and 5.5 miles of distance and can be done in one day rather than two if—and this is a big if—the hikers are in excellent physical condition and have climbing equipment (an ice ax if snow lingers, a staff later in the summer, and belay rope, depending on party experience and training), cross-country hiking skills, and no acrophobia. Permits are required for overnight stays and must be obtained months in advance or by lottery on the morning of departure at the Leavenworth Ranger Station (this is true in 1998; contact the ranger station as far in advance as possible, as changes may occur in the future).

Turn south on the Icicle Creek Road from U.S. 2 half a mile or so west of Leavenworth. Drive 8.5 miles to the road fork. Turn left, drive through the Bridge Creek Campground, and continue to the large parking area at the Lake Stuart trailhead; there is room for about fifty cars here.

The trail goes up moderately on the east side of Mountaineer Creek for about 1.8 miles and crosses the creek on a bridge at this point. There are campsites at about 0.25 mile and near the bridge. The signed trail junction to Colchuck Lake is reached at about 2.5 miles, after a walk of an hour. Turn left here and drop down slightly to a nice campsite near Mountaineer Creek. Cross the creek on a footlog; notice the splendid view of Mount Stuart reflected in the clear waters of the creek at this point. Climb upward—80 percent of the time on moderate switchbacks, and 20 percent of the time on steep scrabble trail—to reach the west end of Colchuck Lake. It is an estimated 2 miles and an additional hour of hiking time to the lake. The elevation at the lake is 5,570 feet, so the altitude gain to this point is roughly 2,200 vertical feet. The maintained trail ends at the west end of the lake. There are a number of good campsites in this area.

If going to Aasgard Pass, pick up a scrabble trail to the right (west) side of the lake and follow it up and down, in and out (when in doubt, stay high), over timber, talus, slide alder, and brush, passing a side bay and a satellite lake en route to reach the east end of the lake. At this point, there are several nice campsites, a pretty beach, and a splendid view to the west. The walking time from one end of the lake to the other is approximately 50 minutes. Only those in good to excellent physical condition with some knowledge of rock climbing, boulder hopping, and route finding should proceed beyond this point.

Pick up the small scrabble trail from the beach and follow it about 150 yards through the trees to the talus slope. The entry to the slope is marked by both a cairn and flagging tape. Proceed up this steep slope the easiest way, which generally means following a number of inapparent divergent and convergent trails. About 25 percent of the way up the slope, there are alternatives, but all the routes are difficult. A left trail proceeds upward through but not into the slide alders to the cliff on the left and stays on the left (north) side until approximately 60 percent more of the slope has been climbed. It then contours to the right (south) underneath a rock wall, goes up through trees and larch for about 300 vertical feet, and contours to the north (left) about 100 feet above a tarn early in the season and a dry lake late in the season to a large boulder and grassy col; follow this col to the top, turn left across another dry lakebed, and pick up a faint scrabble trail on the north side, which leads to the north end of the highest Enchantment Lake 100 yards farther.

An option that may be somewhat quicker and shorter but is more difficult is to go to the base of the first large rock where the waterfall is and climb two or three pitches that are moderately difficult (if wearing a heavy pack) to the left of the waterfall or scramble up fairly steep granite to the right of the waterfall. Cross the creek (if taking the latter route) and proceed upward through meadow and scree to the rock base, at which time you may turn left, which is the easiest route to the pass, or, less desirably, turn right and follow that route to the crest. If you take the right route, you must walk roughly half a mile over the top of a talus- and boulder-strewn area to reach the lakes. The wilderness manager of the Leavenworth Ranger District states, "We prefer to direct people to the left away from the lower falls when ascending Aasgard."

The upper lake contains large, fat cutthroat trout, beautifully colored, which will bite on salmon eggs. Campsites are difficult to find around the several upper lakes, since there is little level terrain; at most, there is room for six to eight campsites. This area is quite exposed to wind and weather and unusually cold in comparison with surrounding areas.

From Aasgard Pass, the views to the west are spectacular. Sloan, Pugh, White Chuck, and Mount Baker are visible; Colchuck Lake sparkles in the afternoon sun below.

Those with moderate climbing skills will have no difficulty ascending Little Annapurna, either via snow or by following rock approaches on either side of the peak, and then contouring to the summit. Visible from here are Mounts Adams, St. Helens, Rainier, Baker, and Glacier Peak; below, the whole complex of the Enchantment Lakes spreads out like a string of sparkling jewels in a 180-degree arc.

Dragontail (known as Dragging Tail by the fatigued) Peak, about 8,700 feet high, is also climbable without undue difficulty. Views from here are also impressive.

As the hiker proceeds downward on the scrabble trail from the higher Enchantment Lakes to the lower, better and better campsites become apparent.

The hiker passes Isolation Lake and associated cold, deep lakes with no campsites, then some lovely tarns and granite waterfalls in a larch meadow, and then a scenic waterfall descending over granite base rock. This cataract, about 1.5 miles and 400 feet below Aasgard Pass, is a junction point.

From here, the tread drops down a steep col, losing considerable altitude, to Inspiration Lake. A southward trek of half a mile through a notch, dropping about 200 feet, brings the hiker to Perfection Lake. At the north end of the lake is the junction with the trail to Prusik Pass. A side trip to the east of the pass leads to scenic Gnome Tarn, immediately beneath Prusik Peak. Lakes Viviane, Leprechaun, and Temple, blue gems in a granite bezel, lie below. From these lakes, the trail again descends to the Snow Lakes and then Nada Lake.

Approximate time to climb Little Annapurna: 1 hour and 15 minutes up, 30 to 40 minutes down. Walking time from the highest lake to Gnome Tarn: down, 1 hour and 15 minutes; up, 1 hour and 45 minutes. Up-time from Colchuck Lake to the highest Enchantment Lake: 2 hours and 15 minutes; down-time, 1 hour and 15 minutes. Down-time from Colchuck Lake to the trail junction is 40 minutes; from the junction to the parking lot is 50 minutes.

The upper Enchantment area is similar to the High Sierras geologically and scenically.

Clearly, compared with the access time via Snow Lakes, this is a faster and easier route, in spite of the horrendous 2 hours and 15 minutes required to ascend from Colchuck Lake to the top of the Aasgard Pass.

The estimated distance (via the scrabble trail) from one end of Colchuck Lake to the other is 1.5 miles. The linear distance from the lake to Aasgard Pass is about 0.8 mile, with an altitude gain of roughly 2,230 vertical feet.

(September 1973)

ENCHANTMENT LAKES (AASGARD PASS; SNOW CREEK)
Elevations

Trailhead:	1,300 feet
Destination:	7,800 feet (Aasgard Pass)

Other Significant Locations: Upper Snow Lake, 5,500 feet; Viviane Lake, 6,785 feet

Altitude Gain   6,500 feet (including ups and downs)

Walking Time   In: 16 hours   Out: 10 hours

Trail Length   12 miles; Nada Lake, 5.2 miles; Upper Snow Lake, 6.5 miles; Lake Vivianne, 9 miles (one-way)

Accessibility   Early August to early October

Difficulty   Strenuous

Pack   Full, trailhead to Upper Snow Lake; light, Upper Snow Lake to Lake Viviane

Topographic Sheets   USGS: Mount Stuart, Liberty
                         Green Trails: The Enchantments, Washington

There are several important facts that hikers should consider before planning to access the upper Enchantment Lakes and Aasgard Pass: (1) Permits, not easily obtained, are mandatory for overnight entry; contact the Leavenworth Ranger Station, 600 Sherbourne Street, Leavenworth, WA 98826 (509-548-6977) as far in advance as possible to determine permit acquisition policies currently in force. (2) Distances and altitude gain are both substantial; in addition, poor-quality tread slows the pace frequently. The average hiker will require three days to reach Aasgard Pass and two days to descend from the pass. (3) Do not anticipate solitude; the area is popular. (4) Temperatures at night are colder here than in most other places in the North Cascades, and no campfires are allowed. (5) Dogs are prohibited. (6) Designated campsites must be used at both Snow Lakes and Nada Lake; in the Enchantment core area, already impacted sites away from trails and lakes must be used. (7) Strategically placed toilets are scattered throughout the area and should be used by all visitors. (8) group size is limited to eight people.

To compensate for these restrictions, the upper lakes are gorgeous, particularly in late September and early October when the larch needles have turned yellow and glow when backlighted.

To reach the trailhead, turn south at the west outskirts of Leavenworth from U.S. 2 onto the Icicle Creek Road. At 4.4 miles, turn left into the Snow Lakes parking area, which will accommodate about forty cars.

The trail descends to cross Icicle Creek, and then switchbacks upward moderately steeply through an extensive burn area. This is best ascended in the early morning, since temperatures usually are hot here in the afternoon.

None of the footpath is brushed. Fireweeds bloom in the fire-scarred area. The Alpine Lakes Wilderness is entered at about 1 mile. To the right, the Snow Creek Wall looms above the hiker. At 1.5 miles, the footpath begins an upward traverse, and enters forest at about 2 miles. Three nice campsites adjacent to Snow Creek are passed in the next quarter mile. Intermittent thick brush overhangs the footpath. Another small camping area is passed about 0.7 mile farther. Tread quality deteriorates thereafter. A boulder and brush "crawl" for about a quarter mile is miserable walking. After about 3.5 hours, Snow Creek is crossed on a bridge. There is a fair campsite near the crossing, and another about 0.2 mile farther. Another upward slog on rocks, over boulders, and through brush follows. After 4.5 hours, a campsite to the left and relatively level terrain herald arrival at the west end of lovely Nada Lake. The scenery of the peaks and descending waterfall is impressive, but somewhat less appreciated due to the swarms of mosquitoes. There is a good campsite adjacent to the day-use vision point on the lakeshore. The footpath then follows the lakeshore for about half a mile; a stream crossing is necessary, either by ford or less-than-secure footlogs. Another poor tread and brushy set of switchbacks leads upward to the pass between Nada Lake and the Snow Lakes. A gentle descent from the pass brings the hiker to the concrete dam between the two Snow Lakes. The footpath crosses this dam, in spite of the 2- to 6-inch flow of water over the top of the 150-foot dam; gaiters are useful to keep the feet dry during the crossing. All of the campsites located near the shore of the upper lake are nice. To summarize, there are six designated campsites around Nada Lake, five sites on lower Snow Lake, and thirteen camping areas near Upper Snow Lake. Hiking time from the trailhead to a midlake camp area at Upper Snow Lake (including lunch, rests, and viewing at Nada Lake) was 7 hours and 5 minutes.

The trail to the south end of Upper Snow Lake crosses a number of bogs on footlogs. The footlog crossing the inlet stream has collapsed; replacement was scheduled for late 1997. It takes about 40 minutes to walk from one end of this lake to the other. After the crossing, tread follows the creek for about a half mile, and then starts upward steeply away from the stream. Tread is scrabble and is marked by rock cairns. The ascent is steep and many times requires hands-on ascents on somewhat exposed granite. With a full pack, the route is very strenuous. Acrophobics should avoid this section of the trail. A long, impressive waterfall cascades down from Lake Viviane. At one slickrock crossing, steps have been hacked out of the granite. The lake nestles in a granite bowl, with the summits of Little Annapurna, Prusik Peak, and McClellan Peak rising above. The exit stream must be crossed to continue upward to Leprechaun Lake; the one narrow footlog in place is precarious (it is hoped that the trail crew will improve this crossing in the near future.) Several tent sites

Prusik Peak

can be found on either side of the crossing with a reasonable search. Snowpack on the steep granite on the south side of the lake precludes further safe upward exploration. Up-time to Lake Viviane with a light pack from the inlet stream crossing is 1 hour and 45 minutes. Descent time is only 5 minutes shorter. Descent time from Upper Snow Lake to the trailhead, including lunch stop and ogling and photo time is 5 hours and 25 minutes.

I have not walked the approximately 1-mile section of trail between Lake Viviane and the north end of Perfection Lake. See data about the upper lakes in the Colchuck Lake–Aasgard Pass trail description.

Snow lingered about 4 weeks longer than average in the 1997 summer. In a more normal year, or later in the summer, the multiple other lakes can be explored en route to Aasgard Pass. Note the spire of Prusik Peak. Enjoy a side trip to Prusik Pass and Gnome Tarn, directly beneath Prusik Peak. Consider a not-too-difficult ascent to the summit of Little Annapurna, from which all the great peaks of Washington can be seen on a clear day. Enjoy the views of Mounts Baker, Sloan, Pugh, and White Chuck, and of Colchuck Lake sparkling in the afternoon sun below, from Aasgard Pass.

Considering the technical difficulty of carrying a heavy pack up either route to the upper Enchantment area, the limited campsites in the upper basin, the low temperatures at night, and the fragile nature of the high meadows, many elect to camp lower and visit the high country carrying only a day pack. Other recommendations from the Leavenworth Ranger District follow:

1. Due to the fragile nature of the Enchantments, it is imperative that users diligently apply "minimum impact" or "leave-no-trace" practices.
2. Visitors should not urinate on vegetation. Mountain goats will paw up the plants and soil due to their desire for the salt in human urine. If a privy is not available, hikers should urinate on large rock slabs where the urine will evaporate.
3. Do not place trash in the toilets; pack it out.
4. Avoid walking on vegetation; use existing trails or try to walk on snow, rock, or sand.
5. Above the Snow Lakes, use only existing campsites.

(July 1997)

INGALLS LAKE

Elevations

Trailhead:	4,200 feet
Destination:	6,463 feet (Ingalls Lake)
High Point:	6,500 feet (Ingalls Pass)
Altitude Gain	2,500 feet in; 300 feet out (including ups and downs)
Walking Time	In: 2 hours 45 minutes Out: 2 hours 30 minutes
Trail Length	5 miles one-way
Accessibility	Mid-July to mid-October
Difficulty	Moderately strenuous
Pack	Light
Topographic Sheets	USGS: Mount Stuart
	Green Trails: Mount Stuart

In 1996, restrictions imposed on this heavily used trail included the following: (1) no camping at Ingalls Lake; (2) permit acquisition required at the trailhead; and (3) dogs prohibited (but allowed on the Esmeralda Basin trail). Additional restrictions are probable in the near future, which may include pre-registration for overnight camping. Hikers planning a trip to either Longs Pass or Ingalls Lake should contact the Leavenworth Ranger District, 600 Sherbourne Street, Leavenworth, WA 98226 (509-548-6977) to ascertain current regulations for entry.

Take the Teanaway River Road off U.S. 97 east of Cle Elum. The pavement ends after 13 miles. Ten miles of gravel road, one-lane with turnouts, follows.

Drive with caution, particularly on holidays and weekends. Turn left at 1.6 miles. At 4.2 miles, elevation 3,000 feet, is pleasant Beverly Campground; 5.8 miles farther, the road ends at the trailhead. The parking lot holds about thirty cars; on summer weekends, thirty to forty more cars park along the access road. There is a privy at the trailhead. Several picnic tables are located by a nearby cataract.

The trail follows an old roadbed alongside waterfalls and cataracts for 0.25 mile. At the junction of the Esmeralda Basin and Ingalls Lake trails, about 100 feet of the Ingalls tread was washed away by a recent flood. Turn right and follow the gully until the tread becomes apparent. Ascend thereafter on switchbacks. The Esmeralda Peaks come into view after about half an hour. Another 12 minutes (1.5 miles from the junction) brings the hiker to the Longs Pass junction; take the left trail.

Five minutes farther, the fine scree and slanted tread above a steep slope for 150 feet create a potential injury area; use caution. Half a mile farther, water is available 25 feet west of the footpath; a bivouac site is present above the stream. Five minutes farther, Mount Rainier is first seen through a notch in the Esmeralda Peaks; views of the volcano improve as altitude is gained. One hour and 45 minutes after leaving the trailhead, Ingalls Pass is reached. There are great views here of Mount Rainier. The hiker enters the Alpine Lakes Wilderness at the pass. Lyall's larch trees appear. The trail forks here; the tread to the left leads to the lake, and the trail to the right leads to tent sites below the pass. Use caution crossing the talus slope en route to Headlight Basin, a scenic area with water about 200 feet lower than the pass. Four designated campsites are located here, and there is a privy south of the tread.

After leaving the basin, tread quality deteriorates. Watch carefully for cairns to locate the route, which ascends steeply at times. This section of the trail is not for novice hikers. The trail tops out at a narrow pass; Ingalls Lake is 150 feet to the west. Several snowbanks were present around the lake, but it was ice free (melted out about August 1 this year, according to a ranger). Travel around the lake is difficult. Mount Stuart rears upward in the background. The rock around the lake is orange, which contrasts with the black fang of the mountain. The lake evokes atavistic feelings and gives the impression of having just emerged from ancient glacial ice. Wildflowers bloom in places around the lakeshore. This is one of the world-class viewpoints of the North Cascades. To preserve this mystical atmosphere, do not visit on weekends or holidays, when the area is crowded.

There are only ten designated and marked campsites. If these are occupied, campers must descend to any site at least half a mile from the basin or lake. There is also one tent site accessed by the Ingalls Creek trail located to the northwest of the lake.

(August 1996)

LONGS PASS

Elevations

Trailhead:	4,200 feet
Destination:	6,300 feet (Longs Pass)
Altitude Gain	2,100 feet (including ups and downs)
Walking Time	In: 1 hour 45 minutes Out: 1 hour 5 minutes
Trail Length	3 miles one-way
Accessibility	July to late October
Difficulty	Moderate
Pack	Light
Topographic Sheets	USGS: Mount Stuart
	Green Trails: Mount Stuart

In 1996, restrictions imposed on this heavily used trail included the following: (1) no camping at Ingalls Lake; (2) permit acquisition required at the trailhead; and (3) dogs prohibited (but allowed on the Esmeralda Basin trail). Additional restrictions are probable in the near future, which may include pre-registration for overnight camping. Hikers planning a trip to either Longs Pass or Ingalls Lake should contact the Leavenworth Ranger District, 600 Sherbourne Street, Leavenworth, WA 98826 (509-548-6977) to ascertain current regulations for entry.

Take the Teanaway River Road off U.S. 97 east of Cle Elum. The pavement ends after 13 miles. Ten miles of single-lane gravel road follows. Drive with caution, particularly on holidays and weekends. Turn left at 1.6 miles. At 4.2 miles, elevation 3,000 feet, is pleasant Beverly Campground; 5.8 miles farther, the road ends at the trailhead. The parking lot holds about thirty cars; on summer weekends, thirty to forty more cars park along the access road. There is a privy at the trailhead. Several picnic tables are located by a nearby cataract.

The trail follows an old roadbed alongside waterfalls and cataracts for 0.25 mile. At the junction of the Esmeralda Basin and Ingalls Lake trails, about 100 feet of the Ingalls tread was washed away by a recent flood. Turn right and follow the gully until the tread becomes apparent. Ascend thereafter on switchbacks. The Esmeralda Peaks come into view after about half an hour. Another 12 minutes (1.5 miles from the junction) brings the hiker to the Longs Pass junction; turn right here. The tread narrows, at times to about 6 inches; use caution. After about 15 minutes, Mount Rainier comes into view to the south; views of this volcano improve as altitude is gained. There is one water source 25 feet to the left of the tread 5 minutes after the first Rainier view; no other water was seen. Shortly after an abandoned roadbed, Mount Adams can be seen in the distance. The tread follows the roadbed steeply for 0.1 mile; the path then veers off the road to the right. About 100 vertical feet below the pass and below the trail, there is a flat area suitable for a tent site; this would be a dry camp unless snow lingers nearby. Longs Pass is only 5 minutes away. On arrival, note the incredible view of the black fang of Mount Stuart, elevation 9,415 feet, looming above Ingalls Creek valley. Several species of wildflowers bloom on the ridge, creating a floral foreground for photographers. A scrabble trail, quite steep for the first 100 feet, connects with the Ingalls Creek trail below. Tread continues to the east along the crest, eventually intersecting the old roadbed. Several scenic tent sites are found along this ridge, but they are waterless unless snow is available for melting. Old silvered trees along the crest are impressive. In short, Longs Pass is an elegant place.

Although car traffic and people are substantial on good-weather weekends, most hikers choose the Ingalls Lake trail, so solitude may be possible at Longs Pass even at high-use times. Even better is to visit on a weekday.

(July 1996)

Wenatchee National Forest

PYRAMID MOUNTAIN VIEWPOINT

Elevations
 Trailhead: 6,600 feet
 Destination: 8,247 feet (Pyramid Mountain)
 Other Significant Locations: Longview Camp, 6,350 feet
Altitude Gain   3,250 feet (including ups and downs)
Walking Time   In: 4 hours 45 minutes   Out: 4 hours 15 minutes
Trail Length   9.2 miles
Accessibility   July 15 to October 1
Difficulty   Moderately strenuous
Pack   Full to campsite; light to summit
Topographic Sheets   USGS: Lucerne
                        Green Trails: Lucerne

Starting at Ardenvoir on the Entiat Canyon Road, drive approximately 20 miles farther up the canyon. After passing the Lake Creek Campground sign, be on the alert for Forest Road 5900, signed Shady Pass, which angles back rather sharply from the paved road. Turn right on this road; at 1.6 miles, pass Halfway Spring. Turn north at Shady Pass onto Road 113 at 8.5 miles. This junction can also be reached, although the drive is more difficult, from the 25 Mile Creek area on Lake Chelan.

Although the road to the north is signed "Limited Maintenance— Unsuitable for Passenger Cars," it was easily drivable in a passenger car in 1980 (check at the Entiat Ranger Station for current conditions). Continue left at 10.5 miles (the road to the right goes to the Big Hill campsite). The left fork terminates 0.3 mile farther in a spacious parking lot, elevation approximately 6,600 feet. Burn scars from the 1970 conflagration are noted from Shady Pass to the end of the first mile of the trail. The trail is open to hikers, horses, and mountain bikers, but not trail machines (as of 1996).

The trailhead slopes downward 25 feet on the west side of the parking lot to the following sign: "Butte Creek Trail 2.5; Pyramid Viewpoint Trail 6; Pyramid Creek Trail 8; Emerald Park Trail 17." After a level 0.1 mile, the trail drops down, losing perhaps 200 vertical feet over the next 0.2 mile, and then turns left off the fire road. There is a post at this point, but no sign. (As of 1980, the fire road was a more direct but steeper route that may be used going upward and is probably the desirable route downward.) At 1 mile, the trail rejoins the fire road and continues along it for an additional 0.2 mile. At 1.4 miles, there is a viewpoint, and this is the highest point that the trail reaches as it bypasses Crow Hill on the west. At 1.5 miles, Poodle Camp, located in a pleasant larch

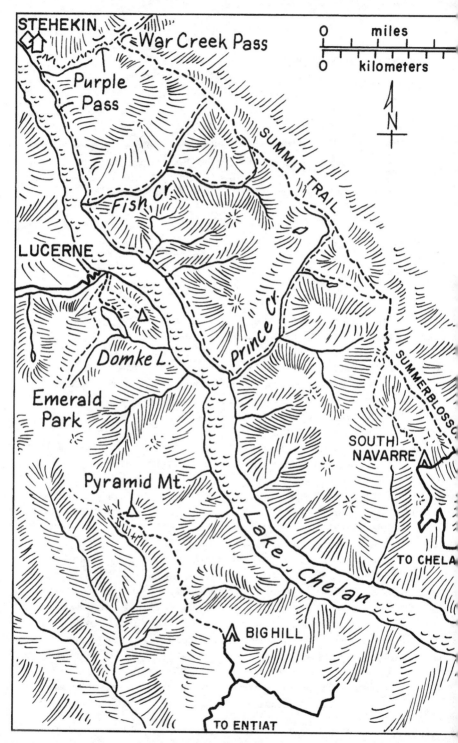

Wenatchee National Forest

forest, is passed; there is no water. The altitude gain from the low point below the parking lot to this point is estimated at 600 vertical feet. One-tenth of a mile past Poodle Camp, the trail passes over a saddle, with views to both the east and the west, and then contours along the west side of Crow Mountain for an additional half mile. It then begins a moderately steep descent to a ridge below. At 3.1 miles is the junction with the Butte Creek trail. There is also a dry campsite at this point. At 3.2 miles, Butte Camp, 100 feet to the left and 75 feet below the trail, is passed; there is no water at this campsite. The trail has now come down from high meadow and is in forest.

Six-tenths of a mile farther, the first water on the trail is found as a small spring 25 feet to the right of the trail, in a patch of wildflowers. Keep a sharp eye out, or it can be missed. Twenty-five feet to the left of the trail, across from the spring, is a campsite with a fire pit and sufficient room to pitch two tents. At 4.1 miles, a better campsite can be found 200 feet to the right of the trail, in a meadow. The trail crosses a very small creek at 4.2 miles, and there is a campsite on the left with a sign on the trail reading, "Longview Camp." A second creek is passed 0.1 mile farther, and again there is a campsite on the left. From here, the trail goes up moderately steeply on rough, difficult-to-walk tread, in switchbacks, gaining approximately 650 vertical feet over the next half mile; mountains to the west and northwest again come into view.

The high point of the trail as it contours around the west side of Graham Mountain is reached at 5 miles. From here, the trail descends 650 vertical feet to a saddle at 5.5 miles. There is a splendid view of Lake Chelan to the east from a rock knob 100 feet to the right of the trail at this point. An additional 0.4 mile, losing 150 more vertical feet in altitude, brings you to water from a small spring just to the left of the trail. An additional 0.1-mile walk across the meadow leads to a suitable campsite a few feet to the left of the trail.

Three-tenths of a mile farther, a second meadow is passed. There is a bit of water here, but it is brackish and not easy to obtain. The trail again goes upward after leaving this meadow, gaining 400 vertical feet, to the junction with the Pyramid Viewpoint trail at roughly 6.6 miles. A sign at this point states that the summit is 3 miles; a letter from the Forest Service put it at 2.9 miles. A Forest Service letter also indicated that it is 7 miles to this point from the trailhead, although it is signed as 6 miles both at this point and at the trailhead. (It is clearly longer than 6 miles—somewhere between 6.6 and 6.9.) Another sign at this point says, "Pyramid Creek 1.5; Pugh Ridge 3; Emerald Creek Trail 10.5 miles."

From this junction, the Viewpoint trail runs on the level for about 0.3 mile and then drops down, losing 200 vertical feet in altitude, to a meadow, where there is water from a small spring and a good campsite 15 feet to the left of the trail. Two-tenths of a mile farther on, there is a second spring and another good campsite with a fire pit 50 feet to the left of the trail. Beyond this point, the upward gradient steepens. At 7.5 miles, the trail crosses an avalanche path; the awesome power of the winter avalanche is apparent from the shattered larch trees above and below the trail.

"Last water" is crossed at 7.6 miles. From here, it is 2 miles upward via switchbacks to the summit of Pyramid Mountain and the site of the destroyed Pyramid Lookout. The trail initially switchbacks up the southwest side of the peak, then goes up the west part of the peak to the north side of the mountain, then switchbacks back to the south side of the mountain, and finally reaches the summit from the south. Before reaching the exact top, a storage cave, primitive bathroom, and horse-hitch area are passed. The foundations of the lookout are clearly apparent, as are fused glass, metallic debris, and a metal structure in the center of the 14-by-14-foot foundation, which presumably held the range finder. The view is fantastic. A bit over 7,000 feet below is Lake Chelan and the mouth of the Prince Creek alluvial fan. To the east are the cliffs of Big and Little Goat Mountains. Both forks of Prince Creek are apparent. To the north is the Bearcat Ridge crest. To the northwest is Cardinal Peak, and beyond it are Pinnacle Mountain and Borealis Ridge. To the west and below is the north fork of the Entiat River, with Fern Lake directly to the west. To the southwest are Duncan Ridge and Duncan Hill. Looking backward to the south are Graham Mountain, Crow Hill, and Big Hill. Far to the northwest, Castle Peak near Stehekin can be seen.

The high ridges are generally cold, even in midsummer. Be prepared with appropriate clothing and a good-quality tent for cold nights and inclement weather. There is plenty of wood for campfires at all of the campsites described. There are no other campsites with water nearby; indeed, there is no other water anywhere on this trail in the late summer or early fall.

The walking time from Longview Camp to the trailhead with a full pack is approximately 1 hour and 45 minutes in either direction. The walking time from Longview Camp to the summit of Pyramid Mountain with a light pack is approximately 3 hours. From the summit back to Longview Camp takes 2.5 hours. The altitude gain from the summit to the trailhead is about 1,850 feet.

From Big Hill, Crow Hill, and Graham Mountain, there are enjoyable vistas. Perhaps one-third of the walk is in timber and two-thirds in meadow, with wildflowers at your feet and scenic panoramas in the distance. There is larch forest along the entire trail, enhancing the views in late September and early October, when the larch needles glow yellow in the rays of the sun. There are some interesting examples of timberline tree growth as the trail ascends Pyramid Mountain. Tree succession and the krummholz phenomenon are obvious as timberline is passed at about 8,000 feet. Still blooming on the summit, however, are several varieties of wildflowers.

For those with more time and energy, there are a number of other loop trails farther up the valleys and ridges, as perusal of a Wenatchee National Forest map will confirm.

(August–September 1980)

EMERALD PARK
Elevations

Trailhead:	1,100 feet
Destination:	5,400 feet (Emerald Park)
High Point:	6,663 feet (Millham Pass)

Other Significant Locations: Mirror Lake trail crest, 6,700 feet

Altitude Gain	4,400 feet (including ups and downs)
Walking Time	In: 5 hours 30 minutes Out: 3 hours 30 minutes
Trail Length	7.1 miles one-way
Accessibility	Mid-July to mid-October
Difficulty	Moderately strenuous to Emerald Park; strenuous to Millham Pass
Pack	Full to Emerald Park; light from Emerald Park to Millham Pass, and Mirror Lake trail crest
Topographic Sheets	USGS: Lucerne
	Green Trails: Lucerne

This is a strenuous hike to the glorious meadow of the mountain king, where a waist-high profusion of closely packed wildflowers fills the valley floor beneath Pinnacle Mountain, Saska Peak, and Emerald Peak.

Take the boat from Fields Point to Lucerne (Lake Chelan). From the dock, follow the road for about 0.25 mile; take the left fork. The footpath goes 0.1 mile up a man-made gully to a trail signpost ("Meadow 7; Pass 9"). After 0.2 mile, there is a fine uplake view from a bluff. Farther is one brief additional view from the east end of the switchback between the Domke Mountain and Domke Lake trails.

At about 1 mile, the junction with the Domke Mountain footpath is passed. The Domke Lake trail is reached at 1.6 miles. At 2.3 miles, enter the Glacier Peak Wilderness area and intersect the Holden Trail junction. A hundred feet up the Holden trail, you reach Cedar Camp, which has water, tent sites, a table, and rounds for sitting. The big cedar grove here is dark and mysterious in comparison with the forest below and above. The drawback to staying here is the plethora of mosquitoes; be prepared to repel bloodsuckers. Half an hour farther, after returning to the Emerald Park trail, note the brief view of Domke Lake below and the ridge of Domke Mountain to the east. After another half hour, the footpath turns and begins its ascent up the Emerald Park Creek valley. Water is available half an hour farther up the trail. After another 1 hour and 10 minutes, the footpath breaks out into meadow. Ten minutes farther, you reach a good campsite to the left of the trail—a welcome sight after about 7 miles and 3,900 vertical feet. Water is available from Emerald Park Creek 200 feet away through brush, which is wet from dew in the morning. There are views 0.1 and 0.2 mile to the west. The trail to the Domke Lake junction is in good condition, except for windfall; thereafter, the tread quality deteriorates, and vegetation impinges on the footpath, especially above 4,000 feet.

From the campsite, the footpath traverses forest interspersed with flower-festooned meadows (Indian paintbrush and lupine). Emerald Park and the junction with the Mirror Lake trail are reached after a 1.2-mile walk that takes a bit over 30 minutes. There is a large campsite under trees on the northeast side of the half-mile-wide Emerald Park Meadow; water is available 100 yards to the west or south. Many tents can be pitched here; a privy is located 0.1 mile north of camp. The Mirror Lake trail junction is at the east end of the camp. To locate this footpath, go through the tent areas into meadow; go north a bit, and look for the sign "Trail closed to stock." Follow the tread from here to the right of two large granite boulders; the tread fades out in the trees here for about 125 feet but reenters meadow and is obvious thereafter.

The trail to Millham Pass crosses the meadow for half a mile; two small streams must be crossed. The greenery is 2 to 3 feet high in places, making the tread intermittently obscure. The floral display is glorious. Unfortunately, there are lots of mosquitoes here and at the otherwise fine camp; come prepared to cope with these pests.

The trail to Millham Pass goes up steeply after leaving the meadow. In late July, several snow patches must be crossed; one required kicking steps. The trail crosses the pass one notch north of the Millham Pass sign. Trees obscure the view from the pass; climb the ridge south of the pass. About 200 feet up are ledges for gazing at Emerald Park below and Borealis Ridge and Fifth of July Mountain to the west. Views improve as altitude is gained; caution is advisable. Rock-climbing skills are needed in places, and there is exposure.

The footpath to the ridge crest en route to Mirror Lake is about 1.1 miles in length, gains about 1,300 vertical feet, and takes 50 minutes to ascend carrying a day pack. There are good views of the Emerald Park Meadow below and of Mirror Lake to the north. Climbers with an ice ax may wish to ascend Pinnacle Mountain from here. There is no water from meadow to ridge, and the tread is of poor quality the entire distance. (I did not visit the lake but was advised by others who had been there that fishing was good and that there were good campsites near the lake.)

During my three days of exploration here, I saw no other people. Those desiring a combination of beauty and solitude may wish to consider this area. Good physical condition is essential, considering the distances and the altitude gain.

Other walking times: Emerald Park Meadow to Millham Pass, 1 hour and 20 minutes; pass back to meadow, 1 hour; Mirror Lake ridge crest down to meadow, 35 minutes.

(July 1991)

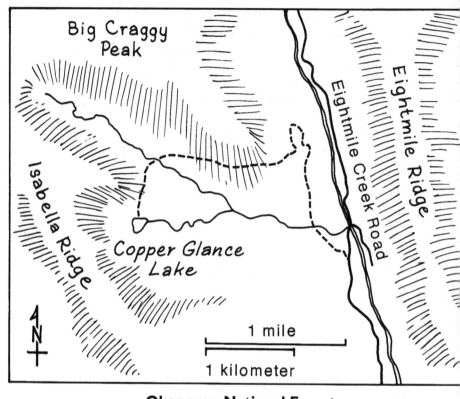

Big Craggy Peak

Isabella Ridge

Copper Glance Lake

Eightmile Creek Road

Eightmile Ridge

N

1 mile

1 kilometer

Okanogan National Forest

Okanogan National Forest

COPPER GLANCE
Elevations

Trailhead:	3,840 feet
Destination:	6,100 feet (Copper Glance Lake)
High Point:	6,200 feet

Altitude Gain   2,500 feet (including ups and downs)
Walking Time   In: 2 hours   Out: 1 hour 30 minutes
Trail Length   3.3 miles one-way
Accessibility   Early June to mid-October
Difficulty   Moderate
Pack   Light
Topographic Sheets   USGS: Billy Goat Mountain, Mazama
                    Green Trails: Billy Goat Mountain, Mazama

From Winthrop, drive north on the West Chewuch Road about 9 miles; turn left onto Eightmile Creek Road. Pass the Honeymoon Campground at 9.5 miles. This is a good place to stay before or after if day hiking. The trailhead is 3.5 miles farther up the road (13 miles altogether). Trailhead parking is limited (two to three cars).

Ascend steeply on an abandoned roadbed for 1.5 miles (53 minutes). Early on (15 minutes), cross Copper Glance Creek on a bridge. The road ends at the mine sites. The trail begins here and ascends steeply, soon reaching a scenic meadow (views and wildflowers). At 1.9 miles, the upward gradient lessens. At 2.1 miles, Copper Glance Creek is crossed on a footlog; water is available. At 2.4 miles, top out; descend to a tarn 100 feet below, where there is a good campsite. Then ascend a steep scree slope, culminating in a second top-out at about 6,200 feet. There is another campsite on this ridge, where Copper Glance Lake is first visible. The tread then descends to the lakeshore. A large rock, with a small larch growing on it, is a good spot from which to fish or eat lunch, or you can swim in the cold water.

A walk around the lake, mostly on talus, takes 15 minutes. There is a superb tent site on the southeast side about 20 feet above the lake by a small greenery-surrounded stream. The lake is malachite green in color—a gorgeous gem in a bowl, surrounded by the summer greens and the fall yellows of the alpine larches.

For better views of the lake and surrounding peaks, ascend cross-country to the west and northwest, gaining about 400 vertical feet in about 0.3 mile. A wide-angle lens is useful here to photograph the lake, flowers and surrounding peaks.

Unfortunately, the trail was open to horses, mountain bikes, and trail machines as of 1991.

(August 1991)

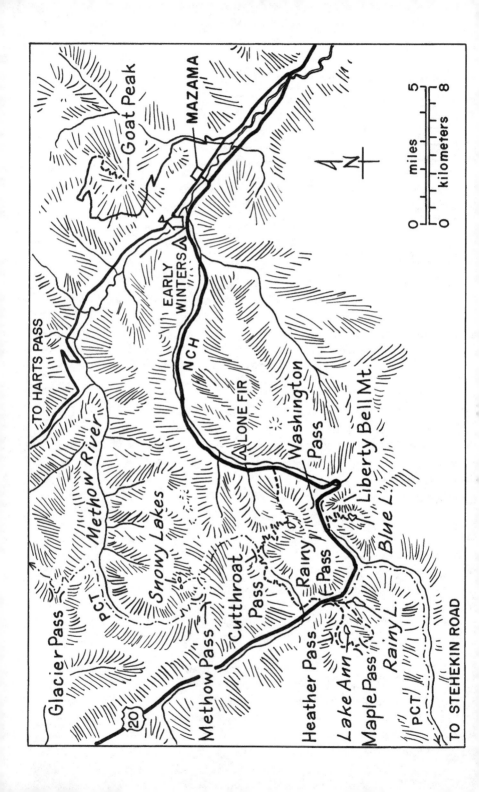

Goat Peak

MAZAMA

EARLY WINTERS

NCH

LONE FIR

Washington Pass

Liberty Bell Mt.

Blue L.

TO HARTS PASS

Methow River

Snowy Lakes

PCT

Glacier Pass

Methow Pass

Cutthroat Pass

Heather Pass

Rainy Pass

Lake Ann

Maple Pass

Rainy L.

PCT

20

TO STEHEKIN ROAD

N

miles
kilometers

0   5
0   8

Okanogan National Forest

BLUE LAKE (WASHINGTON PASS)
Elevations
Trailhead: 5,200 feet
Destination: 6,300 feet (Blue Lake)
Altitude Gain 1,400 feet (including ups and downs)
Walking Time In: 1 hour   Out: 45 minutes
Trail Length 2.3 miles one-way
Accessibility July 15 to early October
Difficulty Moderate
Pack Light
Topographic Sheets USGS: Washington Pass 7.5'
Green Trails: Washington Pass

The trailhead is located on the south side of the North Cascades Highway 0.8 mile west of Washington Pass. The parking area is at mile 161.5 alongside the highway, with the trailhead 0.1 mile to the east. The trail parallels the road eastward for about 150 yards and then turns to the south, ascending in a gentle and prolonged series of switchbacks. At the 1.5-mile mark, where the trail crosses an avalanche meadow, the cross-country climbing route for the Early Winter Spires departs to the southeast. The trail crosses the outlet stream below the lake before reaching the north end of the deep blue lake, surrounded by a forest of subalpine larches.

Near the lake outlet is a deteriorating cabin, a relic of the Blue Whistler Mine. The lake has been stocked with trout. It is possible to circumnavigate the lake cross-country without difficulty. Views from the south end of the lake—looking northward, with the lake in the foreground and Cutthroat Peak in the background—are spectacular. The area is most scenic in late September and early October, when the larches about the lake have turned golden yellow.

On the ridge to the west above the lake, there are two beautiful tarns, each of which offers photographers nice reflection shots of the surrounding peaks. It is possible to climb higher for even better views and to photograph Blue Lake in the foreground with Liberty Bell and the Early Winter Spires in the background. A wide-angle lens and color film are necessary to do photographic justice to the Blue Lake area. Blue Lake is well named; it is a deep cerulean blue. Water is available from several creeks en route and at the lake.

The lake and its environs are day-use areas only; the surrounding meadows are too fragile to permit overnight camping. Since the hike is popular, it is best to go on a weekday, if possible.

(September 1987)

CUTTHROAT PASS (EAST APPROACH)
Elevations
    Trailhead: 4,500 feet
    Destination: 6,800 feet (Cutthroat Pass)
    Other Significant Locations: Cutthroat Lake, 4,935 feet
Altitude Gain   2,350 feet (including ups and downs)
Walking Time   In: 2 hours 40 minutes   Out: 2 hours
Trail Length   5.4 miles one-way
Accessibility   July to mid-October
Difficulty   Moderately strenuous
Pack   Light
Topographic Sheets   USGS: Washington Pass 7.5'
                          Green Trails: Washington Pass

Proceeding eastward from Winthrop on Highway 20, drive 1.5 miles beyond the Lone Fir Campground to the access road; if coming from the west, the access road is 4.6 miles from Washington Pass. In either case, turn west and proceed up a moderately steep one-way road with turnouts for about 1 mile. There is parking for approximately ten cars to the right near the trailhead; located around this parking area are a number of picnic tables and a rest room. There is parking for approximately twenty additional cars in a large, undeveloped parking area on the south side of the loop. Camping in this area is restricted to only one night for hikers planning to take the trail the next day. No camping is allowed at Cutthroat Lake.

The trail leaves from the western end of the loop. After 100 feet, turn right at the bulletin board, and 100 feet farther, cross the bridge onto the north side of the creek. From this point, it is 1.9 miles to the lake, 5.5 miles to Cutthroat Pass, 10.5 miles to Rainy Pass, and 31.5 miles to Hart's Pass. The trail enters the woods briefly but breaks out after 0.3 mile; intermittently, there are fine views of the mountains to the south and west thereafter (Cutthroat Peak, 7,865 feet; other unnamed peaks, a bit over 7,000 feet).

There is a nice waterfall visible to the south at 0.5 mile. At 1 mile, a creek must be forded or crossed on a footlog or jerry-built bridge. At 1.8 miles, there is a junction; the left trail goes 0.1 mile to the outlet of Cutthroat Lake, and the right trail switchbacks upward to Cutthroat Pass. During the spring runoff, it is difficult to reach the east side of Cutthroat Lake; in the summer and fall, water levels are lower, so the outlet can be crossed on rocks and timber. There are fish in the lake. In the summer and early fall, the area is quite buggy, and it is important to bring insect repellent. The lake is beautiful and nestles in a cirque under higher peaks. Water is no problem on the trail in the late spring and early summer, but it is a substantially drier trail later in the year.

If going to Cutthroat Pass, 0.1 and 0.3 mile past the junction, creeks must be forded. Early in the year, the second ford presents formidable difficulties; however, these two areas may be bypassed by going upward cross-country, beginning east of the two bridges on the lower trail to the lake. One-tenth of a mile through the woods and a gain of 150 vertical feet puts you on the trail to the pass without having to make the hip-deep ford. There are no significant creeks beyond this point. Again, in the spring and early summer, water is available in many areas, but in the late summer and early fall, this is a dry trail, and water bottles should be filled at a stream near Cutthroat Lake.

The trail switchbacks upward steadily but never steeply, gaining approximately 1,900 feet in altitude from the junction to the pass. The up-time from the junction is approximately 2 hours. About 2 miles from the junction, where the trail passes through a relatively level area before switchbacking higher, there are a number of primitive campsites. From here, follow a faint way trail westward about 0.3 mile, losing 200 feet in altitude, to a creek from which water should be obtainable all summer, under normal circumstances. There is no other place to camp until Cutthroat Pass is reached.

Proceeding upward, note a huge white bark pine on the north side of the trail at approximately 4.5 miles. As altitude is gained, views improve and trees become more scattered. Larch is the dominant tree as the trail contours across meadowland to reach Cutthroat Pass, where there are a number of good camping areas; however, water here can be a real problem, unless there are snowfields still unmelted in the area. Note the classic krummholz composed of white bark pine, alpine larch, and mountain hemlock approximately 150 feet north of the pass. The trees in this area resemble lowland shrubs; higher branches that protrude from the winter snowpack have been pruned by high-velocity winds. Views from the pass are impressive in all directions, particularly in late September and early October, when the needles of the larch forests, both near and at the pass, have turned a golden yellow and glow in the fall sun. Cutthroat Peak looms to the south. Cutthroat Lake nestles under the high rocks far below. The surrounding rocks have an orange tinge; all the mountains in this area were etched from the Golden Horn batholith. To the west, down the Porcupine Creek Valley, the darker peaks sculpted from the Black Peak batholith can be seen in the distance.

This is a more scenic approach to Cutthroat Pass than the route from Rainy Pass to the west. Once Cutthroat Pass is reached, the Pacific Crest Trail is intersected. This trail goes down to Rainy Pass, 5 miles to the south, or northward about 1 mile, with minimal gain or loss in altitude, to a viewpoint above Granite Pass. From here, Methow Pass, Azurite Peak, and some incredibly beautiful mountain country can be seen to the north; it is an impressive vantage point.

The up-time to Cutthroat Lake is 40 minutes; down-time is approximately the same, perhaps a minute or two faster. Altitude gain from the trailhead to the lake is about 500 feet.

(August 1990)

CUTTHROAT PASS (WEST APPROACH–PCT)
Elevations

Trailhead:	4,860 feet
Destination:	6,800 feet (Cutthroat Pass)
Altitude Gain	2,000 feet (including ups and downs)
Walking Time	In: 2 hours Out: 1 hour 30 minutes
Trail Length	5 miles one-way
Accessibility	July 15 to mid-October
Difficulty	Moderate
Pack	Light
Topographic Sheets	USGS: Washington Pass 7.5'
	Green Trails: Washington Pass

To reach the trailhead, turn east off the North Cascades Highway onto a side road at the summit of Rainy Pass; follow this road 0.2 mile to its termination in an extensive parking lot. The trail starts at the north end of the parking area, beyond the horse ramp. Initially, the trail switchbacks upward to the north through moderately deep timber. Brief views of the peaks and cirques to the west are obtained at approximately 0.8 and 1.3 miles, when the trail breaks out into open rocky knolls for a short distance. Wildflowers and succulent rock plants grow in these areas. The trail then turns northeastward and reenters the deep woods; Porcupine Creek is crossed on a bridge at the 2-mile mark. The trail enters open meadow at about 3.2 miles; a waterfall descends from the north and crosses the trail near this location. This is a good place to fill water bottles, since in late summer and early fall, water is scarce beyond this point. After another brief reentry into forest, the trail again breaks out into meadow and remains in splendid alpine country thereafter. Scenery improves as altitude is gained. The only good campsite on the trail is at the 4-mile mark; look for a sign directing hikers downward by means of a way trail 0.1 mile to a flat area west of the main trail. Small springs provide water, except under drought conditions. Beyond the camping area, the trail switchbacks upward in a southerly direction, then goes eastward; a few additional switchbacks bring you to the crest of Cutthroat Pass. The tread is faint to nonexistent for the last several hundred feet of the trail near the pass.

In addition to the opportunity to continue northward on the PCT or to descend via the trail to the east, there are opportunities for cross-country walking on ridges to the south and northwest. If two cars are available, keys can be exchanged at this point, and each party can descend via a different trail than that ascended.

Refer to Cutthroat Pass, east approach, for a description of that trail and for a more extensive discourse about the Cutthroat Pass area itself. In addition, recall that this is an exposed location, and wind velocity can be substantial during storms. Wood supplies are very limited, and the area is ecologically fragile. Campfires should not be attempted at the pass; carry stoves for cooking.

(July 1992)

GOAT PEAK
Elevations
Trailhead:	5,600 feet
Destination:	7,000 feet (lookout)

Altitude Gain   1,400 feet (including ups and downs)

Walking Time   In: 1 hour 20 minutes   Out: 1 hour

Trail Length   2.5 miles one-way

Accessibility   July to October

Difficulty   Moderate

Pack   Light

Topographic Sheets   USGS: Mazama
Green Trails: Mazama

Take the north loop of the North Cascades Highway. Two miles east of Mazama (about 11 miles west of Winthrop), turn sharply to the north on Road 52. From this point, it is 12 miles to the trailhead. At 2.7 miles, turn left. At 9 miles, turn right. The trailhead is signed. A primitive road continues to the northeast past the trailhead. Road quality deteriorates past the starting point of the trail. There is parking space for approximately ten cars where the trail begins. There is one nice viewpoint on the road, roughly 6 miles from the pavement on the left (south) side.

The footpath goes up along a rocky ridge and then makes a sharp right turn to the west at about 0.5 mile. A sign on a tree indicates the location of the first junction; another trail continues onward from here, so be sure to make the correct turn. The trail goes briefly through timber and then breaks out on a wide scenic ridge. In the late spring and early summer, there are blooming glacier lilies and other flowers on the ridge crest. After leaving the ridge, the trail switchbacks up the northeast side of a rather steep bluff to reach the north end of Goat Peak ridge and follows the ridge crest roughly half a mile south to the lookout.

The trail is interesting from a botanical viewpoint. At the trailhead, there are subalpine fir and even Douglas fir, but at the exposed summit, white bark pine, larch, and Englemann's spruce at the only trees able to survive.

If the lookout station is manned (as is often the case), the fire watcher might invite you in for a cup of coffee. The opportunity to inspect the inside of the lookout should certainly be taken. Early and late in the season, or if the fire hazard is considered to be low, the lookout is locked and cannot be entered.

The views from the fire lookout are breathtaking in all directions. The Methow valley lies at your feet. The villages of Winthrop and Twisp can be seen to the east. Sandy Butte in the foreground and Gardner Mountain in the background rise up to the south. The road to Hart's Pass can be seen to the west; the North Cascades Highway is directly below. Silver Star Mountain rears rocky spires into the southwestern sky. The great peaks of the Pasayten Wilderness, on the skyline to the north, extend as far as the eye can see.

There are several places where it is feasible to camp along the trail. After the snow is melted, finding water is a major problem for campers. Indeed, water should be carried by day hikers.

(Late June 1980)

MAPLE PASS LOOP (AND LAKE ANN)

Elevations

Trailhead:	4,860 feet
Destination:	6,600 feet (Maple Pass)

Other Significant Locations: Lake Ann, 5,475 feet; Heather Pass, 6,100 feet

Altitude Gain	1,800 feet (including ups and downs)
Walking Time	In: 2 hours Out: 1 hour 30 minutes
Trail Length	4 miles one-way (Maple Pass)
Accessibility	July 15 to October 15
Difficulty	Moderately strenuous
Pack	Light
Topographic Sheets	USGS: Washington Pass, Mount Arriva 7.5'
	Green Trails: Washington Pass, Mount Logan

Turn southward at the crest of Rainy Pass off the North Cascades Highway and park 0.2 mile farther in the extensive visitor parking areas. Walk back on the access road 0.1 mile to pick up the trailhead, which begins rather surprisingly by switchbacking upward away from the lake but eventually moves toward the southwest. The trail is muddy in places. At about 0.6 mile, it breaks out into an open area, crosses a talus slope (where there is considerable avalanche risk in snow conditions), and contours in a long half-circle to reach a ridge crest to the south. At this point, the now abandoned original trail to Lake Ann is intersected; 0.2 mile farther, the trail bifurcates. The lower trail to the left crosses meadow and terminates on the shores of Lake Ann about 0.6 mile farther. The Lake Ann basin is a day-use area only. Fishing is often good. The lake area is scenic, particularly with the tree-studded island projecting from the waters of the lake. The distance to Lake Ann from the trailhead is about 1.8 miles, and the walking time upward is about 1 hour; allow 40 minutes for the return trip.

Returning to the junction, the right, or higher, trail gains altitude progressively crossing talus slopes and meadow. Above Lake Ann, there are switchbacks. A short way trail to the right (north) brings the hiker to the Heather Pass area. This junction is not signed and is not obvious, so keep a sharp eye out when nearing the top of the ridge. At Heather Pass, there is a broad meadow with a number of campsites. To the northwest of Heather Pass is a scrabble trail terminating 0.4 mile farther in an extensive boulder and talus field. Experienced wilderness travelers may proceed beyond this point to campsites at Lewis and Wing Lakes to the northwest. Mountaineers use this route to reach the base of Black Peak.

Returning to the main trail, the footpath switchbacks upward through fairly steep meadow for slightly over a mile from the Heather Pass turnoff before reaching the crest of Maple Pass. The scenery from this point is splendid. Corteo Peak is seen to the northwest, and Mount Benzarino is directly to the west; between the two peaks is Last Chance Pass. Lying below, to the east, is the Lake Ann valley, with Whistler Mountain, Liberty Bell, and the Early Winters Spires in the distance. Below, to the west, is the Maple Creek valley, and farther in the distance are the valley of Bridge Creek and the great peaks of the wilderness alps of the Stehekin. Glacier Peak looms in the distance to the southwest.

Camping is allowed at both Heather and Maple Passes. There are a number of level places for campsites. Late in the season, obtaining water can be a problem at both areas. Wildflowers and fall color are both splendid in season. Marmots and pikas add their whistles and cheeps to the wilderness aura of the North Cascades high country.

Wood is scarce to nonexistent at either pass, and both areas are too fragile to permit fire-pit construction. Carry a stove for cooking, and forgo the pleasure of a campfire in order to leave the areas pristine.

Lake Ann is a classic cirque lake, surrounded on three sides by meadows, mountains, and snowfields. The depression in which it lies was gouged out by the now melted and departed glacier.

At some time in the future, the Pacific Crest Trail (PCT) may be routed down Maple Creek to join Bridge Creek. If that occurs, this trail will become part of the PCT or an alternate route for the PCT. At the time of this writing, a final decision about this possibility had not been made.

In 1994, a second access trail to Maple Pass created a scenic loop. To ascend the south footpath from the Rainy Pass parking lot, follow the Rainy Lake trail for 0.4 mile. Look for a trail sign to the right of a boardwalk. Turn right here; be prepared for steep, slippery tread. The first viewpoint is reached in 26 minutes from the turnoff. Fifteen minutes farther, there is a view of Rainy Lake below. Lake Ann can be seen below in a bit over an hour; there is also a nice view to the northeast from the same location. Alpine larches appear here. The tread tops out at the ridge crest 15 minutes later. The approximate distance from the turnoff is 2.5 miles; altitude gain is 2,500 vertical feet. There is a splendid view of Lake Ann below from this ridge. I found no water during the climb up, but it was a drier than usual summer. At best, one or two poor-quality tent sites were noted on the way up. The top-out is about 500 vertical feet above and 0.7 mile away from Maple Pass. The prior scrabble trail from the pass to the top out has been replaced with standard constructed tread. Faint tread goes 0.1 mile to the south; those wishing to go higher must rock climb from this point. The descent to Maple Pass takes about 25 minutes; views are superb along the way.

If doing the loop—particularly during or following rain, when the tread will be muddy and slippery—it is best to ascend from the south and descend from the north.

Both trails attract many hikers on summer weekends and holidays. The loop is about 7 miles in length; average walking time with a light pack is about 5 hours.

(September 1994)

RAINY LAKE TRAIL
Elevations

Trailhead:	4,800 feet
Destination:	4,800 feet (Rainy Lake)
Altitude Gain	100 feet (including ups and downs)
Walking Time	40 minutes
Trail Length	2 miles round-trip
Accessibility	July to mid-October
Difficulty	Easy
Pack	None or light
Topographic Sheets	USGS: Washington Pass
	Green Trails: Washington Pass

The trailhead is on the west side of Rainy Pass, 50 yards from the North Cascades Highway, along a side road to the parking area and rest rooms at the pass. The trail is black topped for the entire 1-mile distance to Rainy Lake. It is level, moderately easy, and suitable for wheelchairs. There is adequate parking 0.1 mile north in the parking area. There are scrabble trails around the lake in either direction. The lake is inviting and impressive, with a splendid waterfall descending from the snow-clad peaks to the south. Overnight camping is prohibited in the area. The trail can also be reached without crossing the highway by the Bridge Creek–Pacific Crest Trail. In the fall, the colorful mountain ash provide excellent color contrast with the azure blue of the lake and the gleaming white of the snowfields on the peaks above and beyond. Walking time is about 20 minutes in either direction. Water is available at the lake and at the trailhead. There is a paved viewing platform at the end of the trail. Do take time to read the interpretive natural history signs alongside the footpath.

(September 1994)

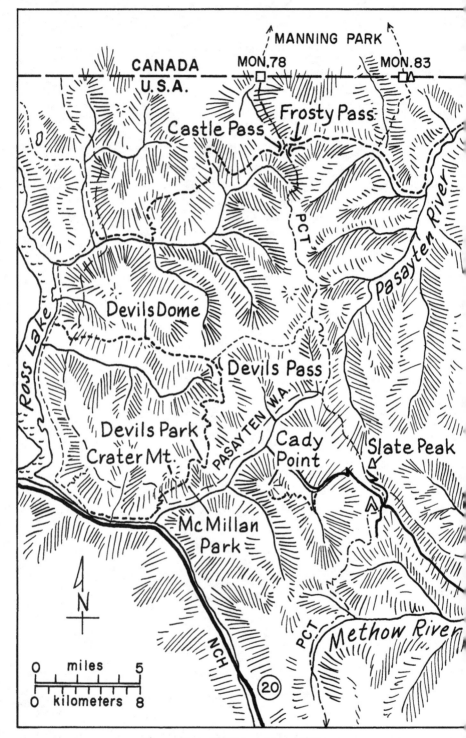

Pasayten Wilderness–West

Pasayten Wilderness–West

BOUNDARY TRAIL

Elevations

Trailhead:	Irongate (east), 5,800 feet; Ross Lake (west), 1,600 feet; Castle Pass (west), 5,500 feet
High Point:	7,600 feet (Cathedral Pass)
Altitude Gain	East to west (preferred route), about 14,000 feet (including ups and downs)
Walking Time	7–10 days
Trail Length	94 miles one-way (Irongate to Ross Lake)
Accessibility	Early July to October 15
Difficulty	Strenuous (in segments)
Pack	Full
Topographic Sheets	USGS: Horseshoe Basin; Bauerman Ridge; Remmel Mountain; Ashnola Mountain; Ashnola Pass; Tatoosh Buttes; Frosty Creek; Castle Peak; Ross Lake; Skagit Peak
	Green Trails: Pasayten Peak; Jack Mountain; Coleman Peak; Billy Goat Mountain; Ross Lake; Horseshoe Basin

The east access to the Boundary trail from Irongate Camp to Louden Lake is described under Horseshoe Basin (Pasayten).

There is some disagreement about whether the section of trail going from Castle Pass to Ross Lake should be considered a portion of the Boundary trail, but I consider it to be an integral part of this footpath. I have not personally walked two small segments of the Boundary trail—namely, from Bunker Hill to the junction with trail 482 that leads to Monument 83, and the steep descent from elevation 6,128 feet to the Little Fish shelter. Information on these two sections has been obtained from maps and from other sources believed to be reliable.

From Louden Lake, it is 0.4 mile to a good campsite north of and below the trail. A mile beyond the lake, there is a fair campsite near a tarn. At 3 miles, the footpath goes upward; there is a tarn with a nearby table and a good tent site in an insect-infested meadow. At 5 miles, cross a stream; there is a good campsite 50 yards to the northwest. Half a mile farther, another stream is crossed; nearby is a nice campsite located under some dead silver-colored trees. Snow Sled Camp is located in a small meadow 1.3 miles farther. An additional mile brings the hiker to the crest of a ridge (which we named Silver Forest Ridge because of a magnificent stand of bleached tree trunks on both sides of the ridge crest). There are also alpine larches in this area. A campsite is located approximately 50 yards south of the trail; watch for it, because the location is not obvious. For the next 2.2 miles, there are no places to camp. Water is scarce; water bottles should be filled at every available opportunity.

Seven-tenths of a mile past the Silver Forest, the trail turns from west to north; Cathedral Peak comes into view. A mile and a half farther, there is a campsite complete with table; water is available from a spring about 100 yards to the south. A 100-yard bushwhack at this point to the west brings you to the banks of a beautiful tarn, where there are also level, pleasant campsites for those who wish to camp farther from the trail. The elevation at this point is 6,800 feet. Westward from this camping area, the Boundary trail goes downward fairly steeply in switchbacks, losing approximately 500 vertical feet in about 0.6 mile. The footpath passes about 200 yards from Scheelite Lake (it is suspected that this is the location of the true pass; a sign higher up on a tree 0.6 of a mile back stated that the pass was at that location).

No-see-ums, mosquitoes, and occasional deerflies are a constant problem along the trail.

The walking time, light packed, from Louden Lake to Scheelite Pass is 3 hours and 50 minutes. The estimated altitude gain going west is about 1,000 feet; going east, 1,500 feet. The trail is high most of the time, and at least 8 of the 10 miles are very scenic, making this portion of the Boundary trail a memorable walk. Hikers with full packs should allow approximately 6 hours for this 10-mile segment of trail (9.5 miles to the Scheelite Pass sign and campsite).

In an average year, the area is reasonably snow free somewhere between June 30 and July 10. Finding water can be a problem in late summer and early fall. In addition, sheep grazing is still allowed in the area intermittently. For these reasons, the ideal time for walking this segment of the trail is between July 4 and July 20.

Westward from near the Scheelite Lake area, the trail drops down into a forested area, crosses a small creek, and begins ascending a high ridge. After 1.5 miles, most of the altitude is gained, and the trail stays high for a splendid 1.5 miles to the Tungsten Mine. At this location is the junction with the trail to 30 Mile campsite at the end of the Chewuch Road. Buildings in the area are infested with rodents but have watertight roofs; they are therefore good places to head for in a downpour. (However, staying in rodent-infested cabins is now considered unwise because of the risk of contracting Hanta virus lung infection.) There are campsites around the building areas if you prefer a tent to the wooden bunks. There is also a nice campsite on the left, half a mile west of the mine buildings. It is 1.8 miles from the mine area to Apex Pass, where there are a number of splendid specimens of alpine larch and a level area suitable for a dry camp. From this point, it is a fairly easy class 2 walk to the top of Apex Peak. Most impressive are the views to the west from this point of the great triangular spire of Cathedral Peak (elevation 8,600 feet). After crossing the pass, the footpath makes a long, gentle descent to below Cathedral Pass and then switchbacks up to reach the highest point on the Boundary trail; Cathedral Creek is crossed en route. It is 2.5 miles between Apex and Cathedral Passes.

Climbers interested in summiting Cathedral Peak should start at the pass. The ascent is not particularly difficult, but there is an interesting move across an approximately 4-foot gap a few feet below the summit. The views from the top of Cathedral Peak can only be described as incredible in all directions. To the north are the ridges and peaks of Cathedral Provincial Park. To the east, Windy Peak is easily visible. Lying below are the splendid Cathedral Lakes. To the west are Sheep Mountain and, beyond that, the great peaks of the spine of the Cascades. To the south is Remmel Mountain.

Returning to Cathedral Pass, descend to perhaps the most beautiful lake in the North Cascades. Past a shallow tarn, a way trail to the left leads to the east shores of Upper Cathedral Lake; the main trail passes small tarns and pools in the exit stream to reach a campsite on the west side of the lake. The lake is situated beneath the sheer granite scarp of Amphitheater Mountain, 0.8 mile from the pass. Both the lake and the streams abound with trout. The granite ramparts light up and glow in the evening sun; the area is spectacular. Be sure to plan at least one overnight camp in this area.

The trail loses altitude below Upper Cathedral Lake and then crosses underneath a granite cliff. After 0.7 mile, the junction of the half-mile-long trail to Lower Cathedral Lake, about 400 vertical feet below, is intersected. There is a high meadow campsite about 2.5 miles westward from the upper lake. Three miles from the lake is the junction with the trail to Remmel Lake. At this point, there are options. The shortest route westward is to follow the Boundary trail directly onward to Spanish Camp. The most scenic route is to take the Remmel Lake bypass; there are fine campsites at the lake. Slightly over a mile farther is the junction with the Andrews Creek trail and the Forest Service administrative cabin at Spanish Camp, altitude 6,250 feet. There are multiple campsites in this area.

Another 3.3 miles farther down the trail is a high pass on Bald Mountain. If time permits, leave packs at this point and enjoy a glorious ridge saunter eastward. Look for deer in these high meadows. At the very least, plan a rest stop at this point to enjoy the vistas before proceeding further. The trail reaches an altitude of almost 7,400 feet at this location. After a walk over a high plateau for a mile or so, the trail enters timber and switchbacks repetitively downward into the valley of the Ashnola River. From the high point at Bald Mountain, almost 2,400 vertical feet of altitude are lost in this jarring, nonscenic descent.

Near the bottom of the valley, the trail to Black Lake 14 miles away is intersected. A half mile farther is a trail shelter in excellent condition that sleeps four (another good place to head for in storm conditions). One-tenth of a mile farther is the Ashnola River, which must be forded. It is about 4.1 miles from the high point on Bald Mountain to the Ashnola ford. The water was about 18 inches deep in a relatively low snow year. This ford could be difficult and dangerous if the water level was significantly higher. Probing the depth with a staff, and using the stick as a third point of contact with the stream bottom lessens the likelihood of falling. The belly band of the pack should be unclipped before starting the ford to facilitate a rapid removal.

Beyond the ford, there is a miserable slog upward in deep woods, as the altitude lost on the east is regained on the west. Two miles from the ford, a fair campsite is passed. After about 3 miles and 1 hour and 30 minutes, the trail again breaks out into meadow after regaining about 2,000 vertical feet of altitude. There are a number of trails in this meadow, none of which are signed. At the first fork, take the upper trail. There is a good campsite a bit over 3 miles from the ford, to the south about 100 vertical feet below the trail.

The main trail, marked with pointed stakes, contours around the meadow to the north, gradually gaining altitude. Surprisingly, there are no good campsites in this meadow (except the one mentioned above) until PeeVee Pass is reached, 4.6 miles from the ford of the Ashnola River. There are several level camping areas at PeeVee Pass; water can be obtained from a small stream 0.2 mile south on the Larch Creek trail to Billy Goat Pass. From this junction, it is a bit over 18 miles to the Billy Goat Corral, 13 miles to Hidden Lake, and 14 miles to the Pasayten River. The elevation of the pass is 6,800 feet.

The next 8 miles west of the PeeVee junction are perhaps the most scenic and enjoyable segment of the Boundary trail. About half a mile west of PeeVee Pass is the junction with the trail leading to Park Pass and Ramon Lakes to the north. From this junction, the main trail proceeds westward; 1.5 miles farther, the 1-mile way trail to Quartz Lake is intersected. There are campsites at the 6,741-foot-high lake. Proceeding westward, the main footpath contours beneath the south and west faces of Quartz Mountain, maintaining an elevation of slightly over 7,000 feet. Farther westward, the upper portion of Dean Creek must be forded. The footpath then gradually gains about 600 feet in elevation to reach the summit of Bunker Hill, 7,239 feet high. All the trails described in this paragraph run through splendid high alpine meadowlands.

Alas, such elegance cannot continue. Three-tenths of a mile west of Bunker Hill is the junction with the trail descending into Dean Creek. Half a mile farther is a high meadow campsite. From this point, the trail descends initially in meadow, then in progressively deeper timber. There is another campsite 3.2 miles from the top of Bunker Hill. Five miles below the summit, Bunker Hill

Creek must be forded. Another 1.7 miles farther is the junction with the trail to Hidden Lakes and a bridge crossing the east fork of the Pasayten River. There is a campsite here. Six-tenths of a mile farther, the Pasayten River itself is crossed on a bridge; there is a tenting place at the bridge and another one inland a short distance. From here, it is about 1 mile to the junction of the abandoned footpath that followed Harrison Creek upward to Monument 83 and Manning Provincial Park. This way trail was last maintained in 1984. Substantial blowdown has occurred since then. Tread still exists; turnpike failure has created muddy areas. The footpath is probably passable for the intrepid bound for the Canadian border.

The Boundary trail now continues southwestward, reaching Harrison Creek and Harrison Camp adjacent to the Pasayten River about 0.25 mile farther. From this tenting area, it is 4.7 miles to the abandoned Pasayten airstrip. There is a junction here; cross the north end of the airstrip and pick up the Soda Creek trail. Dead Lake will be passed after about 3 miles; there are no good campsites here. Another mile is required to reach the campsite at the junction with the trail descending from Monument 83. Just before reaching this potential overnight stop, Frosty Creek is crossed on a bridge. There are multiple campsites at this location, which is in the deep woods with minimal views. Abandoned cabins nearby are too deteriorated to be of any use as shelter in inclement weather.

From the tenting area, the Boundary trail continues westward, gradually ascending through dense forest. After about 1.6 miles, there is a difficult ford of Frosty Creek. During spring high water, crossing the stream at this location can be a major problem. At 3.6 miles from the junction, there is a campsite 0.1 mile south of the trail, but the creek must be forded to reach the camping area. At 3.7 and 4.3 miles, the creek must again be forded. The junction with the easily missed side trail to The Parks is at 4.4 miles. This way trail is overgrown; look for a sign on a tree about 50 feet from the junction. The way trail to The Parks is about 3 miles long and gains roughly 1,200 vertical feet.

Three-tenths of a mile farther along the main trail is the Frosty Lake campsite, located 100 yards north of the lake. The altitude gain from the Chuchuwanteen–Frosty Creek junction to this point has been about 700 vertical feet. A rough guess as to mileage, based on walking times, is 4.7 miles. (There is considerable discrepancy between Forest Service figures and personal experience in this section of trail; the actual distance may be as short as 3.5 miles or as long as 6 miles. Reader input is requested.)

From this point, the trail switchbacks up fairly steeply. Half a mile from Castle Pass, or roughly 1.5 miles from the Frosty Lake campsite, is a superb campsite in high alpine meadow. Water is obtainable 0.2 mile down the trail from a stream. Half a mile farther is Frosty Pass, elevation 6,500 feet. This level ridge offers multiple level areas for tents, but there is no water available after the winter snows have melted off the ridge crest. To the north rises Mount Winthrop (7,860 feet), an easy climb from the pass. Immediately below is a small tarn, the source of Frosty Creek. Blizzard Peak is to the south. Joker and Castle Peaks lie to the west. Everyone will want to spend considerable time at this location, and plans should be made accordingly.

The trail to the west descends steeply, some of the poor-quality, badly eroded tread has been replaced by a long switchback. The Pacific Coast Trail (PCT) is intersected 0.2 mile south of Castle Pass. About 1,000 vertical feet are lost in the about 1.5-mile descent. (See the PCT and Monument 78 trail in Manning Park with regard to routes after this junction is reached.)

The walking time from the PCT to Frosty Pass is 45 minutes with a full pack. From Frosty Pass to the Frosty–Chuchuwanteen junction, the walking time, again full packed, is 3 hours and 15 minutes. Estimated distances are as follows: PCT to pass 1.2 miles; pass to Frosty Lake campsite, 1.9 miles; campsite to junction 5 to 6 miles. In reverse order, allow 4 to 4.5 hours from junction to pass and 30 minutes for the descent to the PCT.

(Note: This footpath was affected by a substantial forest fire in 1995. Anticipate postfire changes in the surroundings west of Castle Pass.)

From Castle Pass westward, the trail drops about 100 vertical feet in timber over half a mile and then switchbacks upward; dead trees and nice flowers are present here. After an hour, reach a saddle with good views of peaks to the northwest and Hopkins Pass to the southeast. The tread then goes upward, reaching a flowered meadow bowl; there is a good campsite at the east end, with water available below the camp. Pushing onward, after two ridge crests, the footpath tops out on a scenic knoll, where there are great views in all directions and a fair but dry camping place. The trail descends, passing several level areas; water may be available via a way trail from the lowest site. Altitude is gained going north, and then a gradual descent into the Big Face Creek valley occurs. Spring water crosses the trail after 25 minutes of descending; 100 yards farther, a way trail goes down 200 feet to reach two scenic campsites in the trees; 150 feet farther down the main trail, a small stream is a water source. With a full pack, the hiking time to this point is 3 hours and 35 minutes, and the estimated distance from Castle Pass is 7.6 miles.

Switchbacks descend from here for about 1 mile. Thereafter, the tread alternates between timber and high, thick brush. After 45 minutes, Big Face Creek is rock-hopped across. Again, there is intermittent brush and forest. After a slide alder transit, the trail goes straight up in brush; the tread is not visible at times. After this ascent, the trail turns left south of a stream; this is the last water source. The tread then switchbacks upward through alternating forest and meadow; the junction with the way trail to the 6,898-foot knob south of Joker Mountain is passed; this is a walk up but gains about 900 vertical feet. Not far from the way trail, the main trail tops out at Elbow Pass, elevation about 6,400 feet. Light packed, from the campsite, the hiking time to this point is 2 hours and 20 minutes, and the estimated distance is 4.5 miles.

No tread is present for the next 100 yards; go northwest to a sign on a tree that says, "Elbow Basin ¼ mile; Ross Lake 13 miles; Castle Pass 10 miles." Faint tread goes downward from here for 200 feet and then stops, presumably to Elbow Basin. The footpath to Ross Lake goes up past the sign; there is no tread for 50 feet. It then contours to a high saddle; there are glorious views from here. Again, there is no tread for 0.2 mile; go southwest, watching for cairns. Tread becomes apparent in a copse of alpine fir trees. The trail then traverses a ridge above Freezeout Lake about 600 feet below. Scrabble tread in places to the lake can be seen; a probable campsite is noted on the west end of the lake. Walking time from Elbow Pass is 1 hour. The trail descends steeply to a lower saddle and then down to a lower meadow; the tread is faint in places. Fifty-three minutes past Freezeout Lake, switchbacks start the descent to Three Fools Creek far below. The estimated distance from Elbow Pass to this point is 3.5 miles, and the hiking time is 2 hours. There are level sites for setting up a tent in the lower meadow, but except for two snow patches, no water source is obvious.

More apparent tread is present on the fifty-five switchbacks down to the creek. The Little Fish shelter is about 1 mile after the downward march ends. There are several tent sites in the vicinity of the shelter, the first overnight stopping place since the beginning of the downward slog. The shelter roof leaks, but dry areas were present in 1987.

From the shelter, it is 2.2 miles to the Pasayten Wilderness boundary and 3 miles to the Lightning Creek trail. A trail post marks the junction. Turn left (south) here; the Lightning Creek trail drops down at this point, crosses a small bridge, and shortly thereafter crosses the sturdy bridge across Lightning Creek. On the other side of the bridge is the Deerlick Cabin, a horse-hitching area, and level but somewhat muddy ground for pitching a tent. The cabin roof is quite mossy and has a few holes, but it would make a reasonable rain shelter (as of June 1980). This is a pleasant, scenic area; two huge cedars tower above the cabin and bridge. The cabin is often used by Park Service trail crews.

Going westward from the bridge and cabin, the trail goes upward for roughly 0.9 mile, gaining about 350 vertical feet. Near the cabin, the trail is in dank, deep forest. Shortly thereafter, it is in very dense young forest; the homogeneous growth at this point is probably due to uniform regrowth following a burn. A bit farther on, a number of extensively branched lichens (Old Man's Beard) can be seen hanging from most of the tree limbs in the area.

The trail levels off about 500 feet above Lightning Creek and continues westward for a bit over 2 miles without gaining or losing much altitude. About 1 mile away and approximately 900 vertical feet above the Lightning Creek Campground, it begins a switchbacking descent to the lake. At the high point, there are good views of the lake to the west and south of the Eastbank trail bridge over the mouth of Lightning Creek directly below, and of Mount Prophet to the west. The junction with the Desolation Peak trail is 0.15 mile from the campground, marked by a trail post. A few yards farther, again marked with a trail post, is the junction with the Eastbank trail, running to the south and crossing a sturdy suspension bridge over the mouth of Lightning Creek a few feet away. A short way trail 0.1 mile long leads from this junction to the Lightning Creek Campground, where there are tables, rest rooms, and campsites for five or six parties. Walking time from the Deer Lick Cabin to the campground is 1 hour and 30 minutes. From the campground, the North Cascades Highway (NCH) can be reached via the Eastbank trail (described elsewhere in this book). Alternatively, arrangements can be made in advance for a boat pickup to return the hiking party to the Ross Lake Resort located about 1.5 miles from the NCH.

The distance from Castle Pass to Ross Lake is somewhere between 21.9 and 25 miles. The former distance is from the Green Trails maps; the latter is from data provided by the Forest Service. This section of trail is for experienced wilderness travelers only, since route finding can be a problem in several locations. However, it is ideal if solitude is the goal; seeing anyone between Castle Pass and Little Fish shelter is unlikely. The downside is that hikers must be prepared to cope with any emergency that may occur.

Fossils are abundant in the area around Dead Lake. Good lake and stream fishing is available in many areas. The peace and quiet of the deep wilderness, the fantastic beauty of the hills, and excellent opportunities for mountain photography mark this unusual wilderness route. The length and isolation of this trail make it unique within the continental United States.

Although access to the Boundary trail is not easy anywhere, the footpath can be done in segments rather than in one sustained march. If possible, the descents into the Ashnola and Pasayten River valleys should be avoided, since they are the least enjoyable portions of this wilderness walk.

(Louden Lake–Scheelite Pass, July 1975; Scheelite Pass–PeeVee Pass, July 1977; PeeVee Pass–Bunker Hill, July 1986; Castle Pass–southeast of Skagit Peak, July 1987)

CADY PASS AND CADY POINT

Elevations
  Trailhead: 3,800 feet
  Destination: 6,542 feet (Cady Point)
  Other Significant Locations: Cady Pass, 6,000 feet
Altitude Gain   2,800 feet (including ups and downs)
Walking Time   In: 3 hours   Out: 2 hours 30 minutes
Trail Length   6 miles one-way
Accessibility   July 15 to October 15
Difficulty   Strenuous (one-day, round-trip)
Pack   Light
Topographic Sheets   USGS: Azurite Peak
                         Green Trails: Washington Pass, Mount Logan

Access Harts Pass (see Pacific Crest Trail—Harts Pass to Cutthroat Pass). From the pass, drive westward and downward 5.5 miles to the trailhead on the left, adjacent to the closed bridge over Slate Creek. There is space for five to seven cars to park. The road is steep and difficult in places; four-wheel drive is useful but not essential, but it is a road for experienced back-road drivers.

There are several fair tent sites in the vicinity of the trailhead. The trail is actually a deactivated mining road, gated at its beginning. It is closed to all motorized vehicles.

At 1 mile (30 minutes), a bridge crosses the south fork of Slate Creek. At 1.8 miles, water is available. There is fallen rock in the road here, but there is no difficulty bypassing it (50 minutes). A campsite is passed at 3 miles; the last water available is nearby, as is an abandoned mining location (1 hour and 25 minutes). The roadbed is rougher beyond this point. First views occur at 3.4 miles. Cady Pass is reached at 5 miles (2 hours and 15 minutes). The road continues downward into the Mill Creek valley.

Cady Ridge is scenic in both directions. Crater and Jack Mountains are impressive to the west; the Slate Peak Lookout is in view to the east. Elegant weathered dead trees are scattered about the glorious meadowland.

From the pass, follow intermittent tread westward for 1 mile to reach Cady Point, elevation 6,542 feet. Four concrete foundations are all that remain of the forest fire lookout that once stood here. A helicopter landing location is still present near the lookout site. Views in all directions are extraordinary. The up-time from pass to point is 40 minutes; descent takes 32 minutes. Going up, the altitude gain is 700 feet; descending, it is 200 feet.

If time and strength permit, go eastward on the ridge from the pass toward Mount Ballard for a great meadow ramble. Blueberries along the high route turn a brilliant red in early September. There are many level places to pitch a tent, but all are waterless after the snow has melted.

This footpath is little used. If solitude is your desire, it is probably achievable here. There is little to see for the first 1 hour and 30 minutes up, but the rewards on the top are well worth the effort. Allow a full day for lunch, photography, meadow ambling, and mountain gazing; if you can carry enough water, plan an overnight stay.

(September 1994)

MCMILLAN PARK AND DEVIL'S PARK
Elevations
  Trailhead: 1,650 (Panther Creek Bridge)
  Destination: 5,850 feet (Devil's Park)
  High Point: 7,054 feet (Crater Mountain lookout site)
  Other Significant Locations: Confluence Granite and Ruby Creeks, 1,900 feet; McMillan Park, 5,500 feet; high point on Jacketa Ridge, 6,840 feet
Altitude Gain 4,900 feet (including ups and downs)
Walking Time   In: 6 hours 30 minutes   Out: 3 hours 45 minutes
Trail Length   7 miles one-way
Accessibility July 15 to October 15
Difficulty   Strenuous
Pack   Full
Topographic Sheets USGS: Crater Mountain, Shull Mountain, Jack Mountain; Azurite Peak
                        Green Trails: Mount Logan, Jack Mountain

The trailhead is just west of the Panther Creek Bridge on the North Cascades Highway (NCH), 32.8 miles east of the village of Marblemount and 55.1 miles west of the village of Winthrop. There is a large parking area at the trailhead. The trail drops down and crosses Ruby Creek on a large foot and horse bridge. Turn right at the junction immediately after the bridge is crossed. From this point, it is 0.9 mile to the recreation area boundary and 3.5 miles to the McMillan and Devil's Park trail. Ruby Camp is 50 feet away, by the river; there are two nice tent sites close to the rushing water. A toilet is located on the hill above the camp.

The trail follows the north side of Ruby Creek, gradually gaining altitude. The walking time to the McMillan Park trailhead is about 1 hour and 30 minutes. A shorter alternative may be available to reach this trailhead. Drive 2.9 miles farther east on the NCH to the junction of Canyon and Granite Creeks.

There is a bridge allowing hikers to cross Granite Creek. Follow the trail on the east side of Granite Creek to the confluence. At low water in the fall, it is possible to ford Canyon Creek without great hazard, although the ford is impossible in late spring and early summer. At times, it is also possible to cross the creek on a footlog (one was present in 1996). If this route is feasible and safe, it saves about 2.5 miles.

From Canyon Creek, the trail switchbacks up steeply, with water available only at 1.2 and 3.3 miles. This is a steep, hot climb, topping out at 3.8 miles where the trail forks; the right fork leads to McMillan Park, and the left fork leads to Crater Mountain.

Formerly, there were two lookout buildings on Crater Mountain—an older structure on the true summit and a newer building on a ridge substantially east of the true summit. Both lookouts have been destroyed by the Forest Service.

To explore the Crater Mountain area, switchback upward through beautiful alpine meadow. Five miles from Ruby Creek, the trail forks. The right fork leads to the Crater Mountain ridge 1 mile farther over good tread. From this high ridge, there are good but not spectacular views of the surrounding areas. The left trail (at the 5-mile junction) goes to the true summit of Crater Mountain. This trail is less well maintained, is difficult to locate in places, and requires a class 2 to class 3 rock climb for about 400 feet to reach the summit; route finding is facilitated by following fading yellow paint markings on the rocks. Distance from the junction to the summit is about 2.7 miles.

The view from the true summit of Crater is one of the best in the entire Cascades. The hiker-climber can see portions of Diablo and Ross Lakes, Jack Mountain, Mount Baker, Mount Shuksan, and the entire sweep of the western and eastern Cascades; the vista is mind-boggling.

The dramatic climatic demarcation along the Granite Creek valley is quite obvious. The mountains to the west are heavily glaciated. Those to the east have far less snow and ice. It is apparent from this viewpoint that much of the precipitation brought into the mountains by storms generated in the Pacific Ocean is deposited on the mountains to the west, leaving far less to reach the mountains to the east.

Mountain goats are often seen in the Crater Mountain area. There are campsites on the ridge crest (water is scarce late in the season) and in the lower meadows.

Returning to the 3.8-mile trail junction, the right fork leads to McMillan Park, 4 miles from Canyon Creek. The park is a 1-by-1.5-mile area of high alpine scenic meadow, with numerous campsites. Deer are common in the area. Mosquitoes are ubiquitous and can be intolerable without protection.

Repellents and mosquito netting are essentials for those planning to camp in McMillan Park.

The footpath continues through McMillan Park. The up-time from Canyon Creek to McMillan Park is about 3 hours; an additional 2 hours are required to reach the Crater ridge; to reach the true summit, allow 3 hours.

A word of caution: McMillan Park is hunted heavily by parties on horseback during the High Cascade hunting season. Visitors are relatively few at other times. It is wise to check the dates and visit the area before the arrival of hunting parties. (Hunting season usually begins around September 10.)

After the northeast portion of McMillan Park is reached at about the 5-mile mark, the trail drops about 500 vertical feet in half a mile. From the crossing of the creek bottom to the Devil's Park shelter is an additional 1.4 to 1.5 miles, with an estimated altitude gain of approximately 1,000 feet. After leaving McMillan Park, water is scarce or nonexistent until you reach the shelter, where a small but reliable stream 100 feet to the east provides a good water source. Adequate wood for campfires is available in the Devil's Park area. The Devil's Park meadow extends about 0.8 mile and offers spectacular views of Slate Peak, Harts Pass, Crater and Jack Mountains, Hozomeen Mountain, and the Pickets to the west. The shelter sleeps four people; it was structurally sound in 1984.

From the shelter, the trail goes southeast through the meadow approximately 0.4 mile. Tread is faint to nonexistent here. The footpath then makes a curve to the east. Tread becomes apparent when the trail turns northward and begins the ascent of Jackita Ridge. If you are unable to follow the trail from these directions, simply go directly east from the Devil's Park shelter and climb the meadow. You will intersect the trail after about half a mile and an altitude gain of approximately 600 feet. From here, the trail gradually climbs along the ridge for an additional 2 miles. The footpath immediately below the first of two prominent knobs then drops down sharply, losing about 500 feet in altitude, and goes through the woods; it meanders in a westerly direction, losing further altitude and going almost on the contour line out on the ridge. From here, it returns eastward to near the ridge crest and follows the ridge crest closely to Devil's Pass.

The views from Jackita Ridge are superb, and since this area is seldom visited, wild game is seen frequently, particularly deer.

From the junction of the Crater Lookout and McMillan Park trails to the Devil's Park shelter is slightly over 3 miles. From the Devil's Pass shelter to the point on the ridge where the trail drops down sharply is an additional estimated 2.5 miles. The time from the Crater–McMillan trail junction to the shelter is about 1 hour and 45 minutes; it takes an additional 1 hour and 15 minutes to proceed 2.5 miles farther along Jackita Ridge. The altitude gain from the Devil's Park shelter to the Jackita Ridge dropdown is about 1,000 feet. With packs, allow 5 hours from Granite Creek to the Devil's Park shelter. The descent can be done comfortably in 2.5 to 3 hours. In McMillan Park, there are many good campsites and water is available from several sources. If the Devil's Park shelter is occupied, there are a number of excellent campsites in the surrounding meadow. Jackita Ridge is too steep and too dry to permit camping.

Insects, particularly mosquitoes, are often a substantial problem at Devil's Park; be prepared to cope with these pests. Patches of blooming gentian are found near the shelter. However, neither meadow produces superb floral displays.

(August 1984)

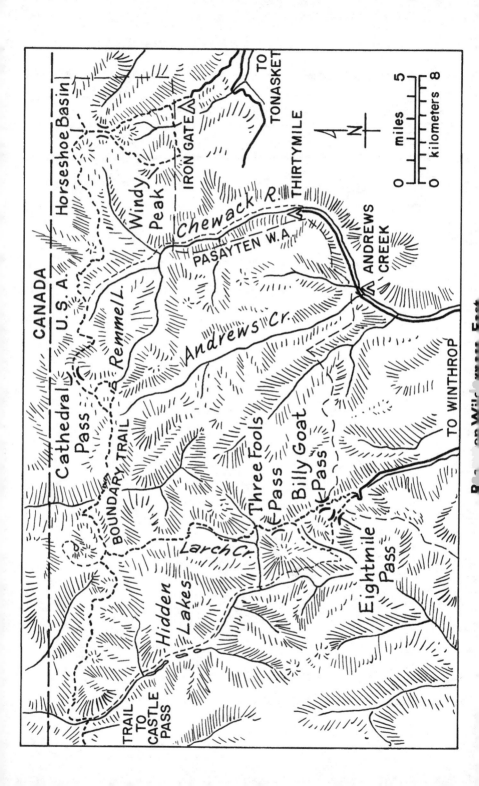

Pasayten Wilderness, East

Pasayten Wilderness–East

HORSESHOE BASIN
Elevations
  Trailhead: 5,800 feet
  Destination: 7,100 feet (Louden Lake)
  High Point: 7,200 feet (Sunny Pass)
Altitude Gain   1,500 feet (including ups and downs)
Walking Time   In: 3 hours   Out: 2 hours 40 minutes
Trail Length   6.6 miles one-way
Accessibility   Early July to mid-October
Difficulty   Moderate
Pack   Full
Topographic Sheets   USGS: Horseshoe Basin
                         Green Trails: Horseshoe Basin

The best access route to the trailhead involves leaving U.S. Highway 97 at Tonasket and driving 11.6 miles to Loomis. From the post office at Loomis, follow the paved road northwest. Turn left at 2.2 miles and left again at 10.8 miles; Stay on Forest Road #39. Enter the Okanogan National Forest at 15.5 miles, and then turn north 16.2 miles from Loomis on a primitive side road signed Irongate; 5.9 miles up this one-way road with turnouts is the trailhead. The road should be driven with considerable caution in wet weather. There is parking for approximately thirty cars at the Irongate trailhead, as well as campsites and toilets. The turnoff road to the trailhead can also be reached via primitive roads from Winthrop and Conconully.

The first part of the trail follows the Tungsten Mine Road. The Pasayten Wilderness is entered at 0.2 mile. At 0.5 mile, there are junctions with trails leading to Deer Park and 14 Mile Camp to the east and to the Windy Peak trail to the west (see Windy Peak trail description). At 2 miles, there is a water source. At 3 miles, a wooden fence must be bypassed. The trail breaks out into meadow at 4.5 miles. There is a good campsite at this location. From here, the trail goes up more steeply to reach Sunny Pass, 5 miles from the trailhead. The pass area is scenic. The left trail at this point is part of the Windy Peak Loop. The Horseshoe Basin or Boundary trail contours north and slightly east. Six miles from the trailhead, Horseshoe Pass is reached. There are a creek and a tarn at this location. The Long Draw trail goes eastward at this point toward Goodenough Peak. There is also a 0.8-mile way trail to Smith Lake, perhaps the only water source in the area in late summer or early fall. The Boundary trail turns left at this point and passes through splendid meadowland; three-quarters of a mile farther is Louden Lake, with a number of excellent camping areas. Two-tenths of a mile past the lake is another good campsite, north of and below the trail.

From a base camp at Louden Lake, you can cross-country northward to reach a high plateau. From this area, border markers 103 and 104, the great 20-foot slash cut along the border, and the intermittent fence marking the border can be inspected. Half a mile north of the border, there are two beautiful lakes some 500 vertical feet below, which contain fish. Views from the mile 103 marker are spectacular to the west; the scenery from the mile 104 marker is good to the east. It is also possible to continue along the Boundary trail to the west as far as time and energy permit.

The splendid high meadowland of Horseshoe Basin is best visited in late June or early July. Later in the year, water access is a substantial problem. In addition, domesticated animals are still allowed to graze in this area, and flocks of sheep can intrude on the wilderness experience. If planning a visit after July 15, check at the Methow Valley Visitor Center in Winthrop to determine if domestic animals are presently in the area. Mountain goats, bighorn sheep, and deer may also be seen in Horseshoe Basin. Rather surprisingly, considering the distance of the trailhead from a major population center, visitation may be substantial on weekends and holidays.

See the Boundary trail description for information on the footpath beyond Louden Lake.

(July 1975)

WINDY PEAK
Elevations
Trailhead:	5,800 feet
Destination:	8,384 feet (Windy Peak)

Other Significant Locations: Junction Windy and Boundary Trails, 7,200 feet

Altitude Gain	3,100 feet (including ups and downs)
Walking Time	In: 2 hours 40 minutes Out: 2 hours
Trail Length	6.5 miles one-way
Accessibility	July 15 to October 1
Difficulty	Moderately strenuous to summit and back in one day; strenuous if entire loop is done in one day
Pack	Light
Topographic Sheets	USGS: Horseshoe Basin
	Green Trails: Horseshoe Basin

See Horseshoe Basin (Pasayten Wilderness) for details about access to the trailhead. Continue up the Boundary trail half a mile to the cleared rectangular area containing granite rocks. The way trail to Windy Peak is unsigned but cairned and leaves near the northwest end of this cleared area; the connecting loop is called Clutch trail 343. (You can also reach Windy Peak from the Long Swamp Campground at the end of the pavement of Long Swamp Road 39 via the Windy Creek trail.)

The Clutch trail drops down moderately steeply, losing about 600 feet in 0.7 mile, to reach the middle fork of Toats-Coulee Creek. There is a satisfactory campsite at this point. Cross the creek on a footlog or, if necessary, ford it. About 0.2 mile beyond the creek, there is an unsigned trail junction; take the left or more heavily used fork. Midway up the canyon walls, the hiker breaks out into view areas containing grass and flowers. Contour upward on switchbacks to gain the top of one ridge, cross over it, and continue upward, eventually crossing the top of the second ridge. At about 2.5 miles, there is one small spring. At 4 miles, this trail intersects the Windy Peak trail. There is a dry campsite at the junction, presumably Two Bear Camp. Do not stop here. Turn right (north); at about 4.8 miles, there is a beautiful campsite amid larches in a delightful meadow, which I have named "First Larch Camp." There is a scenic green grassy ridge to the northeast from this campsite. The trail disappears at about this location, and no tread can be seen for approximately 200 yards. Follow cairns upward and northeastward through the meadow, picking up the trail again by locating the Pasayten Wilderness sign on a large larch tree. The trail is somewhat difficult to locate over the next mile beyond this sign; if in doubt, look for cairns. The footpath goes up through a boulder field and past krummholz trees, eventually reaching a flat at about 5.6 miles. Views from this area are exceptional; it would make an ideal campsite, if not for the lack of water.

Going northward from this point, there is a high trail that follows the old phone poles and leads to the summit of Windy Peak. A lower, more apparent trail bypasses the summit to the west. The last 200 vertical feet to the summit is trailless on class 2 rock. There is a scrabble trail to the summit from the west, which leads up from the hikers' trail; this is probably the Windy Creek trail.

The view from the summit at 8,334 feet is one of the most splendid in the North Cascades. To the northwest is the spire of Cathedral Peak. To the north are Arnold Peak and Goodenough Peak; to the west is the vast expanse of the Pasayten Wilderness, seemingly extending forever. The broad meadowland of Horseshoe Basin is impressive to the northeast.

From this point, you can retrace your steps or continue northward on what I have termed the "Windy Peak Loop." After picking up the hikers' trail to the west of the summit of Windy Peak, continue northward, drop down and turn left at the first rock knoll, contour underneath it, and go through the next notch to the northwest (right looks correct at this point but is not). Dropping further downward, roughly 0.2 mile of cross-country travel brings you to shallow

Windy Lake. There are several good campsites in the meadow near the lake and at elevated areas around the lake. The lake seems barren of fish. Another half hour farther, or roughly 9 miles from the trailhead, a stream is crossed in a meadow where there are campsites; this is the bottom-out, or low point. The trail then goes moderately upward and eventually connects with an old road about a mile from Sunny Pass; the turnoff from the road to the trail is signed. From Sunny Pass, return to the point of beginning via the Boundary trail. The loop distance is approximately 15 miles. The altitude gain for the loop is roughly 4,000 feet. A strong hiker with a light pack can make the loop in 6 hours and 30 minutes, but most would want to make a two-day trip.

The junction with the Basin Creek trail is signed, indicating that it is 6 miles to the Chewach River; this junction is located near Windy Lake and Topaz Mountain.

Although a fair number of people visit Horseshoe Basin, few visit Windy Peak. Winter comes early here, because of the substantial elevation. The area is most scenic in late September, when the larch needles are turning gold.

(August 1978)

Cathedral Provincial Park, British Columbia

CATHEDRAL LAKES: GENERAL INFORMATION

The turnoff from Canada Highway 3 is 15.2 miles east of Hedley or 2.6 miles west of the Keremeos left turn to Osoyous. The turnoff is signed. Almost immediately, cross an unusual one-lane bridge over the Similkameen River. Base camp for the Cathedral Lakes Resort is 13.5 miles (20.1 km) from the turnoff.

Canada uses the metric measuring system; all distances are posted in meters or kilometers. A meter is about 39 inches. Eight kilometers (km) are roughly 5 miles. To convert miles to kilometers, multiply miles by 1.6. To convert feet to meters, multiple feet by .305.

The public trailhead is reached by turning left at 14.8 miles and proceeding 0.4 mile to a parking area large enough to handle about twenty-five cars. There are several campsites by the Ashnola River, 100 feet away from the parking area. The trail crosses a footbridge at this point and joins the jeep road about 0.5 mile after the river is crossed; there is a 300-vertical-foot altitude gain in this half mile. From this lakeview trailhead, it is about 8.5 miles to Quiniscoe Lake by road and perhaps 9.5 miles by trail, with an altitude gain of about 4,000 vertical feet.

The jeep road is exactly 9 miles long from the base camp to the lodge at Quiniscoe Lake. Here is a road log: 1 mile—road joins trail; 2 miles—Lakeview Creek is crossed on a bridge (hikers should obtain water at this point, since there is no water between here and Lindsey Creek, several miles farther by trail); 2.6 miles—trail goes to the right, jeep road to the left; 4.4 miles—Sheep Camp (water available from creek to east); 9 miles—lodge and campground.

The people who run the lodge provide round-trips from the lodge to the lake for hikers and backpackers with advance reservations (1996 cost, $55 Canadian per person). There are usually three trips a day, at 10, 2, and 4 o'clock, with additional trips on heavy-use weekends or three-day holidays. Four-wheel-drive transportation saves a full day up and a half day down through areas that are generally hot and not scenic, so its use is strongly recommended. Private cars are not allowed to use the road.

The trail is 1 mile longer than the jeep road and takes 7 to 8 hours. The jeep road takes 6 hours up. There is a campsite on the trail at Lindsey Creek. Hikers may use either the trail or the road. The lodge staff prefers them to use the trail but takes no action against those walking the road.

As inspection of the map shows, a number of trails in the area offer several loops and circle hikes. The lakes, in order of scenic beauty, are Ladyslipper, Glacier, Quiniscoe, Scout, Pyramid, and Lake of the Woods. The Cathedral Rim trail, from its start at Lake Quiniscoe to its termination near Grimface

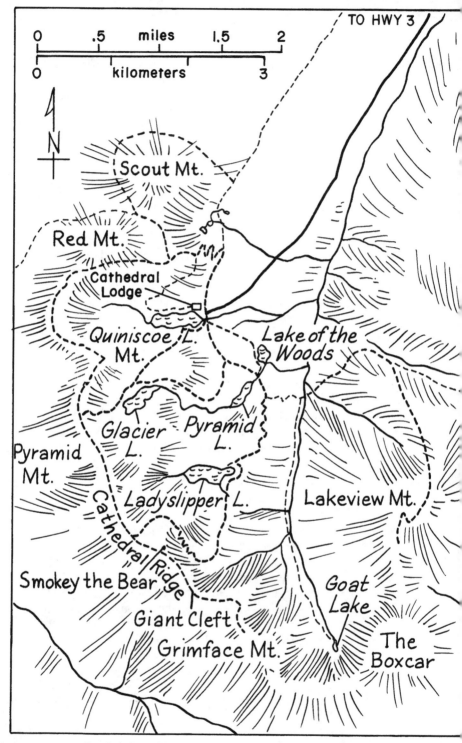

Cathedral Provincial Park, British Columbia

TO HWY 3

0 .5 miles 1.5 2
0 kilometers 3

N

Scout Mt.

Red Mt.

Cathedral Lodge

Quiniscoe L.
Mt.

Lake of the Woods

Glacier L.

Pyramid L.

Pyramid Mt.

Ladyslipper L.

Lakeview Mt.

Cathedral Ridge

Smokey the Bear

Goat Lake

Giant Cleft

Grimface Mt.

The Boxcar

(McKeen) Mountain, and the Lakeview Mountain–Centennial trail are the superior footpaths in the area and are described in detail below.

The Diamond trail around Scout Mountain offers a moderately scenic, less strenuous footpath than the rim hikes. Wildflowers in the summer, and fall displays of glowing yellow larch, can be seen from the above-timberline sections of this walk. The trail starts and ends at the lodge. Only 20 minutes of step retracing is necessary. Distance is about 4 miles (6 km), altitude gain about 750 feet (225 meters), and average hiking time about 3 hours.

Unfortunately, there are substantial discrepancies in the names used by the lodge, the provincial park, and the British Columbia topographic sheet. For example, the Cathedral Provincial Park staff advises that "the names of Quiniscoe Mountain, Red Mountain, and Scout Lake are incorrect on the B.C. topographic map. They are correct on the B.C. park brochure." Therefore, in the descriptions that follow, two names may be used if they match the location. Where different names exist for the same location, the name provided by the Cathedral Provincial Park staff is used.

Camping in the core area of the park is permitted only at Quiniscoe Lake, Pyramid Lake, and Lake of the Woods. Seventy campsites are available. Campfires are permitted only at Quiniscoe Lake. As of 1996, camping fees were $2 (Canadian) per person per night from July 1 to Labor Day. Dogs and mountain bikes are not permitted in the core area of the park.

In 1997, substantial upgrading of several of the park footpaths was accomplished. Expect improved tread in a number of locations.

Those interested in transportation from base camp adjacent to the Ashnola Road or reservations at Cathedral Lodge should contact the Cathedral Lakes Resort, Ltd., Site 4; Comp. 8, Slocan Park, British Columbia, VOG 2E0, Canada; phone 250-226-7560, or 888-CLL-HIKE.

CATHEDRAL LAKES–LAKEVIEW MOUNTAIN
Elevations
Trailhead: 6,775 feet (2,066 meters) (Quiniscoe Lake)
Destination: 8,622 feet (2,630 meters) (Lakeview Mountain)
Other Significant Locations: Lakeview Creek (low point), 6,300 feet (1,921 meters)

Altitude Gain 2,400 feet in; 400 feet out (including ups and downs)
Walking Time In: 2 hours 15 minutes   Out: 1 hour 45 minutes
Trail Length 4.5 miles one-way
Accessibility Late July to early October
Difficulty Moderately strenuous
Pack Light
Topographic Sheets Ashnola River 092H/01 British Columbia

Follow directions for the south section of the Cathedral Rim until the Ladyslipper Lake–Lakeview Mountain junction is reached. Turn left and follow the switchbacks downward. At 0.5 mile, the signed junction with the Goat Lake trail is intersected at the southern end of a switchback (estimated distance from the lake to the junction is 2 miles). At 0.8 mile, the bridge across Lakeview Creek is reached; this is the low point of the trail. Walking time from Quiniscoe Lake to the bridge is 19 minutes.

Going upward, the trail is muddy and in poor condition in approximately eight to ten places. Two areas of substantial puncheon must be crossed. Use caution when it is wet or frosty, since it can be quite slippery. Fifteen minutes after starting up, there is a small bridge and available water. At 26 minutes, there is water on the left, as the creek from the meadow is first intersected. From here on, there are splendid alpine flowers. The trail parallels the creek upward and 8 minutes later breaks out into full meadow, although intermittent trees continue for a substantial distance. The estimated distance from the bridge to this point is 1.2 miles. This is a gorgeous wildflower area. The tread becomes faint to nonexistent hereafter. The Centennial trail follows the creek upward to the crest and then turns left in the high meadow, passing beneath the Twin Buttes and ultimately descending to Mountain Goat Creek below; it does not go down to Mountain Goat Lakes, easily seen when the crest is reached.

The Lakeview Mountain trail goes southeastward. There are several good campsites at the breakout point and nearby in the tree-line area. The route to the mountain can be found by following cairns upward, but any way is the right way. Perhaps easiest is to go directly up the ridge rather than going left to the saddle and then up the ridge. It takes about 1 hour and 5 minutes from the tree line to the summit; the estimated distance is 1.5 miles. The summit is cairned and has a post on top. It can best be reached by contouring around to the east side and going up the south side over talus. The views are splendid. To the southeast is Haystack Mountain. Immediately to the south are the two elevated ends of the Boxcar. To the north is a broad, grassy ridge that invites one to roam at will among the high alpine flowers. Most splendid of all, to the west, the entire Cathedral Rim, from Grimface Mountain on the south to Red Mountain on the north, is visible. Lady Slipper, Glacier, Quiniscoe, and Pyramid Lakes are clearly visible.

To look down on Goat Lake, go south a bit west of the crest half a mile. By clambering out on a rock knob at this point, you can see Goat Lake nestled in its cirque beneath the Boxcar–Denture Ridge, Matriarch Mountain, Macabre Tower, and Grimface Mountain. Also note a chute to the left of this rock knoll but to the right of the main ridge that leads downward, allowing a cross-country scree, talus, and meadow traverse on the lake and a round-trip from there via trail back to the trail junction above Lakeview Creek.

More enjoyable, however, is a leisurely walk down the ridge crest to the saddle, taking in the view of Mountain Goat Lakes below. From there, wander over the high ridge, drinking in the splendid panoramas in all directions and now and then gazing down at the equally splendid, seemingly infinite varieties of flowers that carpet the expanse of this broad ridge in season. Note the dramatic change in wildflowers at timberline, where the clusters of foot-high lupines give way to the small tundra flowers. Also note several scenic and photogenic dead larches between the breakout point and timberline. Unfortunately, moderate numbers of mosquitoes and no-see-ums are also present.

It is of interest that though the creek at the breakout point has no obvious snowfield source, it has adequate water. Where the water comes from is an interesting question. There are also a few small tarns on the crest near the Centennial trail, from which you can obtain water.

The altitude gain (round-trip) is 2,800 feet. The distance is 4.5 miles to the summit and 5 miles to the Goat Lake viewpoint (one-way). The hiking time to the summit is 2 hours and 15 minutes; the return time from the summit is 1 hour and 45 minutes. Allow an additional 30 minutes to reach the Goat Lake viewpoint and return to the summit.

If possible, allow forever to enjoy the splendor of the surroundings!

(August 1980)

CATHEDRAL RIM (NORTH SECTION)
Elevations

Trailhead:	6,775 feet (2,066 meters) (Quiniscoe Lake)
Destination:	8,369 feet (2,553 meters) (Bomford Mountain)

Other Significant Locations: Quiniscoe Mountain, 8,100 feet (2,470 meters); Glacier Lake, 7,250 feet (2,211 meters); Scout Lake, 6,950 feet (2,120 meters)

Altitude Gain	2,000 feet (including ups and downs)
Walking Time	4–5 hours (loop)
Trail Length	7.4 miles (loop)
Accessibility	Late July to early October
Difficulty	Moderately strenuous
Pack	Light

Topographic Sheets Ashnola River 092H/01 British Columbia

The trailhead to Scout Lake is on a side road 150 feet north of the lodge. A 15-minute walk of 0.7 mile through the woods brings you to the junction. At this point, it is 0.2 mile farther northward, and an additional 0.2 mile on a side trail to the west, to reach Scout Lake. Scout Lake has several good campsites, but camping is no longer permitted here.

There are lots of lupines growing around the lake. After inspecting Scout Lake, return to the junction and proceed upward in switchbacks along the beginning of the Cathedral Rim trail. Eleven minutes of walking over 0.4 mile of ascending switchbacks brings you to the tree line, and views are splendid thereafter. After an additional 0.4 mile, the tread disappears. Follow the rock cairns upward. Scout Lake can be seen below at this point. Two-tenths of a mile farther is a sign indicating the junction of the Centennial and Cathedral Rim trails. At this point, there is another good view of Scout Lake below. The Cathedral Rim trail crosses high meadow near a tarn (where there is a good campsite), contours under Red Mountain (which the Cathedral Rim trail is about to ascend), and goes westward several miles through meadow before dropping down to the Ashnola River.

The Cathedral Rim trail continues upward through high, flowered meadow. Follow the cairns, since in most places there is no tread. For that matter, you can wander in this area (and most of the other high areas) at will, since vegetation is of the tundra type and you are above timberline. Scout Mountain, the peak to the north of Centennial trail 0.5 mile, can be climbed without difficulty.

The Cathedral Rim trail ultimately requires a talus scramble and then runs the ridge crest for 0.5 mile, mostly in meadow but occasionally on rock. There are many flowers in this area and several summits, all of about the same altitude. Ptarmigan are often seen in this area. The trail then drops 300 vertical feet in 0.3 mile to a broad saddle and reascends up Quiniscoe Mountain, gaining perhaps 550 vertical feet to the summit of the 8,369-foot peak. If desired, the summit can be bypassed to the west, saving 200 vertical feet in altitude gain.

Descend from the mountain, following rock cairns, through a meadow alternating with talus slopes to the Glacier Lake trail junction in a saddle perhaps 0.6 mile to the south. If desired, roam at leisure on the broad fingers of meadow extending westward. Ultimately return to the junction and descend fairly steeply on scree, meadow, talus, and snow to the shores of Glacier Lake. This splendid larch-lined alpine lake, altitude 7,250 feet, is a day-use area only, and camping and fires are prohibited. It is about a mile from the ridge crest to the lake exit stream; 0.9 mile, first through meadow and then through woods, to the junction with the Pyramid Lake trail; and 0.7 mile through woods back to the point of beginning at Quiniscoe Lake.

Even in relatively good weather, a cold wind is frequently present on the Cathedral Rim, and extra clothes are strongly advised, even if the weather is warm at Quiniscoe Lake. Snow may occur in this area any day of the year, and appropriate precautions with regard to hypothermia are important before hiking anywhere in the Cathedral Lakes area. This loop can be walked comfortably in 4 to 5 hours, but most people will want to make it a full-day trip to allow time for lunch, exploration, wildflower photography, wildlife observation, and simply sitting and looking at the splendid panoramas in the distance and the profusion of small alpine flowers surrounding the trail. Over 200 varieties of wildflowers have been described and catalogued in the Cathedral Lakes area by botanists from the University of British Columbia. Around August 1, the height of the season, flowers are literally everywhere. There is a striking change in flower type as timberline is reached. Below timberline, lupine and paintbrush predominate. Near timberline, shrubby cinquefoil is most common. Higher up, various types of tundra flowers, including moss campion and golden fleabane, predominate.

Once the rim is reached, the vista of the peaks of the Pasayten Wilderness lying to the south and west unfolds dramatically. Peaks and ridges stretch forever, like waves in a stony sea. Vistas are superb. As frosting on the scenic cake, view the jewel of Glacier Lake, an aquamarine gem surrounded by a bezel of subalpine larch.

(August 1980)

CATHEDRAL RIM (SOUTH SECTION) VIA LADYSLIPPER LAKE

Elevations

Trailhead:	6,775 feet (2,066 meters) (Quiniscoe Lake)	
Destination:	8,000 feet (2,440 meters) (end of Rim trail)	
High Point:	8,570 feet (2,614 meters) (highest point on Cathedral Ridge)	

Other Significant Locations: Ladyslipper Lake, 7,200 feet

Altitude Gain   3,200 feet (including ups and downs)

Walking Time   7 hours 30 minutes (loop)

Trail Length   12 miles (loop)

Accessibility   Late July to early October

Difficulty   Strenuous

Pack   Light

Topographic Sheets   Ashnola River 092H/01 and British Columbia Cathedral Provincial Park brochure

Follow the trail from the lodge 0.1 mile, crossing the outlet stream of Quiniscoe Lake to the Pyramid Lake trail. It is 1 mile through woods to the Lake of the Woods trail junction, and an additional 0.3 mile, passing the north end of Pyramid Lake, to the junction with the Ladyslipper Lake–Lakeview Mountain trail. The trail loses perhaps 120 feet of altitude to this junction. It is about 1.1 miles to Ladyslipper Lake from the junction. The trail breaks out into meadow at 0.7 mile, and after 26 minutes of walking from the junction, there is a fine view from a knoll above the lake. The trail goes up to a high point of 7,500 feet and then drops down to the lake at 7,200 feet. This is the prettiest lake in the entire Cathedral Lakes and is also the best for fishing. Camping and campfires are prohibited at this lake; it is reserved for day use only.

Follow the trail half a mile around the east side of the lake and cross the outlet stream. Drink deeply and fill water bottles here. The cairned footpath continues south; the tread is faint in places. It remains almost level for 0.5 mile, then switchbacks up steeply to the west, turns northwest, and terminates with a final scrabble up scree and talus to Cathedral Rim. This trail segment is about 1.5 miles long and gains about 1,000 vertical feet. Walking time from the lake is a bit under 1 hour. Watch for mountain goats on this segment of trail. One-tenth of a mile from the top-out point, the Centennial Rim trail is intersected. From here, turn left, or southeast, and follow the rim trail through interesting granite formations. Approximately 0.5 mile from the junction is Smokey the Bear, a granitic formation resembling the legendary Forest Service fire-fighting bear or, perhaps more appropriately, Yogi the Bear. It is possible to climb above this formation without difficulty, allowing one to put a human figure in photographs for scale. It is perhaps another half mile to the Giant Cleft. The trail immediately preceding the cleft is vague, and in one place, a descent of about 150 vertical feet of class 2 rock or scree is necessary to bypass a 10-foot obstruction in the trail, which can be up-climbed with difficulty, but which the average hiker cannot down-climb. The trail terminates on a knoll about 0.1 mile from Grimface (McKeen) Mountain. The gain and loss of altitude between the junction and the knoll are perhaps 500 vertical feet in each direction. This is a good spot to eat lunch; water, which is scarce on the ridge, may be partially replaced from nearby snowfields. It is important to get water at Ladyslipper Lake before starting upward.

From this knoll, there is a splendid panorama of Boxcar Peak, Lakeview Mountain, the Deacon, Orthodox Mountain, and across the border, Cathedral Peak, Remmel Mountain, Sheep Mountain, and the other peaks of the Pasayten Wilderness. From this point, the adventurous can drop down to the south into a valley; ascend a ridge; follow the ridge crest, crossing what appears to be a somewhat technical pass; drop down into the valley on the other side; and go farther cross-country to join the Boundary trail near Cathedral Lakes or Cathedral Pass. Also, the adventurous can drop down a scree slope at this point to reach Goat Lakes in the valley below. The lake cannot be seen from the knoll. Most hikers, however, will retrace their steps to the junction.

From this point, the rim trail is followed northwestward. It passes through an area of interestingly eroded granite called Stone City. Shortly thereafter on the ridge crest, the Devil's Woodpile, a fractured lava (probably andesitic) dike, is noted. From this point, there are views down to Ladyslipper Lake, and mountain goats are frequently seen in the meadow and talus below. The trail then goes up to the ridge that leads to the summit of Pyramid Mountain. Hikers have the choice of summitting Pyramid or continuing on to Glacier Lake. Mountain goats are often seen on Pyramid Mountain. Descend the rather steep initial portions of the Glacier Lake trail, but midway along the lake, turn left and cross-country along the alpine ridge, following a generally north-eastern direction. If you wish, go straight north for a view of Quiniscoe Lake below. Eventually you will pick up the flagged and blazed but somewhat less than obvious trail that descends directly to Quiniscoe Lake. It is about 0.7 mile to the ridge cutoff and 1 mile from the cutoff to the lake via this route, thus saving a mile compared with the return route discussed under the north section.

This is a strenuous walk; hikers attempting it should be in good physical condition and knowledgeable about cross-country travel.

(August 1980)

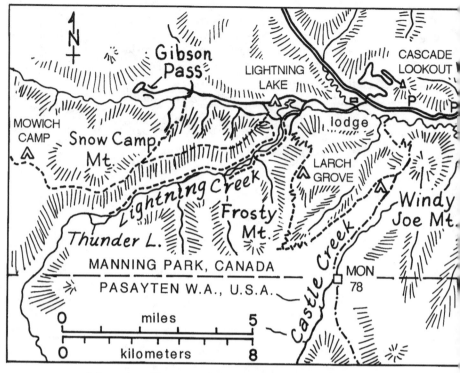

Manning Provincial Park, British Columbia

Manning Provincial Park, British Columbia

FROSTY MOUNTAIN
Elevations
Trailhead: 4,100 feet (1,250 meters)
Destination: 7,900 feet (2,408 meters) (Frosty Mountain)
Altitude Gain   3,900 feet (1,180 meters) (including ups and downs)
Walking Time   In: 3 hours 30 minutes   Out: 3 hours
Trail Length   7.5 miles (11.1 km) one-way
Accessibility   August to early October
Difficulty   Strenuous
Pack   Light
Topographic Sheets   Manning Provincial Park PS-M1 25-meter contour map

Go west from Manning Park Lodge. Park at the east end of the Lightning Lake day-use area. Cross the green bridge and walk southward on the dam on the east side of the lake. The signed trailhead is obvious. There are two trails here; take the one that goes up; do not take the level trail around the lake.

The trail goes up fairly steeply through deep forest. At 1.3 miles, a junction with an old trail from Lightning Lake is intersected. At 2 miles, there is a fair view of Strike and Flash Lakes to the west. At 2.5 miles, there is a better view of these lakes, since there are fewer trees in the way. At 3.5 miles, the trail levels out for about 1 mile. At 4.1 miles, while passing through a meadow, note the sign that says "Wilderness Campsite 1 kilometer." At 4.6 miles, the campsite is reached. There is a shelter here with an intact roof but with little in the way of other amenities. There are also an outhouse and four tent sites, with a trickle of water nearby on August 31. This area is in deep conifer forest, without views. At 5 miles, reach the first subalpine larch, a deciduous conifer. At 5.9 miles, the footpath passes along a broad ridge crest. This is a scenic area, with blooming heather and wildflowers below and green (or in the fall, glowing gold) larch needles above, plus scenic views in most directions. Tree-ring dating studies indicate that the largest trees in the larch forest are 1,500 or more years old. At 6.6 miles, there are elegant views to the north of the Brothers Mountains. Water is available near the trail here.

At 6.7 miles, pass a warning sign and ascend a rough scree and talus scrabble trail via switchbacks. At 7.1 miles, the Windy Joe trail junction is reached as the ridge crest is gained. Follow the crest southward and then westward to reach the summit at 7.5 miles. Cairns mark the high route to the summit. Rock walls scattered over the summit area provide shelter if high-velocity winds are blowing.

There are great views in all directions. Three lookouts can be seen (Windy Joe, Monument 83, and Desolation Peak). The south peak of Hozomeen, Mount Shuksan, and Mount Baker are all in the same direction to the southwest. Crater, Jack, and Three Fools Mountains lie to the south, and the Brothers to the north make for an elegant view. You can follow with the eye the tread of the crest trail for miles to the south. For scenery, this is the premier trail in Manning Park.

(August 1987)

CASTLE PASS–USA/MONUMENT 78 (MANNING PARK) B.C.

Elevations

Trailhead:	4,200 feet (1,281 meters)
Destination:	4,400 feet (1,342 meters) (Monument 78)
High Point:	5,380 feet (1,641 meters)

Altitude Gain   1,250 feet (including ups and downs)
Walking Time   In: 3 hours 25 minutes   Out: 3 hours 15 minutes
Trail Length   7.9 miles (12 km) one-way
Accessibility   Late June to late October
Difficulty   Moderate one-way; strenuous round-trip same day
Pack   Full
Topographic Sheets   USGS: Castle Peak, Frosty Peak 7.5'
Green Trails: Jack Mountain, Pasayten Peak
Manning Provincial Park PS-M1 25-meter contour

There are two trails that access Monument 78 as of 1997. The trailhead for the footpath to be described at length is about 0.2 mile east of the visitors' center and is signed "P.C.T." and "Windy Joe." The other trailhead is about 1 mile east of the visitor center, and is signed "Monuments 78/83." Both are about the same length. The Windy Joe trail gains more altitude but does have a campsite en route to the border. This footpath is also more scenic. Printed descriptions of both trails are available at the Manning Park Visitor Center located about 0.5 mile east of the Manning Park Lodge.

The Windy Joe route to Monument 78 initially passes the sewage treatment plant, and then drops down to cross the Similkameen River on a bridge. After the bridge is crossed, the trail proceeds moderately steeply upward on a fire road for approximately 2.4 miles until the Frosty Mountain trail is intersected on a sharp curve. The walking time to this point from the current trailhead is about 1 hour. The altitude gain is about 1,250 feet. There is no water for about 2 miles after the river is crossed. Leave the fire road at this point, and follow the Frosty Mountain trail approximately 0.7 mile to a junction, which was unsigned in 1979. The right fork continues to the summit of Frosty Mountain; take the left fork to Monument 78. One-tenth of a mile farther, there is another fork. The left fork leads 0.1 mile to a campground; a poor-quality water source is available adjacent to the trail junction. Unless you wish to camp, take the right fork and proceed over a footpath of fair quality, which gradually descends as it proceeds northward. Scars of a prior logging operation can still be seen in the valley to the east. About 7.6 miles from the trailhead, a delightful creek is crossed on a bridge. There are several campsites in the deep woods on the east side of this creek. The walking time to this campsite with a full pack is 3 hours and 20 minutes. Three-tenths of a mile farther, Monument 78, located on the U.S.–Canada border, is reached. The triangular brass monument is obvious, located a few feet to the west of the trail; beyond that, a treeless swath 10 feet on either side of the border clearly delineates the location of the international boundary. At this point, the U.S. boundary and the Pasayten Wilderness boundary are the same. A few feet into the Paysayten Wilderness is a trail register. The trail makes two fairly steep switchbacks immediately after entering the United States and then contours gradually upward through timber and forest fire burn areas to reach Castle Pass, 4 miles from the monument or 11.9 miles from the trailhead. The altitude gain over these 4 miles is exactly 1,000 feet. At 2.8 miles from the monument, there is a fair campsite 50 feet off the trail to the east, suitable for one tent only, with a water supply nearby. Three-tenths of a mile north of Castle Pass, subalpine meadow is entered. A way trail to the right (west) descends 0.1 mile, where there is a good campsite adjacent to a small stream. There are level but waterless campsites at the pass itself. At the pass, the junction with the west-going Boundary trail is intersected; from here, Big Face Creek is 10 miles and Ross Lake is 25 miles. The walking time from the monument to the pass upward is about 1 hour and 40 minutes; the down-time is 1 hour and 20 minutes. Two-tenths of a mile south of the pass on the second switchback, the Frosty Creek trail (the east-going Boundary trail) is intercepted.

The Pacific Crest Trail continues southward from this point to Hopkins Pass and Hopkins Lake.

Views are fair from the Castle Pass area but nowhere near as impressive as they are from Frosty Pass, a bit over 1 mile to the east and 1,000 feet higher. The main reason for walking this section of trail for most people is to complete the northernmost section of the Pacific Crest Trail or to make the loop trip via Monument 83.

The prevailing customs regulations on both sides of the border must be observed and cannot be waived. Every person crossing the international boundary must report directly to the nearest customs house in the country into which he or she has crossed.

Camping in Manning Park is restricted to designated sites only.

(August 1987)

SKYLINE II

Elevations

Trailhead:	4,500 feet (1,372 meters)
Destination:	5,500 feet (1,675 meters) (Mowich Camp)
High Point:	6,150 feet (1,875 meters) (ridge of Lone Goat Mountain)

Altitude Gain   2,100 feet (630 meters) (including ups and downs)

Walking Time   In: 3 hours 40 minutes   Out: 3 hours 10 minutes

Trail Length   7.5 miles (12 km)

Accessibility   Mid-July to mid-October

Difficulty   Moderately strenuous

Pack   Full

Topographic Sheets   Manning Park and Skagit Valley Recreation Area 25-meter contour

Drive eastward from Manning Park Lodge toward Gibson Pass. Park at the Strawberry Flats parking area, where there is space for about fifty cars. Follow the trail half a mile across Strawberry Flats and take the left fork. The trail starts gaining altitude about 0.2 mile from the junction and goes up through deep timber. Water is accessible at 1 mile from a small stream and from poor-quality tarns at about 2.5 miles. The trail is muddy with lots of roots, so walking is both slow and slippery. After passing the tarns, the trail ascends to a ridge and then goes southward, with the tread etched into the side of a cliff. It is about 3.5 miles to the junction with the Skyline I trail, which ascends from Lightning Lake and traverses the summit ridge above Strike and Flash Lakes.

From the junction, the trail drops down via switchbacks, losing about 400 vertical feet; crosses Despair Pass; and then regains the lost altitude as the slopes of Snow Camp Mountain are ascended. After 1.1 miles, the trail reenters meadow. The trail then passes around the south side of Snow Camp Mountain, descends a bit, and then reascends to the high point on the south side of Lone Goat Mountain. The scrabble trail to the summit of Lone Goat starts at the high point.

After the high point, the trail descends above a lovely meadow, with elegant views of Mount Hozomeen in the background. It then contours around a second, lower meadow. Three hundred feet below the trail in the second meadow, there is a small spring providing good water. After leaving the second meadow, the trail descends through progressively deeper forest to reach Mowich Camp, losing about 800 vertical feet from the high point. There is a shelter in good condition at the camp, and there are multiple campsites. Water is available but is sparse in dry years. Deer are frequently seen in the area. The trail distance from the junction to the established campsite is 4.5 miles. The only designated campsite on this trail is at Mowich Camp. Manning Park regulations forbid camping in other locations.

Both Snow Camp (elevation 6,494 feet; 1,980 meters) and Lone Goat Peak (elevation 6,577 feet; 2,004 meters) can be easily climbed without technical difficulty. The access to Lone Goat is from the south. Snow Camp can be climbed from either the east or the west but is easier from the east. Snow Camp is quite flat on top. Views are superb in the open meadows beneath these two peaks and from the summits of both peaks.

From the junction, Skyline I trail runs 5.3 miles (8.5 km) to Lightning Lake. The first 0.2 mile from the junction is through woods, then the trail traverses a half-mile-long meadow and scrabbles up to a saddle and then below two knobs; it then crosses a knoll, drops about 400 vertical feet, and reascends to a higher knob. The first knoll, about 2 miles from the junction, requires about 45 minutes of walking with a light pack. The views are nice but not as good as from Lone Goat and Snow Camp Mountains.

(August 1987)

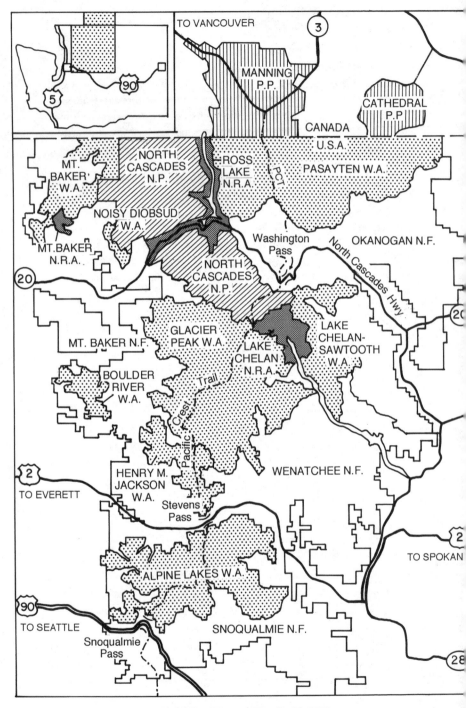

Pacific Crest Trail (PCT)

Pacific Crest Trail (PCT)

Elevations

Trailheads: 3,000 feet, Snoqualmie Pass (south); 4,200 feet, Manning Park (north)

Supply Points: 4,061 feet, Stevens Pass; 4,800 feet, Rainy Pass; 1,600 feet, High Bridge Stehekin Valley

High Point: 7,100 feet (near Hopkins Lake)

Low Point: 1,600 feet (High Bridge [Stehekin])

Altitude Gain Approx. 37,100 feet (including ups and downs)

Walking Time 2.5 to 4 weeks

Trail Lengths 245 miles total (plus 7 miles in Canada); Stevens Pass to Stehekin, 98 miles; Stehekin to Canadian border, 80 miles.

Topographic Sheets USGS: Stevens Pass, Labyrinth Mountain, Benchmark Mountain, Poe Mountain, Glacier Peak 15', Holden 15', Agnes Mountain, Stehekin, McGregor Mountain, Washington Pass, Mount Arriva, Azurite Peak, Slate Peak, Pasayten Peak, Castle Peak

Green Trails: Snoqualmie Pass, Kachess Lake, Stevens Pass, Benchmark Mountain, Glacier Peak, Holden, McGregor Mountain, Stehekin, Washington Pass, Mount Logan, Pasayten Peak, Jack Mountain

U.S. Forest Service: Pacific Crest National Scenic Trail–Washington Northern Portion, Snoqualmie Pass to the Canadian border (1986)

Canadian Maps: Manning Provincial Park PS-M1 25-meter contour

Readers wishing more information on the PCT may consult volume 2 of *Pacific Crest Trail* by Schaffer and Selters (see the Bibliography). Data may also be obtained from the Pacific Crest Trail Association, 5325 Elkhorn Boulevard, Suite 256, Sacramento, CA 95824; phone 800-817-2243.

Portions of the Pacific Crest Trail between Snoqualmie Pass and Canadian Highway 3 in Manning Park have been described elsewhere as separate trails. These include Snoqualmie Pass to Park Lake; Stevens Pass to Lake Valhalla; Smithbrook Road to Janus Lake and Grizzly Peak; Agnes Creek from the Stehekin Road to Suiattle Pass; Bridge Creek from the Stehekin Road to the North Cascade Highway (NCH); NCH to Cutthroat Pass; Manning Park to Castle Pass.

The remainder of the PCT will be described as follows: (1) Grizzly Peak to Suiattle Pass; (2) Harts Pass to Cutthroat Pass; (3) Harts Pass to Castle Pass; (4) Park Lake to Stevens Pass.

GRIZZLY PEAK TO SUIATTLE PASS

Leave flat-topped Grizzly Peak reluctantly. It is a splendid place for wild-flowers in the summer and for the reds and yellows of autumn. Descend one switchback into the saddle between an unnamed summit to the north and Grizzly Peak. Contour northward beneath the summit, gradually losing altitude. Half a mile north of the summit, the trail crosses from the west to the east side of the ridge crest and drops down until it crosses Wenatchee Pass. From here, there is a gradual ascent, including a gain of about 300 vertical feet past a waterfall, to reach Pear Lake. One and a half miles south of Pear Lake is the half-mile-long way trail to Top Lake to the east. Top Lake becomes ice free earlier in the year than Pear Lake does. There are nice campsites on the southeast and north sides of Top Lake and at the northeast end of Pear Lake. The walking time from Grizzly Peak to Pear Lake is about 1 hour and 40 minutes; in the reverse direction, it takes about 2 hours (with a light pack). Snow remains late along this particular section of the PCT. (The Wenatchee National Forest reports that the PCT has been rerouted to a location east of the tread location described here. Pear Lake and Fortune Ponds have been bypassed by the new section of the footpath.)

Leaving Pear Lake, the trail switchbacks up on the west above the lake to Frozen Finger Gap. Well into midsummer, there is a steep snow slope in this area that must be traversed; an ice ax is mandatory, since steps must be cut early in the day or kicked later in the day when the snow has softened. The trail then descends via switchbacks by a tarn, crosses a creek at its lowest point, and goes upward across magnificent flowered meadow. Three miles farther, there is one campsite by a stream in the meadow. The trail tops out on a ridge crest, descends into a forested area, and then goes up to reach Saddle Gap 3 hours and 15 minutes from Pear Lake with a full pack. The trail then contours north and slightly west about half a mile, passing the West Cady Ridge trail junction. The footpath then descends in switchbacks until it reaches Pass Creek, where the way trail to the west (North fork of the Skykomish) joins it. Three-tenths of a mile farther is Cady Pass, with its eastern way trail to the Wenatchee River Road.

The trail then goes upward, gaining about 1,100 vertical feet. Foggy Camp is passed en route, but a better name would have been Soggy Camp, since the runoff from melting snow was flowing through the middle of the camp area. Ten minutes farther, there is another single campsite. From Saddle Gap, Pass Creek is 55 minutes, Cady Pass 1 hour and 5 minutes, Foggy Camp 2 hours and 30 minutes, and Lake Sally Ann 3 hours and 45 minutes (in August 1974, it was necessary to cut steps almost continuously over fairly steep snow slopes for the last 2 miles to Lake Sally Ann). There are at least eight nice campsites around this almost continuously frozen little lake. The area is quite scenic; this is a recommended overnight stopping point. Four-tenths of a mile north is

Cady Ridge, which requires a descent. There are good camping spots on the ridge, with the added bonus of splendid views of Glacier Peak and Kodak Peak to the north. It is also possible to wander cross-country eastward on Cady Ridge for a substantial distance without difficulty. The tread of the Cady Ridge trail may or may not be obvious.

From Cady Ridge, the trail turns to the northeast and goes up over Ward's Pass. This portion of the trail was solid snow, requiring step-kicking upward, a crossover north of the summit knob from the west to the east side of the crest, and a glissade down the snow slopes to Dishpan Gap, where the Bald Eagle trail can be seen contouring beneath June Mountain to the northwest en route to its junction with the PCT.

Considering the ascents and descents from Pear Lake to Lake Sally Ann, the estimated altitude gain for the 11 miles is 3,500 vertical feet, approximately 40 percent of which was done on snow on August 8. Route finding was a problem at times. Invaluable under snow conditions are topographic maps of the area and a reliable description of the trail.

After leaving Dishpan Gap, the trail goes northeast to the flank of Kodak Peak. It then passes through a lovely meadow to a ridge crest, where the Glacier Peak Wilderness is entered. Approximately half of the trail from the gap to the wilderness boundary was snow covered. From here, the trail goes northwest to Indian Pass, a large, pretty meadow with a small stream. From Indian Pass, the trail gains several hundred vertical feet while traversing forest for approximately half a mile and then breaks out on the meadowed west flank of Indian Head Peak, where there is a magnificent view down the Sauk Valley.

Way trails from the east reach the PCT at both Indian Pass and lower White Pass. From Lake Sally Ann to lower White Pass takes approximately 4 hours under the snow conditions described previously; it is about 6.8 miles.

Reflection Pond can barely be discerned through the deep snow. There are six or seven nice campsites on the ridge above the pond that are snow free. Glacier lilies bloom in profusion between lower and upper White Passes, as the snow melts from the meadows. The PCT goes northward and a bit to the west to reach upper or true White Pass. Campers are asked to camp at a bench west of the pass rather than in the pass itself. There is splendid meadow walking in this area, although considerable portions of the meadow are boggy, and the camping areas tend to be a bit damp until all the snow has melted.

Half a mile from White Pass to the northwest is the junction with the trail coming up from the north fork of the Sauk River. Red Pass is 1.5 miles farther to the northwest. In snow conditions, experienced wilderness travelers can cross-country up to the top of the meadowed ridge half a mile or so before Red Pass is reached and glissade down the snow slopes on the other side, saving over a mile of walking with only a couple hundred feet of cross-country travel upward; an ice ax is mandatory for a safe descent. Even in mid-August 1974, an ice ax was necessary to descend the solid, steep snow on the north side of Red Pass (or to ascend it if coming from the north).

There is a good campsite near trees 100 yards east of the cinder cone, but no water close by. The PCT descends below and east of this campsite. Half a mile north of this point, the trail was lost in snow near a stand of silvered tree trunks. The trail goes west of campsites near these trees and does not follow the main creek. Locating the trail under snow conditions is quite difficult at this point; go westward cross-country to pick it up in meadow half a mile from the main large creek below the campsite (the headwaters of the White Chuck River). The trail descends further, crosses the White Chuck River on a bridge, then enters forest. There are brief views from a meadow about 2.5 miles beyond the bridge. It is 3 hours from the cinder cone to the Sitkum Creek crossing. From this point, it is 2 miles to Kennedy Hot Springs, 9 miles onward to Fire Creek Pass, and 8 miles backward to Red Pass. Fill water bottles at Sitkum Creek.

It takes another hour of walking to reach the Kennedy Ridge trail junction, about 0.4 mile after crossing Kennedy Creek. From this point, it is a steep, dry 1.9 miles up to Glacier Creek (Kennedy Creek is milky and not a satisfactory source of water); full packed, the ascent to Glacier Creek takes 1 hour and 15 minutes. There are several campsites below the crossing of the PCT with Glacier Creek, with good water available. It is an additional hour to Pumice Creek. An additional hour and 15 minutes brings the hiker to a nice campsite just below the switchbacks leading up to Fire Creek Pass. One-tenth of a mile west of this camp is an enjoyable view down the White Chuck Valley.

From this campsite, a constant upward walk for 50 minutes, on snow for the last 10 to 15 minutes, brings you to Fire Creek Pass. This is the most technically difficult pass on the PCT, since snow usually persists well into September. In cloudy and rainy conditions, with unbroken snow underfoot, route finding downward is exceedingly difficult and potentially hazardous.

Under snow conditions, descend about 30 degrees to the left of north down moderately steep snow, then continue down to a flat area (losing about 600 vertical feet), where there are occasional patches of rock and heather visible. Two or three short sections of trail may be apparent on the way down along the ridge to the left of Fire Creek Pass. Having made the descent to this point, there are two potential routes: to the right or east, and to the left or west; the latter is the correct one. A level 100 yards brings the hiker to a rock where Mica Lake can be seen below; the lake cannot be seen from the crest of Fire Creek Pass. Descend moderately steep snow to the east side of Mica Lake and contour just above the lake to its outlet on the north. Climb up about a 20-foot snowbank. The PCT can be seen in places to the west of the outlet, but under snow conditions, the best route is to stay east of the outlet and glissade moderately steep snow down about 400 vertical feet and 0.2 of a linear mile almost due north, to where the footpath enters the relatively flat valley below from the east.

If the trail is apparent and the snow has melted, simply follow the tread. However, expect problems either ascending or descending Fire Creek Pass in an average year until Labor Day, and carry an ice ax for this section of the trail.

From north of Mica Lake, the gentle switchbacks seem never-ending, broken only by an avalanche valley where there is a campsite (the only one between Fire Creek Pass and the Milk Creek Bridge). This leads the hiker to the junction with the Milk Creek trail between 3.5 and 4 miles and 1 hour and 30 minutes of walking time beyond Mica Lake.

After leaving the junction with the Milk Creek trail, elevation 3,800 feet, the trail switchbacks up the east wall of the canyon. Heavy alpine vegetation overhangs the trail. If the trail has not be brushed recently and the plants are wet, they will saturate the hiker from the waist down. Rain pants help but do not keep off all the water.

After gaining about 2,000 feet over 2.5 miles, a ridge crest is reached; near a small pond, there is a campsite in open meadow. To the south is Kennedy Peak, a spire on the north ridge of Glacier Peak.

The footpath now contours eastward, slowly gaining altitude. One and a half miles farther, there is a campsite 100 yards below a small knoll. After crossing a boulder field and then a ridge at about 6,100 feet, another campsite is located below and to the north of the trail. Shortly thereafter, the multiple switchbacks down to Vista Creek begin. After a few of these, the Dolly Creek campsite, nestled among a few protective mountain hemlocks, is located. Water is 100 yards downslope. There is another campsite half a mile farther on Vista Ridge. At 2.6 miles farther, elevation 3,650 feet, is a campsite beside Vista Creek. This stream is crossed on a sturdy bridge about 2 miles farther and 750 feet lower. At the crossing, there is a good campsite.

The PCT now contours eastward across a gentle slope to cross Gamma Creek 0.8 mile farther. Seven-tenths of a mile beyond this crossing, the junction of trails 791 and 798 is reached. The PCT then turns north and after about 1 mile crosses the Suiattle River on a 50-yard-long horse bridge. Just after the river is crossed, there is a junction: the Suiattle River trail goes to the northwest; the PCT turns east. There are campsites near this junction. The PCT then switchbacks upward as it ascends Middle Ridge. The footpath from Buck Creek Pass is intersected 4.4 miles from the river. The PCT continues upward, crosses Miners' Creek, and reaches the Image Lake–Suiattle Pass trail 2.3 miles from the prior junction. From here, it is 1 mile farther east to Suiattle Pass.

The distance between Milk Creek and Suiattle Pass is roughly 23 miles. Slightly over 3,000 vertical feet are gained from the Suiattle River crossing to Suiattle Pass.

(Grizzly Peak to White Pass, 1977; White Pass to Milk Creek, 1983; Milk Creek to Vista Creek, 1987)

HARTS PASS TO CUTTHROAT PASS

To reach the trailhead, drive to Mazama, which is 74.4 miles east of Marblemount and 13.5 miles west of Winthrop, on the North Cascades Highway. If on the southern loop, take the half-mile road to reach the junction to the north. If on the northern loop, the road intersects at the grocery store and gas station at Mazama. From Mazama, drive westward.

The road, fairly good at first, becomes tortuous, narrow, and in one place, downright airy. It is 19.4 miles from Mazama to the guard station at the pass. Slightly east of the summit, turn south and drive approximately 2 miles to the trailhead. There is parking for approximately six to seven cars at the trailhead itself, plus a substantial parking area at the campground 0.7 mile from the trailhead.

For the first half mile, the PCT goes moderately upward through larch and alpine fir forest to a ridge crest, gaining about 300 vertical feet. Views from the crest are impressive. The footpath then contours gradually upward to the west, reaching another crest at approximately 2 miles, after an altitude gain of another 500 vertical feet. From this ridge, there is an excellent view to the north of the Slate Peak lookout. The trail descends gradually over the next 2 miles, losing about 300 to 400 feet in the process. At 4 miles, the Tatie Basin campsite immediately beneath Tatie Peak is reached. The first water source since beginning the trail is located at this excellent camping area. Over the next 1.5 miles, the PCT gains approximately 500 vertical feet to reach a ridge crest from which there is a splendid view of Mount Ballard and Azurite Peak to the west. (From Harts Pass to this viewpoint makes an excellent one-day, light-packed hike for an above-average, well-conditioned hiker; the round-trip distance is 11 miles.)

On the Green Trails map, this high point is often referred to as "Grasshopper Pass." This segment of high trail is particularly attractive in late September and early October, when the larch forests glow golden when backlighted by the autumn sun.

From here, the footpath switchbacks downward, losing about 1,300 vertical feet over the next 2 miles. Forested Glacier Pass is 8 miles from the trailhead. "Pass" is somewhat of a misnomer, since a clear-cut crest in the usual sense does not exist. South of Glacier Pass, the trail drops gradually into Brush Creek, so named because of the slide alders in the area. At roughly 9.3 miles (a 4-hour-and-30-minute walk, full packed), the trail reaches the first campsite since Tatie Basin. There is space for about four two-person tents in this area. Wood for campfires is adequate, and water can be obtained 100 yards to the west from Brush Creek. Bears are common in this area, so be sure to hang food supplies. The altitude loss from "Grasshopper Pass" to the campsite is about 2,000 feet. Beyond this camp, the PCT drops gradually downward, losing an additional 800 feet in the process. Ten miles from the trailhead, it intercepts the way trail ascending from the east along the Methow River. A few feet beyond the junction, the trail crosses Brush Creek on a footlog. This is the low point of the PCT between Harts Pass and Cutthroat Pass. Immediately east of the creek is a campsite that accommodates only four people.

After the creek crossing, the trail goes gradually upward near the Methow River. Twelve miles from the trailhead, there is a good campsite approximately 200 feet south of the trail in a meadow adjacent to Jet Creek, known as Horse Heaven Camp. One-tenth of a mile farther, the way trail to 3-mile-distant Mebee Pass comes in from the west. At 12.8 miles, the footpath crosses the Methow River on a bridge. Nearby there is a rudimentary campsite, good water, and probably good stream fishing. Willis Camp is passed at 13.5 miles. The trail gradient is now substantially steeper. At 17 miles, a fair campsite is located in a meadow north of Methow Pass. Methow Pass, elevation 6,600 feet, is reached 18 miles from the Harts Pass trailhead. There are good campsites at the pass, but water is obtainable only from snowfields. Nine-tenths of a mile beyond the pass, there is an excellent campsite with good water—the recommended stopping point in the area. From this campsite, there is a scrabble trail that ascends to the Lower and Upper Snowy Lakes, roughly 0.5 and 0.7 mile away, and 500 and 600 vertical feet higher. The upper lake is especially scenic, since Mount Hardy is framed and reflected in its waters. There are wonderfully scenic camping areas around both Snowy Lakes; the altitude of the lower lake is 6,735 feet and the upper is 6,839 feet. Above the lake lies the orange granite of Tower and Golden Horn Mountains, both well above 8,000 feet in elevation. From Upper Snowy Lake, an unnamed ridge between the lakes and Methow Pass may be climbed to obtain better views. Almost all the mountains in the vicinity are sculpted from the orange granite of the Golden Horn batholith. To the west can be seen the darker rock of Black Peak and adjacent spires. (The Okanogan National Forest advises that the Snowy Lakes are being adversely affected by overuse. Visitors are urged to practice no-trace camping here, which includes forgoing the pleasure of a campfire.)

Continuing southward, the footpath makes a high traverse to reach 6,300-foot-high Granite Pass 2.5 miles to the southeast. Hikers should use caution in this area, since sections of the footpath have been sloughing, leaving narrow, exposed tread. From the pass, the trail switchbacks up steeply, gaining 600 vertical feet over the next half mile. The PCT then contours the east side of an unnamed ridge at about 6,900 feet in altitude; snow can persist here until well into the summer. Early summer hikers should carry an ice ax and be experienced with kicking steps into snow slopes. Once the south slope of the ridge is reached, there are no technical problems until Cutthroat Pass is reached 23 miles (more or less) from the Harts Pass trailhead. (See Cutthroat Pass for further data.)

Except for the approximately 9 miles in the Methow Valley, viewing is splendid throughout this PCT segment. The best campsites from a scenic viewpoint are at Tatie Basin and Snowy Lakes.

It is substantially easier to do this segment of the PCT from north to south, since the altitude gain is considerably less. With full packs, actual walking time is about 13 hours.

(August 1971)

HARTS PASS TO CASTLE PASS

To reach the trailhead, turn right at the crest of Harts Pass and drive a bit over 1 mile up the road toward the Slate Peak lookout. The trailhead is located on a sharp curve. Parking in this area is limited; if there is no parking space here, overflow parking is available adjacent to the toilet and bulletin board area, midway between Harts Pass and the trailhead.

For an overall introduction to the area, it is suggested that hikers visit the Slate Peak lookout, elevation 7,440 feet. From this area, the route of the trail can be visualized for a number of miles, and walkers can become familiar with the lay of the land.

Returning to the trailhead, the PCT contours northward beneath Slate Peak, gradually losing altitude and passing a suitable campsite with access to water at about 2 miles. The elevation at the trailhead is 6,800 feet. Windy Pass, 4 miles from the trailhead, is at 6,257 feet. A hundred feet north of Windy Pass is the boundary of the Pasayten Wilderness.

From the trailhead to Windy Pass, views to the west are marred by scars of prior mining activity centered around the ghost town of Barron. Indeed, jeep trails still reach almost to Windy Pass; miners' cabins are located in Indiana Basin below the pass. However, the views in the distance of Mount Baker, Crater Mountain, and Jack Mountain help to compensate for the intrusions into the wilderness by gold seekers of the past.

Evidence of mining activity is left behind after the Pasayten Wilderness is entered. Half a mile beyond Windy Pass is Windy Basin, where there are good campsites and water. The trail switchbacks upward after Windy Basin, reaching a ridge crest at about 5 miles, with an altitude gain of about 500 vertical feet. The PCT then descends equally steeply in approximately the same number of vertical feet to reach Oregon Basin and its excellent campsite with water at roughly 5.5 miles. Foggy Pass is reached at the 6-mile mark. The footpath then gains a bit of altitude on the west side of the ridge, reaching a grassy knoll at about 6.5 miles. This is a good place for lunch or can be the turnaround point for vigorous one-day hikers. There is a major campsite at about 200 vertical feet below the ridge. The trail then goes around the east side of the ridge, ultimately reaching another ridge crest at about 8 miles north and slightly east of Devil's Backbone. Switchbacks go downward thereafter, with about 400 vertical feet lost. At 8.7 miles, there is a good water supply. Notice the impressive winter avalanche slope to the northeast at this point. An immense amount of snow pulled off Jim Peak and Devil's Backbone, depositing avalanche debris well down into the Shaw Creek valley.

For the next 4.3 miles northward, hiking is mostly in forest rather than meadow. At 10.1 miles, the trail turns west and begins a 2.1-mile downward set of switchbacks to reach Holman Pass, 12.2 miles from the trailhead and 5,150 feet high. The Holman Creek trail leaves to the east, destination the former Pasayten airstrip. An alternative route back to Harts Pass via the west fork of the Pasayten exists; it is less scenic but offers the possibility of a loop trip. At Holman Pass, there are tent sites, but there is no water and no view. Also at Holman Pass is the junction with the Devil's Ridge trail to the west.

From Holman Pass, the PCT again gains altitude, gradually leaving forest and entering meadow. At 2.3 miles north of the pass is the Goat Lakes Basin, a truly lovely area, although adversely affected by horsemen during hunting season. There are multiple quality campsites in this meadow and at least three or four dependable water sources. A walk of half a mile to the southeast brings the hiker to Lower Goat Lake, where there is a secluded, sheltered campsite. Upper Goat Lake lies 500 vertical feet above the lower lake; walking time is half an hour. The basin and the lakes are the recommended overnight camping areas and are the best locations to overnight since Oregon Basin.

The PCT continues northward, gaining altitude across Goat Flat Meadow to reach Rock Pass, elevation 6,491 feet, about 1 mile from the center of Goat Flat Meadow. There is a tent site at this point, but no water; there are lots of marmots in the area.

The PCT bifurcates at Rock Pass. The lower trail loses about 500 feet in altitude but is technically easy; the upper trail is covered with scree, talus, and in places, steep snow without runouts. Almost everyone should use the safer lower trail, since the upper trail is considered dangerous by the Okanogan National Forest personnel. Hikers with climbing experience and an ice ax may elect the upper trail at their own risk. Both trails lose some altitude. The trails rejoin after about 1 mile on the upper trail and 2 miles on the lower trail. The recombined trail then switchbacks up moderately steeply to reach Woody Pass, elevation 6,624 feet. About 200 feet south of Woody Pass, there is an excellent campsite with water available from a snowfield. En route to Woody Pass, the Rock Creek trail, leading into the Coney Basin and ultimately reaching the middle fork of the Pasayten River, is intersected.

From Holman Pass to Woody Pass, the basic rock is a conglomerate. It takes about 40 minutes on the high trail to go from Rock Pass to Woody Pass. North of Woody Pass, the trail makes a long, high, level contour beneath Three Fools Peak. The views to the west are spectacular from this segment of trail. Crater, Hozomeen, Baker, Shuksan, Spickard, Joker Mountain, and Castle Peak can be seen without difficulty.

Three Fools Peak can be climbed with relative ease. Views from the 7,965-foot-high summit are among the best in the North Cascades. A beautiful, shallow, emerald green lake surrounded by larches is noted below and to the north. Lake of the Pines can be seen to the east, as well as the other great peaks of the Pasayten Wilderness.

Returning to the PCT, continue northward beneath Three Fools Peak. Note another impressive avalanche path below. About 2 miles north of Woody Pass, the PCT makes a sharp turn to the right (east). A scrabble way trail below loses several hundred feet to reach Mountain Home Camp; another way trail connects the camp with Lakeview Ridge. The PCT starts upward at this point, eventually topping out on a knob slightly over 7,000 feet in altitude 1.5 miles to the north. The trail then drops down sharply, losing 300 feet in altitude, to access Lakeview Ridge. The PCT contours on the level for a time along the ridge crest and then switchbacks downward, losing about 600 vertical feet to reach Hopkins Pass (elevation 6,122 feet), slightly over 22 miles from the trailhead. This descent is called the Devil's Stairway. From Lakeview Ridge, there are splendid views of 6,171-foot-high Hopkins Lake below.

Three-tenths of a mile south of Hopkins Pass is the way trail to Hopkins Lake, where there are excellent campsites and good views of the mountains to the east, framed in the waters of this delightful, inaccessible, and uncrowded high alpine lake. There are also a number of excellent campsites in the vicinity of Hopkins Pass. The hiker can drop down 0.1 to 0.2 mile to the headwaters of Chuchuwanteen Creek and find a number of campsites by tarns or by a small stream.

It is 3 miles from Hopkins Pass to Castle Pass, with an altitude loss of about 650 feet. If going down, the walking time is 50 minutes, compared with 1 hour and 30 minutes coming up from the north. The trail becomes progressively less scenic as it descends.

See the Monument 78 trail description for data on the PCT from Castle Pass to the border and on the trail from the border to Canada Highway 3 in Manning Park.

There is no water from Woody Pass to Hopkins Lake, although there are several satisfactory dry camps. It is best to stay overnight below Woody Pass or continue to the preferred campsite at Hopkins Lake or to the slightly less desirable campsites a bit below Hopkins Pass.

Strong, fit hikers can reach the Goat Flat Meadows in one day from the trailhead. Hopkins Lake or Castle Pass can be reached the second day, and the Canadian road the third. Average hikers can walk this segment of the PCT from Harts Pass to Manning Park in four days with three overnight camps. (August–September 1974)

PARK LAKES TO STEVENS PASS

After leaving Park Lakes, the trail gains a bit of altitude as it ascends a ridge crest. Past the crest, there are views of Spectacle and Glacier Lakes below. The PCT then descends on multiple switchbacks, reaching the Spectacle Lake trail 2.9 miles from the junction with the Mineral Creek trail. There are two side trails leading to the lake. Spectacle Lake lies in a scenic glacier-carved basin. The PCT continues downward to cross Delate Creek on a bridge. There are campsites where the trail crosses Lemah Creek. The footpath ascends Escondido Ridge and then loses about 2,200 feet of altitude as it descends to the junction with the Dutch Miller Gap trail. The descent is through an area scarred by a forest fire about seventy years ago. The Waptus River is crossed on a bridge; a way trail leads to the shore of Waptus Lake, where campsites abound. The PCT gradually turns northeast to enter the Spinola Creek drainage basin, where there are many wildflowers in season. A way trail on the west side of Deep Lake leads to a number of camping places. From here, the trail goes upward to reach Cathedral Pass below impressive Cathedral Rock. Near the junction with trail 1345 is a campsite that is pleasant in fair weather but exposed in foul. The next campsite northward is beside a creek about 2 miles away. Early in the hiking season, a stream descending from Mount Daniel to the west may create a hazardous ford by afternoon on hot days; it is wise to cross this creek early in the day. Deception Pass (4,500 feet) is about 1.8 miles past this creek. At 1.4 miles north of the Deception Pass junction is a campsite with water access even late in the summer. After a 500-vertical-foot altitude gain, the Deception Lakes are reached; a campsite is located at the middle lake. The PCT gains another 1,000 feet of altitude as it contours upward around the west side of Surprise Mountain to reach Pieper Pass, a bit under 6,000 feet high. The descent from the pass to Glacier Lake loses about 1,000 vertical feet. Camping may be restricted within 100 feet of both Glacier and Surprise Lakes. If so, there are good places to camp both north and south of Glacier Lake.

Where the PCT proceeds north after descending from Pieper Pass, look for the no-longer-maintained tread to Surprise Gap, and from there to the summit of Surprise Mountain. Views from this high point are well worth the side trip upward.

After passing above Surprise Lake, the PCT gains altitude en route to Trap Pass. Seven-tenths of a mile northeast of the pass, the 0.25-mile way trail to Trap Lake is intersected; there are many good campsites at the east end of this lake. The PCT then loses altitude en route to buggy, unimpressive Hope Lake; there are campsites here, but it is best to push on to nearby Mig Lake, which is prettier and less buggy. There are good places to camp on both the east and west sides of Mig Lake. After leaving Mig Lake, the PCT gains altitude, crosses the Cascade Crest above Swimming Deer Lake, and drops down a bit to the west side of Josephine Lake. There are campsites adjacent to the southeast shore of this lake, reached by the Icicle Creek trail. Small Lake Susan Jane is then passed half a mile north of Josephine Lake; there are campsites on the north side of this lake. North of here, civilization intrudes. The trail passes under the power lines and then descends through the ski slopes below the chair lifts to reach the trailhead by the Stevens Pass ski area parking lot.

The midportion of the PCT between Snoqualmie and Stevens Pass can be accessed by forest road 4330 to the Tucquala Meadows campground and trailhead. From here there is a direct route to Deception Pass as well as by the longer but more scenic route via Cathedral Rock. This latter access is discussed in the description of Peggy's Ponds elsewhere in this book. There is also a southern access via the Mineral Creek trail. There are two northern access routes from U.S. 2, which connect with Surprise Lake to the west and Hope Lake to the east.

The approximate distances (in miles) from Park Lakes to Stevens Pass are as follows:

Park Lakes–Mineral Creek trail junction to second Spectacle Lake trail junction: 3.4
Spectacle Lake trail junction to junction with trail 1329C: 10.5
1329C junction to Dutch Miller Gap trail (DMGT) junction: 4
DMGT junction to Deep Lake trail (DLT) junction: 7.6
DLT junction to Cathedral Pass (CP): 3.2
CP to Deception Pass (DP): 5.5
DP to December Lakes (DL): 3.7
DL to Pieper Pass (PP): 1.4
PP to Glacier Lake trail (GLT) junction: 2.4
GLT junction to junction with trail 1060A: 1
1060A junction to Hope Lake: 4
Hope Lake to Josephine Lake: 3.5
Josephine Lake to Lake Susan Jane: 0.5
Lake Susan Jane to Stevens Pass: 4.1
(1987)

Resources

CONSERVATION ORGANIZATIONS
Sierra Club National Office
85 Second St.
San Francisco, CA 94105

Sierra Club Northwest Office
1516 Melrose Ave.
Seattle, WA 98122

The Wilderness Society
900 17th St. NW
Washington, DC 20006

National Parks and Conservation Association
1776 Massachusetts Ave. NW
Washington, DC 20036

National Audubon Society
700 Broadway
New York, NY 10003

Washington Environmental Council
1100 2nd Ave.
Seattle, WA 98101

Washington Wilderness Coalition
4649 Sunnyside Ave. N #242
Seattle, WA 98103

Washington Wildlife Federation
PO Box 1966
Olympia, WA 98507

Friends of the Earth
4512 University Way NE
Seattle, WA 98105

Wildlife Conservation Trust
PO Box 176
Bow, WA 98232

Conservation International
1015 18th St. NW, Suite 1000
Washington, DC 20036

LAND MANAGEMENT AGENCIES

When requesting information from land management agencies, be aware that the quality and accuracy of the data provided vary, depending on the agency and the knowledge of the staff person on duty at the time. Weekend staff often consists of individuals who work only part time. For accurate data, contact the agency well in advance of your trip by letter or phone, so that your question can be researched accurately.

Mount Baker–Snoqualmie National Forest

Forest Supervisor
21905 64th Ave. West
Mountlake Terrace, WA 98043
206-775-9702

Mount Baker Ranger Station
2105 State Road 20
Sedro Woolley, WA 98284
360-856-5700

Darrington Ranger Station
1405 Emmens St.
Darrington, WA 98241
360-436-1155

Skykomish Ranger Station
74920 NE Stevens Pass Highway
PO Box 305
Skykomish, WA 98288
360-677-2414

North Bend Ranger Station
42404 SE North Bend Way
North Bend, WA 98045
425-888-1421

Glacier Public Service Center
1094 Mt. Baker Highway
Glacier, WA 98244
360-599-2714

Verlot Public Service Center
Granite Falls, WA 98252
360-691-7791

Wenatchee National Forest
Forest Supervisor
215 Melody Lane
Wenatchee, WA 98801
509-662-4335

Cle Elum Ranger Station
803 West 2nd St.
Cle Elum, WA 98922
509-674-4411

Chelan Ranger Station
428 W. Woodin Ave.
Chelan, WA 98816
509-682-2576

Entiat Ranger Station
PO Box 476
Entiat, WA 98822
509-784-1511

Lake Wenatchee Ranger Station
Star Route 109
Leavenworth, WA 98826
509-763-3103

Leavenworth Ranger Station
600 Sherbourne
Leavenworth, WA 98826
509-548-6977

Okanogan National Forest
Forest Supervisor
PO Box 950
Okanogan, WA 98840
509-826-3275

Methow Valley Visitor Center
PO Box 579
Building 49, Highway 20
Winthrop, WA 98862
509-996-4000

Tonasket Ranger Station
PO Box 466
Tonasket, WA 98855
509-486-2186

Twisp Ranger Station
PO Box 188
Twisp, WA 98856
509-997-2131

North Cascades National Park Complex
Superintendent's Office
2105 State Road 20
Sedro Woolley, WA 98284
360-856-5700

Marblemount Wilderness Information Center
728 Ranger Station Road
Marblemount, WA 98267
360-873-4500

Visitor Center Newhalem
502 Newhalem St.
Rockport, WA 98283
206-386-4495

Stehekin Ranger Station
PO Box 7
Stehekin WA 98852
360-856-5700, ext. 340

Chelan Ranger Station
PO Box 189
Chelan, WA 98816
509-682-2549

Outdoor Recreation Information Center
915 Second Ave
Suite 442
Seattle, WA 98174
206-220-7450

British Columbia, Canada, Provincial Parks
Cathedral
PO Box 399
Summerland, BC VOH 1ZO
Canada
250-494-6500

Manning
Box 3
Manning Park, BC VOX 1RO
Canada
250-840-8836

Bibliography

Beckey, Fred. *Cascade Alpine Guide Series: Climbing and High Routes.* Vol. 1, *Columbia River to Stevens Pass,* 1987; vol. 2, *Stevens Pass to Rainy Pass,* 1989; vol. 3, *Rainy Pass to Fraser River,* 1995. Seattle: Mountaineers Books.

Copeland, K., and C. Copeland. *Don't Waste Your Time in the North Cascades.* Berkeley, CA: Wilderness Press, 1996.

Darrington Ranger District Hiking Guide. Seattle: Northwest Interpretive Association, 1994.

Darvill, Fred. *Mountaineering Medicine and Backcountry Medical Guide,* 14th ed. Berkeley, CA: Wilderness Press, 1998.

———. *North Cascades Highway Guide.* Seattle: Northwest Interpretive Association, 1986.

———. *Stehekin—A Guide to the Enchanted Valley.* Mount Vernon, WA: Outdoor Publications, 1996.

Gardner, C., et al. *Potential Volcanic Hazards from Future Activity of Mount Baker, Washington.* Open-file report 95-498. U.S. Geological Survey, 1995.

Graydon, Don, ed. *Mountaineering: The Freedom of the Hills,* 6th ed. Seattle: Mountaineers Books, 1997.

Harcombe, Andrew, and Robert Cyca. *Exploring Manning Park.* Seattle: Mountaineers Books.

Iron Goat Trail. Seattle: Mountaineers Books, 1993.

Kirkendall, Tom, and Vicki Spring. *Cross Country Ski Tours—Washington's North Cascades,* 2d ed. Seattle: Mountaineers Books, 1996.

Kresek, Ray. *Fire Lookouts of Oregon and Washington.* Fairfield, WA: YeGalleon Press, 1985.

Mathews, Daniel. *Cascade–Olympic Natural History.* Portland, OR: Raven Editions, 1994.

Miles, John. *Impressions of the North Cascades.* Seattle: Mountaineers Books, 1996.

Prater, G. *Snowshoeing,* 4th ed. Seattle: Mountaineers Books, 1997.

Schaffer, Jeff, and Andy Selters. *The Pacific Crest Trail,* 5th ed. Vol. 2, *Oregon and Washington.* Berkeley, CA: Wilderness Press, 1990 (1997 supplement available).

Spring, Ira, and Harvey Manning. *100 Hikes Series: Alpine Lakes,* 2d ed. 1993;
  Glacier Peak Region, 3d ed. 1996; *North Cascades National Park Region,* 2d ed.
  1994. Seattle: Mountaineers Books.
Strickland, Ron. *Pacific Northwest Trail Guide.* Seattle: Writing Works, 1984.
Waitt, R., et al. *Volcanic Hazard Zonation for Glacier Peak Volcano, Washington.*
  Open-file report 95-499. U.S. Geologic Survey, 1995.
Washington's Back Country Almanac. Seattle: Mountaineers Books, 1997, Annual
  Editions.
Wilkerson, Jim. *Medicine for Mountaineering,* 4th ed. Seattle: Mountaineers
  Books, 1992.
Wisberg, Saul. *North Cascades—The Story Behind the Scenery.* Las Vegas: KC
  Publications, 1988.

Index

NOTES

NOTES

NOTES

NOTES

NOTES

NOTES